A Deeper South

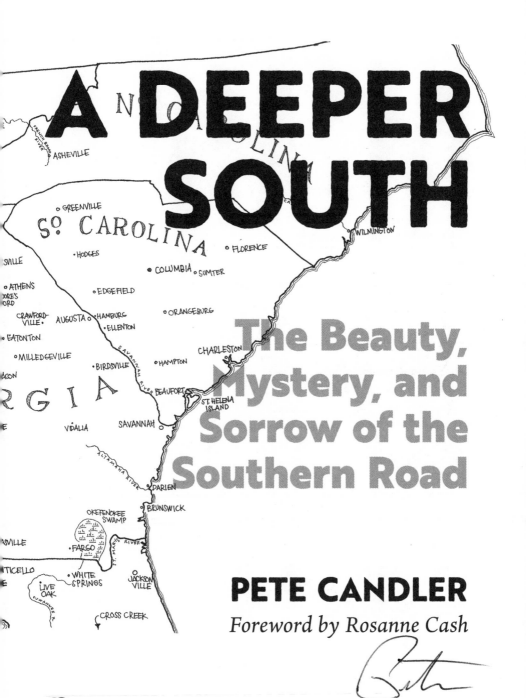

A DEEPER SOUTH

The Beauty, Mystery, and Sorrow of the Southern Road

PETE CANDLER

Foreword by Rosanne Cash

THE UNIVERSITY OF
SOUTH CAROLINA PRESS

© 2024 University of South Carolina

Published by the University of South Carolina Press
Columbia, South Carolina 29208

uscpress.com

Printed in the United States of America

Library of Congress Cataloging-in-Publication Data
can be found at https://lccn.loc.gov/2023057913

ISBN: 978-1-64336-479-7 (paperback)
ISBN: 978-1-64336-480-3 (ebook)

To my wife
Meredith
and our children
Henry
Charles
Oliver
and
George—
the geniuses of this place

You cannot love what you do not know.

—St. Augustine, *On the Trinity*

here there is no place
that does not see you.

—Rainer Maria Rilke,
"Archaic Torso of Apollo"

Contents

Foreword

When my dad died in 2003, I got dozens of personal condolence letters from his friends and admirers. I was touched by the kindness, and I made an effort to read all of them over time. There were also hundreds, if not thousands, of obituaries, tributes, and testimonials in the months after his death in every kind of publication. I made it a point to read very few. It was emotionally treacherous territory. But a friend sent me an essay and said he thought I should read it. He said it was different. It was by a professor of theology, Peter Candler. The "theology" part made me a bit wary—I didn't want to hear anyone else tell me how my dad was "in heaven" and was "looking down on me." But there was none of that. I was struck by the wise, gentle tone in the essay. It read like a letter from my dad to me—it had a quiet acceptance, and an acknowledgment of my dad's dual nature (what Kris Kristofferson had described as a "walking contradiction.") It was pure and generous and completely lacking in self-referential—and what I had come to see as "industrial"—grief. It was—as he said of my father—authentic, as well as spiritually grounded. I was so moved by the piece that I asked my friend if he could connect me with Pete.

Pete and I began a correspondence that sustained me in some hard times. He offered a sense of poetry that was different from mine, and it gave me a sense of liberated calm. He also espoused the ideas that doubt can be cherished, that mysteries are mysterious by definition and can be relaxed into, rather than figured out, and that God has a thick skin, should you test Him or Her. As well as those ineffable gifts, he offered a solid connection with my own Southern history that had real love in it, by way of acceptance of the terrible with the terribly beautiful.

Pete and I have been corresponding for twenty years now, and I have read countless of his essays and pored over his photographs. He is a quintessential storyteller, in the great Southern tradition of which he describes, but a storyteller of magnificent largesse of spirit: one whose heart is so large that you feel he has forgiven us for pain we don't remember inflicting, and pain we don't recall enduring, in both a cultural and personal sense. I don't know why that is. I only know that his large heart beats through every sentence, but his intelligence and elegant facility with language underscores his writing in a way that your mind can unhinge itself from some very rusty entrenched patterns and grievances. Pete writes, "an honest sense of one's own history is necessary to human well-being." His vision and dissection of the South, and what it means to be a Southerner, even if one has not called it home for several decades, has challenged me to get more honest with myself about my ancestry, my birthplace, the characters who surrounded me, and the elemental, as well as metaphoric, sweat, blood, and tears.

There are multitudes of nuanced beliefs and feelings within the tropes about the South, and Pete unpacks all of them through the lens of his own complicated, storied, and quintessentially American personal history with compassion and clear insight: the violence, the redemption, the vitriol, the humor, the regression, the vision, the love, the loss, and what it means to have a home and a past that you must sometimes reject before you can embrace, as we both did. What is unacceptable and what is cherished are both held to the light to reveal a larger story about who we are and where we come from, through the prism of the story of the South.

Pete writes that at some point, while in academia, he realized he was living a smaller, lesser version of himself. I also learned that to come into the fullness of our own potential, we must know our own history. This book—as elegant in its recounting of the deep roots Pete has in the South, and as rich in vision as it is—is at center a story of self-*recovery*. As Pete did, I squeezed my eyes tight, or saw through a vague cloud of shame my own history and the provenance of my Self. In midlife, we may feel the urgency to know, to accept, to recover what was there all along, and this is what he has done. It is liberating for those of us who are taken on his journey, particularly when there is so much love, wisdom, and honesty in every paragraph. "Revisiting takes work," he writes. Indeed it does. Part of the work is pure courage, and part is the hard business of blowing away the smoke of shame and awkwardness to fully address and accept one's own ancestral chains and threads, and to know which to break and which to bind. *A Deeper South* is a longer wise and gentle letter, similar to the one written in the form of a eulogy to my father that was the occasion of the beginning of our friendship. It is a letter to his forebears, to the South as a whole, and to all of us who yearn to recover and be revealed to ourselves. Where we come from is a window to the future. Travel both directions with Pete Candler, and, as he writes, "a little time here can help to loosen the hold of even the most possessive of American myths."

Rosanne Cash
June 2023

Opening Fracture

There is a crack in my name.

Before, it just sat there, whole and untroubled on the corner of my desk, painted around the side of a white porcelain mug that is at least a century old. It is flanged out at the top and bottom, gilded around the rim and hand-painted with my grandfather's name, a name he disliked so much that he chose to go by another, which became my name.

Now, the mug is broken. While writing a section of this book about the importance of family history, I clumsily knocked it off the shelf and onto the floor, where it shattered into pieces. Across the broad side of the mug, where you would wrap fingers around to warm up a cold hand, a fracture cuts across the name. What pieces of the keepsake I was able to salvage are now gathered into a Ziploc bag and tucked away somewhere less vulnerable. At some point, maybe, I will be able to put it back together.

I came by it by default. No one else in my family wanted it, so I adopted it just as I have other items that once belonged to my grandparents and other members of my family: pieces of furniture, plastic cups, stereographs, old cameras. I even have a packet of Knox gelatin and a small jar of McCormick's peppercorns that they held on to for a comically long time. For some reason, I have become the de facto custodian of these things to which no one else in my family seems to attach much value, and why I do is still a mystery to me.

This tendency to hang on to things could be a genetic trait; it could also have something to do with the fact that I come from a region that is obsessed with it. The American South is a story-rich and storyteller-rich environment. Hanging-on-to and handing-on-to is what we do. The term "storyteller" is almost an honorific, denoting a certain—perhaps fading—social status that few of us can pretend to. We even hold contests to decide who is the best at it this year. Not many of us can claim that mantle, but the truth is that whether we are good at telling stories, every human being is a story bearer. All of us, no matter where we call home, are bearers of a finite number of stories that make us who we are individually, and those stories are part of much bigger local, regional, and national stories, and ultimately a part of an infinitely varied story of all things.

What makes Southerners unique as a breed of storyteller is that we have never really shied away from trying to tell a story of the whole region. I must confess ignorance on the subject, but my suspicion is that head scratching, hand wringing, or soul searching over what constitutes "the Northern mind," or the "Pacific Northwestern way of life" is a rarity. The eternal quest for Southern self-understanding, such as it is, is usually framed over against "the North," that perennial other that is both the South's great bogeyman and a useful antagonist in a national culture that both pushes back against and thrives on dualisms.

Not too long ago, serious writers regularly took their own shots at a sort of Southern metanarrative that would distill the "essence" of the South, or attribute to it a single "mind." For over a century, the narrative of the South (at least as told by white people) was of a region nobly devoted to a politico-religious Lost Cause whose lostness was, the story went, no fault of its own. Quite the contrary: that lostness was a function of its devotion to a supposedly unimpeachable moral goodness, which is reflected in the oft-repeated refrain that the South, both during and after the Civil War, was put down and kept down by a less righteous but more heavily armed force. There is a great appeal in this kind of story, not only because it casts its protagonists and their descendants, its storytellers, as innocent and morally pure victims, but also because it is easily digestible: the South means X (a convenient variable that also translates visually to the Confederate Flag as representing some idea of "heritage" as opposed to a symbol with a concrete and deeply troubling history).

There are plenty of people who still believe the story. Those who don't tend to be aware of how damaging it is to the humanity of those whom that story often erases, especially Black Americans. But it is also damaging to those who tell it, because of the deliberate acts of intellectual, psychological, and spiritual self-amputation required to sustain it. The price of maintaining the integrity of this version of "the South" is a potentially catastrophic loss of personal integrity, because an honest sense of one's own history is necessary to human well-being, and that honesty is often the first casualty of "the Lost Cause." It may well be that an aspiration to comprehensiveness is itself untruthful, since no single person in themselves can tell, embody, nor even remember any story in its wholeness. It is, I believe, better to tell a story in many true fragments than to tell an all-encompassing one that is false.

To tell the story of the South truthfully requires a multiplicity of voices, perspectives, tones, accents, styles, vocabularies, and dispositions. One problem with big, comprehensive stories is that they do not allow you to be troubled by them, so long as you are inside them. From outside, the Lost Cause story is quite obviously troubling on so many levels, but only to those who aren't telling the story to begin with. One of the gifts of Southern storytellers have given us is their ability to unsettle, to displace us from what we thought we knew as home, to make the world appear stranger (and all the more wonderful and mysterious for it), and ultimately to make us confront the conflict that is internal to every human heart, which is one reason why the Lost Cause version of Southern history—or any of its multitude of reboots and remixes—is not a very good story. If you are inside of it, the story itself does not give you the resources to interrogate the source of your need to believe it. If you are to ask why you need to believe this story, you will have to break it apart from within, and look outside of that story.

As will become clear, I am a white male of privilege who has descended from some very gifted storytellers (if not fabulists and mythologists), and I have inherited a version of that large, overarching story of the South. I only became aware, more or less by accident, how many stories that Official Version left out—or indeed how many fragments the violence of an Official Version produced—and how much more interesting, more difficult, more necessary, are some of those other stories that have been left largely unmarked on the thoroughfare of American public memory. This book is an attempt to gather some of those fragments into something resembling a more complete story of the place.

This is a gathering of stories about the South. But it is also a set of stories about me, about my attempt to reassemble the pieces of a fractured self. When I left academia ten years ago, I felt that I had become a truncated version of myself, and that the highly insular culture of academia had discouraged me from interests that have really driven who I am from a young age. That sense began to set in early in my first semester as an untenured assistant professor, when a colleague not at all subtly wondered aloud to me, with a distinct tenor of suspicion, why I was writing an article about Johnny Cash; it culminated a decade later when I found myself seriously considering taking an anonymous reviewer's advice to make my writing more boring and anodyne, so as to appeal to that handful of scholars who might or might not care about my argument. That moment brought a small but consequential revelation that I was less than the person I wanted to be.

My work in photography, narrative nonfiction, and even my flailing attempts to write a comic novel or two belong to a larger attempt to reassemble the pieces of a self-dismembered by both academic culture and my own blindness to recover the fragments of personality and reassemble them into something more like a whole.

This process has taken a number of different forms that are simultaneously creative and personal. My wife and I moved our family back to the Southeast. I began relistening to the music I had enjoyed as a younger person, perhaps in an attempt to recover who that person was before I had become disintegrated by academic life. Through regular visits to the library they left behind, I began to try to understand my paternal grandparents, who were themselves both disintegrated by Alzheimer's disease before I really got to know them. I tried this in the only way I really know how: by writing about it.

But returning to the back roads of the American South along with my good friend John Hayes, with whom I had begun exploring the region in 1997, meant recovering stories and fragments of stories of both my region and myself that I did not even know existed, and writing about it has been less a kind of reportage from the road than an ongoing discovery post-factum. The mysteries of the American roadside and the genie-souls who lurk there continue to reveal themselves long after we have shaken that very particular dust off our shoes. I came to learn that there were, particularly in my native Georgia, broken shards of stories about my own family that had been buried so deep that by the time of my parents' generation they had been effectively lost from collective memory. Recovering some of those stories has meant not just being able to tell a fuller picture from the outside but from within, coming to learn a perspective on myself, my family, my city, my region, and my country, that parts ways with the typical Southern posture of self-justification or defensiveness.

Although it cuts against my years of training in the you-make-a-better-showing-with-your-mouth-shut school of Southern decorum to admit it, my own family, on my father's side, was prominent in the development of the "New South" and influential in the shaping of twentieth-century Atlanta. The Candler name is all over the place, its ubiquity in inverse proportion to my own knowledge about "my people." Until this project began, I only knew them like game pieces for *Clue*, with little more than titles to differentiate them from one another. If my family's story were a play, it might begin with a list of the dramatis personae who sometimes seem to represent character types more than actual people:

William Candler, "the Colonel"
Martha Beall Candler, "Old Hardshell"
Milton Anthony Candler, "Uncle Milton"
Asa Griggs Candler, "Asa"
Warren Akin Candler, "the Bishop"
John Slaughter Candler, "the Judge"
Asa Warren Candler, "the Major"
Allen Daniel Candler, "the Governor"

For decades, this was all I knew about them. My children, who have been raised in a different school of Southern behavior than I was, and also because they are too young to be burdened with that enveloping cloud of insecurity that prevents you from fully disclosing yourself to others, do not share my learned reticence about these people. They think of them as interesting people who did interesting things, human beings with complicated stories that we should keep telling because they understand intuitively that their stories are ours, too. My wife and children have been as responsible as any other factors for helping me to break out of that tenacious cloud and to breathe more naturally. As the reader will learn, my great-great-grandfather, The Judge, is a paradigmatic case of how white Southern amnesia is erosive of the memory of both vice and of virtue. What that regime of forgetfulness withheld from me was a mountain range of stories about him that were by turns disturbing and ennobling, somber and hilarious, but almost always illuminating. By the time I had received them, many of those condensed histories had already gone through generations' worth of dulling, softening, and flattening-out, a process that had deprived them of their power to reveal.

When the name-bearing mug broke, I contacted a friend of a friend who is a kintsugi master, skilled in the ancient Japanese art of repairing broken tea vessels with gold. In that tradition, such vessels are more valuable as broken and restored than they were in their original state. I asked him if he could repair the mug for me. Yes, he said, but it would be a while.

That waiting was providential, in its way. In the interim I learned that the mug was not for him to repair. It would be my job to put it back together. Or maybe not. I am told that some Japanese families will hold on to a broken tea pot for generations until the time is right for them to mend it. In the same way, the mug's time was not yet. The hour of its reconstitution lay still in the future then, as it still does now. It may fall to generations after me, to my children's children.

The same is true for me, and for the South: while I still pursue a version of myself, my region, and my country, that is more whole because more honest with itself, less bashful about its own injuries and less cagey about its own sins, to gild the wounds of that fractured name and story is not for me, not yet. This work is, I hope, an attempt to gather some of those fragments into one, and like those families in Japan, simply to hold them together.

I cannot offer here a mended story, much less a mended name. I do not promise a resolution, nor do I know if it is even wise to hope for one. What I can do in the meantime is to gather the broken shards of a once whole yet illusory story, to collect what I can find from among the fragments, that what has been discarded and forgotten can, even as fragments, show us something true about ourselves, in the hope that someday a more whole story awaits its arrival upon ears that will be ready for it, hearts that will be open to receive it.

Bike taxis outside Halls Chophouse, Charleston, South Carolina. Photo by the author.

STEAK DINNERS AND GRADY MOMENTS

I was a twenty-four-year-old graduate student at an English university, fresh-faced and out of place, when I met my first Canadian over a steak dinner. At least I assumed it was steak. The meat-and-potatoes dinner meal was what one would expect in England: cooked for too long, and with little inspiration. I had known enough about England to anticipate that much, but I had never had enough interaction with Canadians or the idea of Canadians to have any expectations of them. They simply never entered any discussion of any kind in in my youth in Atlanta, Georgia. I am sure there were Canadians about then, but I hadn't ever heard one speak a word of any language until the one sitting across from me at dinner said,

> You know, the thing about America is, you can travel everywhere and the accents all sound pretty much the same.

I was too busy choking on my aggressively unsalted roast potatoes to protest this outrageous thesis with words. To be fair, had I given any thought to it at the time, I probably would have thought that Canadians all talked the same, too, eh? Ignorance, it turns out, is no respecter of geography. It is, however, curable: the only problem is that you have to recognize your ignorance as ignorance if you would like to be cured of it.

Within a year of this jarring episode, I shared a house with a different Canadian, and quickly came to discover that not all Canadians share such a monolithic view of their neighbors. Canadian Number Two was doing a doctoral dissertation on Anglo-American relations during the Civil War, so despite having traveled 4,000 miles to study theology at a medieval institution, it turned out that I hadn't made it very far from home at all.

One of our house mates, who was from the Home Counties—in England, not Canada—often suggested we have "a barbecue" at the row house we co-rented on St. Luke's Street. I tried in vain to explain that barbecue is something that you eat, not something that you host, but it was wasted breath trying to correct an English person on how to use the English language. Instead, I directed my voluntary diplomatic efforts on behalf of my home region to disabusing Canadians, English people, and other Europeans of their New York–centric view of the United States and their apparent prejudicial aversions to the American South. *In the inevitable event that you should come to the United States,* I tried to persuade them, *sure, sure, you should visit New York. But also go see Charleston, Savannah. Mobile, even.* Everyone goes to New York, but not everyone sees it, of course. More people should visit Savannah and Charleston. *Like you, long-lost Canadian linguist friend. You should definitely visit Savannah. Then you would stop saying that all Americans talk the same.*

Defensiveness is often the default position of Southerners, especially when they find themselves outside of the South, assuming the role of ambassadors for their region against the prevailing prejudices against the place, often correcting unbelievably durable misconceptions by exaggerating the region's best qualities with an almost religious fervor. But both postures reflect a basic *it's-not-what-you-think* sort of approach. If even supremely tolerant and overeducated Canadians are prone to those prejudices, then no one is safe from them. And defensiveness was the posture I assumed when faced with what was clearly an empirically falsifiable theory. *You should see Charleston,* I said. I thought I knew then what I was actually recommending.

Had I myself ever actually *seen* Charleston?

It's possible that in talking up the South's most photogenic cities to my Canadian and English friends, I was succumbing to a temptation as dangerous as ignorance: the desire to be taken seriously, as if to say, "Look, we have beautiful eighteenth-century planned cities, too, trees older than Keith Richards—hey, we also drink tea—and an air of refined antiquity that will not only be surprised but make you feel right at home."

Why is it so important to you that a tourist feel at home in the South? I failed to ask myself at the time. Was the impulse wrong? Where did it come from?

The South I would come to know later, after spending at least two decades wandering around its less-traveled roads, might not feel quite so homely to an English or Canadian person—or even a Southerner. Many visitors come here looking for something they have already seen, whether in a movie or an in-flight magazine. What many seek is often some version of the Tara myth, an idealized and whitewashed and domesticated rehash of the "Old South" that makes for attractive book covers and postcards and blockbuster motion pictures, if not for self-informing history. All of which might amount to little more than a toothless fancy, were we Southerners not so obliging in catering to market demand for such manufactured nostalgia—or if we didn't invent the myth in the first place.

At the time of my apologia for Charleston and Savannah, I had not seen that much of the South myself, and my suggestion that others do so was founded on pretty slim lived experience. Perhaps I was simply confirming the Tara myth to them, replacing one tabloid version of my region with another.

So after the presumably-steak dinner, I returned to my spectacularly unfurnished room, silently bemoaning the ignorance of my Canadian colleague, sublimely oblivious to the depth of my own. I knew enough about my native region to balk at the idea that there is only one American accent, but I remained as yet unhaunted by the brooding phantasms of history—my region's, my city's, my family's, my own.

There is a history to everything, including the desire to represent the South to the rest of the world in a way that plays up its virtues and plays down its vices. My own gestures of Southern diplomacy in England, I would discover later, were not at all original. Even my encounter with Canadian Number One was a kind of reprise of William Faulkner's *Absalom, Absalom*, in which the Mississippi-born Quentin Compson ends up at Harvard with a Canadian roommate named Shreve McCannon. It is probably no accident that it is also a Canadian who, in Faulkner's great novel, serves as Compson's Grand Inquisitor, an "outlander" whose curiosity prompts the brooding Compson to explain himself to himself (*"Tell about the South. What's it like there? What do they do there? Why do they live there? Why do they live at all?"*)[1], which culminates in a final posture of self-defensiveness framed by the "iron New England dark."[2]

In the lowering dark of October in the old England, my Shreve may have lacked the distended curiosity of Compson's, but still managed to beckon from me a similar urge to make it make sense. In my case, an instinct for self-promotion was bred in the bone, a congenital condition originating from the pathologically self-promoting city of my birth. Despite coming to England to study an ancient and venerable discipline, within a few days I had already become an ad man. Unawares, I was already part of a history I had yet to know, much less interrogate for myself.

It all begins in a smoky hall at the corner of Nassau and Frankfort Streets on the Lower East Side of Manhattan in 1866. Atlanta news-paperman Henry W. Grady evoked the scene in a now-famous speech he gave twenty years later. Besuited men in muttonchops mingled in the gin-scented company of other besuited men and several probably besuited ladies, whose presence encouraged shows of virtue. They exchanged toasts suitable for the occasion, and one by one took their seats in antici-pation of the evening's scheduled animating Oration. Up on the dais, Boss Tweed, the imperious Grand Sachem of Tammany Hall, leaned back into a festooned armchair, his waistcoat stretched tight across an increasingly bulging belly, his signature diamond brooch pinned to the middle of his shirt. On the other side of the dais, the guest speaker from middle Georgia, a few miles south of Monticello. The Grand Sachem— who needed no introduction to the denizens of Tammany Hall—stood to introduce his guest, fluffed the lapels of his coat and strode to the podium. "Benjamin Harvey Hill," he bellowed to the crowd. "But we call him 'Ben.'"

Ben Hill was the sort of Southern politician they liked on the Lower East Side: a unionist who voted against secession in 1861, and whose advocacy for industrialization of the South was music to northern ears. When the applause died down, Hill cleared his throat, flapped out the tails of his worsted wool coat, and "by one of those happy paroxysms which sometimes makes him of great usefulness,"[3] as the *Cincinnati Enquirer* reported, began:

> There was a South of slavery and secession—that South is dead.
> There is a South of union and freedom—that South, thank God, is
> living, breathing, growing every hour.
> [APPLAUSE]

It is charming to imagine that it went down this way in Tammany Hall in 1866, but it most certainly did not. In his retelling of the episode, Grady indulged in a peculiarly Southern penchant for a) not remembering history very well, and then b) building an entire platform, if not a meta-physical system, on that convenient forgetfulness. Despite what Grady claimed, Hill did not give the speech in 1866 but in September of 1880, at which point Hill was a US Senator, and Boss Tweed had been dead for two years. The event was far from a glowing success, either. According to *The New York Times*, in comparison with a similar meeting of Republicans the previous week, the Tammany Hall event was a "wretched failure."[4]

In any event, it was Hill who first took to the North to spread the gospel of the "New South." To proclaim the "South of slavery and secession" as "dead" in 1866, just months after Appomattox, would have taken cojones, for sure. It wouldn't be dead for a long time yet, but Hill helped to inaugurate a new kind of Southern mythology—which was less a mythology in the strict sense than a PR campaign, a brazen marketing strategy with little interest in the technicalities of history or the realities of political life. What mattered was money—a language that Boss Tweed and the patrons of Tammany Hall spoke with seasoned fluency.

Hill wasted no time in revising the story of the South, confidently burying the just-barely past and dusting his hands of "the recent unpleasantness." Hill was eager to claim the abolition of slavery through the war as an act of divine justice (and not deliberate political or military action). In a revealing passage in which he borrowed the voice of William Shakespeare's Hamlet, he said, "In the revolution of 1861 there was a divinity that shaped our ends, rough hew them how we wanted; and we are indebted for the abolition of slavery not to the Republican Party but to that divine power which directs human events contrary to human will."[5]

At the same time, he may have overdone it a bit when it came to characterizing the mood of Southern white men in 1880: "Southern people," he claimed, "have been the most benefited and are the most contented with the abolition of slavery." A bit of a stretch, yes. Hill wasn't a full-blown Lost Causer per se, but he began to tweak the story of recent history in an unabashedly self-flattering and insouciant way, and to set the tone for what was to follow.

What did follow, six years later, at the annual meeting of the New England Club at Delmonico's Restaurant at 2 South William Street, was another Southerner on a kind of mission trip to New York: Henry Grady, the managing editor for the *Atlanta Constitution*. Delmonico's was an auspicious site for Grady's New York visit: the restaurant claims to have originated eggs Benedict, Baked Alaska, lobster Newburg, and Chicken á la King, in addition to its famous eponymous steak. Three days before Christmas 1886, it was the site of another invention: the "New South."

It started with Ben Hill, but Grady made the concept famous. When he began his after-dinner speech in Lower Manhattan in late 1886, Grady borrowed Hill's burial proclamation for the Old South as the opening salvo of his now-celebrated address. Hill's comment was more than just a handy intro for Grady; it was scripture, and his speech at the New England Club was an expository sermon. "These words," Grady said, "true then and truer now, I shall make my text tonight."

Grady was a hit that night at Delmonico's. He won them over from the start, with classically chummy and endearing anecdotes of both domestic and biblical caste, before turning to praise Abraham Lincoln as the exemplary type of the American life. He conceded the defeat of the Confederacy without resentment and even with wit, claiming that Sherman is "considered an able man in our parts, though . . . a kind of careless man about fire." The fawning gesture was classic Grady: General Sherman himself, tidied up in a black civilian suit, his wild wartime hair now combed and kempt, was in the audience.

It was a calculated and ingenious move: with a single aside, Grady appeared to have swiftly dispatched the "sectional differences" that divided North and South. The hatchet ostensibly buried, Grady slid into his real object, the South's economic promise. "We have fallen in love with work," he said. Grady propagated the mythology of the Lost Cause while simultaneously promoting a surprisingly radical vision of the new South as a "perfect democracy," in which there are "a hundred farms for every plantation, fifty homes for every palace."[6] He appealed to an imagined brotherhood of victorious northerners and chastened southerners, who by divine justice got what they deserved but still had nothing for which to apologize.

Ever the newspaperman, Grady knew how to sell a story, even if in its finer details it was undercooked. But before the streaks of demi-glace even began to congeal on the bone China plates in front of them, the guests at Delmonico's were already entertaining visions of a radiant, sun-warmed industrial paradise in the South, and discreetly whispering Grady's name as vice-presidential material. The speech was summarized or reprinted in full in newspapers across the country, from the *New*

Orleans Daily Picayune, to the *Ironton County Register* (Missouri), from the *Yorkville Enquirer* to the *Salt Lake Herald* and the *Chicago Tribune*.

And, of course, the *Atlanta Constitution*.

Not everyone took a shine to Grady's appeal for northern investment in southern lands. Tom Watson, the notorious populist firebrand and agrarian, and the "New South's" most obnoxious political troll, resented Grady's kowtowing to northern industrialists. But Grady's vision ultimately won, for a time. Watson had the support of grassroots populists, but Grady had a newspaper.

Grady knew what deep-pocketed Yankee industrialists (and the former commanding general of the US Army) wanted to hear. He knew his claim that the "relations of the southern people with the negro are close and cordial" would be mutually flattering to both Northern and Southern self-images. He was playing to his audience, just as he did, in a very different mode, a year later at the Texas State Fair in Dallas. Facing a very different crowd than the coterie of Boss Tweed, Grady was among friends in Dallas, and shifted his tone to exploit his home-field advantage:

> Those who would put the negro race in supremacy would work against infallible decree, for the white race can never submit to its domination, because the white race is the superior race. But the supremacy of the white race must be maintained forever, and the domination of the negro race must be resisted at all points and at all hazards—because the white race is the superior race. This is the declaration of no new truth. It has abided forever in the marrow of our bones, and shall run forever with the blood that feeds Anglo-Saxon hearts.[7]

He went on. And on. In a speech before the Boston Merchants' Association at Faneuil Hall two years later, Grady was only slightly more circumspect. He styled himself an apostle of the New South, hoping "to plant the standard of a Southern Democrat in Boston's banquet hall."[8] He opened, as he often did, with a paean to the natural beauty of the South. It was a tried, and clever, move: delivered like a romantic ode to the verdant pastures of his "section," it was meant to be received as a mouth-watering resumé of the South's exploitable natural resources. When he practically swooned over "mountains stored with exhaustless treasures" and rivers that "run wanton to the sea," it was clear what he was trying to communicate. Grady was no less shrewd in playing his hand on the question of slavery. Don't be too hard on the South, he implied: "the slave-ships of the Republic sailed from your ports, the slaves worked in our fields." He cast "The Race Problem" (also the title of his speech) as a national issue, and not simply a sectional one. It is an early example of subtle whataboutism: *you may have abolished slavery well before we were forced to*, Grady implied, *but you're not so innocent yourselves.* He pointed out, for example, how incarceration of Black people was three times higher in the north than in the South. He wasn't wrong—but underneath both the Dallas and Boston speeches is a slow-burning but red-hot negrophobia.

Interestingly, the notes of White supremacy were, if more rhetorically subdued in Boston than in Dallas, no less prominent. The theme of White superiority was as self-evident in Boston as in Texas, and in 1889 Grady foreshadowed the terms upon which the full (White) reunion of the divided nation would be effected around the time of the First World War. *We love the Negro,* he claimed, but asked his New England audience to consider what an impossibly superhuman task was set before the South. He concluded the speech with two visions: the first of his own "old black mammy" blessing him from her eternal home; the second of a loyal black slave at his wounded master's bedside, "ministering with uncomplaining patience, praying with all his humble heart that God will lift his master up." Together these twin vignettes of plantation mythology were meant to indicate the "love we feel for that race," as Grady put it.[9]

His final, rousingly purple paragraph extolled the "uplifting force of the American idea," strained at the "spectacle of the Republic, compact, united, indissoluble in the bonds of love . . . serene and resplendent at the summit of human achievement and earthly glory, blazing out the path and making clear the way up which all the nations of the earth must come in God's appointed time!"[10]

Such a stirring defense of American nationalism may be surprising coming from a Southerner just under twenty-five years after the end of the Civil War, but the racial terms of the American idea were as unquestioned in Georgia as they were in Massachusetts: it is the duty of the White race to uplift the Negro because the White race is, by nature and by divine ordination, superior. And all Grady's high-blown rhetoric served an economic motive that had a secondary benefit. "When you plant your capital in millions," Grady said, "send your sons that they may know how true are our hearts and may help to swell the Caucasian current until it can carry without danger this black infusion." This first principle of the new American nation, still in utero in 1889, would be enshrined in the Black Codes and Jim Crow laws of the next decade and reinforced by the intensifying regime of White terrorism in the form of lynching. The editor of Grady's speech notes that "The Race Problem" "electrified his audience," and was met with "great applause." But the editor is silent on the real effect that Grady desired: how swiftly the Boston audience whipped out their checkbooks. As the guests departed the Hall, bellies full of filet mignon à la Richelieu, they were not talking about the other speakers, Andrew Carnegie or Grover Cleveland. They were talking about Grady.

Eleven days later, Grady was dead. The Southern Mythology Machine quickly rattled to life. Pneumonia had finally claimed the life of not just a famous newspaper man, but of an entire state. "Georgia's Dead!" proclaimed the headline of his own newspaper, the *Atlanta Constitution*. "The Awful Affliction Brings Universal Grief," read the subheadline. The entirety of the first five pages of the December 24 issue of the paper were given over to coverage of Grady's death, and to responses from readers around the nation. To many it was the end of a promising future.

Grady had been slick as canvasback duck in New York, and the *Times* rewarded him with a laudatory obituary. "To his teaching and his example, as much as to any other single influence perhaps, the South owes the impulses of material advancement, of downright hard work, of that well-nigh complete reconciliation to the conditions and duties of the presented the future that distinguish her today," the paper proclaimed.[11]

Perhaps the tireless evangelizing, spreading the gospel of the New South around Yankeedom, undid him. *That's what he gets*, Watson may well have been thinking at the news of his great rival's passing at thirty-nine. Ten years after the Delmonico's speech, Grady was long gone, and it was Watson whose name was now being bandied about as a presidential running mate, this time on the 1896 Democratic ticket alongside William Jennings Bryan. They both lost.

But Grady's vision survived Watson's ascendancy, his increasingly racist and nativist populism, and his decline. Atlanta had already permanently marked its course as a forward-looking metropolis with not only an indifference to history but a forthright dedication to forgetting it. William Hartsfield, later a mayor of Atlanta during the 1940s, famously declared Atlanta as "the city too busy to hate," a turn of phrase Grady would surely have loved.

It would take me years to realize it, but that night over dinner with the Canadian, maybe I was pulling a Henry Grady myself. Grady had toured the northeast after the Civil War and told deep-pocketed industrialists up there what a wise move it would be to bring their plants down to Atlanta. Real estate is cheap, the people are warm and friendly, etc. I had come to England with a not very different message. It's possible I was trying to counter someone else's ignorance with an appealing but illusory dose of my own.

What happened at that steak dinner in Cambridge would determine the next twenty years—but not at that moment. Like many such life events, it took a long time to percolate. That episode in October 1995 could be seen in retrospect as a kind of moment of grace. I suppose the ignorance I thought I witnessed in My First Canadian was simply a dim reflection of my own. It may have prompted me in some small way to try to repair that lack of knowledge by firsthand experience of the region I thought I understood, opened up a gap in my own awareness I was not aware existed. I had come 4,000 miles to begin to discover that my ignorance had made the trip with me.

Today a monument to Henry Grady stands on Marietta Street at the very heart of downtown Atlanta. The celebrated newspaperman is depicted in orator mode, on a pedestal of granite quarried—appropriately—in Constitution, Georgia. Four blocks to the northeast on Forsyth Street, almost eighty years after the dinner at Delmonico's, another steak dinner in Atlanta revealed how Grady's vision had endured, and tested how serious it was about its commitment to a postracial South. The dinner was in many ways a revelation of who Atlanta was, and is, and might become.

The Dinkler Plaza Hotel on Forsyth Street seemed to attract intrigue. In January 1961, Carling Dinkler, president of the Dinkler company, threw himself from the window of his suite on the twelfth floor of his hotel. In 1963, a woman murdered her lover in New Orleans and then attempted to kill herself in the Dinkler.

Like most, if not all, White-owned hotels in Atlanta at the time, the Dinkler Plaza Hotel remained officially White-only until the mid-1960s. In 1962, it refused to let a room to the diplomat and political scientist Ralph Bunche, who in 1950 became the first African American to be awarded the Nobel Peace Prize. In June 1963 the Dinkler, along with about a dozen other hotels in Atlanta, agreed to a limited desegregation plan, but that did not stop the hotel from hosting Governor George Wallace to address a Citizens' Council meeting in one of their ballrooms. Hundreds of African American students protested outside, while indoors Wallace bitched about commies and John F. Kennedy, and his host, former governor Marvin Griffin, took racially innuendoed potshots at progressive Atlanta Mayor Ivan Allen, Jr., who could not attend because he was in Africa.

When the Dinkler was given a second chance to host an African American Nobel Peace Prize winner, the hotel approached the opportunity differently. The Dinkler was chosen as the host site for a January 1965 welcome-home banquet for Atlanta native Martin Luther King, Jr., upon his return from being awarded the Nobel Prize in Oslo. At first, the response of Atlanta's White business leaders was cool: few RSVP'd that they would attend. It was looking like it would be a huge embarrassment for the Dinkler, for Ivan Allen, and for the city's self-curated reputation as the "city too busy to hate." At the urging of Coca-Cola Chairman Robert Woodruff—the most powerful man in the city—J. Paul Austin, the president of Coca-Cola, hastily convened a meeting of White business leaders at the Piedmont Driving Club and gave them a humiliating dressing-down. "The Coca-Cola Company does not need Atlanta," he said. "You all need to decide whether Atlanta needs the Coca-Cola Company."[12] Two hours later, the event was sold out.

The gala occasion was, in the end, a success story in a typically Atlanta style: presented as an exemplary moment of racial harmony and shared aspirations, the dinner would not have happened at all without moneyed interest. What ultimately swayed the White attendees of the dinner was not good will or racial reconciliation, but a fear of bad press.

The dinner at the Dinkler was among the most significant—and revelatory—social functions in the city's history. Henry Grady still looms imperiously over Marietta Street, but four blocks away, on the lot where the Dinkler once stood is now an impossibly nondescript parking deck. Dunkin' Donuts occupies the street-level retail space. Today, the subterranean rumble of MARTA trains pulling into or out of Peachtree Center Transit Station is the only reminder that the real stories of places like this are deeper underground.

I have been informally trained as a White son of privilege to see the world in a certain way, to trust the aboveground versions of reality, perhaps, to focus attention on particular strains or interpretations of history that tend to underwrite, not challenge, the form of life in which I have been raised. This is, perhaps, what most kinds of education do: concentrate our intellectual activity, such as it may be, on what is set right in front of us. This kind of direct vision tends to form us in the mode of observant spectators, not agents implicated in the reality of historical existence. Peripheral vision, by contrast, as the Finnish architect Juhani Pallasmaa writes, "envelops us in the flesh of the world."[13] One thing I was not taught—from high school to graduate school—is an ability to see peripherally, to see the contexts—often anonymous, inarticulate, unannounced, unmarked—that form the organic ecosystems in which ideas live and are put into practice.

In this book I want to present such a view of the South, to suggest the range of what we need to see widely if we are to see up close. In a way, this book is an attempt to correct or at least qualify my recommendation to my Canadian colleague many years ago in England, the words I wish I had had available to mind before I opened my mouth. It offers a peripheral view of the region that avoids the classical loci of writing about the South—although some of those loci are impossible, for good reasons, to avoid. Much of the stock imagery of the South—"graceful" plantations, "scenic" landscapes, or even urban blight—has become fodder for perpetuating bored and unhelpful stereotypes about what the South is, who lives here, and how we talk. They feed preestablished ideas about the region to be deployed whenever it is convenient to think about the South as hopelessly and irredeemably backward—or irresistibly charming and elegant. These images are often resourced for a few moments to support what one has already chosen to believe. But they are mainly in the mode of the spectator.

I believe that history is not a spectator sport. One thing every American has in common with every other American is that, insofar as we inhabit the peculiar culture of American life at this late stage, we are inheritors of a certain history, and as agents in the continuation of that history, we all have an obligation to attend to the ways in which we remember it. Many of us daily inhabit an atmosphere that we do not pay regular attention to, because it is more marketable or profitable or comfortable or simply easier to concentrate on a readily digestible article of cultural consumption that does not demand a fundamental reorientation of our diet. For centuries American existence has depended on a certain necessary condition of forgetfulness, such as the fact that "our land" was not really "ours" to begin with, and only a very small minority of people could originally lay claim to belonging to the "we" that could claim ownership over it. In *A Deeper South*, I want to offer a view of the region that allows readers to divest themselves of a defensive sense of ownership, and instead envelops them in the rich, difficult, and all-too-human flesh of the region. Maybe it will spare you, reader, from a Grady Moment of your own.

But this book also represents a movement, from peripheral vision to directed attention. The arc of this whole project is a series of concentric circles of increasing intensity and focus, or a gradually contracting spiral that tries to see the region widely before seeing my own place within it up close. The widest orbital is national memory. Amnesia is an especially American disease, but in the South, we excel at it, if one can excel at a disease. If there is a cure for amnesia, Southerners are especially well-trained at repelling it. The South is simply the most highly concentrated example of a condition that is not unique to it. Whether we have taught this habit to the rest of the nation, I am not sure, but we have done a hell of a job perfecting it. The bulk of this book traces the routes across the region by which I have come to unlearn—often against my own will—this ingrained forgetfulness.

Having circled the South multiple times in multiple directions, I move in the second section to deal with five "satellite" cities that are all within Atlanta's metropolitan orbit. They are all roughly forty miles from my hometown, and each of them plays an important role in this second stage, not least because each town is associated in some way with a significant ancestor. This second circle is that of my own family history, large and dramatic portions of which I was completely oblivious to until a fateful lunch with a friend at a now-defunct restaurant in Asheville. It is fitting, I suppose, that the restaurant is no longer in business, because it ended up being the site of a kind of forfeiture of a latent ignorance about my family's history. That ignorance remained in a state of potency, latent like an image exposed on an undeveloped roll of film, invisible until it was processed. Through the mysterious alchemy of the road, that potency turned to act.

Self-knowledge is, I suppose, the gravitational force that draws this story to its most narrow and concentrated focus. The final circle is that of my own personal ignorance of history, and what it might have to do with my present, and with my future. As became clear to me, the important thing about all of this was what I would do with it. Thus the final chapter approaches—without fully entering into—my own hometown. It narrates the story of a journey to Atlanta with my second son Charlie, and offers a meditation on what all this wandering, all this learned ignorance, might have to do with him and his brothers, how the next generation of Americans will be shaped with a wider field of vision, a deeper understanding of the subterranean currents of our history, and how to spot the realities that remain unmarked on the national, regional, or local landscape.

I have a great deal to say about my hometown now, much more than I did when we set out on what seemed like an innocent quest twenty-five years ago. But this book stops at the frontier; it concludes at the edge of the city that in a profound way is the source of my being, a place I will spend the remainder of my life attempting more fully to understand. If anything my appreciation and love for my home city has only deepened as a result of coming to know it better. I have come to learn both through formal education and personal experience that St Augustine was right: "You cannot love what you do not know."

This book arises out of an experience of the American South unguided by travel brochures or tour directors who offer a curated view of the region for the consumption of their clients. It is rather the fruit of a kind of search for something that could not initially name itself—and possibly still can't. It is driven less by maps and guidebooks than by the nose, by an intuitive sense of trust of the road itself, that if you yield to its inbuilt sense of direction and privilege it over your own, it will lead you where you did not expect or want to go, and reveal to you connections you could not have predicted. It is an attempt to go beyond tourism—not just to "see the place as locals see it" (because locals are often the ones most heavily invested in preserving a deliberately obscurantist version of their hometowns) but to seek out—or to be found by—unmarked intersections of history and self-knowledge. And one beauty of the American South is that those kinds of junctions are prolific.

You should see Charleston, I had said.

You should probably unsee it first, I should have said, to myself.

A Deeper South is about unseeing, unlearning, and unforgetting. It is a negative exercise in coming to dispense with the myths and illusions that many of us who grew up in the South took in with our morning grits. This book is also a positive endeavor: an attempt to clear for the reader's imagination the space for a confrontation with the beauty, mystery, and sorrow of the Southern Road, an invitation to think the American South differently, alongside forgotten and suppressed voices, and into a new American future.

"Dixie Highway." Dougherty County, Georgia. Photo by the author.

INTO HISTORY THROUGH THE SERVICE ENTRANCE

It began with an ending. We did not realize at the time how fortunate we were to see Johnny Cash one last time. His career was riding tailwinds then, and he sounded in full voice, but there were portents in the air. His own breath sometimes came up short. I did not know that August 10, 1997, at the Chastain Park Amphitheatre in Atlanta, would be the last time Johnny ever played my hometown.[1]

I grew up barely a mile away from the venue, on Pineland Road. Atlanta was then still riding Olympic winds, about to become the subject of *A Man in Full*, the sprawling satire by Tom Wolfe. Newcomers were arriving every day, it seemed, and on Atlanta's rapidly changing and increasingly congested streetscape in the late 1990s, native Atlantans like me distinguished ourselves from gridlocked newbies with the gnosis, a proudly esoteric knowledge of back-ways and shortcuts. It was like a kind of religion, whose chief dogma is that there are many routes to salvation, but none of them involve the Downtown Connector.

My friend John grew up over near Lenox Square Mall, and he had the gnosis, too. We were at Chastain together for Johnny's last show, and the next morning, we set off on a twelve-day road trip across the South with a vague sense of a place that was in the middle of losing something. We wanted to seek out the backroads that we didn't know, to get a little lost in other places that we knew even less than our own, or not at all.

We were looking for endings: vestiges of a South we had not known in Atlanta, a city that lacks the geographical moorings of many older American cities. It did not develop along a river or coastline and retains no memory of itself as born on and bound to a specific spot of earth for a specific reason.

Atlanta is an accidental metropolis: it grew up around a railroad crossing, and as a result developed an unsentimental attitude toward history
and place. Being famously burned to the ground by General William T.
Sherman's troops in 1864 didn't help that attitude, either. After the war,
Atlanta gave itself the motto *Resurgens*—"rising from the ashes"—and
adopted the mythological phoenix as its official mascot.

The tradition of detachment from history may or may not have set
in thanks to the effects of General Sherman, but nowadays in Atlanta,
the ashes are often self-made. The city prides itself on being "too busy
to hate," presumably because it is too busy issuing demolition permits.
Atlanta erases about one historic structure every week, and most of it goes
unnoticed. Loew's Grand Theatre—where *Gone with the Wind* premiered
in 1939—was summarily razed after a fire in 1978. The physical markers
of Atlanta's origins, its birthmarks, are all but untraceable now. The rail
depot that was once the heart and the raison d'être of the city itself was
demolished in 1864, but what replaced it has never occupied the center of
the city's spatial imagination. The site of the Zero Milepost where the rail
lines that gave Atlanta its life once intersected is now almost impossible
to access, inside the security office of a parking garage.[2]

Sometimes it seems as if the urge for preservation in Atlanta is about
as futile as changing the formula of Coca-Cola. At other times, it is as if
even the city's buildings themselves desire oblivion. Derelict throughout my childhood, the home where Margaret Mitchell wrote *Gone with
the Wind* somehow managed to survive the rapacious redevelopment of
midtown in the 1970s and '80s. The home Mitchell affectionately called
"The Dump" seemed cursed: It burned twice, most recently—and almost
entirely—in 1994. Each time it was rebuilt, less like the original home
than before. The resulting, sad simulacrum of the original structure
became a metaphor for Atlanta in the late twentieth century: a semblance of history in a city that didn't seem to want either the semblance
or the history anyway. It gets more emblematic: Mitchell's twice-rebuilt
"Dump" survived through fierce local support, but mainly through the
largesse of Daimler-Benz, who used the site for their base during the
1996 Olympics. For better or worse, Atlanta is stuck with it.

On the other side of the Downtown Connector, sites of equal or
greater historical importance have not benefited from the preservation-
ist strain. Established in the 1940s, Aleck's Barbecue Heaven on West
Hunter Street on Atlanta's Westside was famous for smoked ribs and its

proprietary Come Back sauce, but more famous for the people who came back there over and over again in the 1960s. Martin Luther King, Jr., Andrew Young, Ralph David Abernathy, and other leaders of the civil rights movement met regularly at Aleck's to gormandize and strategize. As a general rule, they started the day at Paschal's—an equally legendary Vine City restaurant—and ended it across the street at Aleck's, often lingering late into the night. The location of Aleck's was convenient: Abernathy's church, West Hunter Street Baptist, was next door. When King moved back to Atlanta from Montgomery in 1960, he bought a home on Sunset Avenue, only a few blocks north. Soon after, he persuaded Abernathy to take the job at West Hunter Street. It is not inconceivable that it was all part of a plan for the two old friends to be close to Barbecue Heaven. The ribs were that good. By the late 1980s, when I ate there with my brother for the first time, a picture of King hung by the door, and his regular booth in the back had become a kind of sacred memorial. Aleck's became a sort of image of the quest for justice itself: a moment of restoration, when its leaders were fed and filled, in the same way humans ought to be filled out, restored to their full selves. Aleck's was a pilgrimage site, and not just because the ribs were a foretaste of heaven, but because of what it represented, who had eaten there, and what revolutionary plots were hatched in the dim, hickory-smoke light emitting from the black-and-white television set behind the counter.

Aleck's was a tangible, sensory connection to a living history that people like me, my brother, and John were not wholly exposed to in school. Only when each of us had left home and come back did we realize how strange it was that our elite education had made so little of the local culture of the city we had grown up in, so little of its most famous native son, so little of its own past. Maybe these subjects were meant to be the provenance of familial history and folklore rather than school, the kinds of stories you are supposed to hear in front of a fireplace, not a chalkboard. But we didn't hear them in either place, and felt as though we had been cheated out of something important, ourselves casualties of the peculiarly American form of amnesia of which Atlanta is, in many ways, the not-so-shining exemplar. In 1997, John and I set out on the road, to try and capture some of that memory while it lasted.

By 1998, it was already too late. Aleck's was gone.

We were both in our mid-twenties on that first trip. Both sons of privilege, private school White boys who had stumbled into evangelical Christianity in high school and then stumbled back out of it during college. We'd trod many of the same paths together through high school and college. In 1994, we fell for the same woman, who'd end up changing everything for both of us.

By the time we both took a seminar on her in 1994, we had only barely heard of Flannery O'Connor. Both natives of Georgia, we wondered with astonishment and maybe a pinch of resentment how we'd managed to make it into our twenties without ever being introduced to the greatest writer the state has produced. She showed a South that was refreshingly wild, Christ-haunted, shot through with violent grace, darkly hilarious—a South that the two of us missed out on, and were only just discovering.

We looked for the South that she knew, the hidden South that the eight lanes had bypassed, the towns bled dry of life by the ever-swelling big box stores and fast-food chains that made every town in the South like every other town. Atlanta had become the exemplar of the "doughnut-hole effect," its city center essentially evacuated by a complex array of forces drawing development away from the historic center of town into rapidly expanding "edge cities" and suburban residential "communities."

It was a different era when we started making these journeys. There was Kodachrome. We shot a lot of it, and even more rolls of black-and-white film. There were camera shops, and what we didn't print ourselves in darkrooms or mail off to Kodak we took to them for processing. We rode in John's 1977 Ford F-150 pickup. We used pay phones. We used paper maps. In a dumpy motel room in Conway, Arkansas, we watched Bill Clinton earnestly tell America that he actually did do what he had previously said he had not done.

It is now twenty-six years since that first tour. I was dating the woman who would become my wife in a few years. John would later, after we wrapped up the fifth and final tour, marry as well. We both went through endings, too: for John, of a marriage; for me, of a not very promising academic career for which I turned out to be supremely unfit. John has always been the more sensible one: He remains employed as a professional historian. I, by contrast, left a tenured professorship, and moved back to the Southeast to write fiction and essays, which seemed like a good idea at the time. I went through a series of dramatic, alcohol-inspired weight fluctuations; for twenty years John has remained a solid buck-forty.

In the interim, my wife gave birth to four boys, and the prospect of doing another tour together seemed to have disappeared behind the mad rush of professional and domestic life. Perhaps because of that madness, it also began to reemerge as a kind of urgent necessity. We could talk for the rest of our lives about doing another tour, say to each other that we should really do that again sometime, secretly knowing but refusing to admit that it would never happen.

Or we could hit the road.

Which, in early 2018, we finally decided to do. We blocked out two weeks in July, and reestablished the rules from our first trip: 1) Never, unless absolutely necessary, use interstates; 2) never stay in hotels, unless absolutely necessary. On our first tour, we took one atlas and two relevant guidebooks published in the 1930s by the Federal Writers' Project of the Works Progress Administration (henceforth the "WPA Guides"). We planned only that we would make it to New Orleans and then make the turn back home. We did not know how we would get there, or what we would see on the way.

We made concessions to a new era: I'd bring a laptop, and one digital camera, for video. We decided early on to shoot film again, which meant ordering it in advance. We talked about where we wanted to go this time, what sites we wanted to return to, and what new places we would like to see.

Revisiting takes work. A first experience of a place is primarily an act of reception, of taking in what you had never seen before. But going back a second time requires the additional work of reckoning the fact that you are not the same person you were the first time, and neither is the place itself. The South is different now. So are we. This time, we take the minivan.

By 2018, the exurban trend we were worried about in 1997 has at least partly reversed itself. Downtowns like Montgomery, Memphis, even post-Katrina New Orleans, are buzzing. You can get avocado toast in

Greensboro, Alabama, and sip locally roasted espresso in the public amphitheater in Thomasville, Georgia.

That's not all that's different this go-round. We agree early on that sleeping outside in Mississippi in July is not really necessary. We get decent hotels this time, because we would need the Wi-Fi connection, right? I didn't know what I would see in 1997, and knew even less about what I would miss. That would come much later. But what's new in 2018 is the chance to look again, more closely, to resist the "Oh, that's cool" response, to slow down long enough to let your heart be troubled a little bit, maybe a lot.

This year, we decide to shoot film again, if for no other reason than a shot at the set of micro-experiences that shooting film makes possible: the patient setup, the anticipation and excitement that your film will come back from the lab as good as you hope, the fear that it won't come back at all, the wonder at seeing colors and tones on film that you had not seen in person, the occasional hits and the more common misses, and the dashed hopes and the unforeseen surprises. Despite the fact that film photography is an art of seeing, so much of it depends upon the invisible: mechanical operations, chemical reactions, mathematical equations. The click of the shutter is the sound of trust, the acoustic element of an act of faith that your calculations are correct and that the camera is going to respect them, which it does not always do.

A cardboard box in the back of the minivan holds a couple dozen rolls of film, and a half-dozen WPA Guides, their literary analogues. WPA Guides were built for road trips. And, like the now-antique 35mm cameras John and I both pack, they don't have to be charged.

Published between 1937 and 1941, the guides were the products of FDR's Federal Writers' Project, which put thousands of jobless writers and researchers back to work producing a guidebook to each state in the Union. While the Writers' Project was a national program, each volume was produced by a state agency and staffed by home-state writers, many of whom became canonical American novelists: Richard Wright, Ralph Ellison, Saul Bellow. Eudora Welty took photographs for the guide to her native Mississippi. Unlike contemporary travel books, the WPA Guides are fastidiously backward-looking acts of cultural preservation, works of literature wholly uninterested in being au courant. If Lonely Planet guides are the traveler's equivalent of tourist information offices, the WPA Guides are their National Parks.

The fruits of society's leftovers, they are both a record of an era and an indispensable resource to the forgotten hinterlands of American self-understanding. They were produced at a time of a profound cultural breakage—on the eve of a world war—when a confident narrative self-description about what it meant to be a (White) American was a political and cultural desideratum for a depressed nation seeking understanding of itself. They are an expression of a need to define American identity over against rising European—especially German—movements rooted in a deep, if manufactured, sense of national selfhood. The guides for the Southern states go even further, taking great pains to define White Southern culture over against "the Negro."

In 1945, America was at the beginning of a state of existential crisis: It celebrated itself as a beacon of justice and freedom, the "last, best hope" for the world in defeating tyranny in Germany and Japan. But at home, many of its citizens were still disenfranchised, and did not enjoy the fruits of liberation that American troops were bringing to Europeans. The Soviet Union exploited this contradiction between America's self-image and the reality of race relations in the nation, and it became a valuable weapon in the Soviet Union's PR campaign against American colonialism. In the United States, the contradiction became too potent to ignore. By 1947, W. E. B. Du Bois was appealing to the world, through the United Nations, "to witness that this attitude of America is far more dangerous to mankind than the Atom bomb."

The WPA Guides were supposed to represent the best of America, but in reality—in many of the Southern guidebooks at least—they reproduced the mythology of "the Negro Question" in such a way that only reinforced the caste system. African American readers were often left to fill in the conspicuous blanks left by the writers of the guides.

In the guides to the Southern states, there is no such chapter devoted to "The Indian" or "The Jew," even though hostility towards both was often just as fevered (the most notorious lynching in Atlanta's history was of a Jewish man). But the presence of chapters in the WPA Guides devoted to "the Negro" is an indication of how necessary this opposition is to the idea of "Southern culture." For one thing, my education tended to be more honest about Indian Removal and (although it was never called that in those days) genocide, because centuries of political maneuvering and geographical confinement had made Native peoples nonthreatening to White sensibilities. They were literally removed from

the scene. It was possible to be (slightly) more forthcoming about violence against Native Americans than against Black Americans because,
during the time of both the WPA Guides and of my upbringing, they did
not represent an active threat to the White status quo.

Toni Morrison powerfully illuminated the ways in which the idea
of American newness, innocence, and peaceableness needs the idea of
Black bondage, an image of Black unfreedom that conditions and determines and makes possible images of White freedom.[3] A White regime
needed to invent Black inferiority, degeneracy, and therefore the natu-
ralness of slavery not only to defend the political order but to invest the
idea of freedom with an opposite. The WPA Guides reflected this even
as they pushed back against it, by enriching 1) the collective treasury
of stories that constitute the American experience, and 2) broadening
the sense, range, and aspirational character of that very American word,
"we." The guides attempted to provide a sort of narrative national self-
understanding founded on the specificity of place, proceeding on the
assumption that there was actually an integral national self to understand. The project was virtually impossible then, and even more so
today. If the nation has anything to learn from the ways in which Southern "culture" is haunted by its history takeaway, one lesson could be how
unhaunted our national history has been by collective failure to be the
reality many of us so casually appeal to in our use of that word.

The final frame on the last roll of black-and-white Kodak film from 1997
is of the golden dome of the Georgia State Capitol in Atlanta. It is evening. The mercury vapor light of Miss Freedom's torch atop the dome is
visible against a darkening August sky. In shadow in the foreground: the
horse-mounted figure of Confederate General John B. Gordon. It is the
last photograph I took on the first tour.

After twelve days in the sweltering heat of the Deep South in July
2018, from Augusta to Fargo, Georgia, to a near-death experience with
a leather-vested, Crocodile Dundee–style, knife-wielding biker in north
Florida to a manhunt in Thomasville, to Montgomery, a strange encounter with the president of the United Daughters of the Confederacy (UDC)
in Selma, across the Black Belt into Mississippi, up the Delta from
Yazoo City to Dyess, Arkansas, to make the turn at Memphis, across
northeast Mississippi from Holly Springs to Okolona and back east via

Birmingham, we end up here again, on the grounds of the Georgia State Capitol. Through a strange coincidence or subconscious convergence, my last photograph from this trip is of the same view as my last one in 1997, of the Capitol dome. It is seven in the evening. The light is harsher this time, but unusually crisp for Atlanta in July. Gordon is not in shadow, but in the bright but waning sun. The light of Ms. Freedom—as she is now known—is washed out by the hot light of Georgia summer.

The Georgia State Capitol has always looked a little imbalanced to me. The showy dome layered with Georgia gold and the Indiana limestone of the main structure go together about as well as you might imagine Georgia and Indiana would. It's a combination of ambitious pretense with no-nonsense pragmatism. But more than that: the disparity between the bling of the dome and the comparably spartan structure that holds it up could be a metaphor for the oppressive social and political structures that have propped up the image of Georgia and its capital as models of progress grounded in the amnesic pursuit of wealth.

The Capitol grounds are shaded with native trees—Southern magnolia, pecan, live oak—but there is less shade than there used to be. After an infestation of starlings came to roost in the 1960s, then–Secretary of State Ben Fortson waged a protracted and mostly unsuccessful war against the birds with tin cans, shotguns, flares, and Roman candles. He lost, and so did three huge magnolias that Fortson had removed. Like the Confederate monument in Tuskegee, the dozen or so monuments to Georgia's political past on the Capitol grounds are more exposed now.

When we were here in 1997, the entrance on Washington Street had been guarded by a statue of "the fiery agrarian Senator Thomas E. Watson," as the WPA Guide to Georgia puts it, "with upraised fist in an attitude of forensic vehemence." (The WPA Guide to Atlanta, published two years after the state guide, interestingly, and perhaps characteristically, softens "forensic vehemence" to "oratorical eloquence.")[4] Whatever the attitude, the message seems to be "get the hell off my lawn." In 2013, Watson himself was removed from the lawn, turned 180 degrees, and set in a park across the street so that now the incendiary agrarian populist raises his fist toward the Capitol itself, not as its gatekeeper but as its benighted exile.

There is a certain kind of Southern mythologist who reveres Watson as the model of the protective, gun-toting, father figure who would sooner coldcock a Yankee industrialist than see his maidenly agrarian

South "outraged" by unwanted advances upon her virginal purity. Watson was also a racist firebrand who became increasingly hostile toward African Americans over the course of his forty-year career in politics. In 1913, he wrote, "In the South we have to lynch him [the Negro] occasionally, and flog him, now and then, to keep him from blaspheming the Almighty, by his conduct, on account of his smell and color."[5] Even if that were the only such comment he had ever made about the matter, it would be enough to question the wisdom of a statue of Watson in front of the entrance to the state capitol. But Watson had his own newspaper, the *Jeffersonian*, in which he fumed prolifically about the evils of Jews, Catholics, Black people, and Coca-Cola. He used it to stoke populist anger against Leo Frank, a Jewish businessman who in 1915 was awaiting a death sentence in the state pen in Milledgeville for the murder of Mary Phagan, a White woman. When Frank's sentence was ultimately commuted to life in prison, a mob of White men, prodded on partly by Watson's editorials, lynched Frank on the town square in Marietta in August 1915.

Watson has been reassigned, but others remain, like Governor Joseph Brown, mustache-less Shenandoah beard down to his midsection, patrician hand on the shoulder of his downcast wife. They are the picture of an antebellum marriage, which surely still brings a nostalgic tear to some eyes around here: he—overcoat draped over one arm, clutching a rolled-up document of some official nature—the pragmatic man of action, business, leadership; she—Bible in her lap, not daring to look up beyond her immediate footprint—the picture of domestic piety and Southern womanhood, the steadfast and matronly guardian of home.

Brown led the state during the Civil War, and after it was over he ran a mining operation in northwest Georgia, and made a fortune off of convict labor, a system that Douglas Blackmon has described as "slavery by another name."[6]

The main entrance to the capitol that Watson once guarded is still flanked by four large plaques, erected by the UDC in 1920, narrating the "sanguinary" siege of Atlanta by federal troops in 1864. Their effect is more Lost Cause mythmaking than history: they tell how, with a "heroism worthy of Sparta, the inhabitants stood the supreme test," enduring a "fearful siege which, lasting for six weeks, was veritably a reign of terror."

Despite everything else I have seen in the last two weeks—and over the last twenty years—the presence of these plaques is still hard to believe.

The White supremacist regime in Georgia politics once ensured that you did not cross into the shrine of government without passing the image of a pissed-off Tom Watson and four skewed accounts of one moment in the city's history. In the same way that Confederate memorials were often placed on courthouse lawns, the symbolism of the architecture of the state capitol was surely no accident: it implies that by entering this building you are tacitly accepting or submitting to an order of things in which history, politics, and law serve White people, to the explicit misfortune of African Americans.

But for every main gateway, there is a service entrance.

At the northeast corner of the building, facing the intersection of Capitol Avenue and the boulevard named for him, there's a new statue of Martin Luther King, Jr., in a quiet corner of the capitol grounds. Like Joseph Brown on the other side of the building, overcoat draped over one arm, he clutches not the Bible but documents, in the prosaic form of a folder full of papers. The monument is barely a year old. The front of the capitol is for White people who supposedly made history, but the back side is the Black section.

A few steps away from the new MLK statue is another monument to African American history in Georgia. Titled *Expelled Because of Color,* the 1976 sculpture by John Riddle tells the story of African American experience in Georgia from images of slavery to the ballot box. The title is a reference to an event in state history that I am hearing about for the first time.

During Reconstruction in Georgia, dozens of newly enfranchised African Americans were seated in the state legislature and thereby given hitherto unknown political power. White resistance kicked in. Thirty-three African American legislators were kicked out of the capitol on the unsurprisingly spurious grounds that their eligibility to hold office was not established by law. The real reason, of course, is obvious.

It's an episode that did not make it into my education. I had to go around back, seek it out.

In *Black Reconstruction in America,* W. E. B. Du Bois describes the episode. Led by a White Democratic senator, "a movement was started to declare that since Negroes were not citizens, they could not hold office."[7] The motion was eventually struck from the record, but the damage was done. Shortly thereafter the push to have African American members removed from the Senate and House succeeded.

The White Democratic senator who led the movement: Milton A. Candler.

My great-great-grandfather's oldest brother, Milton Candler represented the 5th Congressional District of Georgia in United States House of Representatives 1875 to 1879. The same seat that John Lewis held over a century later. Milton was a Democrat, but not like Lewis. In the late nineteenth century, the party was dramatically different than it is today; it largely represented the White elites, and acted the main engine of resistance against the new enfranchisement of African Americans during Reconstruction. I know nothing of Milton's personal political views, but I have a decent idea. Nothing of his story has been passed down to me through family lore. If any of my forebears know anything about Milt, they aren't telling.

I didn't know about Milt at all when John Lewis came to speak at our high school. I only knew slightly more about Lewis, but not much. I knew that he had marched in Selma. I knew that he upset Julian Bond in the Democratic runoff in 1986, and then won easily in the general election. But what I remember from the time he was running for Congress is that his opponents criticized Lewis for the way he talked. He lacked the stately rhetorical polish of Bond. It was not difficult to see, even then, the thinly veiled racism behind those criticisms. But when Lewis came to speak to us, I sensed that something was different from the standard dispensation of Important Information at the weekly Tuesday assembly. He didn't have to come talk to us, and had little to gain by doing so. He knew so much more than he could share with us in fifty minutes. One subject I am sure he knew more about than I did was Milton Candler.

We spend the hot afternoon of the final day of our 2018 tour on the sprawling Atlanta University campus, the largest contiguous consortium of African American colleges in the nation. Arguably the center of African American higher education in the United States, the site is comprised of several historically Black colleges and universities: Clark Atlanta, Morehouse, Spelman, the Interdenominational Theological Center, Morehouse School of Medicine. This is the first time I have set foot on the campus. I am forty-six.

I had to go to North Carolina to first hear the name Flannery O'Connor, who had lived less than a hundred miles from where I grew up. We never read Martin Luther King, Jr., in high school and never heard about Du Bois, both of whom had lived within ten miles of the elite private high school where I did not learn about them.

Atlanta is especially skilled at not making much of local heroes—it is too busy, you will recall. But King and Du Bois were both threatening to the White establishment to which my family belongs and which schools like mine have educated. But they were also two thinkers who offered the possibility to imagine a different way forward: an honest, sober self-examination of White indifference and its costs, and a way to localize and personalize the struggle for civil rights as a project that belonged to Atlanta as a whole, and not just one section of it. In my own case, ignorance about Du Bois is more acute. He's taught me more about my own family history than I have learned from my own flesh and blood.

He taught for twenty-three years on this campus in west Atlanta, and wrote two masterpieces in this place. And while this is my first time to see Atlanta University, it's not as though I was never exposed to the area. Atlanta's Westside was a regular stop on the elementary school field trip circuit. But when our school took us to this part of town, they took us to the other side of the university complex, to the West End, a historically Black section of town along a boulevard named for Ralph David Abernathy.

But we didn't go to West End to see the epicenter of African American culture in Atlanta. We went to visit the Wren's Nest, the stately Victorian home of Joel Chandler Harris, one-time associate editor of the *Atlanta Constitution*, and the author of trickster tales he "wrote" from 1880 until his death in 1908, attributed to a formerly enslaved raconteur called Uncle Remus.

The freckle-faced redhead son of an Irish immigrant mother and an unknown father, Harris was bullied as a kid, and even as an adult. Whatever the cultural impact of his stories was to be a hundred years later, he felt at least some qualified sense of kinship with the slaves on Turnwold Plantation near Eatonton, where he first heard the stories he adapted into the Uncle Remus tales. Du Bois, who was then teaching at Atlanta University, sought Harris out in 1899. In *Dusk of Dawn*, he describes going to meet him: "[I] started down to the *Atlanta Constitution* office, carrying in my pocket a letter of introduction to Joel Chandler Harris. I did not get there. On the way news met me: Sam Hose had been lynched, and they said that his knuckles were on exhibition at a grocery store farther down on Mitchell Street, along which I was walking. I turned back to the University. I began to turn aside from my work. I did not meet Joel Chandler Harris nor the editor of the *Constitution*."[8]

The episode was traumatic for Du Bois. He had been writing a "careful and reasoned statement concerning the evident facts" of the case, and evidently planned to submit them to the *Constitution*. But the sight of Hose's knuckles in the grocery shop window was "a red ray which could not be ignored." Du Bois became convinced that "one could not be a calm, cool, and detached scientist while Negroes were lynched, murdered, and starved."[9] The event changed his life.

None of this made it into the presentations on our field trips to west Atlanta. The red rays were withheld from us. A whole history of the city might as well have never happened. We never heard about W. E. B. Du Bois, never heard that the nation's most prominent African American intellectual lived and taught in this same neighborhood, and certainly never heard about Sam Hose. Atlanta has a history of razing historic buildings, but an even more troubling history of erasing the memory of its most consequential figures, especially when they are Black. Naming streets for some of them may be a good way of honoring them, but it is a better way of ensuring that they will never be talked about.

The house on Sunset Avenue where King spent his last eight years belongs to a different family now. There is no sign to mark it out, except for the conspicuous No Trespassing signs in the yard. I can hardly blame them. Maybe they've had enough of the gawkers, the snoopers, and the past.

Parking is free, however, at the Wren's Nest. It sits—oddly enough—next door to the West Hunter Street Baptist Church, where Ralph David Abernathy moved his congregation in 1973. Fronting the boulevard named for Abernathy, Joel Chandler Harris's house is a conflicted outlier, like its owner and his body of work. To many people that work represents a soothing mythology of half-truths, to others a nefarious White appropriation of Black culture.

A high school education can only give you so much, it is true, and it would be churlish to expect too much from it. But what we were given was less an incomplete set of historical facts than a distorted view of reality in which Joel Chandler Harris is a more noteworthy local celebrity than King or Du Bois. We were given the residue of a deliberate choice to pass over in silence an essential portion of our own city's history.

Truth has not been especially well remembered in a city that has made forgetfulness a marketing strategy. Du Bois has been a victim of that oblivion far more than King has. Even if we had been taken on a field trip to Clark Atlanta University in the 1980s, we would have seen no visible signs of Du Bois's presence. The bust of him in front of Harkness Hall was erected only in 2013. The University did not—until relatively recently—go out of its way to highlight its most famous former faculty member. Du Bois had been kicked off campus in 1943, and died in self-imposed exile in Ghana in 1963, one day before the March on Washington.

I knew nothing about Sam Hose in 1997. It would be twenty years before I learned about him.

"There's a book you should read," David tells me over a lunch in November 2017. David is a Southern historian. A real one, unlike me. So when he tells me there's a book I need to read, I pay attention. "It's called *At the Altar of Lynching*," he says. It's about the lynching of Sam Hose, a Black man accused of murdering a White man in the town of Palmetto in Coweta County, Georgia, in April 1899.

"I think it will interest you," David says. "It concerns your family."

I put off taking him up on his recommendation for months. His cryptic comment about my family did not make me exactly eager to pick it up. He was right. It does concern my family. My great-great uncles are in there. So is my great-great-grandfather.

And it's not just that book, either. Characters from my family's past start to pop up in connection with events I can't believe it's taken me forty-six years to learn about. Philip Dray's *At the Hands of Persons Unknown: The Lynching of Black America* opens with an account of Du Bois seeing Hose's knuckles in a shop window.

On page four: "Georgia governor Allen D. Candler, widely known to endorse lynching as a method of controlling black criminality, termed the Palmetto murder 'the most diabolical in the annals of crime' and declared its details 'too horrible for publication.'"[10]

But the details were published, over and over again. The lynching of Sam Hose is one of the most well-documented events in Georgia criminal history. And it's impossible to tell that story—one of America's most notorious acts of White terror—without mentioning Allen

Candler. My family name is front and center in the history of lynching of African Americans in the United States. How am I only just now hearing about it?

Allen Candler was the leader of the state at a time when his first cousin, my great-great-grandfather, was a colonel in command of a regiment of the state militia and a superior court judge, and his brother and another cousin powerful figures in state politics. As a candidate for the state legislature in 1882, Allen was endorsed by the *Atlanta Constitution* as a "man of the people...whose election would be an honor to the whole state."[11] In the run-up to the 1898 gubernatorial election, the *Marietta Journal* joked that Candler, the "One-Eyed Ploughboy from Pigeon Roost" who had lost an eye in the Battle of Jonesborough, "has the bulge for the governorship. He has one eye on it, at least." With "the largest majority ever received in Georgia," he easily defeated the incumbent William Atkinson, a native of Newnan who as governor had vigorously lobbied, unsuccessfully, for anti-lynching legislation.[12] When the Georgia legislature voted in 1899 to segregate Pullman rail cars, Du Bois and a "committee of the Negroes of Atlanta" personally approached Candler in his downtown office, and pressed him to refuse to sign the legislation into law. Despite initial assurances to Du Bois, Candler ultimately signed the bill creating separate Pullman cars for White and Black people.[13]

On April 12, 1899, Sam Hose, a twenty-one-year-old African American man, killed his boss, Alfred Cranford, with an ax and fled the scene. There was powerful evidence he was acting in self-defense, but that made no difference. For weeks, the Atlanta papers carried news of the sensational event and speculated on Hose's whereabouts, until he was apprehended on the twenty-second. A crowd of thousands, including many who traveled from Atlanta on a specially commissioned train, watched as Hose was tortured and burned alive the following day in a field outside Newnan.

Asked for comment about the lynching of Hose (a.k.a. Sam Holt), Allen Candler put the onus of responsibility on African Americans. He said:

> The negroes of that community lost the best opportunity they will ever have to elevate themselves in the estimation of their white neighbors. The diabolical nature of the double crime was well-known, and they owed it to their race to exhaust every means of bringing Holt to justice. I want to protect [negroes] in every legal right and against

mob violence, and I stand ready to empty every resource of the state in doing so; but they must realize that in order to merit and receive the protection of the community, they must show a willingness to at least aid in protecting the community against the lawless element of their own race.[14]

One month later, Governor Candler delivered the opening address at the Fourth Conference for the Study of the Negro Problems, organized by Du Bois and held at Atlanta University. In the name of the state of Georgia, he expressed affirmation for and loyalty to the work of the university. He urged African Americans to be modest in their expectations, however: "[I]t is unreasonable to suppose that a race emerging from a state of servitude should accomplish in one generation what it has taken our race six hundred years to accomplish."[15]

The presumption that Africans had no culture before they were brought in chains from their native lands was a convenient mythology to serve the logic of White supremacy, and the governor was hardly alone in holding this view. While his official statements on the subject of Black education were predictably high-sounding, his private sentiments seem to have been less enthusiastic.

Two years after the lynching of Hose, Candler was approached at an event in Savannah and pressed for comment about Northern industrialists then touring Atlanta with a view to endowing colleges and schools for African Americans. The governor expressed approval for what Booker T. Washington was doing in Tuskegee, but added that education of African Americans should not go beyond agriculture. "I do not believe in the higher education of the darkey. He must be taught the trades. When he is taught the fine arts, he is educated above his caste, and it makes him unhappy."[16]

Those comments would have surprised no one in 1899. They were expressions of a view that Allen Candler's constituents voted into the state's official pulpit in 1898. It's in this context that Du Bois wrote *The Souls of Black Folk*, whose chapter on Atlanta in particular includes a vigorous defense of a humanistic ideal of the university, whose vocation is finally not technical skill but the pursuit of truth, by the whole person. That is not a coincidence.

I read Du Bois now under the shadow of my distant cousin. I am not especially surprised that my family has never mentioned Allen Candler.

Nor am I surprised to learn that he was a racist. What is surprising is that, even in my own tight-lipped family, an event of such local and national significance should have been so completely passed over in silence.

It ended with a beginning. Aleck's is long gone. There is no trace of it, no smoke-tinged vestige of either the barbecue or the American history that was made here. In its place, a sidewalk leading to a Walmart parking lot.

The West Hunter Street Baptist Church is still there, barely. It sits vacant and boarded up, as if in preparation for a hurricane. At the east end of the boulevard, the gigantic über-modern Mercedes-Benz Stadium looms incongruously like an oversized spaceship in port.

Among the last stops: a return visit to Hillcrest Cemetery on US 78 in Villa Rica, where my great-great-great-grandfather Samuel is buried next to Old Hardshell. I know more about him this time than I did the last time I was here twenty-one years ago. I know now what I did not want or lacked the mind to know then. I now know one of his sons tried to get African Americans removed from the Georgia Senate in 1868. I now know that his nephew Allen did a lot more than just compile historical records. I now know that Samuel himself was one of the largest slaveowners in Carroll County until the end of the Civil War.

On the grounds of the capitol in mid-July 2018, beneath the diminished shade of oaks and magnolias that are not as grand as they are supposed to have been, I find something else I did not see in 1997: a reduced history—my city's, but also my own. The bronze-cast monuments to public history are the crystalized and gathered residue of collective memory but more of collective forgetting. They serve more to occlude than to disclose. The codification of memory, whether public or personal, tends to serve the work of amnesia more than of living remembrance. What the condensation of memory into cold monuments and fixed family fables leaves out, whether through oblivion, time, or self-interest, however, is the more interesting—and, paradoxically, more hopeful—matter.

O'Connor's work helped introduce me to a South I had little experience with. But she also introduced me to the idea that hope—for oneself, for one's city, for one's nation—is only to be found in an honest, and often violent, confrontation with the past—one's own, one's city's, and one's nation's. Mythologies may be soothing, and even good for tourism, but they cannot save us. O'Connor showed me that there is no future for any of us without a clear-eyed and unsentimental reckoning with our own complicity in the suffering of others. That there is nothing more terrifying, exciting, and liberating than the unlearning of untruths, the dethroning of the self and its enabling illusions, the freedom of spaces newly opened up where lies once were.

On the last day of the 2018 tour, I am seeking out the bust of Du Bois, a new presence. I think I know how to get there, but as I make a turn down the wrong street, I realize that I am not as familiar with my hometown as I used to be. I begin to wonder whether I really have the gnosis anymore, or if I ever did. I turn onto a street I do not recognize. It is possible that it was not here the last time. I do not know if it is the right road, but it will—I hope—get me where I think I am going. I do know, however, that if I am going to get to know the place of my birth this time, I am going to have to get lost again. A lot.

Georgia Girl Drive-In, Woodbine, Georgia. Photo by the author.

GEORGIA I
US 19 South, the Road Out

Due south of Atlanta, US 19 unfolds like a ribbon out ahead. Wave on wave of yellow-striped blacktop, each one smaller and more distant than the one before, as the Appalachian piedmont dies out like the last echoes of a global cataclysm five hundred million years ago. Edged with bare red clay on either side and tufted here and there with some sort of grass that looks dead. The kind of grass you normally see on sand dunes. What it's doing here I don't know. But maybe grass knows something.

The road traverses the line of a porous geological boundary that runs from Augusta to Columbus. On one side, the undulating piedmont; on the other, the pancake-flat coastal plain. Along this stretch where the low-sloping ridges of the mountains intermingle with the widening branches of the state's great fluvial systems like the intertwining fingers of two hands at prayer. This transitional band of ancient geological history is rife with decrepitude: at seemingly regular intervals, the roadside is punctuated with decaying roadside barns, periodic mementos mori along the *cammin de nostra vita*, as Dante calls it. They're not pretty—not debutante ball pretty, anyway—but they are beautiful in a way that only time and weather can produce. They are a harbinger of death and decay up all around this boundary, but of a different kind.

Forty-five miles south of Atlanta, the town of Griffin has now been absorbed into the gargantuan Metropolitan Statistical Area and has been lately injected with a new jolt of life by commuters to the city. The tree-lined boulevards that intersect at the center of town are the sort that travel writers even more sentimental than those behind the WPA Guide might describe as "graceful" or "leafy." The WPA Guide is content to leave it at "clean, attractive." It is that: the sort of camera-ready small town that film producers love, especially when they are half an hour from the world's busiest airport.

The dark past is rarely self-evident, especially in "charming" Southern towns like Griffin. At the end of the twentieth century, Griffin was home to a little over 20,000 people. But at the end of the nineteenth, Griffin could claim roughly 7,000 souls. A small railroad town on the Macon and Western rail line with an outsized reputation for racial violence, Griffin is not likely to have been described as "quaint" by African Americans in the late 1890s, when at least five Black men were lynched in or near Griffin.

Griffin in the 1890s represented the forthright preemptive defense against the imminent race riot that was the stuff of White southerners' daily fears, stoked regularly by scandalous news reports from the *Atlanta Constitution* and *Macon Telegraph* about the potential for a Black takeover by some of the 7,000 African American troops stationed in the South. In 1898, President William McKinley's War Department had established four special regiments for the Spanish-American War, each led by a White officer and comprised entirely of Black men who were believed to be immune to yellow fever. After the Treaty of Paris in August of 1898, these regiments began to be disbanded. One of these regiments, the Tenth Immunes, were stationed at Camp Haskell in Macon, and began to be mustered out in March 1899. On the eighth of the month, they passed through Griffin. White citizens fed on a diet of racial paranoia were waiting for the train when it pulled into the station at mid-day.

Lieutenant Colonel Charles Withrow was one of the White leaders of the regiment. As he reported in a letter to the governor, when the train carrying his troops arrived in Griffin, they were met with armed soldiers lining both sides of the tracks. As the train began to pull away, someone discharged a pistol near the front of the train. The soldiers lined up alongside the tracks then opened fire on the sleeping car, which held officers and their wives, some of whom were sitting in the windows when bullets began flying. The rear brakeman, G. L. Agee, was struck by the gunfire, and died from his wounds that night in Atlanta.[1]

The reports from local papers in Griffin, naturally, diverged wildly from the testimony of Lieutenant Colonel Withrow. The *Griffin Daily News and Sun* carried a report saying that "There is nothing that the true Griffinite delights in more than to give instructions to all sojourners in her midst, and if two sections of the 10th Immune Regiment did not learn a lesson here yesterday it was only because Booker Washington is mistaken in the idea that his race is capable of the most rudimentary instruction."[2]

The *Atlanta Constitution* was no more sober: the African American soldiers "Left Macon Ready for Trouble," it proclaimed.[3] They were "in a mood to create trouble and in their drunken condition were ready for any kind of disorder." The main headline across the front page read: "Riotous Colored Troops Cause Trouble by Firing at Citizens."

The rhetoric surrounding the "Griffin Incident" followed a familiar pattern in Jim Crow Georgia: Black people were troublemakers—called in various reports "disorderly," "insatiable brutes," "black despera- does," and "half-drunken fiends"—and White people were the stalwart defenders of law and order ("innocent men," "law-abiding citizens" who had simply "done their duty," "forced" to take extreme measures). The appeal from Withrow was met with derision by many of Griffin's White citizens, members of the Griffin Rifles, the mayor, and the governor of Georgia, Allen Daniel Candler, who accused the lieutenant colonel of making an "imperious and ill natured demand" of him. The Governor's verdict: "The occurrence was deplorable, but those disorderly negroes alone are responsible."[4]

It's not the first or the last time that Allen Candler will blame vio- lence against African Americans on them. Nor is it the last time his name during this trip or its aftermath that I will have a belated encoun- ter with the Governor.

Griffin may be movie-set adorable now, but racially motivated kill- ings are not just ancient history.

On October 9, 1983, the body of Timothy Coggins, a twenty-three- year-old African American man, "was found in a grassy area adjacent to a high-tension power line on Minter Road in the Sunny Side area,"[5] just a few miles north of Griffin on US 41. He had been stabbed mul- tiple times and dragged behind a truck for several miles. No one was ever charged with the crime. If anyone knew anything about the murder, they weren't talking. There was reason in Griffin to be afraid to be too forward about a dead black body.

Thirty-four years later, those fears had become an itch. People had begun to talk. New evidence emerged that revealed that Coggins had been killed for "socializing with a white female." In November 2017 the GBI and Spalding County Sheriff charged two White men in their fifties with the crime, and three other White adults with obstruction. For decades, Franklin Gebhardt and his brother-in-law William Moore bragged about the deed and threatened anyone who spoke of it with the same treatment they had given Coggins. Moore allegedly pined for "the good ole days when you could kill a black man for no reason."[6] In June 2018, Gebhardt was sentenced to life plus twenty years in prison; two months later Moore pled guilty and was given twenty years. There is no reason to describe the murder of Timothy Coggins as anything other than a lynching.

The details of Coggins's murder closely resembled those of James Byrd's in Jasper, Texas, in 1998. Byrd's case made international headlines, and ultimately led to federal hate crime legislation. But the town of Jasper remains haunted by the horrific episode, and even the name Jasper, Texas, seems tainted with the blight of old-school White terrorism. I once knew a priest who had served a parish in Jasper. When I met him, my first thought was of James Byrd. But in Griffin in 1997, I never once thought of Timothy Coggins. Why?

Not only did Coggins's case not make headlines in 1983 the way Byrd's did fifteen years later, but Georgia newspapers also barely mentioned it. The silence over Griffin in 1983 is not inconsistent with the ethos of New South Atlanta in the 1890s, which held that it is more important to look ahead to the future than to look back into the difficult past. In the years following the Civil War, the powers and principalities in Atlanta had made a collective bargain to emphasize the city's progressiveness, at the price of living memory. Just as Griffin has been absorbed into the Metro Atlanta Statistical District, it has been drawn into the capital city's culture of forgetfulness. In many ways, Timothy Coggins is as much a victim of this selective public memory as he is of violence at the hand of two White supremacists.

Memory tends to work like this, by crystallizing a complex history or life into a single, graspable episode. The ancient practice of the art of memory—a part of the art of rhetoric, specifically oration—put this to good use: by associating a specific memory (part of an argument, an episode to be recalled, etc.) with a concrete object in a specific context it is possible to reconstruct a speech entirely from memory so that it could be delivered without a written text. Public memory often partakes of this crystallizing process: we remember Timothy Coggins as a victim of violent racial hatred. At one time, Griffin was infamous as "the lynching capital of the 1890s." It is easy for the brain to work this way, but there are obvious casualties of this reductive process: we forget far more than we recall, such as the life of Timothy Coggins, which deserves to be remembered far more than does his death. Alternatively, when the historical past is condensed into distilled episodes, they not only become easier to remember; they become much easier to forget.

Eugene Talmadge was born in Forsyth, thirty miles south of Griffin on US 41. In the summer of 1946, Ol' Gene was running for governor again. He had served in the office twice before, and in 1946 he saw an opening. In Georgia, as in many other southern states, Democratic primaries had been for White people only for decades shortly before the end of the war. *Smith v. Allwright*, a 1944 US Supreme Court decision, declared the practice in Texas unconstitutional. Two years later, in *King v. Chapman*—a lawsuit initiated in Columbus, Georgia—lawyers for the NAACP, including Thurgood Marshall, argued successfully against the practice in Georgia before a US District Court of Appeals in New Orleans.[7]

The 1946 gubernatorial election would be the first time that African Americans were allowed to vote in the Democratic primary. In Talmadge's mind, *King v. Chapman* was a classic case of Washington interfering with local politics, a textbook example of professional bureaucrats sticking their noses in things that were none of their business. The enfranchisement of African Americans was fuel for Talmadge's staunchly segregationist brand of states' rights politics and gave him the opportunity to stir up racist sentiment among his diehard supporters in rural Georgia.

Canvassing the state in the Georgia summer in shirtsleeves and pleated trousers, Talmadge was handsome and dapper, trim and tan in tortoise-shell frames, black-and-white Oxford wingtips, and—never one to play it safe—both suspenders and a belt, gesticulating from festooned rail depot platforms, courthouse steps, town square gazebos, claiming that "Two million white Georgians are being attacked at their strongest point—their determination to survive as a white State—and they will slap down the decadent 'reformers' by the greatest avalanche of votes ever seen in this State by voting for Eugene Talmadge on July 17."[8]

African Americans took the new opportunity to turn out at the polls in droves, too, but they did not vote for Talmadge. Over 135,000 African Americans were added to the voting rolls in 1946, but Talmadge was not about to let that new enfranchisement stand without a fight. He encouraged White citizens—and when available, sympathetic county registrars—of their legal rights under the Code of Georgia, Title 34, Section 605, to challenge any voter's qualifications, and to call them out if they were "not of good character," or unable to read and offer a reasonable interpretation of any paragraph of the US Constitution.[9] As many as 16,000 registered Black voters were purged from the rolls before the election. In Savannah, polls were closed, while thousands of Black voters remained in line waiting to cast their ballot.

Where voter suppression or psychological intimidation was not wholly effective, "Georgia's demagogue" resorted to threats of violence.[10] Leading up to the election, in a speech in Swainsboro a week before the election, Talmadge openly warned Black people of dire consequences if they tried to vote in Georgia's primaries. "Wise Negroes will stay away from the white folks' ballot boxes on July 17," he said. "We are the true friends of the Negroes, always have been, and always will be as long as they stay in the definite place we have provided for them."[11] He repeated the threat the next day in Cochran, south of Macon, saying, "I think it would be extremely wise for Negroes to stay away from the white folks' ballot boxes on July 17, for neither the U.S. Attorneys nor [Talmadge's opponent in the 1946 gubernatorial race] Jimmie Carmichael will have a corporal guard to back them up."[12]

It wasn't empty political rhetoric. The atmosphere at polling places on July 17 was tense, even where there were separate voting locations for Black and White people (as Black people often requested, out of concern for their own safety). The *Atlanta Constitution* reported the day after the primary that in Cochran, where Talmadge had spoken four days earlier, "not a dozen Negroes went to the Bleckley County Courthouse to vote but left with their ballots after a crowd of white men 'gathered around them,' Sheriff John Smith told the Associated Press."[13] In Meriwether County, between Atlanta and Columbus, there were reports of picketing intended to prevent African Americans from voting.

Talmadge's words carried leaden weight. Roger and Dorothy Dorsey Malcom, and George and Mae Murray Dorsey worked as sharecroppers on Loy Harrison's property in Walton County. George Dorsey was a decorated veteran of World War II, having served in the Pacific theater with the United States Army. George's brother-in-law, Roger Malcom, had been held in the county jail in Monroe for allegedly stabbing a white man during an altercation when Harrison picked him up on bail. On his way back home, Harrison was stopped on a bridge at the county line by a mob of White men, who blocked him in and demanded he hand Roger over to them. As the Malcoms and Dorseys were dragged out of their car at the Moore's Ford Bridge on July 25, one man in the White mob called out to Dorsey, "I bet you're one of those niggers who voted the other day."[14] The mob bound all four of them and took them to woods nearby and murdered them all (including Mae Dorsey's unborn child).

The intersection of Talmadge's violent words with Black lives was not limited to Walton County; a similar incident is south of Griffin, where US 19 crosses Georgia 64 at Butler. Inside the Taylor County Courthouse in Butler there are two plaques in the lobby in memory devoted to the veterans of World War II: one labeled "WHITE," and one "COLORED."

I don't know if Maceo Snipes's name is on one of those plaques. Snipes spent two and a half years with the US Army, and, like George Dorsey, fought in the Pacific Theater in World War Two. Honorably discharged in 1945, he returned to Taylor County to live with his mother, Lula, and work his late father's sharecropped farm. On July 17, 1946, he was the first Black person to vote in Taylor County. The next day, during dinner with Lula, four White men, allegedly local Klansmen, drove up to his house in a pickup truck and called into the house, summoning Maceo away from the supper table. Outside, Snipes got into a scuffle with Edward Williamson, who shot Maceo in the back. Snipes stumbled back into the house, bleeding from the stomach, and then staggered with his mother toward the main road in search of help. Snipes died later in the hospital, having been refused a blood transfusion because there was "no black blood" on hand.

A jury found Williamson—unsurprisingly—innocent of murder, ruling that he had acted in self-defense. Snipes's friends and family were apparently warned that if they held a funeral for Snipes, they would end up the same way he did.[15] He was buried in an unmarked grave somewhere in Butler that his surviving relatives don't even know how to find. To some of Snipes's family, his killing was the last straw. They left for Macon, and caught the next train for Ohio.[16]

White people chose to keep quiet about the whole affair, to bury it along with all the other dark secrets of Taylor County. But others saw the rank hypocrisy of a nation that proudly championed its defeat of fascism in Europe as a sign of national virtue, but which at home could not offer its own citizens of color the dignity and legal protection that White people enjoyed, not even the ones in uniform.

But at least one person wanted to talk about it. Less than three weeks after Snipes's murder, in August 6, a young Martin Luther King, Jr., a student at Morehouse College in Atlanta, wrote to the *Constitution*:

> We want and are entitled to the basic rights and opportunities of American citizens: the right to earn a living at work for which we are fitted by training and ability; equal opportunities in education, health, recreation, and similar public services; the right to vote; equality before the law; some of the same courtesy and good manners that we ourselves bring to all human relations.[17]

It was the first piece King ever had published. To many White people, King and the movement he came to be identified with originated with Maceo Snipes of the US Army voting for the first time in Butler, Georgia. Snipes's murder represented the uniquely American confluence of two equally American but unequally acknowledged activities: a free democratic election and White terrorism.

It goes without saying that insofar as we were taught about King in school, it wasn't this letter that we were told to read, because doing so would have opened up a whole lot of questions that too many people did not have answers for.

American Trilogy: Sumter County, USA

There is little of Friendship left in Georgia now. What remains is just the intersection of state roads 30 and 153, and the customarily disproportionate number of Baptist churches. On a hot August night in South Georgia in 1898, Mary McGarrah and her son James Boone were brutally murdered in Friendship with an ax. Within a day Hamp Hollis had been ratted out by his own wife and lynched for the crime, which he allegedly committed in response to being accused of stealing a slab of bacon. The story is rife with both improbable details and the over-the-top language characteristic of the subject matter at the time. "A more revolting, damnable crime was never committed by fiend incarnate," reported the *Atlanta Constitution*.[18]

Friendship is on the northwestern limit of Sumter County, a region of South Georgia that is rife with contradictions, where sin rides shotgun with Jesus. The county is home to three towns that are identical with contrary poles of American experience: in less than 500 square miles are sites associated with globally recognized humanitarian organizations, a hammer-wielding nonagenarian ex-president of the United States, a wartime concentration camp, a baseball pariah, and Christianity of almost every stripe. All of America's favorite vices and virtues are condensed within the borders of Sumter County: pride, charity, lust, humility, courage, cowardice, violence, pacifism, racial equality, and racist hatred. And baseball. Its county seat is, appropriately, named Americus, because Sumter County, Georgia, may be the most American county in the land.

Americus

Americus, Georgia, is not an obvious spring break destination, but that's where I spent mine in 1992. An opportunity arose to go hammer nails and dig drainage ditches for Habitat for Humanity, but that's not why I went. There was a girl I had an incurable crush on, and she was going. She was dating another guy, but he didn't go to Americus that spring. I drove down to South Georgia from North Carolina because sometimes eros can inspire acts of unintentional virtue.

Five years later, I wanted to see Americus again, but not just to relive the memories of young love or of a time when I did something for other people. I wanted to see the road again.

There is one stretch in particular I wanted to revisit: a sweeping, leftward curve in US 19 north of Americus that affords an expansive view of the last of Georgia's hills, a bucolic vista of white-planked farmhouses and dilapidated barns in the signature rust and weathered-oak palette of the deep South. I'd hoped to get a photograph of it this time, capture it on film the way I'd remembered it, secure it, and lock it down for future reference. But I never took the shot. Maybe I was driving, maybe the old view did not register this time the way it did five years earlier. Sometimes seeing something for a second time is not seeing it at all.

Americus is supposed to have been named for General John Americus Smith, Amerigo Vespucci, or the "merry cusses" who settled here, depending on whom you believe. The speculative etymology is an apt example of how much any single version of American history depends on its sources, and how much of a market there is and has always been for rank nonsense. However it came to be, the name is especially apropos,

because Americus is a microcosm of American virtues and vices, concentrated in part around the town's history with baseball.

Americus has been home to a number of professional baseball teams
since the beginning of the twentieth century, starting with the bottom-
dwelling and macabrely named Pallbearers of the Georgia State League.
The Pallbearers finished—appropriately—dead last in the league, and
the team was not revived for the 1907 season. The *Atlanta Constitution*
reported in June 1906 that "[D]espite the discouraging aspect of the situ-
ation Americus fans are loath to surrender their baseball franchise . . .
Americus has an excellent team now, and having weathered the disasters
of the opening of the season with its alleged incompetent management,
is inclined to stay in the game if possible."[19] In a classic case of mixed
messaging, the paper reported on the very same page that the team failed
to show up at the previous day's game against the Waycross Machinists.
After the umpire gave the Machinists a 9–0 victory, because a baseball
field with a loaded gallery is a terrible thing to waste, "two scrub teams
played to a fairly large crowd."[20]

Covering the Pallbearers for the *Constitution* must have felt like pun-
ishment to whoever got stuck with the job. A game against the Columbus River Snipes was "unmarked by special feature."[21] Later that June,
the reporter was in Valdosta where the Pallbearers went up against the
Stars. "Both sides played indifferent, careless ball today and Americus
won an uninteresting game by a score of 5 to 4."[22] The league folded in
July. But resurrection was in the future, thanks to a blacklisted baseball
messiah.

In 1919, Joe Jackson was the Pete Rose of Major League Baseball. A
first-class hitter with a career average of .356, "Shoeless Joe" was dis-
graced by his alleged involvement in the notorious Black Sox scandal
of 1919 and banned for life by then-Commissioner Kenesaw Mountain
Landis. But Joe didn't let much infield dirt gather on his feet, shod or
not. Using fake names, the "former Chicago White Sox gardener"[23] continued to play small-time ball in minor leagues up and down the east
coast, an itinerant slugger wandering the country in disguise.[24] In 1923,
the Americus "Looseknit Ball Club" was not interested in Landis's judgment nor Jackson's aliases.[25] They signed Jackson for $75 a week.[26]

Not everyone was thrilled by Joe's arrival in Americus. "Joe Jackson
is Disrupting Baseball," a headline in the *Tampa Tribune* declared.[27] "Still
a Thorn in Organized Baseball," said the *Jackson Clarion-Ledger*.[28] While

baseball officials argued over Jackson's eligibility, locals in Americus could not have cared less. They formed "practically an all-day welcome at his hotel, calling there to talk with the former 'big leaguer'" on his arrival in Sumter County.[29] Hitting a "three-bagger" in his first at-bat, he turned the struggling squad around, and led them to a victory over Albany in the league championship.

It was a pyrrhic victory for the club. The unorganized South Georgia League disbanded in August, and some blamed its demise on Shoeless Joe. The league was thriving before he got to Americus, the *Berkshire Eagle* claimed. "Jackson was forced on the league; after the curiosity to see this confessed thrower of games was satisfied the fans quit the games and the backers threw up the sponge."[30] "Jackson's home run hitting has broken up many a ball game," claimed the *Shreveport Times*, "but is now credited with packing enough punch in the willow to break up a league."[31]

Joe Jackson was a blight on the story of American baseball as a site of national purity, a pain in the ass for the keepers of the flame of the national game. But people in Americus didn't seem to mind Jackson's moral turpitude: tarnished or not, he was a major league star in a definitely minor league town. Forgiveness was beside the point: Americus gave him welcome because he could help them win.

Americus has long had an on-again-off-again affair with baseball (off since 2002), but its relationship to Christian charity has been more abiding. In 1942, Clarence Jordan and his wife Florence established the Koinonia Farm here, a "demonstration plot for the Kingdom of God." The Jordans built an intentional Christian community modeled on the very early church, sharing resources and property in common. The multi-racial community farmed together, ate together, prayed together. In South Georgia—home to segregationist Gene Talmadge's base in the 1940s—the idea of Black and White people intermingling like this was anathema to many. Townspeople boycotted the farm.

In 1957, the sheriff of Sumter County was not having it, either. "The people have had it up to here," he said. "We get reports of whites and Negroes strolling down the streets together in Americas. One report said a white girl and two Negro boys walked down the street eating popcorn out of the same bag. They're operating more openly now than ever before and somebody's going to get hurt."[32] The mayor of Americus said Koinonia was "like a cancer on the community and we ought to get rid of it."[33]

In January of that year, a roadside produce stand operated by the farm was destroyed by dynamite thrown from a passing vehicle. The next month, "night riders blasted out floodlights" on the farm property and burned a cross in the yard of an elderly African American couple.[34] The Ku Klux Klan sought to buy the property and drove a seventy-car motorcade onto the farm in a curious show of interest. Two days later, it emerged that the FBI and the Georgia Bureau of Investigation had long been looking into the community for "subversive activities." Paranoid suspicions that Koinonia constituted "a conspiracy to overthrow the government" were not supported by the evidence, in spite of how hard many locals and Klansmen may have attempted to manufacture it.[35]

In April 1957, a Sumter County grand jury alleged that Koinonia has "close friends among known Communists and has entertained known Communists," but lacked sufficient evidence "to convict of communism in a court of law."[36]

That month, Dorothy Day, the founder of the Catholic Worker Movement, was in Koinonia for an extended stay. One night, she and another woman kept watch by night at the entrance to the farm. She wrote an account of it for the *Catholic Worker* newspaper: "Friday nights are bad nights, many cars passing. Usually we get out to let them see people are on hand. But this time, at one thirty, we were sitting in the first and second seats of a station wagon, under a floodlight, under a huge oak tree, and a car slowed up as it passed and peppered the car with shot. We heard sounds of repeated shots – a regular gunfire, and we were too startled to duck our heads."[37]

In 1965, a young couple named Millard and Linda Fuller visited Koinonia Farms. Fuller sold his share of a direct-mail marketing operation to his business partner, Morris Dees. Dees went on to establish the Southern Poverty Law Center; Fuller gave his wealth away and eventually moved his whole family to Americus. With Jordan, the farm turned its attention to the Fund for Humanity, a "partnership housing" project aimed at building decent homes for people who otherwise might not be able to afford them. In 1973, four years after Clarence Jordan died suddenly, the Fullers left Koinonia for Zaire, where they implemented the Fund's principles. Three years later they returned to Americus and established Habitat for Humanity, which in 2018 dedicated its world headquarters in Americus to Clarence Jordan.

Few, if any, would have predicted in 1942 that this remote corner of peanut country in South Georgia would become a kind of epicenter of radical hospitality and a revolutionary model of intentional community—or, in the view of its detractors—a hot bed of communism. There are alternative versions of Christianity on offer in Americus, too, if you prefer the more predictable, billboard variety.

At the junction of US 19 and Millard Fuller Boulevard, Granny's Kitchen promises "Down Home Cookin." On this day it is served with an appetizer of religious admonition. A white van parked in front proclaims:

> SINCE THE SECULAR HUMANIST, ANTI-CHRIST SYSTEM HAS
> DEPRIVED YOU OF LEARNING GOD, THE CREATORS MORAL
> PARAMETERS FOR ALL OF MANKIND:
> HERE IS WHAT THEY DON'T WANT YOU TO KNOW

It's followed by the Ten Commandments in stenciled red paint. The VIIth, the one against adultery, is glossed with the word FORNICATION, just so we're clear.

At this intersection, Millard Fuller Boulevard becomes US 280, which takes you to Plains, ten miles away. We take the other way, for a detour via Georgia 49 to Andersonville.

Andersonville

Being educated is supposed to mean being aware of the things you aren't educated about, becoming cognizant of the gaps in your own knowledge of the world. In 1992, Flannery O'Connor was one of those gaps. Being introduced to her in my early twenties was like finding an extra present behind the Christmas tree that you had overlooked. It was a kind of unbelievable gift, that this woman who'd change your life was right in your living room the whole time.

Andersonville, Georgia, was one of those gaps, too. But learning about it was like finding a cigar box full of Nazi memorabilia in your grandfather's closet. You wish you hadn't.

I experienced, if not quite a crack-up, certainly a moment erosive of the accumulated silt of assumption and ignorance, at the northeast corner of Sumter County at Andersonville, the site of a notorious Confederate prison camp during the Civil War. I didn't learn about Andersonville formally in any of the high-priced classrooms where I was taught, but first heard of it in a song on *The Killing Floor*, a 1992 masterpiece by the Vigilantes of Love, one of the greatest bands to come out of Athens. I heard them play at Ziggy's in Winston-Salem around that time, when *The Killing Floor* began to turn me out of an unfortunate NutraSweet-country phase I had been suffering under since high school. Head Vigilante Bill Mallonee sang about Andersonville, but I didn't realize what he meant until I ended up there on a visit in August 1997.

> We were locked in hell in Andersonville
> In shebangs hot and stinking
> The stream we use as our latrine
> Gives water for our drinking
> And a hundred of us daily die
> To fill those fresh-dug graves[38]

Andersonville wasn't quite in my living room, but it was basically in the backyard, a hundred and twenty miles south of Atlanta in a deliberately remote part of the state. Conditions were horrific at Andersonville. Union prisoners were starved and diseased, forced to drink from the same shit-swamp in the middle of the camp that held their own excrement. Contemporary descriptions of the place resemble those of Nazi labor camps in Poland during World War Two, and the likeness is not entirely an accident. Camp Sumter, as the concentration camp in Andersonville was officially called, was a precursor to the camps of the Third Reich. The military tribunal that tried Andersonville commandant Henry Wirz was a model for the Nuremberg trials eighty years later.

Born Heinrich Hartmann Wirz in Zurich, twenty-six-year-old Wirz left his wife and kids in Switzerland and ended up in Louisiana, where in 1861 he enlisted with the Confederate Army. In 1864 he was given command of Camp Sumter, which he ruled with an iron hand. Rumors that he murdered prisoners were not unheard of, nor suppressed. He was arrested in May of 1865. In Annapolis that year, Walt Whitman witnessed a "large boat load" of newly freed, emaciated captives returning from Southern prisons. "Can those be *men*?" he asked. "The sight was worse than any sight of battle-fields, or any collection of wounded, even the bloodiest." He said that the treatment of prisoners of war in places like Andersonville "steeps its perpetrators in blackest, escapeless, endless damnation."[39]

For Whitman, it was a sign of contradiction. "Reader," he asked, "did you ever try to realize what starvation actually is?—in those prisons—and in a land of plenty?"[40] That November, hundreds of Union soldiers on the grounds and onlookers on nearby tenement roofs and balconies watched as "the Demon of Andersonville" was hanged from a stockade in Washington within sight of the Capitol. As his body dropped from the gallows, some in the crowd cried, "Remember Andersonville!"

Wirz is one of only a handful of men during the Civil War to be convicted and executed for war crimes, but outside the boundary of what is now the Andersonville National Cemetery, in the middle of Church Street in the tiny village of Andersonville, there is—naturally—a large obelisk in his honor of Wirz, erected in 1909 by the UDC to "rescue his name from the stigma attached to it by embittered prejudice."

The UDC has long been the chief organ of Lost Cause mythology, which still has a strong hold on the imagination of many people in this isolated outpost of Georgia's upper coastal plain. In other cities and towns, statues of Lee, Jackson, Davis, "Silent Sam," and other monuments to White supremacy have been removed, but the monument to Wirz still looms over Church Street. There have been—as far as I know—no marches for its removal, no op-eds in the local paper arguing that its time has long passed. On the contrary: the local chapter of the Sons of Confederate Veterans (SCV) holds an annual memorial service for Wirz on the anniversary of his execution.

The effect of the UDC's continued propaganda mission to "set the record straight" about Wirz (and countless other Confederate figures), however, is to forestall the kind of crack-up that America most desperately needs: a consequential confrontation with the most unsavory truths about ourselves and with the potentially irresolvable errors inherent in our national self-image. The real monument to Wirz is not, however, the marker on Church Street, but the thousands of white marble headstones for the Union prisoners who did not have to die here. Which leaves the obelisk to Wirz on Church Street to serve another purpose: as a monument to collective forgetfulness, to selective outrage, to the most threatening disease that bedevils American culture at this hour: amnesia.

Plains

Clear across Sumter County from Andersonville, Plains didn't even make the 1940 WPA Guide to Georgia. It was a relatively young town then, incorporated only in 1896, when, like so many towns in America, the laying of rail lines determined which intersections would be the generative loci of life. What is now Plains was originally called Plains of Dura, one of the three settlements that became one in the nineteenth century.

According to the Book of the prophet Daniel, "King Nebuchadnezzar made an image of gold, whose height was sixty cubits and its breadth six cubits. He set it up on the plain of Dura, in the province of Babylon."[41] It's difficult to imagine a stranger namesake for this town. Plains is decidedly lacking in gold, and Sumter County has voted blue in the most recent elections. One of the poorest counties in the state, where two-thirds of African American residents live below the poverty line, it belongs to the 2nd Congressional District, and has been represented by Sanford Bishop, a Democrat and African American, since 1993. It has not been represented by a Republican since Reconstruction and cannot realistically be called Trump Country. In many unexpected ways, Sumter County complicates the widely shared perception of the South as monocultural or monopolitical. But more than that: a little time here can help to loosen the hold of even the most possessive of American myths.

Plains is well-preserved, if not exactly lively. White wooden structures dot the area around the old depot. A fragment of a Main Street, not a full block long, two-storied brick structures fronted by a uniform rusted tin-roof veranda held up by painted four-bys. East into the bend on 280, silver-toned silos and elevators of grain mills, the silver water tower. All of it is postapocalyptically quiet.

It's also hot as hell. The center of Plains is the synapse of two parabolic curves—one for US 280 and the other for the railroad—which almost kiss each other at Bond Street, right next to Billy Carter's Service Station. On my first visit to Plains in 1997, a marquis out front stood unsteadily on an arid patch of gravelly soil, amid occasional pine seedlings and burned-out grass. The light bulbs were all gone from the marquis, which delivered either a cryptic message or the remnants of one: I L LILIY. On the building, a white OPEN sign hung a-kilter from a nail next to the door. On the other side, a Pepsi machine, slightly incongruous for South Georgia. On our return here twenty years later, the gas station has been restored and converted into a museum. The 90's Pepsi machine is gone, replaced by a more regionally accurate vintage Coke machine. Inside is every manner of Billiybilia, including cans of his famous Billy Beer, whose status as an icon of Americana was forever solidified when it made an appearance on *The Simpsons.*

I turned five years old a few weeks before Jimmy Carter was elected president in 1976. It was the bicentennial year, when myths of American innocence and nobility were probably at an all-time high. Not that I noticed much: in the years to come, I would hang on to the bicentennial quarters I'd come across, the ones with the colonial drummer on the tails side. They weren't worth any more than regular quarters, but I'd think twice before I stuck one into the coin slot of *Asteroids* or *Pac-Man* at the Timeout arcade at Lenox Square Mall. But if you absolutely had to use one of these special coins, you told yourself it just might get you a high score, or your initials onto the scoreboard. Maybe I implicitly believed somehow that the nobility of the tricorned figure and the cause whose drum he dutifully beat would redound to my benefit, however trivial.

For most people who know about this sort of thing, there was not much worth remembering about Carter's presidency. I remember almost nothing, but what I do is colored with the hot light of the Middle East: OPEC-induced lines of Buick sedans and Oldsmobiles at gas stations, a protracted hostage crisis, Anwar Sadat and Menachem Begin shaking hands in front of the White House, and the shah of Iran, whose name was emblazoned on a burlap bag of uneaten pistachios that sat in our kitchen counter for probably the whole of Carter's presidency. But not much else. Presidential politics did not intrude into most little boys' lives in 1977 the way it does into everyone's life now whether we like it or not. If few people—including a lot of Georgians—were not all that happy with Carter in the late seventies, I wouldn't have known it.

The white-clapboard railroad depot that served as the headquarters for Carter's 1976 campaign is emblazoned with a sign indicating as much. The depot faces the rail lines expectantly, as if waiting for Jimmy to roll in again someday. It's a bit of a ruse. Jimmy still lives here.

In the window of one of the stores, a laser-printed leaf of white paper announces the dates Jimmy will be teaching Sunday School at the unassuming Baptist Church up the road.

Inside the depot is a fittingly unvarnished, raw timber museum to Carter's Presidential Campaign. In the foyer is a case of campaign buttons, including one announcing, "JIMMY CARTER LUSTS . . . FOR ME!" It's a reference to the famous interview Carter did with *Playboy Magazine* in 1976, in which he confessed, "I've looked on a lot of women with lust. I've committed adultery in my heart many times."[42] Which, naturally, initiated a bona fide shitstorm in Georgia and Texas and elsewhere where much of the electorate was shocked to learn that *Playboy* printed interviews with words.

It seems quaint now that a president should have once been pilloried for an unexpected act of honest introspection. Carter was not universally rewarded—much less absolved—for his confession, especially among those who thought then that religion was a private matter between you and God and not you and the readership of *Playboy*.

In 1975, he was "Jimmy Who?" But now he has the universal appeal of a rock star, but one whose life has been given over to people who haven't fared as well as he has. Nowadays people generally don't seem so insistent on keeping religion a private matter, as long as it agrees with their ideas of what a religion is supposed to be for. In 1976, Carter's frankness about his faith did not play well everywhere; today he is for many a model of what a public, lived Christianity can look like. Jimmy seems to embody an idea I once heard the novelist Marilynne Robinson put into words: "I am a Christian, but I am not angry at anybody." The Carters have deep roots in the soil of Sumter County—both its contradictions and its best aspirations—and from the area's peculiar culture of lives in service to others. They could easily be cooling their heels in some Florida high-rise, but they haven't chosen that life.

Friendship is not entirely absent from Sumter County now. Even now there are images of alternative lives, of people determined to make America otherwise, crack-ups that lead the other way from despair. One is Jimmy Carter, ninety-five, his right eye bruised and stitched up after a fall, tapping nails into someone else's home on one day, on Sunday sitting in a packed sanctuary at the Baptist church teaching about kindness to the friendless. A contradiction, perhaps, but a hopeful one: wounded and frail, bloodied and bandaged, but a servant of others, a living *nevertheless*.

In 2018, twenty-one years after my first visit here, we drive past the Carter compound en route to the screen-porched Sears-Roebuck house where he spent his youth. We pass Jimmy and Rosalynn walking along the four-lane to dinner at the retirement home next door. It is 5:30. Rosalynn is ninety, Jimmy is ninety-three, same as the temperature. They could have had food delivered. They could share the parasols the casual security detail behind them is using, or ride with the guys in the black Tahoe with the A/C on. But soberly, determinedly, they walk.

Albany: The King is Gone

I first rode a motorcycle near Albany sometime in the 1980s, when my friend Sammy invited me down for a weekend at his family's place amongst the prolific pecan groves of Dougherty County. I assume his father was off shooting quail with other grown men and bird dogs, but it wasn't important. We rode his miniature Honda motorbike around the fields and slalomed in between pecan trees, shot up Coke cans with a bolt-action .22 rifle. It was Tom Sawyer freedom—exhilarating, fun as hell, and totally illusory.

The countryside around Albany has long been home to playgrounds for wealthy Atlantans, some of whom maintain lush quail hunting "plantations" in the area. It is no accident that when Tom Wolfe needed an airstrip-equipped quail plantation for Charlie Croker, the title character of A Man in Full, he put it in South Georgia near Albany. It's not fiction, though. There are dozens of massive tracts of privately-owned South Georgia woodlands owned by fabulously wealthy White men with connections to the too-busy-to-hate world of Atlanta commerce. Robert Woodruff bought 29,000 acres southwest of Albany in the 1920s. Doug Ivester, former CEO of the Coca-Cola Company, owns an 18,000-acre tract near Albany. Ted Turner has one half that size (but don't feel bad for ole Ted; he owns more land than any American apart from two or three people). Most of these sites—Pine Hill, Wynfield, Abigail, Nonami—still call themselves "plantations," and while some of them, like Woodruff's Ichauway Plantation, are devoted to research and conservation, many of them cater to that set of Garden & Gun subscribers for whom ads for expensive, Italian-made Beretta shotguns, bespoke hunting vests, and Kodiak leather gun bags are deliciously alluring. Whatever it is that wealthy hunters take back with them on their private jets back to Atlanta, it is not likely the local past, or even the local present.

When W. E. B. Du Bois traveled here by train from Atlanta at the turn of the twentieth century, he encountered a land of stretched shadows and creeping specters, the crumbling detritus of collapsed empire. "A resistless feeling of depression falls slowly upon us," he wrote, "despite the gaudy sunshine and the green cotton-fields. This, then, is the Cotton Kingdom,—the shadow of a marvelous dream. And where is the King?"[43]

Cotton is no longer King in Dougherty County. It had already gone into decline by the time Du Bois passed through, when the now legendary pecan trees that hatch the landscape in patterned rows were mere saplings. Pecans have been the cash crop for over a century now, and until 2017 Georgia was the largest producer of pecans in the country, accounting for a third of the national crop.

The storied pecan groves around Albany still flourish and nourish romantic visions of a more quaint order of reality than the frenetic commercial life of the distant capital city, but even now there are suggestions available to the attentive that not everything in Dougherty County is fodder for luxury lifestyle marketing copy.

If Albany was "a lively sports town," a "popular stop-over for visitors" when the WPA writers visited in 1940, it sure doesn't feel like it when we stop here in 2018. We do not find "the sidewalks gay with beach pajamas, slacks, and flannels," nor the streets "crowded with shiny, stream-lined cars full of recreation-seekers." Already reeling from a 2017 tornado that killed five, a few months after we visit Albany it will be slammed by Hurricane Michael. A category five storm when it made landfall in and comprehensively destroyed Mexico Beach, Florida, Michael was still a category three storm when it hit Albany, 150 miles inland. Albany's already-staggering economy was knee-capped. Thousands were left without power, buildings were damaged, and the local pecan and cotton crops crumbled. After Michael, pecan production in 2019 had made it only to 20% of what it had been the year before. Du Bois' words in 1903 seem strangely resonant in the immediate aftermath of Michael in Albany in late 2018: "All is silence now, and ashes, and tangled weeds."[44]

The Flint River flows southward out of Albany and forms the eastern boundary of Baker County. On the north side of the river, Robert Woodruff's Ichauway Plantation at one time hosted an annual barbecue "for Negroes only." In 1963, Charlie Ware, one of three thousand Black attendees at the event, allegedly got too friendly with the mistress of Guy Touchtone, Ichauway's White overseer and major-domo of the barbecue. Touchtone complained to Sheriff L. Warren "Gator" Johnson, who called at Ware's home later that night. Finding Charlie not at home, he beat his wife instead until he returned home. The Sheriff then beat Charlie Ware and arrested him, drove him to the jail in nearby Newton, seat of the county known to local African Americans as "Bad Baker."

Parked outside the Baker County jail, with Ware handcuffed beside him on the front seat, Johnson picked up his radio transmitter and said, "This nigger's coming on me with a knife! I'm gonna have to shoot him." He fired two .32-caliber bullets into Ware's neck. "He's still coming on! I'm going to have to shoot him again," said Johnson, and fired a third time.[45]

Somehow, Ware survived the shooting, and sued the sheriff of $150,000, but the case did not go to trial until 1963. In the meantime, the civil rights movement had already come and gone in Albany, and its most uncelebrated campaign left the White status quo virtually intact. So when a jury in Columbus acquitted Johnson that April after less than half an hour deliberation, it was clear evidence that little had changed in Albany even since Du Bois's train journey through here sixty years earlier. Ware's attempt at legal justice not only failed in the usual way: in 1943 the sheriff of Baker County, Claude Screws, arrested Robert Hall, a Black man, for stealing a tire. In front of the very same jail where Charlie Ware was nearly killed by Screws's successor, "in public view, Screws beat Hall with first and blackjack for at least fifteen minutes, then dragged his lifeless corpse into a jail cell."[46] A federal grand jury ultimately acquitted Screws and two other accomplices who participated in the beating death.[47]

Sixteen years later, however, at least one thing had changed. In 1945, the Screws verdict was not met with protest marches or boycotts. In 1961, some local Black activists responded to the acquittal of Gator Johnson by boycotting a grocery store in Albany's Black neighborhood operated by Carl Smith, a member of the White jury. But it went about as well as previous attempts at justice in Baker and Dougherty Counties. The protest lasted an hour before Albany police chief Laurie Pritchett shut it down. In August 1963 the Department of Justice indicted nine civil rights workers for obstruction of justice for picketing Smith's store, which closed due to the loss of Black patronage.[48] The episode, which Howard Zinn called at the time "[p]robably the most shameful act of the Department of Justice in the recent history of civil rights crises," made it into John Lewis's speech at the Lincoln Memorial three weeks later during the March on

Washington.[49] The short protest at Smith's Supermarket was, according to Taylor Branch, "the most significant single picket line of the entire civil rights movement," but it's the kind of story that is not likely to make it into the glossy brochures on the desk at the posh quail plantations near Albany, but it is an episode revealing of the imaginative fissures between what Albany is for White people and what it is for Black people.[50]

Specter of Camilla

Back on US 19 South to Camilla, John tells me about his paternal grandfather, Eben Hayes. He was originally from Marion County, South Carolina, and ended up in Camilla around 1909. Eben was a Democrat during the war, but after it was over he joined the Republican Party. In 1870 the *Charleston Daily News*—not a pro-Republican newspaper—called him "an old uncleanly white man." It was a courageous move for a White man in 1870 South Carolina, and brought Hayes a lot of enemies. One of them was the planter-publisher of the *Marion Star*, who once offered a bounty for Old Eben's head, and refused to capitalize his name in print. The paper called him "a pretended minister of the gospel." Eben was mocked for his advanced age, but in the state house it was a sign of his seniority. He was thought of as "the Patriarch of the House."[51]

Hayes's story is an amazing tale of conversion, turning against the grain of Southern White society. Five years after the war, Reconstruction was not universally popular in the Low Country bulwarks of the Lost Cause. A change of heart, or an act of moral conviction that might have cost him a lot. Eben Hayes was a scalawag.

I don't have any similar family stories of moral courage in this period of our history, when a family member stood on a principle so contrary to local mores. Camilla represents for John a story of nobility, of principled morals. It's the kind of story I don't really have much access to: when my family members were sitting in Congress or in the halls of elected power, they were in the ruling class, not in the dissenting one. They were Democrats, and generally speaking accepted—either explicitly or tacitly—the logic of White supremacy and did not question it. Some—like the Bishop and the Judge—may have come later to try to upset that logic, but my family history in 1870 is on the opposite side of history from Eben Hayes, and Camilla is where that line is drawn.

On September 19, 1868, a "speaking" was to be held in Camilla for the Republican Party. Basically a political rally with a fife-and-drum band, it drew hundreds of newly enfranchised Black voters along the road from Albany into Camilla, the seat of Mitchell County. Word spread that White people in Albany were stockpiling weapons and preparing for war. Some of the Black people who marched into Camilla that morning were carrying rifles and shotguns out of habit, but few of them came with ammunition. White people in Mitchell County spread rumors of an armed Black insurrection, the looming race war that would come to terrorize paranoiac White consciences for decades. When the African American delegation, led by representative Philip Joiner, arrived in Camilla, they were met by an armed mob at least fifty strong. Embittered and trigger-happy White men began firing on the marchers. Chaos ensued—Black people fled on horseback and sought shelter in the heavily wooded swamps or "among the gallberry bushes and bamboo briars &c. hanging over from the banks," as James Washington did.[52] When it was over ten or more African Americans where dead, thirty more wounded. Those that survived and still believed in the democratic process were intimidated into sitting out the general election later that November.

Joiner had been one of twenty-nine African American members of the state legislature who had been removed from office at the beginning of September 1868, just a few weeks before the act of terror in Camilla. White men like those who massacred African Americans in Camilla had been energized by the removal, and by the idea of White people "retaking their government," an idea first proposed in the Georgia Senate by Milton Anthony Candler.

So Camilla is a dividing line: it marks where the words of one man with whom I share a name and an ancestor led ultimately to the deaths of innocent victims.

The year 1868 marked a kind of conversion for Eben Hayes, but not for Milton Candler. Six years later, Milton Candler was on the Democratic ticket for the 5th United States Congressional District. He had been out of public life for two years, but voters still remembered him. In 1874, he was still riding on the strength of his political gestures six years earlier, when he had initiated a motion to have three newly seated Black senators removed from the Georgia Senate. The motion failed, but Democratic voters remembered Milt. "A pale, low-browed, slender individual; he possessed a full, sonorous voice and an unusual energy of expression and delivery,"[53] a contemporary said of him. At a barbecue in 1874, he used that energy and played to his strength: exploiting White fears. The Republicans, he said:

> are not satisfied with simply degrading the whites, and depriving some of the best and most intelligent of the right to vote, or have any influence in the government, but they propose to grant that power to the ignorant and degraded negro, and to make him competent to vote and hold office. And your dearest interests and rights are to be entrusted to the colored people, who have already demonstrated to the world their incapacity to administer any civilized government—a race without virtue or intelligence, who exercise political power not for their own good. No, my friends, that is not the secret. The reason is that they may perpetuate power in that party that hates you and does not love them—a party that hates the constitution of our fathers.[54]

"The War of Northern Aggression" was not just a quaint, tongue-in-cheek expression for Milton. He attributed the "desolation" of the war explicitly to the Republican party, who "inaugurated and carried [it] on." "They make war on the whole white race of the south," he fumed, "destroyed everything hitherto held sacred by our wisest and best men." He railed against the proposed Civil Rights Bill because it would force Black and White people to socialize together. "You will not be allowed to say to a negro when he takes a seat by your wife or daughter that you object," he said.[55]

I have no way of knowing whether Milton was a member of the Klan, but he sure as hell had the resumé of one. After Milton was elected to the US House in 1877, "the men of Decatur held a torch-light parade from the town out to the farm, some on foot, some on horseback, their torches flickering up through the trees of the avenue."[56] And in his home at 146 South Candler Street, the Agnes Lee chapter of the UDC was organized in 1901.[57] Milton's daughter Claude was a member, and as president of the chapter, his daughter-in-law, Mrs. Charles Murphey Candler, led the fundraising campaign for the Confederate monument in Decatur.[58] And if Milt wasn't a Klansman, he certainly hung out with people who were. On Sunday afternoons in the 1870s, former Confederate general and Georgia governor John B. Gordon would ride his horse over from "Sutherland," his Tara-esque mansion in Kirkwood, to Milton's farm in Decatur to talk politics. It is generally accepted that Gordon was the de facto head of the Klan in Georgia. What he and Milt likely talked about on the veranda is—well, you do the math.

Gordon was only the de facto head because the organization of the Klan was "never perfected," as Gordon testified before Congress in 1870. "I was spoken to as the chief of the State," Gordon testified. While he defended the organization as "a brotherhood of the property-holders, the peaceable, law-abiding citizens of the State, for self-protection"[59] against Negroes who "were being incited throughout the South to antagonism and violence,"[60] Gordon denied—unconvincingly—knowledge of any acts of violence committed by disguised vigilantes against Black people. In an intense line of questioning, Representative John Coburn, a Republican from Indiana, presented Gordon with a series of examples of "outrages" against African Americans designed to prevent them from voting in the recent election. Gordon denied any knowledge of any such intimidation, and held firmly to his belief in the "kindly" relationship between Black and White people generally. But one exchange revealed Gordon's memory of racial harmony might not be so trustworthy:

> Question. You said something about jurors. Do you say that, as a general rule, whites and blacks serve together on juries in Georgia?
> Answer. O, yes, Sir.
> Question. Do you know that to be a fact?
> Answer. I have seen blacks and whites on juries together.
> Question. How often?
> Answer. I have never seen any juries often.
> Question. Where did you ever see a black man on a jury?
> Answer. I think I have seen them on juries in Atlanta.
> Question. Are you sure of it!
> Answer. No, sir; I am not.[61]

Gordon's appearance before Congress ended with one final series of questions. James Burnie Beck, a Democrat from Kentucky, asked Gordon about a ruling in the Georgia legislature that removed Black legislators from the general assembly. It was a leading question: Beck—a vigorous defender of the "late insurrectionary states," was teasing out from Gordon how Republicans had supported the move as well. "Governor Brown," Gordon replied, "who is now the chief justice of Georgia, and who is considered one of the best lawyers we ever had, took the position emphatically all over the State that the negroes could not hold office; and I believe that the best lawyers of his party agreed with him."[62] Gordon's response echoed the language of Milton Candler in his introduction of a resolution in the Georgia Senate a few years before, which appealed to Governor Brown, "one of the ablest lawyers of the Republican Party of Georgia," as implicit bipartisan authorization of the expulsion. And then, after hours of interrogation, it was over. I do not know if, as Gordon gathered his papers, smoothed the front of his coat, and walked out of the House chamber, the specter of his friend Milton Candler hung in the air. But it does now.

Thomasville

The WPA Guide describes Thomasville as one of those quaint Southern towns where winters are "short and mild," a fragrant, rose-garlanded small city where "the streets are lined with Red Radiances," a beneficiary of the disposable income of northern capitalists who "built palatial winter homes, which are maintained in the manner of old southern plantations and provide employment for an average of three hundred people each." In Thomasville, Henry Grady's new southern chickens came home to roost: in 1940 Thomas County could claim "sawmills, tobacco markets, cotton gins, an iron foundry, a concrete-pipe plant, and a crate and basket factory," and apparently not even the irresistible march of enlightened northern progress could resist the allure of packaged southern nostalgia. Not long after Grady was appealing to deep-pocketed Yankees in Tammany Hall, Georgia became the world's largest producer of naval stores: lumber, pine gum, pitch, turpentine, rosin.

The WPA Guides occasionally hint at a world that perhaps only fiction can show truly. In their subject matter and descriptive style, they tend toward the picturesque. They stop at the margin of the grotesque, but do not cross into it. That is Flannery O'Connor's world, where the darker interior life of the South seems to brood in the deep shadows of dense woods, hidden away like unshriven sin. It is the territory of her short story "A Good Man Is Hard to Find," in which an Atlanta family is about to set off on a multigenerational road trip to Florida. In the opening scene, the relentlessly chatty grandmother flails the newspaper about her son's bald head, about to knock sense into him.

"Here this fellow that calls himself The Misfit," she says, "is aloose from the Federal Pen and headed toward Florida and you read here what it says he did to these people. Just you read it. I wouldn't take my children in any direction with a criminal like that aloose in it."[63] Her son does not listen to her, of course, and the trip does not end well.

North of Thomasville, we stop for gas. It's Sunday. Waiting in line to pay for the gas, I pick up a copy of the *Thomasville Times-Enterprise*. The headline: "MANHUNT UNDERWAY."

Turns out the suspect, Robert Lee Carter II, has taken three members of a family hostage in their own home, tied them up, and bolted out a back window. Carter is still on the lam in South Georgia. Countless state troopers in hot pursuit want him for aggravated assault, and in connection with the disappearance of the seventy-year-old Deanna Shirey.

I fold up the newspaper and tuck it behind the driver's seat. We stop to take pictures of wall murals at George's Grocery on Main Street in Ochlocknee, north of Thomasville. George tells us that Carter has just been captured, not a mile away in Ochlocknee.

We learn later that Carter murdered Shirey and buried her in a shallow grave behind his house. As fitting as it is to feel as if we are inside of an O'Connor story, in the circumstances it feels better to be outside of one.

As in the era of the WPA Guide, the region is rife with longleaf and slash pine, pecan groves that stretch to the horizon. And while the naval stores industry is a shadow of its former self, the area retains its allure for people with money to burn. Cap'm Charlie Croker, former Georgia Tech football hero, filthy rich Atlanta developer, and the eponymous title character of Tom Wolfe's *A Man in Full*, owns a massive tract of South Georgia property that he calls Turpmtine Plantation.

Almost as if it were an avatar of Thomasville's wealth, the "Big Oak" is one of the state's oldest trees. Born in roughly 1680, the canopy of the massive live oak occupies almost an entire city block. It's the kind of feature that turn-of-the-century industrialists could not find back at home in Massachusetts and New Jersey. It's spectacular, and almost impossible to capture adequately on film. I try a few different angles and give up. But if you want your picture taken under the shade of the Big Oak, you can dial a telephone number from your smart phone and a camera atop a light pole across the street will snap a photo of you under the giant tree.

The wonder of a travel photo in 2019: you don't even have to be there for it.

It's not the only way Thomasville has slid on into the twenty-first century. The historic town center along Broad Street is paved with cobbles, and lined with the kind of shops you see in towns that aren't dead yet. Thomas Drug Store has been in operation since 1881. The improbably hip Grassroots Coffee Shop opened in 2009 and has been roasting their own beans since. Naturally, we stop for a to-go cup. The chipper barista fills up the bougie YETI travel mug someone gave me because no one ever admits to buying anything YETI for themselves. The place is thriving, full of life. It's not what we expected of Thomasville, nor is the cheese shop across the street. The Sweet Grass Cheese Shop opened about the same time as the coffee shop, and they serve up old-world cheeses made from their own cows at their dairy farm up the road on US 19. I revise whatever half-baked rule of thumb I may or may not have had about urban health. There can now be no more definitive indicator of a town's well-being than the presence of a cheese shop. What's more, in Thomasville we find our first opportunity to offload the stash of half-crushed aluminum cans, random cardboard and plastic pieces that have accumulated in the belly of the minivan. Thomasville has its own recycling center. Pretty progressive for South Georgia, we both remark, revealing how far south our own Atlanta-bred prejudices can sometimes run.

Thomasville becomes the first real instance of the kind of phenomenon we were hoping to see in 1997, but after the fact: it's evidence of a recent and welcome revival in small towns, a show of local resistance to the forces of homogenization that course along interstates and off exit ramps everywhere in America. But it's also disclosive of a gap that hadn't yet opened up in my understanding then: namely, how the contemporary fortunes of Albany and Thomasville are inextricable from race. Whatever wealth lies out there in the pecan groves of rural South Georgia, it isn't being spent in predominantly-Black Albany but in mostly-White Thomasville. While the latter has made the effort to acknowledge "The Bottom," the town's historically Black commercial section of the town center, it is unclear at this stage how much that acknowledgment amounts to restoration, or how the forces of gentrification have migrated southward from Atlanta to this town on the southern frontier with Florida.

Fargo

There is no cheese shop in Fargo, Georgia. The danger here is not gentrification or homogenization as much as dissolution. Fargo is a border town in two senses. It's the last town before the Florida line, and the last town before the Okefenokee Swamp. It has absolutely nothing in common with the city of the same name in North Dakota, with the possible exception that the Georgia version looks like it could very well be the set of a Coen Brothers film. It's not hard to imagine the sound of woodchippers from the parking lot of the four-room Gator Motel in Fargo at the southern edge of the swamp on the Georgia side, an establishment so implausibly small and inert that one might think it was a mistake. Palm trees and white pines frame the tiny tan structure, but do not give it a tropical feel whatsoever. This motel means business, if your business is sleeping. Or watching television, because the 200+ channel cable TV set is the only amenity they offer. There's not much else to do either at the Gator or in Fargo, which claims to have over 300 residents.

But we do not stay there in 1997. It is almost too posh.

Instead we pitch a tent in Stephen C. Foster State Park, where the old folks in RVs with Pennsylvania plates stay.

In 2018, it's not too posh for us anymore: balding, thicker, slower, more baggy-eyed than before, we are ready for the Gator now. It seems like paradise compared with the other options, which, without a tent or sleeping bags, are precisely none. John calls ahead this time to make a reservation. The place has been run by owner Kevin Hart the same lo-fi way for over thirty years. The Gator is not on Orbitz. Payment is by check or cash left on the bureau in the unlocked motel room. When we arrive, there is a strip of white office paper taped to the door of Room 4 that reads "Hayes." The door is open, the key is on the sideboard. On this night, we are the motel's only tenants. Fargo, such as it is, is not what it used to be.

"Back in the sixties and the seventies we had a chip mill here," Kevin tells us, "where they brought wood in, chipped it up and shipped it by rail to Jacksonville for paper. The chip mill's closed now, and there's just not quite as many people here as there used to be. There used to be around seven, eight hundred people here and now there's about between three or four hundred. At one time there was three or four gas stations here, the grocery store, and now it's just one."

Kevin describes a small town in decline, but not in social terms. "Myself here at the Gator motel and Suwannee River Outfitters, we help each other, we work together. We're all friends here."

Public memory does not seem to be so endangered here: it is processed and transmitted daily on the benches in front of the lone convenience store. It's Fargo's public square now. Robert and Richard, two older White men who look as if they have returned from an early morning fishing trip, sit on one of them. Robert is wearing a ball cap, upturned sunglasses perched on the brim, and a microfiber fishing shirt. He is spitting dip juice into a styrofoam coffee cup. Richard is wearing a black cap, and a camo T-shirt. On the other bench, a wiry, bearded White man, hard pack of Marlboro Lights in the pocket of his T-shirt, hunches forward on the bench, hands propped on his knees as if he is about to get up and go somewhere. He is not. Next to him, an African American woman sits with a dish towel stuck into the collar of her T-shirt, draped over her shoulder. They are not at all reluctant to talk.

"Used to be a booming place," one says. *Spit.*

"Right over yonder you know where that gas pump sit? That was called—shit—Park's Groceries when I was a kid."

"There was a gas station right here, one down there in the fork to the road. Barton's had the ice house and little store, remember where the ice house was? Used to be a snack shop stayed open all night long right there. See them Cypress trees? They was a damn two-story mo-tel right there back in the fifties."

"Right yonder in them trees yonder Emmett Hill had a Gulf station there when I was a kid."

"Mm-hmm." *Spit.* "It was a lot of stuff going on."

"I got my initials wrote in that damn palm tree over yere fifty years ago. Still in it."

"I 'ont know." *Spit.*

The Suwannee River Outfitters is one of the few newish places in town. It supplies local fishermen and women with tackle and cold beer and serves a hot buffet dinner with occasional live music. Tonight a younger goateed dude in a turquoise T-shirt and baseball cap is in the corner of the store, singing contemporary country and some classic southern rock. We retire for the evening to the Gator, where the trouble begins.

John sleeps fitfully all night, hacking and moaning. He's come down with something and struggles out of bed the next morning. He's a festival of congestion and postnasal drip. He heroically rallies, but barely gets above 65 percent for the day.

Back behind the Outfitters, we meet the owner's husband, who also happens to be the town's mayor. He is a burly bear of a man, in a plaid shirt and baseball cap, and arguably the most laid-back mayor in America. He is holding a gigantic Styrofoam cup of iced tea. The version of Fargo he tells echoes Kevin's.

"Well it's a small town, I've lived here all my life, raised here," he says. "We all might have quarrels with each other but if something ever happened to anybody, we all come together, you know, and that's a good thing. Our other mayor, he resigned, and you know, I just got the wild hare to run for mayor," he chortles. "We don't get paid for it, we just do it for—shit, what's it called—"

"Public service?"

"Yeah, public service. 'Cause we love Fargo."

"This is a town where everybody knows everybody," Kevin says. "Everybody's friends and, you know, it's just—it's a real place."

In a country that privileges mobility, cherishes fantasies of dusting off your boots and going west, finally finding the means and the courage to get the hell out of your shit town, few people seem to talk about the courage of people who stay. Who for whatever reason choose to stick it out, to love their towns through their inevitable decline. Towns like Fargo are essentially in hospice now, and the folks who remain are like its nurses. They remain hopeful in the midst of dispiriting trends: "we're losing all our younger kids," the mayor tells me. "We're trying to find some warehouses or something to come in and help us out, but no luck yet."

"When I first got here, there was a lot of people here," the Black woman says. "Then children started growing up and moving out. I raised ten head here—seven of mine and three grands."

They haven't all left. One of them is emerging from the door of the convenience store, and chuckles bemusedly at finding a camera suddenly in her face. "Oh hi . . ."

More people have left than remain, but those who do remain devoted to something endangered, and maybe even unknown to most Americans: a "real place."

Okefenokee Swamp, South Georgia–North Florida. Photo by the author.

FLORIDA
Swamp of Unknowing

Fargo is definitely in Georgia, but the frontier between Georgia and Florida is only clear until about Moniac. Since 1872, the state line has followed the Orr-Whitner Line to the west, but do not be deceived. On the map it appears straight and definite, but it is an abstraction. You wouldn't know you'd even crossed it unless signs told you so. Only the St. Marys River, which forms an appendix-like projection in southeastern Georgia, is a real, physical border, determined by nature and not a committee. Deep black, almost still, framed by longleaf pine and live oak, the St. Marys forms the boundary between the two states for about 130 miles. You would know it if you crossed it. Harry Crews did so as a young boy from Alma, Georgia, relocating with his family to Jacksonville. For him, the "St. Marys River was a border that went beyond fascination." It was the marker between the rural and urban wilds, between home and a foreign land, *all the time keeping everything that was Georgia away from everything that was Florida.*"[1]

This latitudinal band of South Georgia/north Florida is in truth a boundaryless region. The actual line between the two states is porous and indistinct like the mushy peat-bottom of the Okefenokee Swamp. It's easy to feel alienated here, disoriented. One possible reason why so many writers and thinkers have sought it out is for the porosity of its borders. For Crews, the boundary between "everything that was Georgia" and "everything that was Florida" was figurative more than geographical. It delineated two differing existential states: one of belonging, one of estrangement. The Okefenokee marked that frontier for Crews, who spent almost his entire life on either side of it.

Outside of the swamp, it is difficult to tell where the boundary between "everything that was Georgia" and "everything that was Florida" really falls—in either geographical or existential sense. While there is a clear inside and an outside to the Okefenokee, the inside is outside of human dominion.

A row of rental canoes lays unlocked and belly-up on the bank of the swamp canal at Stephen C. Foster State Park at the southern edge of the Okefenokee. Whoever left them that way seemed to assume that no one in their right mind would take a joy ride in one of them, much less haul one off in the back of a pickup truck. "Proceed at your own risk," they seem to warn to any fools dumb enough to try and venture out in a stolen swamp boat. The presence of a solitary sandhill crane seems to offer one final chance to turn back, until it takes flight from the water's edge, a trail of swamp water falling from its drooping feet, as if washing its hands of the world to come. We read this like a telegram: "You're on your own, brother."

The aluminum boat turns over with ease and lithely slides into the water. It shimmies as we step into it, bracing the gunwales with every available hand. We shove off the bank, the boat steadied, and paddle in silence into the narrow canal leading into the swamp. Lily pads line either bank, and creep out into the thin passageway. *What the hell are we doing?* I wonder aloud. I haven't operated a canoe since summer camp on a pond in North Carolina in the 1980s, and there the water was so shallow that if you fell out you could stand on two feet and hoist yourself back in again. But here the water is motionless as death, so who knows when, if ever, you will reach bottom.

The Okefenokee is a different world. Its beauty is unlike anything I have ever seen, especially in the calm, unpeopled twilight when the sense of being far, far away is palpable, increasing even with each minute of fading sunlight. It is a cliché to say that the water is as black as molasses, but that's exactly how it appears: impenetrable and viscous. I do not doubt that there are people who would not hesitate to dip their hand into it. But not me: I am content to imagine that if I were to do so, and lick my fingers, they would taste like sorghum syrup.

We come to a stop in the middle of the river. The eyes of no fewer than nine alligators peer suspiciously at us from just above the surface. Water snakes course a sinuous trail towards the reeds. Surely people have fallen into the Suwannee many times before, and I don't even think gators eat humans, but I know that alligator snapping turtles eat anything that moves. I am not about to test the "they're more scared of you than you are of them" thesis, so my canoeing form is more on point than ever.

The going is shaky at first, but by the time you reach the main river you find your rhythm. A tight canal opens out into a wide section of the Suwannee below where the Middle and South forks join. You turn right, upriver, into a great nave of massive bald cypress bearded with Spanish moss. Their bark is the color of stone in the late evening sun. They guard the riverside like a row of medieval jamb statuary lining the portal to a Gothic cathedral. Their bodies are firm and unyielding, but their green tops sway almost imperceptibly, like the inclining heads of old saints. They are more than just alive; they seem to regard you. On either side the tree walls converge to a point in the distance. The yellowing sky repeats itself identically on the flat glossy face of the water. Together they form an X-shape, whose center point upriver marks, somewhere, the spot of your final judgment.

There is an X-mark deep in the Okefenokee Swamp, but not many people know where it is. Maybe it's not actually the site of your final judgment, but it is named for one. It is an origin in a borderland, a meeting of land and whatever is beneath it, a place with no real identifiable location, a permanently immobile point of crossing-over. Deathless daughter of Ocean, boundary between life and death, the final frontier: this is where the Okefenokee springs. It all begins in a headwater named the River Styx.

Like Queequeg's native Kokovoko in *Moby-Dick*, "It is not down on any map; true places never are."

There is a map-knowledge of a body of water or land that anybody can have just by looking closely, and then there is the kind of knowledge that can only be had from the inside of a thing or a place. You can try, but finding the precise location of the Styx would be difficult, since it is indistinguishable from a massive watershed that has no distinct beginning and no distinct end. Linger here for long enough and the unwritten legend of nonexistent maps will make itself plain to you: here be ancient gods, and their shadows.

The more famous but equally enigmatic Suwannee River has inspired songs and excited hypotheses about the name's origins: it's a corruption of "San Juan." Or maybe "Shawnee," no one really knows. The name's origins are probably as multiple as the swamp's. What St. Isidore of Seville, the seventh-century Spanish theologian who could wring speculative etymology out of a single word like swamp water from a dishrag, could have done with this place. The Suwannee that may or may not be named after the Beloved Disciple leads to the Gulf of Mexico; the Styx feeds the St. Marys River, which perpetually empties itself into the Atlantic. A paradox, perhaps, that the Styx feeds a river named for the virgin God-bearer, but not really: The Okefenokee is an impenetrable mystery that humans have strained to meet with adequate names.

You might assume the site in the swamp is named for the mythological river separating the living from the dead, but it's as easy to believe that the Georgia Styx came first. Moss-laden cypress brood over the face of the waters. Swallow-tailed kites surveil and skim its surface, while other beings more primal still break it from underneath. This place feels ancient, harrowing, and gorgeous. In geological time, it's much younger than it seems: only about 7,000 years old, but old enough to have preceded by a long shot Hesiod and Homer, Herodotus and Tacitus, Virgil and Dante, all of whom imagined the frontier between life and death as an eternal swamp.[2]

In the *Aeneid*, Virgil refers to the "swamp of Styx," and Virgil's most famous disciple borrowed the motif in his own epic poem 1,300 years later. Crossing the swamp in *Inferno*, Dante notes that the "water was deeper dark than perse," an eerie similarity to the depth of hue in the Georgia swamp. At the edge the river is the color of a glass of Coca-Cola in summertime, after the ice has melted—a gradient tone from clear at the surface to amber to dark brown. In the middle it is deep black. (I'm told it's also delicious, and drinking it will fill you, like the lotus flower of Homer's *Odyssey*, with an insatiable desire to return to the swamp.) In Dante, the river-swamp is teeming with souls in violent contest with one another, "faces scarred by rage."[3] Here there are faces like that, too, but not human ones, and you don't really want to see them in that state.

The swamp is enchanted by spirits of its own: indigenous prehistoric reptiles whose eyes you begin to think you see around you everywhere. *Alligator mississippiensis* and *Agkistrodon piscivorus*. Both names are peculiar hybrids, of Latin and Chippewa and Latin and Greek, which give the creatures they name a kind of classical dignity that they don't really need, since they are of a heritage more ancient than Latin or Greek, and inhabit a world that on the surface is as remote from classical influence as it is possible to be. The American alligator alone is so august and majestic that if Homer had ever witnessed one, he would have made it into a god, and the swamp its teeming Olympus.

You don't need to come to the Okefenokee laden with such symbolic baggage. The swamp provides plenty of its own.

Alligator mississippiensis is feared for its power, but like the gods of ancient Greece, its attitude towards human beings is mostly indifferent. Unless, like Prometheus, you provoke them, they are just not that into you. Yet promethean attempts to hoodwink the river-god have often met with the blessings of Mammon: ever since White tourists began tossing money to roadside Seminoles hunting gators for food, wrestling alligators has become a lucrative practice. What began as a set of techniques designed to subdue prey, gator wrestling as a form of entertainment has its roots in an incurable White desire for exotic spectacle. Although still practiced by many Seminoles, the real intention of gator wrestling to magnify the fearsomeness of the reptile, and therefore to magnify the greater fearsomeness of human power. It is Prometheanism as roadside show, human lust for domination as circus act. It may produce in the viewer a sense of respect for alligators, but it is more likely to leave one with a sense that there is nothing in heaven and earth that cannot be dominated by human trickery.

You won't find gator wrasslers here, but you will find vestiges of human guile. And while it should be a self-evident truth that alligators are dangerous, I've seen more than enough kids and adults throwing things at alligators to get their attention to be suspect of human rationality. If there is anything truly scary about the Okefenokee Swamp, it is not really the alligators or the snakes, but its terrifying intensity of life.

Life is everywhere here, but it is mostly hidden from you: in the tangle of moss and mangrove, under the black surface of the river. Back in those recessed dens and hammocks, who can tell what bodies lurk, or what spirits? The Okefenokee is the landscape of unknowing, a terrestrial incarnation of inscrutable mystery, where even the living creatures who deign to reveal themselves to you are familiar yet strange, distant from you but nearer than you think, and, like the Seminoles whom White men forced out of here, "unconquerable," yet in perennial danger.

The Styx of Virgil and Dante is not for the unburied, and the Georgia version isn't either. Its extensions teem with real (if famously exaggerated) mortal dangers that often furnish the mythology of Okefenokee as a land of threat, where people go mysteriously missing by "accident" or where they go to disappear on purpose, to divest themselves of something. The swamp is a site of confrontation: you can't come here and not face something within yourself or within the vast outland beyond its iffy boundaries, within everything that is not Okefenokee. It has a reputation as either actual or potential gravesite, a perpetual natural charnel house where the ancient gods still contend with human desire for mastery.

Loggers and industrialists may have poached lumber and heavy minerals from the swamp, but writers and other word traders have often made off with their own booty of imagery, legend, and mythos. Most of this has been benevolent, perhaps out of an undeniable urge to do this extraordinary wetland some justice in language, but sometimes the mostly negative reputation of the swamp is invoked with more nefarious intent. In 2017, during a Facebook exchange with LaDawn Jones, a Black attorney and state legislator from Atlanta, fellow state representative Jason Spencer took issue with Jones's defense of removing Confederate monuments around the state. Spencer, a White man from Woodbine east of the swamp, warned Jones not to bring her "Bolshevik" "hate" to his region. "People in South Georgia are people of action, not drama," he wrote. He further threatened that anyone who came down there to remove those statues "will go missing in the Okefenokee."

Spencer had bared his figurative White nationalist tuchus for all to see, but it wasn't the last time. In 2018, you will remember, he got punked by Sacha Baron Cohen and bared his actual White ass on Showtime. Baron Cohen, playing a fake Israeli anti-terrorism expert named Col. Erran Morad, convinced Spencer that the best way to repel a homophobic terrorist was to show them your bare ass. Spencer went along, shuffling around the gym with his khakis around his ankles, grunting "America!" and shouting, "I'll touch you with my buttocks!" "USA mother----er!" It aired in July 2018. He resigned within a week. His political career vanished, but not in the Okefenokee.

The swamp is a source, not an end: life comes out of it more than into it. The reward human civilization has paid the swamp for thousands of years of generating life is a particularly industrial kind of death: what does flow into the life-giving swamp these days tends to be in the form of the very real material detritus of human ambition and desire for wealth. What human life does come into it now tends to leave it after a short while, like the thousands of tourists who visit it each year to motor through the Suwannee. Like passing for a moment into and out of the

Heraclitean flux of the river, tourists pass into and out of its particular mode of being. The flux is in a particularly South Georgia mode: unhurried, deliberate, patient, suffering with blithe indifference the impatience of tourists buzzing through the swamp in rented motorboats to survey as much as they can in a few hours.

I get it: the desire to see it all is strong. I've toyed with the motorboat idea myself, and I am sure one day I will spring for one, too. But no place I know of so resolutely resists being finally compassed as much as this swamp. The history of attempts to do so is a history of failure. The swamp is defiantly insistent: you cannot possibly take it all in. Don't even try; instead try to ask what it means for you that you can't.

No river is ever the same river twice, as Heraclitus is supposed to have said. But the Suwannee/St. Marys in the Okefenokee is not even the same river once. It is permanence and transience all at the same time. A gator emerges to cross the river then submerges. A peregrine falcon roosts and dives, an epitome of the swamp itself as a terra peregrina, an unstable and pilgrim driftland of wanderers and permanent residents, originally named "water-shaking," or "the land of trembling earth."

In the nineteenth century, the swamp was regarded by many as a dismal backwater whose unexploited value was a "great waste."[4] One early surveyor, a Frenchman who had served as an aide-de-camp to Napoleon in the Battle of Waterloo, described the site as "emphatically dismal."[5] Draining the swamp was characterized as a "liberation": as if nature was holding itself back from freedom, human agency intervened to set loose the swamp unto its salvation. The Christian God—at least in one version—has also marked this place. Language about the Okefenokee in the nineteenth century echoes John Bunyan's disposition toward boggy wetlands in The Pilgrim's Progress. "The Slough of Despond" served Bunyan as a site of withering despair, an allegory for "the descent whither the scum and filth that attends conviction for sin doth continually run."

Bunyan's spiritual descendants inherited his pejorative metaphorical baggage, but the era's enthusiasm for "progress" did not share his belief that his slough "cannot be mended."

In time, the Okefenokee would become a site for the enactment of Manifest Destiny: an 1847 speech before the Phi Delta and Ciceronian Societies at Mercer University, then barely a decade old, holds the germ of that enactment. The speaker was a young Georgia lawyer whose name was fittingly tinged with the aura of Roman antiquity, Herschel Vespasian Johnson.

The speech is highfalutin, self-consciously erudite to the point of caricature, ecstatic in its praise for the divinely ordained pedigree of the American project, and a classically over-the-top bit of nineteenth-century Southern declamatory rhetoric. It is a tour de force of Enlightened Anglophilic White supremacist Christian colonialism, of the sort which has been having such an energetic—if somewhat less "Ciceronian"—coming out in recent years. It is also highly illuminating for the chilling theological rationale that underpins it. Johnson argued that the "design of God" was responsible for "the progress of the Anglo-American race" and the rapid disappearance of native peoples, which would culminate "when finally the blaze of their council fires shall expire in the darkness of total extermination." Because of their obstinate refusal to cooperate with the White man or to cultivate the earth, "the Indian tribes are thus permitted by the Divine Being, to be driven before the mighty tide of white population."[6]

The speaker got what the speech itself suggests he wanted, apparently: an honorary membership in the Ciceronian Society and the accompanying mantle of the famous Roman himself (as well as publication of the speech). The nominal patronage of the Roman imperator and demi-god Vespasian suited Johnson, who, eight years after this speech, became governor of Georgia. A slaveholder himself and enthusiastic defender of the moral propriety of slavery on Biblical grounds, Johnson believed that "southern slavery is a great necessity of the civilized world, and consequently, those who wage war against it are hostile to the welfare of mankind."[7] For Johnson, "the design of Providence" called for "the substitution of the white for the redman on this continent." In his first term as governor, Johnson initiated a process to reclaim the Okefenokee swamp from the "savages," in order to "improve" the land. On February 26, 1854, the state legislature approved the following motion: "Whereas, the State of Georgia holds the title to a large tract of unimproved, and at present worse than useless land, known as the Okefenoke Swamp [sic]; And whereas, in the opinion of many intelligent persons that said lands could be rendered so valuable by drainage as to yield a large revenue to the State."[8]

It would be another several decades before anyone really followed through with those plans. The state of Georgia eventually gave up on trying to reclaim the swamp itself and began exploring other means to do so privately. But the internal theological logic of reclamation endured.

The value of the Okefenokee was well-known to Indigenous tribes, but—as with most things—White folks had to be educated. They came to the swamp looking not for paradise so much as for profit, and began concocting ways of draining it, putting a railroad through it, and cutting lumber from native cypress trees a millennium old. White engagement with the swamp was almost entirely subtractive: draining, cutting, selling, withdrawing, forcing out. White Southerners—excluding the ones who lived in the swamp itself—typically viewed the massive swamp as a menace of nature to be mastered and controlled, drained into submission.

The *Atlanta Constitution* funded an ongoing expedition in 1875 to explore the "mammoth mystery of Georgia."[9] In September of that year the newspaper published its first dispatch from Valdosta. By the third letter, the explorers had moved from wonder to seeing lucre: "the Okefenokee would be A GOLD MINE if it could be drained. There is no telling what this pond would produce if an industrious and scientific farmer had hold of it."[10]

By 1890 the Okefenokee had "caught the eye of capital" and prospectors and the venture capitalists of the day drooled over the commercial potential of the region. Governor John B. Gordon—former Confederate general and leader of the Klan in Georgia after the war—put the swamp up for sale to the highest bidder. By the time the Okefenokee went on the market, it was drawn into an ongoing debate in the state legislature over the convict leasing system. (Governor Gordon was drawn into it, too, as a beneficiary of the leasing system he supported.) The Okefenokee, some argued, could provide the solution to the intractable debates over the convict leasing system for which many argued, in the form of a permanent supply farm. Some New South advocates believed the Okefenokee could be the next Mississippi Delta with many of the same features: incredibly fertile soil, fabulous riches, and a lucrative convict lease system furnished by a prison farm like Parchman. In his defense of the reclamation project, W. G. Cooper claimed that "Out door work is generally conceded to be best for them," referring to African American workers.[11] Slavery had been outlawed for twenty-five years, but the idea that Black people were oriented *by nature* towards manual labor in the fields and swamps and which drove the chattel slavery economy survived to furnish the era of convict leasing with a putative grounding in racist

anthropology. In both the human and natural economies, jurispruden-
tial and criminal systems were to be put into the service of White wealth.

For just over $63,000, the property went to a newly incorporated
company called the Suwannee Canal Company, led by Captain Harry
Rootes Jackson, Jr., of Atlanta. The digging commenced immediately.
In 1892 a writer for the *Constitution* gushed about how the swamp was
being "transformed into a busy scene of industry and progress, with
sawmills spinning and freight boats adrift all conspire to make this an
interesting study to the scientist and the progressive citizen." Like many
of his contemporaries, the same writer envisioned the draining of the
swamp as a liberation, in which the "waters of famous old Okefenokee
will be turned loose in freedom to run on to the blue waves of the Atlantic."[12] In a telling possible typo, the author described the waters of the
swamp as "damned up."

The "reclamation" project depended heavily on convict labor, in a
reflection of the era's prominent theology of White mastery: inferior to
man, nature was to be tamed, controlled, and even "reclaimed" from
itself, in much the same way that the inborn "laziness" and "brutishness"
of Black people were to be tamed, controlled, and "redeemed" from
themselves. It is no accident that the "salvation" of the Okefenokee coin-
cides with a period in which White Southern politicians thought of their
work as "Redemption." Defenders of drainage also used the language of
"redeeming" the swamp, and the convict labor system that replaced chattel slavery and which would be engaged to do the actual work of draining, was driven by a similar logic of moral improvement.

"[Y]ou cannot fancy at all accurately what it is until you could go and
see it with your own eyes": this could be a motto for the Okefenokee
itself, but Jackson didn't mean the swamp. He meant the buzzing and
hissing battalion of titanic steam skidders, sawmills, and locomotives:
the sounds of progress.

Jackson's ambitious project lasted only five years before the swamp
defeated it. Jackson himself didn't make it that long. He died in 1895, and
the Suwannee Canal Company went under in 1897. The doomed attempt
became known to locals as "Jackson's Folly." Strictly speaking, it should
be known as "Jacksons' Folly:" after Captain Jackson died in 1895, his
father, Harry R. Jackson—a poet and former Confederate General—took
over the Suwannee Canal Company, but he couldn't sustain it either. The
elder Jackson's heart wasn't in the Okefenokee Swamp, anyway. It was

more likely in "The Red Old Hills of Georgia," the subject of his most well-known work of sentimental poetry. The swamp languished.

That was the way of it until a biologist from Cornell visited. Francis Harper—along with his elder brother Roland—had been advocating for the swamp for a while already, but it wasn't until 1912 that the Harpers visited themselves as part of a Cornell research team. For the next twenty-five years, the Harpers became the most powerful advocates for the Okefenokee, and their influence saved the swamp from almost certain death. Francis' wife Jean had been a tutor to the children of President Franklin Delano Roosevelt—who had a close relationship with Georgia already—and through the Harpers' efforts, the Okefenokee was spared a proposed canal connecting the Gulf with the Atlantic and a tourist highway through it (supported by many at the time—including Clark Howell, high-powered editor of the *Atlanta Constitution*, who thought the highway would contribute to the swamp's preservation). In his column for the *Constitution*, "In Georgia Fields and Streams," H. A. Carter of the Georgia Naturalist Society wired his enthusiasm for the Okefenokee from South Georgia to Atlanta readers in the mid-1930s. Carter had drunk the swamp water: "it's in my blood now," he wrote.[13] He became one of the Okefenokee's most ardent defenders in Georgia and an enthusiastic apologist for its preservation. Ultimately, FDR got into the game himself.

That December, Hal Foust, the auto editor for the *Chicago Tribune*, stopped in at Lem Griffis's Fish Camp in the Okefenokee on an epic family road trip from Chicago to Key West and back. The itinerary was supposed to take him along the Gulf Coast from New Orleans to south Florida, but something drew him off-course, and into the swamp. It wasn't easy going for a car and trailer on mostly unpaved roads: "In places the front axle plowed the high center of loose earth with the engine in low gear."[14] Road travel in 1937 was not what it is today, obviously, and also often depended upon the Jim Crow social stratification that even a Chicago journalist could count on: "Shovels and the brawn of six Negroes were needed to move the outfit in one place. At another the car had to leave the roadway to smash its way through sapling pines four to eight feet high and to ford a ditch with two feet of muddy water."[15]

In 1937, thanks largely to preservation efforts by Roland, Francis, and Jean Harper, northerners with the ear of President Franklin Roosevelt, the Okefenokee was spared further devastation through purchase by the federal government and designation as a National Wildlife Refuge. By then most of the native cypress had been hacked down and shipped out. The remains of White settlements and failed attempts to generate White wealth from scouring the swamp are now scarce. The built environment around the swamp—such as it is—bears the visible legacy of both segregation and federal largesse: in a particularly ironic turn of fortune, the roads and facilities that now serve visitors to the Okefenokee National Wildlife Refuge were built by an all-Black unit of the Civilian Conservation Corps.

For the most part, the Okefenokee has managed defiantly to resist the encroachment of the empire of expedience and its graspy gods. But they still skirt along the tenuous borders, even now.

In its final months in office in 2020, the Donald Trump administration dissolved portions of the Clean Water Act, which broadly defined the "Waters of the United States" to include navigable rivers and lakes as well as wetlands like the Okefenokee. Trump had long had his eye on these regulations: In one of his first executive orders, he targeted the 2015 Clean Waters Rule for review. Effective June 2020, the Navigable Waters Protection Rule curtailed federal protection for forty-five million acres of wetlands, including the Okefenokee, opening the door for land-hunting developers and industrialists. It should have been obvious that the intention to protect the nation's waters from environmental damage was all talk. The real intended audience for Trump's new plan was in the audience at the Las Vegas Convention Center where he unveiled it: the National Association of Home Builders.

It didn't take long for industrialists to seize the opportunity. Even before the Clean Water Rule was revised, in 2019 an Alabama Company called Twin Pines Minerals filed for a permit to build a 600-acre titanium mine along Trail Ridge, the Okefenokee's eastern boundary. Protests were swift and loud. The potential threat to the swamp could be serious, and irreversible. But following the new regulation in 2020, Twin Pines went ahead, saying it no longer needed a federal permit to strip mine Trail Ridge. The ruling that made it possible was initially cosigned by the EPA and the US Army Corps of Engineers. But after the Twin Pines proposal threatened the fragile ecosystem of the largest wildlife refuge on the east coast, even the EPA's own regional manager said the mine would "have a substantial and unacceptable impact" on the swamp.[16] The leadership of the EPA vowed in June 2021 to revise the Navigable Waters

Protection Rule, and reintensify federal protections for wetlands like the Okefenokee. The fate of the mine—and the swamp—remains unclear, but as a result of the Trump-era ruling, the Okefenokee/St. Marys River is now considered one of the ten most endangered rivers in the country.[17]

But the object of desire of the proposed Twin Mines project has a perversely classical poetic ring to it. Just what is this precious and sought-after buried treasure along Trail Ridge? Titanium dioxide, a natural mineral compound frequently used in paint pigments to achieve the "whitest white" possible. It's the reason why "Titanium White" is so named. It is a mineral embodiment of the ideal and idol of whiteness, used in toothpaste to achieve that pearly smile, in sunscreens to ward off darker skin and the offending beams of the Sun-God, to communicate the aura of purity in the pages of Holy Bibles, and in whatever devilishly delicious matter constitutes the filling inside of an Oreo cookie.[18]

Named for fallen gods, titanium can claim a fitting patronage for a mineral whose pursuit here has a history of failure. *Nomen est omen*, they say. To name is to destine. According to Hesiod, Titans were those sons of heaven who "strained in insolence, and did a deed for which they would be punished afterwards."[19] In antiquity the Titans were the avatars of defeat, who bore "the characteristics of ancestors whose dangerous qualities reappear in their posterity."[20] Descendants of those deposed gods continue to materialize here on the margins of the Okefenokee, as they have done ever since White men found out about this place. There is, possibly, some solace to be taken from the old myths: banished to Tartarus, the Titans, the "over-reachers," belong to the past, as reminders to the living of the peril of hubris. But deathless Styx is still with us, at least for as long as the unburied cannot locate it.

Outlander

The year 1937 was something of a high-water mark for American interest in the rest of the country, and especially for auto travel. It could be regarded as the birth year of the American romance with the Road Trip. The opening scene of Robert Penn Warren's *All the King's Men*, a canonical work of Southern literature, takes place inside a Cadillac barreling along a Louisiana highway, the elegant "cross between a hearse and an ocean liner" whipping towards the always-receding shimmer up ahead, that alluring yet unattainable heat-mirage that the novel's narrator Jack Burden calls "the dazzle." The scene is set, not coincidentally, in 1936, in a time and a place "where the internal combustion engine has come into its own."[21] The period from 1936 to 1938 marks the first edition of *The Negro Motorist Green Book*, the first Stuckey's, the publication of the first WPA Guide, and its cousin, the Rivers of America Series, which partook of the same wayfaring national curiosity of the WPA Guides. Conceived and edited by Constance Lindsay Skinner and ultimately consisting of sixty-five volumes over thirty-seven years, the series did for American estuaries what the WPA Guides did for American roads. (Skinner herself died at her desk while editing the sixth volume, on the Hudson by New Yorker Carl Carmer, the author of a famous 1934 outlander account of Alabama, *Stars Fell on Alabama*.)

The third volume in the series, published in 1938, *Suwannee River: Strange Green Land*, was written by a botanist from upstate New York named Cecile Hulse Matschat. The book is an evocative description of the land, its history, patois, and inhabitants, human and otherwise.

> In the weird, hobgoblin world of the bays there is perpetual twilight. These bays are flooded forests of close-growing cypresses mixed with a few other trees. They stretch away from the prairies and runs into unexplored depths of shadow and mystery. Even at midday, with a brilliant sun overhead, only an occasional ray pierces the thick green roof of the jungle, spotting the brown water with flecks of gold and lightening the blue of the iris that blooms in the marginal shallows. The bottle-shaped trunks of the cypresses, often twelve feet in diameter at the base and a scant two feet in diameter above the swelling, where they begin to tower symmetrically toward the sky, gleam in tints of olive, silver, violet, and odd greens and blues. Their dark roots protrude above the surface of the water, either arched like bows or in groups of knees. Seeing this malformed forest in the strange green light, one might expect it to be the home of gnomes, with beards and humps. As a matter of fact, it is inhabited by much more sinister personalities.[22]

Suwannee River did much to contribute to the mythos of the Okefenokee as a region removed from the rest of the nation, sometimes forbidding and sometimes diffident about visitors. Matschat writes as a self-conscious outsider. To the locals she becomes known as "Plant

Woman." When one local asks her where she is from, she is met with a characteristic response:

> "New York." The woman sat upon an empty box. "Have you ever been there?"
> "Nuvver heerd of hit. Don' take ary truck with the outland."[23]

But outlanders took a lot of truck with the swamp, hauling off hundreds of millions of board feet of cypress timber until 1930.

The closest the Okefenokee has to local literature is the novel *Swamp Water* by Vereen Bell, published in 1940. Bell was a native of Cairo a hundred miles to the west—in the same latitude as the swamp but by the latter's standards still the "outland." Bell's book was made into a 1941 film for 20th Century Fox directed by the great French auteur, Jean Renoir. The film was shot partially on location in the Okefenokee and represented the first opportunity for many people to see the swamp for itself. Renoir became infatuated with the people of South Georgia and "the land where nature is at the same time soft and hostile."[24] But his experience with Fox soured him on the American movie industry, and he likely sympathized with "Georgians [who] think of Hollywood as a far more distant and bizarre place than France."[25]

In 1941 Renoir took a tour of the swamp with local fisherman and unofficial Charon of the Okefenokee, Lem Griffis. (Griffis's son Alphin still lives in Fargo, where he runs a fish camp and has inherited his father's role as the area's de facto raconteur-in-chief.) Renoir's movie, like Matschat's book, exhibits a particular fascination for the folk-speech of swamp people, but the filmmaker did not find the swamp to be nearly as sinister as Matschat: "In the heart of the swamp I saw a child of ten years fishing all alone, quite peacefully—and this in a place reputed to be the haunt of the very biggest alligators."[26] When the film premiered in nearby Waycross, it drew a bigger audience than *Gone with the Wind* had done two years earlier.

But no one communicated that particular strain of American speech more widely than the outlander Walt Kelly, a native of Philadelphia whose comic strip about a swamp-dwelling possum named Pogo ran nationally for almost twenty-seven years. Entirely free of human characters, Pogo contributes to the swamp's sense of otherness even as it diminishes—or displaces—its famous sense of menace. If it weren't for northern outlanders like the Harpers and Kelly, who recognized the uniqueness of the Okefenokee and campaigned for its preservation, the swamp might not exist in the form it does today.

The same is true of the general area around the Suwannee River watershed, extending from the Okefenokee to the Gulf of Mexico: it is a region whose broad and deep literature is mostly the work of outsiders, visitors or transplants who pass in and out of the bright light and deep shade of north Florida, sometimes returning with stories of their adventures, sometimes pilfering the area's rich and evocative ethos to ornament their own work, sometimes staying to tell the stories of the region itself, and its people. It has been this way ever since Peter Martyr d'Anghiera recorded accounts of returning explorers in Spain in 1520, and since White settlers began steadily forcing Indigenous people out.

Some of the authors who are now identified with North Florida actually came from there. But not all of them stayed. Lillian Smith was born in Jasper, just across the Orr-Whitner line from Echols County, Georgia. Her 1948 book, *Killers of the Dream,* was an unlikely and prophetic critique of the racist culture of the American South. She was often a voice crying in the wilderness, castigating her contemporaries for romanticizing the past and ignoring the evils of racism. While a prominent group of male poets and thinkers centered at Vanderbilt known as the Fugitive Poets or New Agrarians were calling for a recovery of an "agrarian" way of life in the South, Smith rebuked them for turning away from the pernicious realities of Black life under Jim Crow, and seeking refuge in "ancient 'simplicities.'"[27] She did not cotton to their nostalgic sensibility, and recognized the danger of their sentimentality: "No writers in literary history have failed their region as completely," she said of them. She boldly upbraided them for their "failure to recognize the massive dehumanization which had resulted from slavery and its progeny, sharecropping and segregation, and the values that permitted these brutalities of spirit."[28] Her own art dared to do what many of her White male counterparts' did not: directly confront the dark truth of those brutalities, as in her debut 1944 novel about a lynching, *Strange Fruit.*

But Florida couldn't keep Smith. Her fate followed that of naval stores, for decades an economic engine of this region. When his turpentine business fell apart, Smith's father relocated the family to Clayton in the Georgia mountains, where she directed a summer camp for girls from 1925 to 1948, teaching them about African American history, and exposing White children to the legacy of White supremacy long before being "woke" became a thing.

Florida couldn't hold James Weldon Johnson, either. The first Black executive secretary of the NAACP and author of *The Autobiography of an Ex-Colored Man*, Johnson grew up in Jacksonville but during the Great Migration left the South for New York after attending college in Atlanta. His 1899 poem, "Lift Every Voice and Sing," became the text for the "Black National Anthem." In Johnson's *Autobiography*—a fictional account based on his own lived experience—the mixed-race narrator negotiates what Johnson's colleague at the NAACP, W. E. B. Du Bois, famously called "the color line." In the narrator's words: "this is the dwarfing, warping, distorting influence which operates upon each and every colored man in the United States. He is forced to take his outlook on all things, not from the viewpoint of a citizen, or a man, or even a human being, but from the viewpoint of a *colored* man."[29]

As the narrator of *Autobiography* moves from Georgia to Jacksonville to New York, he crosses over the color line and back again, mostly incognito. He "passes" as White, just as he passes "from one world into another." Johnson's narrator is an outlander to stable racial essences: neither fully Black nor fully White, his double-identity is both curse and cover. He experiences both the advantages and burdens of an identity whose fluidity enables him to "choose" Whiteness over "Blackness" in a bid for social mobility.

Zora Neale Hurston was born in Alabama but moved to Eatonville in central Florida when she was young. In the late 1930s, Hurston worked for the Florida Writers' Project and contributed to the WPA Guide to Florida. She is one of a very small handful of individuals—possibly the only one—to have both contributed to a WPA Guide and be cited in one. The section on her hometown of Eatonville—"one of the first towns incorporated by Negroes in the United States"[30]—cites at length from Hurston's description of Eatonville in her now-canonical novel *Their Eyes Were Watching God*, published just two years before the WPA Guide.

Hurston is exceptional in many ways, not least because she is one of the few literary figures from north Florida who was raised there and remained. The literary legacy of north Florida is largely the product of in-migration, mostly of White people from the northeast. Sometimes they lingered for a bit and went back home; sometimes they came to stay, like Hurston's fellow novelist and friend Marjorie Kinnan Rawlings, who moved to the tiny hamlet of Cross Creek in 1928, where she began writing fiction.

Originally from Washington, DC, Rawlings was a contemporary of Lost Generation writers like Ernest Hemingway, F. Scott Fitzgerald, and Thomas Wolfe, with all of whom she shared an editor in the legendary talent hound, Maxwell Perkins. Her novel *The Yearling* won the Pulitzer in 1939. She was every bit their literary and hard-drinking equal: she cussed like a drunken sailor and drove like a bat out of hell. And like Fitzgerald and Wolfe, she flamed out early.

Rawlings's home in Cross Creek is now preserved as a state park. It sits on an isthmus between Orange and Lochaloosa Lakes. Nearby, fishing boats put in at a boat ramp. Entering the property through a thick hedge, you meet a sign that reads: "It is necessary to leave the impersonal highway, to step inside the rusty gate and close it behind. One is now inside the orange grove, out of one world and in the mysterious heart of another. And after long years of spiritual homelessness, of nostalgia, here is that mystic loveliness of childhood. Here is home."

The grounds are like a north Florida version of Flannery O'Connor's Andalusia: chickens free-range it around the rustic henhouse. Spanish moss dangles from a clothesline like the morning wash. The docent on this day, paunch-bellied, barefooted and appropriately transplanted from New York, hands us a paperback copy of *The Yearling*. Like so many before him, he's fallen under the seductive spell of this area. The screened-in porch where Rawlings wrote at a table made by her second husband supports a reproduction of the typewriter she used. Not included in the restoration is the brown-bagged whiskey bottle Rawlings kept by her side as she wrote, nor the role played by Idella Parker, Rawlings's domestic servant, in looking after Marjorie, or literally picking her up off the floor. Outside, under a covered porch, the yellow 1940 Oldsmobile that Rawlings insisted on taking for a spin while under the influence. It may or may not be the same one that she flipped over on one of those joy rides, nearly killing her and Idella both.[31]

Rawlings's fictional work gave a voice to the "cracker culture" of her adopted home, but it and her lifestyle were not exactly the product of a life of back-to-the-land solitude and manual labor—at least not her own. Rawlings's storytelling—and eating and drinking—were enabled by the largely anonymous work of Black laborers, who she often implored to sing spirituals for the entertainment of her White guests.[32]

After her death in 1953, Rawlings's home was donated to the University of Florida. Later that decade, as students at the university, Harry Crews and his housemates at what they called "Twelve Oak Bath and Tennis Club" used the Rawlings home as a regular retreat from Gainesville. They drank in the spirit of Rawlings, along with a lot of actual spirits. Cross Creek was in a dry county, so Crews and co. smuggled Heaven Hill bourbon from across the county line, and holed up in Rawlings' home to get lit, talk shit, and stumble awake in the morning to give hungover tours of the house to visitors.[33] An ex-Marine who attended college on the GI Bill, Crews himself ultimately bought a cabin not far from the Rawlings place. He spent his professional life at the University of Florida, but he was always trying to get his home of Bacon County, Georgia, back. But in the lecture rooms and departmental meetings in Gainesville, he realized his alienation from that world: "For half my life I have been in the university, but never of it. Never *of* anywhere, really. Except the place I left, and that of necessity only in memory. It was in that moment and in that knowledge that I first had the notion that I would someday have to write about it all, but not in the convenient and comfortable metaphors of fiction, without the disguising distance of the third person pronoun. Only the use of I, lovely and terrifying word, would get me to the place where I needed to go."[34]

It was in Florida that Crews discovered that he was an outlander: from academia, from Gainesville, from himself. Somewhere around Cross Creek he found a way to pursue what he believed was a writer's vocation: "to get naked, to hide nothing, to look away from nothing, to look at it. To not blink, to not be embarrassed by it or ashamed of it. Strip it down and let's get to where the blood is, where the bone is."

Maybe "Florida" is built for discovering alienation from the world, from one's history, from oneself. That discovery can be debilitating, which could help explain why so many planned communities exist in the state, as if to fence off the creeping sense that one is not really "where the blood is," to inoculate oneself against the ever-widening impression of distance between the world and oneself, to cultivate in fertilized, irrigated, manicured, and leaf-blown security a feeling of belonging to a manageable world. On the other hand, that distance can be an occasion for what Flannery O'Connor called a "moment of grace." It was for Harry

Crews, who borrowed O'Connor's term to give a name to an experience in Florida "in which I was allowed to see myself." Florida's literary
history is mostly a story of outlanders, like Rawlings, who came here
to make a home. For others—like Crews, Smith, Johnson—it became a
means to discover a way to get there.

Foster's Children

It is almost as dark as the river itself when we row back to the boat basin,
haul the canoe back on to the bank, and turn it over, belly-up like we
found it. The air is thick and resonant, reverberating with deep calls
of wild creatures, some of whom still may not have names. But in this
region of South Georgia and north Florida, one name pops up over and
over again: Stephen C. Foster. The state park that serves as a main portal
into the strange world of the swamp is named for him. So is a cultural
center a little further south, in White Springs, Florida. A small stone
monument in Fargo stands near the river he made famous and probably
never saw.

Stephen Foster was a justly famous nineteenth-century songwriter
with a penchant for place: "I come from Alabama with a banjo on
my knee," "the sun shines bright in my old Kentucky home," and so
on. Foster wrote songs in character, which is important to remember,
because he didn't come from Alabama and sure as hell not with a banjo
on his knee, he had no Kentucky home, and he never once set foot even
remotely close to the park named for him. Almost every school kid in
America knows Foster's music, even if they don't know his name. He
wrote songs for minstrel shows and living rooms, and his lyrics frequently conjure up images of a "simpler" past. Case in point: "Old Folks
at Home," a tune he wrote in 1851, and the song entirely responsible for
his fame in South Georgia and northern Florida.

> Way down upon de Swanee Ribber,
> Far, far away,
> Dere's wha my heart is turning ebber,
> Dere's wha de old folks stay.
> All up and down de whole creation
> Sadly I roam,
> Still longing for de old plantation,
> And for de old folks at home.

The water here seems barely to move at all. It becomes clear Stephen
Foster never saw it, because his lyrics have nothing to do with a real
place and everything to do with a White abstraction.

All de world am sad and dreary,
Ebrywhere I roam;
Oh, darkeys, how my heart grows weary,
Far from de old folks at home![35]

"Old Folks at Home" is written in the voice of a slave pining for South
Georgia (or north Florida). It's a romantic vision of exile, written the
way a White man might imagine an enslaved person longing for home.
Like "Dixie," it's a White songwriter's idea of nostalgia projected onto an
imaginary enslaved character. *Was not "Dixie" written by a black man?*
Foster wrote the song in 1851 at the behest of E. P. Christy, leader of
Christy's Minstrels, a prominent and very successful Blackface group
based in New York who held a standing nightly gig at Mechanics Hall,
a building they owned on Broadway. Foster sold the tune and author-
ship to Christy for the troupe's exclusive use. The "Ethiopian Melody"
became a sensational hit, and vendors of the sheet music struggled to
keep up with voracious demand. By May 1851 it was already in its tenth
edition. One merchant in Buffalo said in June 1852 that the song had
"already met with immense sale and is considered far ahead of anything
in the Ethiopian way ever published." (In 1919, George Gershwin, along
with lyricist Irving Caesar, wrote his own semi-parody of Foster's song
called "Swanee," made famous by America's most famous Blackface
performer, Al Jolson, who recorded it in 1920. It was the most popular
single Gershwin ever wrote.)

"Old Folks" was so fantastically successful that it became a canonical item in American popular culture—so much so that after compos-
ing his Symphony No. 9 ("The New World"), Czech composer Antonín
Dvořák wrote an arrangement for "Old Folks" which he debuted and
conducted at a charity concert in Madison Square Garden in January
1894. Dvořák, who was a studious devotee and apologist for folk music,
thought of "Old Folks" as genuine "negro music." Some reviewers spot-
ted the category error, but some African Americans embraced the song
as a faithful, or at least not egregious, expression of Black sentiment.
W. E. B. Du Bois thought of the tune as exemplary of the way "the songs

of white America have been distinctively influenced by the slave songs or have incorporated whole phrases of Negro melody."[36]

Critics today might say that "Old Folks" "co-opted" or "appropriated" Black musical motifs instead of "incorporating" or being "influenced" by them, but Du Bois was wise to the fact that "Old Folks" belonged principally to the songs of White and not Black America. This has not stopped both Black and White artists from continuing to perform and record it— although more often than not White ones. In this way, it is an important artifact of American culture, in the way the song has been continually reworked, unworded and reworded, rearranged and revised (in the literal sense of "seen again"). The song has been recorded and reimagined by artists from Louis Armstrong, Paul Robeson, Big Bill Broonzy, Chuck Berry, Gene Krupa, the Dave Brubeck Quartet, Mark O'Connor, Itzhak Perlman, the Robert Shaw Chorale, the Mormon Tabernacle Choir, and even the Beach Boys. There is, apparently, something in this music that generations of musicians find worth coming back to, worth arguing about, worth revising.

There is no question that "Old Folks" is a truly great melody. Florida made it the official state song in 1935, and later cleaned up the lyrics of its racial "insensitivities," purged the references to "darkeys," and tidied up its Uncle Remus dialect. The irony is that the Suwannee River basin is by far the most sparsely populated region of the state, and if and when Floridians pine for the Sunshine State, it is probably not the Suwannee River that they are thinking about. But it suits the nostalgic image of the Old Home Place that official songs and anthems are designed to evoke. It's an example of the special kind of amnesia that official, legislated memory intends to induce.

Which is why, if you're looking for a sentimental, nostalgic anthem for Florida, you pick a song written by a guy from Pennsylvania. Foster was born near Pittsburgh and never even set foot near the Suwannee. His identification with the river he made famous is entirely an accident of lyrical exigency: he chose the name "Swanee" when his brother found the river on a map, because the name fit his song better than Yazoo or Pee Dee.

In the 2000s, Florida seemed to realize belatedly that "Old Folks" did not necessarily speak for all the folks in Florida. A movement arose to replace Foster's song with a newer, sunnier version: something that truly represented the self-image of Florida as a sun-soaked, pre-serpent Eden.

So in 2007, the state sponsored a contest to find a new state song. The winner of the contest, "Florida (Where the Sawgrass Meets the Sky)," was written, like Foster's, by a nonnative. It was intended to replace "Old Folks," but in a textbook move of bureaucratic compromise, it was named the state's new official "anthem" in 2008. A more Floridian end is hard to conceive: Foster's song was granted the "emeritus" status and sent to the old folks' home.

The new anthem is even more sentimental than Foster's, if also more apropos of the idea of Florida, as opposed to the incarnated, inhabited place:

> Florida, land of flowers, land of light.
> Florida, where our dreams can all take flight.
> Whether youth's vibrant morning or the twilight of years,
> There are treasures for all who venture here in Florida.[37]

Apart from the obligatory nod to the hordes of retirees in their "twilight of years" who flock to Florida every winter, this is not exactly groundbreaking songwriting. It's certainly not Stephen Foster, and whoever wrote it is not likely to have a state park named for them. "Sawgrass" is a good example of what you get when state representatives commission official music: an entirely sanitized, unobjectionable vision of Florida that conforms to most people's expectations of the place as a land of white sand beaches and dreams fulfilled, music as an arm of the Chamber of Commerce. Granted, state songs are not supposed to remind us that dreams take flight less frequently than they come crashing into the swamp to be eaten alive by alligators who do not give a shit about your dreams, or cruelly shift like the sands on the pristine white beach that Florida is supposed to be made out of.

To be fair, when Foster wrote "Old Folks," he did not intend it to become a state song. Yes, Foster's song is a racially patronizing, hopelessly idealized White vision of Black longing. It is sentimental and nostalgic, in a way that occludes the actual and inherited experience of the people the song is supposed to speak for. But at least the song evokes a real history, even if only a semblance of that history. It summons up a reality that official memory often seeks to dispel: the specter of human cruelty and malice that cannot be whitewashed away.

It is probably no coincidence that Henry Ford was a huge fan of Foster. In 1929 he opened the Henry Ford Museum and Greenfield Village in the heart of the Ford Motor Company's main campus in Dearborn, Michigan. The museum provided a place for Ford to display the company's history, and the village allowed Ford to reconstruct his vision of American history. He purchased Thomas Edison's lab, the Wright Brothers' bike shop, and Harvey Firestone's family farm. Ford's "mecca of Americana" was conceived as a monument to White industry and innovation: conspicuously absent from the collection were the achievements and creative products of Jews and African Americans. In Ford's vision of history, "American" meant "White." In 1916, Black workers represented only 0.1 percent of the employees at Ford (a number that would grow steadily as the Great Migration brought more and more African Americans from the South to Detroit). But more tellingly, the Ford Motor Company's own accounting distinguished "Jewish" and "Negro" employees from "American" ones. Ford's model of American history came in any color, so long as it was White.

Foster was a perfect fit for Ford's vision of America, so Ford purchased Foster's birth home in Pennsylvania, relocated it to Greenfield Village, and dedicated it on Independence Day, 1935.

Paul Robeson, on the other hand, did not jibe with Ford's vision of America. Robeson recorded "Old Folks" in December 1930 as a B-side for *His Master's Voice*. A titanic personality with outsized talent, Robeson was already on Du Bois's radar in 1918, when Robeson was a senior All-American end for the Rutgers football team. In a short profile for *The Crisis* in March 1918, Du Bois highlighted Robeson's achievements on the field, and added, almost as a footnote, that he "is a baritone soloist."[38] Football made Robeson famous, but music made him a legend. By the time he recorded "Old Folks at Home," he was possibly the most popular and celebrated Black singer in the world.

Robeson made his name on the stage and in film by initially playing characters that confirmed White stereotypes of "happy Negroes," and by performing minstrel songs that White audiences took for "perfect Negro songs." After a sojourn in England and the Soviet Union, where he "felt for the first time like a full human being," Robeson came to identify himself as an Afro-American, and when he returned to the United States he became actively involved in campaigning for civil rights. He soured on the old minstrel songs like "Old Folks" and stopped performing them, and put his prodigious, load-bearing voice behind a different vision of America. After the lynching of George and Mae Murray Dorsey, and Roger and Dorothy Malcom at Moore's Ford in Georgia in July 1946, Robeson delivered a speech that September before 20,000 people in a rally in Madison Square Garden calling upon President Truman to act in response to lynchings that summer that had killed fifty-six African Americans. Three months later, Harry S. Truman established the President's Committee on Civil Rights, which ultimately led to the desegregation of the US military in 1948.

During the same season in which Paul Robeson was recording "Old Folks at Home," Ray Charles was being born 130 miles away from the Suwannee River in Albany, Georgia. Ray's mother, Aretha, was from Albany, but lived in Greenville, Florida, in Madison County, about an hour's drive from the Suwannee River. Aretha traveled to Albany for Ray's birth, and then returned to Greenville, where she raised him. Ray could literally cycle the streets of north Florida blind. He knew the area.

Ray Charles statue, Greenville, Florida. Photo by the author.

He made his own, very Ray Charles adaptation of Foster's song in 1957 for the album *Yes Indeed!!* With the Raelettes's antiphonal responses evoking the music of the Black church, it's jaunty and winsome, in every way Foster's version is not, and would have made a decent choice for the Florida state song, but Georgia had already claimed Ray for his cover of "Georgia on My Mind," first recorded by Hoagy Carmichael eight days before Charles was born.

The operative idea in every version of "Old Folks—including Gershwin's derivative "Swanee"—is that the Suwannee River is really, really far, far away. It's a placeholder for an unattainable object of longing, the Southern image of the end of the Earth, about as remote from anywhere as it is possible to get, and definitely distant from the wild urbanity of New York City. But for Charles—unlike Foster—the Suwannee was home.

After he completely lost his vision at age seven, Ray was enrolled in the Florida School for the Deaf and the Blind in St. Augustine, established in 1885, the same year that Florida rewrote its 1868 "carpetbagger" constitution. The new constitution decreed that "White and colored children shall not be taught in the same school." Originally the school was not segregated by race, but after opposition to integrated school teaching and a law initiated by William Nicholas Sheats in 1895, the state ruled that Black and White people could not be taught in the same building together.

Even though many of the students could not see one another, the Black students were assigned to the Florida Institute for the Blind, Deaf and Dumb, Colored Department, where Ray was a student until 1945. The school was not desegregated until 1967.

Ray didn't want to go to St. Augustine. So when he sang about

How my heart is going sad (so sad)
So sad and lonely
Because I'm so far (so far)
I'm far from my folks back home (from my folks back home)[39]

he meant it and felt it. His folks were way back in Greenville. Although the river itself was miles to the east, The "Swanee" was his home. He could sing about it with a depth of familiarity and experience that neither Stephen Foster nor Paul Robeson ever had.

Both Foster's "Old Folks" and the newer "Sawgrass" are about the idea of Florida—and therefore the idea of America—an idea that has been sentimentalized and abstracted and endlessly reproduced, like a Thomas Kinkade painting. "Sawgrass" is all about finding what it is you think you seek. Foster's original at least contains a trace of human longing, of desire for communion, of seeking and not finding. But it is a White man's version of what a White man thinks a Black man wants, and the distance between desire and fulfillment remains determined entirely by White projection, by a White songwriter trying to give voice to Black longing. But in Ray Charles's version, the distance between that longing is real and raspy—if somewhat disguised by the tune's upbeat vibe. It's an act of repossession, of retaking an idea that originated in the mind of a White writer and redeeming it with authentic experience. It's also an example of how the story of American history ought to be told and voiced: again, hoarsely.

Birdsville General Store, Birdsville, Georgia. Photo by the author.

GEORGIA II
Next Door Is a World Away

★ Are Southerners unique in this?

Before I ever heard of Flannery O'Connor, I had heard of Milledge-ville. In Georgia it is a synecdoche for the state mental hospital located there, so one sometimes hears about cousins and in-laws who had a "nervous breakdown" and "went to Milledgeville." A classic instance of ✗Southern indirection, it was a nicer way of saying "looney bin."

The state mental hospital loomed large in the collective imagina-tion as an institution for freaks and misfits, and it seemed fitting that O'Connor's fiction was so heavily peopled with characters who could have escaped from there. But the reality is far more expansive. We both came here for the first time in 1994. We drove down from Winston-Salem to attend a conference on O'Connor at Georgia College. We had both taken a seminar on her recently with Ralph Wood, our professor at Wake Forest who was delivering a keynote at the conference, and the three of us took turns driving the professor's boxy blue Chevrolet Impala. It was our first exposure to the world in which O'Connor lived, but it was exposure at a distance: the farmhouse where O'Connor spent the last thirteen years of her life was not open to the public, and her scrupulously private mother, Regina, still lived in town at her house on Greene Street.

The conference was a big do, more like a festival, really. We attended a reception at the old Governor's Mansion, heard readings by Joyce Carol Oates and Lee Smith, and a performance by Leo Kottke. Throughout the event an ongoing art exhibit displayed works inspired by O'Connor's work and commissioned for the conference, including a striking series of abstract prints on "O'Connor's Treelines" by an artist whose name we both forgot in the intervening years. But the images of some of those prints stuck with me: the sun shaped like a turnip slowly lowering over a jagged wall of pine, a purple sky deepening over a stylized scene of a farm in ruins.

Milledgeville was once the site of the state's mental hospital, and as a result did not enjoy the most glowing reputation within the state. It is no accident that Flannery O'Connor wrote in a world rich with society's misfits and rejects. Andalusia, the farm where she lived with her mother on the outskirts of town, has recently reopened to the public after being gifted to Georgia College. Just off the foyer on the southwest corner of the house, the room where she wrote most of her stories and novels, letters, and lectures: work that had only recently begun to completely screw me up and fundamentally alter the way I thought about everything by the time we first visited Milledgeville in 1994.

Just a few feet away from the small bed where she slept, a stout oak desk supports a typewriter and two wooden boxes repurposed as shelving units. A pair of crutches are propped up against a tall armoire oddly positioned on the other side of the desk, presumably to provide shelter from wandering eyes, even now. I strain to get a decent photograph of her desk, but strain even harder to take in the enormity and consequence of what emerged from this little spot.

In the gift shop in the next room, O'Connor's books are for sale. From a newly built picture rail made of aluminum hooks, wire, and rebar, hang—lo and behold—the last three framed prints from the "O'Connor's Treelines" series that we remembered from 1994. Twenty-four years later, here they are, as if they are waiting just for us, just for this trip. Because the new owners of Andalusia want to redo the gift shop, the prints have been priced to move. And that is exactly what two of them do, right into the back of the minivan.

Pulling down the driveway out of Andalusia and back out onto US 441, across the pond to the right there is a view of the woods. It is the same view Flannery had from her own window or porch. We take O'Connor's treelines with us, a constant exhortation from the back of the minivan to see what she saw.

John and I have both been to Milledgeville before, but this is the first time either of us have set foot on the campus of the State Hospital on the south side of town on State Road 112. Established in 1837 as the Georgia State Lunatic, Idiot, and Epileptic Asylum, by the time it was renamed Central State Hospital in 1967, it was the largest mental health facility in the world.

It is staggeringly enormous, the size and appearance of a heavily endowed college campus, at its heart a leafy central quadrangle edged with red-brick buildings with high-columned neoclassical porticoes. You could even imagine enjoying a loungy picnic on the meticulously maintained lawns on the quad, and get taken in by the brilliant bit of there-are-no-tanks-in-Baghdad groundskeeping trickery. On every side, the buildings of the hospital are uninhabited, crumbling, and roofless. Warning signs proliferate, discouraging intrepid prowlers and the curious from approaching the structures. Bad omens are everywhere.

NO TRESPASSING

UNSAFE BUILDING AND GROUNDS

Light plays weirdly behind broken-glass windows, vines creep through empty panes and up exterior walls, and there is blue sky where there should be a roof. Across the pecan grove quadrangle, the Central Chapel still holds weddings for people with very, er, particular, "Southern Gothic" tastes.

The dusk is deepening as John and I wander in front of the Powell Building on the main campus. A pair of red foxes lurk under the wide branches of a southern magnolia, eye us suspiciously, and flit off. Powell looks more like a state capital than a hospital building: stark, white, and imposing, its weathered bronze dome looms above a three-story porch, held up by four grand ionic columns. The bricks were made with slave labor. Sherman camped his troops here on his way to Savannah. Tonight the building is dark except for one fluorescent-lit hallway deep inside. Out front, the fountain basin is dry, a faded swimming-pool blue.

There is too much to see tonight. We call it a day and come back the next day, first thing. The early morning sun is gold against the Jones Building, which in context does not look as grand as it is supposed to. It has few windows still intact, is overwhelmed with ivy. The Georgia state seal still seems improbably unfaded on the tympanum. Where there was once glass on the main doors there is now stained plywood.

I kneel in the dewy grass to take a photograph of the front of Jones and quickly jump to my feet, my right shin covered in dirt. Except it is not dirt, but a battalion of extremely pissed-off fire ants. The marks they leave on that leg do not go away until well after the trip is over.

In 1959, Jack Nelson, a reporter for the *Atlanta Constitution*, wrote a series of articles for the paper exposing "irregularities" in the operation of the hospital. Nelson found that a nurse had performed a major surgery. People ineligible for surgery—by implication relatives of hospital staff— were operated on, while others who were eligible waited indefinitely. Administrators misappropriated funds. The 12,000-patient facility was inadequately staffed. The superintendent of the hospital, T. G. Peacock, did not take too kindly to Nelson's nosing around. When Nelson pressed Peacock on just how long was the backlog of eligible patients awaiting surgery, the superintendent told him, "I don't think that's any of your business."[1] Peacock telephoned Wallace Gibson, head of surgery and the subject of many of Nelson's stories. "That same damned newspaperman is down here," he said. Peacock was livid. He said that Nelson "ought to be turned over to those patients that handled that other fellow"—an apparent reference to an episode covered in the same day's newspaper, in which two hospital patients attacked an attendant with a shiv, cutting him all over and leaving him "mighty bloody."[2]

Officials at Central Hospital weren't the only ones in a tizzy about Nelson's reportage. In May 1959, Nelson was back in Milledgeville to cover a Baldwin County Medical Society meeting. Some took umbrage to his being there. A doctor from Eatonton, Charles Jordan, complained that Nelson had been dragging Dr. Gibson's name through the mud. They had words. Outside Ray's Drive-In in Milledgeville, Dr. Johnson punched Nelson in the face.

Nelson had the last laugh. He won a Pulitzer for his coverage of the hospital's woes. The institution soon began slowly emptying out, and by 2010 it had all but shut down. In the light of day the vastness of the abandonment becomes apparent. Central State Hospital is huge enough, but when combined with the adjacent Men's State Prison and other now-defunct facilities, it is an almost incomprehensibly sprawling and decaying complex where once an enormous swath of varyingly wayward humanity was managed, treated, rehabilitated, medicated, controlled, and buried.

At the Men's Prison, kudzu has overtaken much of the facility. It is creeping up the four legs of a solitary watchtower, all but inaccessible for the high grass. I crawl through a hole in the chain-link fence. A capsized wheelchair sits in a doorway, surrounded by broken glass. In a large hall like an abandoned set from *One Flew Over the Cuckoo's Nest*, rows of plastic seats are pushed together in one corner. In another, a pile of tan and blue mattresses. Battleship Grey is the common theme.

Milledgeville was not just the state's sanatorium; it had also been the center of the prison system since not long after the city became the state capital in 1807. The State Penitentiary lasted until about the time the capital moved finally to Atlanta in 1868. Its original buildings were demolished in the 1870s, and the rubble-strewn, sixteen-acre site was deeded in 1889 to Georgia Normal and Industrial College, which in 1922 became Georgia State College for Women, which graduated Flannery O'Connor in 1945.

Some people would later say that Marion Stembridge should have gone to the State Hospital, or the prison. In 1949 the local grocer and loan shark and went with a burly colleague to the Shantytown home of John Cooper, an African American, to collect a debt. Stembridge walked up on the porch uninvited, looking for trouble. Emma Johnekin was one of the women on the porch. She turned to Stembridge. "Lord have mercy," she said. "He has got on brass knucks haven't you?' Stembridge turned to go inside the house. "God damn it," he shouted. "What is it to you?"

As Emma testified, "he grabbed me and hit me with his knucks. He hit me on the head. Mary ran where I was and pulled him loose from me. He shot me in the hand, and he shot at Mary. I went on inside the house and sat on the trunk. He came to the door and shot me in the shoulder and in the stomach. I didn't have a gun, neither a knife and Mary had neither gun nor knife."[3]

Emma Johnekin died a few days later, and Stembridge was charged with manslaughter. But it being Georgia in 1949, Johnekin being a Black woman and Stembridge a White man, he managed to never serve time. He maintained his innocence, but the episode festered in him, and it seemed as though he was paying a price anyway. He was later convicted of attempting to bribe two IRS agents, and indicted for perjury.[4] He divorced his wife. He came to feel that the price he was paying was due to other people: he harbored increasing resentment towards Marion Ennis, the attorney who represented his defense until he became "uncomfortable" with the case and quit. Stembridge seethed privately at Pete Bivins, the attorney who he believed was behind the tax evasion charges.[5]

There are NO NATIVES anywhere, unless you can find a group that was lived in the Olduvai Gorge area for the last 7.5 million years

In 1953, Milledgeville was celebrating its 150th anniversary. On May 2, as the town was more decked out and gussied up than it had ever been, as its streets were about to throng with guttural V-8 pickup trucks barely above idle pulling floats of bonneted Georgia girls in billowing hoop skirts, as the asphalt was about to thump with bellowing brass bands and war-dancing ~~Native Americans~~ *Indians* in full ceremonial headdress, Marion Stembridge climbed the steps to Marion Ennis's office on the second floor of the Campus Theatre on West Hancock, and fired three .38 caliber rounds into his back. He then coolly walked back out onto the street, tipped his hat to a group of ladies, and moseyed to Pete Bivins's office. He shot Bivins four times, and then turned the gun on himself.

Not even the mad rampage of the "berserk banker," as the *Chicago Tribune* called him,[6] could cool the "hearts warm with pride, hands warmed with applause" of the over 2,000 high-spirited attendees who helped kick off the festivities the following day. Celestine Sibley wrote, entirely without irony, that "No mother saddened by tragic death in the family in the midst of preparations for a beloved child's birthday party ever rallied more bravely than did the old town of Milledgeville as it hid its grief over the Saturday slaying of two of its leading citizens and put its best foot forward to receive the first of 10,000 visitors to attend the week-long sesquicentennial celebration."[7]

Heaven forfend that a little murderin' should get in the way of a good time. But this classically Southern moment of burying grief deep down where it belongs is where Flannery O'Connor comes in. She was living in Milledgeville at the time, and for all I know was a witness to the pageantry, although she never mentioned it in her published letters. But it must have made an impression, because she used the episode as the basis for her short story, "The Partridge Festival," published in *The Critic* in 1961. Marion Stembridge later became the subject of a full-length treatment in Pete Dexter's novel, *Paris Trout*, which won the National Book Award in 1988. In the opening scene of the book, a young girl—the fictionalized version of Emma Johnekin—is bitten by a rabid fox like the one eyeing me in front of the State Hospital.

Pete Dexter is Milledgeville's second most famous novelist: he grew up here, but lives in the northwest now. I'm sure some people in town still remember him. I don't know how many remember Pete Bivins or Marion Ennis. Or who remembers—or wants to remember—Marion Stembridge. Or Emma Johnekin.

The dead neither remember nor forget. Forgetting is for those who still have life.

Off a cedar-lined dirt lane near the Men's Prison is a field where thousands of the hospital's patients were buried from 1842 onward. The lane leads to and from precisely nowhere. A small gazebo and gate mark one end; at the other a bronze angel stretches a bird-shit–encrusted hand heavenward. Originally, or at least for part of the hospital's history, the dead were buried in this area in separate cemeteries for White and Black people, men and women. Each grave was marked with a small, numbered iron stake like an elongated teardrop. In the 1960s, groundskeepers removed them in order more efficiently to mow the grass. The iron stakes were discovered in 1997, when a group of visitors stumbled upon them in a pile in the overgrown field. Eventually the group established a memorial to the deceased and lined up 2,000 surviving iron stakes in rows like a pecan grove. It is a stark, macabre memorial to society's castaways, and only a partial restoration of their memory. And accidental integration by way of oblivion and anonymity. The dead aren't buried under these markers; they are out there, somewhere, underground. And there are many more than even these small tokens of memory can compass: over 25,000 deceased patients were originally buried here. But no one knows where, or who, they really are.

Next Door Is a World Away

Joel Chandler Harris, whose home, Wren's Nest, I had visited on many a school field trip, was born twenty miles north of Milledgeville in Eatonton, and spent his late teens during the Civil War as a printer's devil on the Turnwold Plantation nine miles north of town. He had applied to work there under the direction of Joseph Addison Turner, who ran maybe the only plantation-based periodical in American history. The weekly *Countryman* was of a piece with Turner's vision for Turnwold as a place devoted to "corn, cultivation, and literature," and enjoyed a wide readership during the war. Turner used the *Countryman* to advocate—unsurprisingly—for slavery and made it into "one of the most passionate and articulate promoters of Confederate nationalism to be found in the seceded states."[8] "Independent in Everything—Neutral in Nothing," the *Countryman* declared itself. And Turner was no less uncompromising about politics than about syntax: "Nothing," he wrote, "save the hellhole at Petersburg, can shock the nerves of a sensitive man, so much as the bad grammar, and terrible typographical blunders which we daily meet with."[9]

Harris worked under Turner for four years, until the *Countryman* collapsed after the war, thanks in part to the fact that Turner had been arrested by Union troops for disloyalty. When he moved to Savannah and then Atlanta, Harris did not seem to have taken Turner's love of political provocation with him. His attitudes toward the people he had spent hours with in the slave quarters on Turnwold diverged from his old mentor's, too. A freckle-faced redhead son of an Irish immigrant mother and an unknown father, Harris was bullied as a kid, and even as an adult. Whatever the cultural impact of his stories were to be a hundred years later, he felt at least some qualified sense of kinship with the people enslaved on Turner's plantation.

He learned the tools of the printing trade there, but it was the people of Turnwold that gave Harris his most fertile material. He heard the formerly enslaved people on the plantation known as Uncle George Terrell, Old Harbert, and Aunt Crissy tell folk tales about crafty creatures, which Harris adapted into Uncle Remus stories.

Harris was at best a kind of amateur folklorist unaware of its practice as a real, albeit very young, "scientific" discipline, but he did more than simply record the stories he heard from enslaved people on Turnwold Plantation. He repackaged and reframed them, and by putting them in the mouth of a narrator with "nothing but pleasant memories of the discipline of slavery,"[10] he made a tacit claim about the nature of enslavement. White readers ate them up, but Black readers did not need them, since they were already part of the oral tradition in Black homes like that of Alice Walker, who grew up hearing her parents tell the stories of Br'er Rabbit and Br'er Fox, but entirely without the mediation of Joel Chandler Harris.

White kids in Atlanta might grow up thinking that the Uncle Remus stories were Harris's invention. We inherited the logic of the WPA Guide, which describes Harris as the "creator" of the Remus tales. He has renamed the narrators, putting his stories at one remove from the actual lives and stories of the people from whom he heard (some might say stole) the stories that made him famous and wealthy.

In another sense, the Remus stories are—whatever Harris intended—often radically subversive tales, detailing in a fabulous style the enculturated forms of clever resistance that made Black survival on plantations possible. This part of the stories is often inaccessible to White readers, who often receive—as I did—the stories as hilariously witty accounts of the "happy Negro," winsome late-afternoon yarns spun by the "elderly, kindly, cottony-haired darkie, seated in a rocking chair," as Walker says.[11]

The image became commodified in Walt Disney's *Song of the South*, released in 1946. The film is, fittingly, a hybrid of live-action and hand-drawn animation, since the Remus stories themselves are a blend of oral history and cartoonish fictionalization. Disney's version—as with all Disney versions of folk or fairy tales—effectively turns the Uncle Remus stories into a mass-cultural product, killing off the living vitality of the stories as a living tradition. It solidified in the cultural imagination the image of the compliant Negro, bluebird on his shoulder, singing zip-a-dee-doo-dah.

When the film world-premiered at the Fox Theatre in Harris's adopted hometown of Atlanta, Walt Disney himself was in attendance. But James Baskett, who played Uncle Remus in the film, was not. In segregated Atlanta, Baskett was barred from the Fox, as well as from gala festivities hosted by the Junior League and others. Two years later— shortly before his death, in recognition of his work in *Song of the South*, Baskett became the first African American man ever to be awarded an Oscar. It was an "honorary" one.

Zip-a-dee-doo-dah.

The film premiered at the Fox Theatre, November 12, 1946, exactly one week after Eugene Talmadge easily won the general election for governor on a segregationist platform. His warnings to African Americans against voting in the primary had led to at least one Black man's death and was associated with the murder of four others. Atlanta was already abuzz with Disney fever, though: while Ol' Gene sat out election night in a hospital room, stars from *Song of the South* like Pinto Colvig, the voice of Pluto and Goofy, were already arriving in town.

The next week, the "gay-a-luh occashun"[12] at the Fox was front-page news. The *Constitution* carried photos of Walt Disney making an entrance, and candids of gussied-up young moviegoers, reviews from a young Celestine Sibley and Doris Lockerman (who two years later would become the first woman associate editor at a major American newspaper). Sibley casually noted that "James Baskete [*sic*], the Negro actor who portrayed Uncle Remus, did not appear."[13]

The film has effectively been taken out of the Disney rotation and has never been released in any home video or streaming format in the United States. Walker saw the film in Eatonton as a young girl, but it did not have the effect Disney desired. "I don't know how old I was when I saw this film—probably eight or nine—but I experienced it as a vast alienation, not only from the likes of Uncle Remus—in whom I saw aspects of my father, my mother, in fact all black people I knew who told these stories— but also from the stories themselves, which, passed into the context of white people's creation, I perceived as meaningless. So there I was, at an early age, separated from my own folk culture by an invention."[14]

Walker did not need Harris's version or Disney's, and definitely not the doubly appropriated *Walt Disney's Uncle Remus Stories*, published by Golden Books to coincide with the release of the film. African American literary material, once purchased with White wealth, becomes handed on from one White owner to the next, with each transfer of ownership a further remove from the source from which it sprang,

In the estimation Albert Murray (a writer I will come to know later, by way of Tuskegee), Harris "was no great shakes as a writer," but "sometime old Joel's ear was not bad, not bad at all."[15] Walker's assessment is more severe. "As far as I'm concerned," she writes, "he stole a good part of my heritage. How did he steal it? By making me feel ashamed of it. In creating Uncle Remus, he placed an effective barrier between me and the stories that meant so much to me, the stories that could have meant so much to all of our children, the stories that they would have heard from us and not from Walt Disney."[16]

A famous White man's home in a famous Black neighborhood, the Wren's Nest remains a conflicted outlier, like its owner and his body of work. To many people it represents a soothing mythology of half-truths, to others a nefarious White appropriation of Black culture. Black and White people both got something from Uncle Remus "in one way or another," as Albert Murray says. Murray and Walker got that something from around the hearth at home in some version of the oral tradition going back ultimately to Africa; White kids like me got them by way of Harris, without ever having any real clue about the difference. Writing of himself in the second person, Murray writes that "there was about as much similarity between your Remus and the one Joel Chandler Harris wrote about as there is between music as you know it and the way Stephen Foster wrote it."[17]

Harris's visible legacy remains outsized in Georgia, even if few people read his versions of the Remus tales anymore. Nearby on Sparta Highway, a smiling cartoon rabbit in a red polo shirt, collar popped preppy-style, is waving at you, pointing you toward the Uncle Remus Museum 9.8 miles away. On the courthouse square in Eatonton, he is dressed in a more formal mood—with a red waistcoat and tobacco pipe—and depicted as a long-eared Bilbo Baggins, a sort of four-legged Odysseus, who "survives forever by his courage and his cunning."

Walker's legacy is far more subdued in her home Putnam County, where she lived scarcely a mile away as the bluebird flies from where Harris heard the stories that would make him famous. Along Old Phoenix Road there is a historical marker indicating the site of Turnwold Plantation, which still stands. Around the corner, on the backside of Turnwold, white-clapboarded Wards Chapel, where Alice was baptized, is still hanging on, barely. Recently derelict and critically endangered, it has been restored, somewhat. The exterior walls have been repainted, and the church windows are covered with plywood painted to look like stained-glass, but weather-grayed wood now competes with bright reds, oranges, blues. Across the road, along with many members of the Walker family, Willie Lee and Minnie Tallulah Walker, the parents who told Alice the stories of Br'er Rabbit and Br'er Fox, are buried. Not far from there, the property where Willie and Minnie were sharecroppers.

Along Ward's Chapel Road are occasional wooden signs highlighting sites from Walker's raising: the church, the graveyard. The farm where the Walkers sharecropped became a wedding venue, then went up for sale. Further on, one of them points across the road to the site of the house where Alice Walker was born. Nothing is there except a bare patch of red clay, two newish transformers at the base of a pole supporting power lines. Two Mercedes SUVs pull out of the crisply manicured gate of Waters Edge, one of the many gated lakefront communities that have sprouted up along Lake Oconee in the last decade. They whizz north up Wards Chapel Road. Past the signs, past the farm, past the past.

We take a crooked route east on GA 15 toward Sparta—one of many Georgia towns whose name is not pronounced the way it looks. Beyond "Sparter," we encounter a name that is everywhere in the late 2010s. In the center of what can scarcely be called the "town" of Warthen, a one-room log cabin of rough-hewn timbers, is the oldest jail in the state. Built in 1783, it held Aaron Burr for one night, as he was being transported on a crooked route of his own, from Bayou Pierre, Mississippi, en route to Richmond, to be tried for treason in 1807.

Birdsville

Eastbound, John reads aloud the passage about Birdsville in the WPA Guide to Georgia, which describes the place as "a small village that grew up about the ancestral home of the Francis Jones family." The manor house was begun in 1762, making it one of the oldest surviving houses in the state. According to the guide, "the avenues about Birdsville are lined with giant oaks almost two centuries old. Still standing at the crossroads are pre-Revolutionary buildings that made the Jones house the center of a small village. The small, gabled frame building was used as the inn, stage stop, and post office; here the members of the community gathered to learn news of the outside world."[18] Frequently, sites described in the WPA Guide have not survived, and have to be reconstructed in the imagination. But not Birdsville. It still looks almost exactly as the Guide has it and feels as removed from the "outside world" as it probably did in 1840.

It's still a private home, so we cannot get to the Jones Family Cemetery behind the house to see the final resting place of the woman the WPA Guide credits with saving the home from Yankee fire. "During the War between the States, General Sherman's men had overrun the plantation, stripped it of its treasures, and started to burn the house. Having no desire to outlive her home, the mistress refused to leave her bed where she lay ill. Because of her persistence the soldiers extinguished the fire, already mounting from a room in the lower story."[19]

The Birdsville story is a great story, to be sure. Whether there is any truth to it or not, it is hard to say. It is also the kind of story that White Southerners during Jim Crow loved, because it's a tale of noble defiance, of virtuous standing-your-ground in the face of the Yankee infidel. It's not hard to see the Lost Cause subtext encoded in the language. Nor is it any mystery which side is the good one in this passage. On one hand there is the wanton, amoral violence of Sherman, whose men "overran," "stripped," and "burn[ed]" the Birdsville plantation. On the other, the "woman" at Birdsville, who "preserved" her home, and "refused" to abandon it, even in her illness. And then the relenting of the Union soldiers to the irrefutably superior moral example of the anonymous woman from Birdsville.

I mention this story because it is so subtle and seductive, but also because it is painfully familiar to me. There is a similar story in my own family's history, but it's not one that was handed down to me. I had to find it on my own.

My great-great-great-grandfather, Samuel Charles Candler, was a prominent citizen in Villa Rica, Georgia, thirty-two miles west of Atlanta. His wife, Martha Beall Candler, was descended from a six-foot-seven Scotsman who fought against Oliver Cromwell, was consigned to indentured servitude in Barbados, and was eventually deeded land in Maryland that became Georgetown. Martha inherited his cast-iron disposition, but not his height. Known as "Old Hardshell," she was barely five feet high, and gave birth to eleven children, including (among her eight sons) a farmer, a bank president, a Methodist bishop and the first chancellor of Emory University, the founder of the Coca-Cola Company and mayor of Atlanta, a Georgia Supreme Court justice, and two United States congressmen. Old Hardshell was a tough and imperious woman, a demanding and overachieving mother you did not tussle with. That seems to have been known to everyone in Villa Rica, but not the Union soldiers who—the story goes—came up to the Candler home one day looking for Old Hardshell's husband.

"I don't know where he is, and even if I did I would not tell you," she is supposed to have said.

"Don't you know what we can do to you?" the soldier said, jabbing a pistol into her chest. "Don't you know that we can send your soul straight to hell?"

"There is not room enough in hell for a Southern lady," Old Hardshell replied. "It is too full of Yankees."

They left her alone, and she lived another thirty-plus years. I do not know if the episode ever happened, but like the Birdsville tale, it's a hell of a story. I have gotten some mileage out of it myself over the years, even if Old Hardshell's Baptist tough-mindedness did not make it all the way down to me.

Two Jameses

North of Birdsville, Augusta is the second-oldest city in the state. On Augusta Common, there are two Jameses. One James has his silk-coated back to the river he sailed up a long time ago, in front of him the town he marked out and named for his boss's mom. He is stylish and even a little campy, in his right hand a rolled-up copy of the charter for the colony of Georgia that could pass as a microphone. From one angle he looks like a tarted-up lounge singer, taking a breath between verses, preening over the city a lot of people think he made.

Half a block away, across a green space and half of Broad Street, another James looks back at him. Smiling in a three-piece suit and cape, he clutches a Shure SM-55 mic close to his chest. He is wearing a wedding ring.

They face each other across Augusta Common, a green space envisioned by James Oglethorpe but realized only in 2003. Of the two, Oglethorpe looks more like the rock star.

Augusta was his idea, but the other James is all over the place. His face and name are everywhere: on a main north-south boulevard, on the arena named for him where just about every famous Black musician in the cosmos came to both pay respects and *get up offa that thing*, right in front of his open casket in 2006. Michael Jackson said a few words then. Standing over the forever stilled and silenced Godfather of Soul, he said that without James Brown there would be no Michael. No Prince, no Usher, no Bruno Mars.

The statue of James Brown on Broad is as tame as Oglethorpe's is brassy and confident. There is no trace of James's ferocious virility, no sign of the agony—sexual, racial, political—that Brown projected from his sweat-soaked face in live performances. He is now a happy crooner, a domesticated, buttoned-up local hero, not the jump-suited, off-kilter–afroed Sex Machine. As much as an honor it is to James Brown to have a statue of him in a town that did not always receive him kindly, the statue seems an attempt to cut him down to size—literally: the statue represents the surprisingly diminutive size of his body, if not his outsized persona. He is immortalized now, a torch-singing family man in bronze, no longer floating above the stage like he once did, his impossibly elastic ankles moving, doing it, you know. He could dance and sing like nobody else and was one of the greatest (and sternest) bandleaders in popular music history. And he could play, too: he plays keys on "Sex Machine."

But you don't get any of that from the statue on Broad, which looks less like a tribute than an attempt at exoneration. Not for James, but for the city that has long been uneasy about him. The message of the statue is less "James Brown invented popular music" than "Look, we gave James a statue, okay? So let it go."

One can imagine how those planning conversations went down in City Council. James Brown was not always Augusta's favorite son, and it isn't hard to see some of the resentment towards him come through in the image of Brown Augusta decided to reify. The current image of Brown on Broad is Brown as the Augusta power-elite wished him to be, not as he was, which is, even still, hard to keep up with. Like James himself: always a beat or two ahead of the crowd and its fashions.

I don't know if anyone did, but I hope someone during those city council discussions about the statue proposed the skin-tight, scoop-neck–jump-suited Brown of the 1970s, mid-split, or even the serviceably patriotic image of Brown from *Rocky IV*. Hell, even the improbably Scandinavian version of a pompadoured Brown in a red-and-white Nordic sweater from the 1965 film *Ski Party* would seem a better compromise to appeal to the country club set in Augusta, but that is not the image they went with. They went with a Black version of Josh Groban. With a cape.

Many of the images of Brown around Augusta seem designed to modify the statue's presentation of him. On the boarded-up storefront of Fuji Wigs, a stylized image of his famous hairdo. On each side of a traffic light switch box on the corner of Broad and the Boulevard named for him, a different black-and-white image of Brown, each as strikingly different from one another as they are from the statue. On the one facing Broad, James is smiling, looking up, a cross around his neck. He is not wearing a wedding ring. He looks here less like the Godfather of Soul than its High Priest, as is meet and right.

As statues go, Oglethorpe got the better hand, in the end. He's the more stylish one. In bronze anyway.

But neither statue in Augusta has the footprint or airspace that a third one does.

On St. Patrick's Day on Broad Street, the crowd is mixed—Black, White, Asian, Hispanic—but everyone is wearing green. A fountain in the middle of Broad Street spews up emerald green. In front of the notorious Confederate Memorial not a block away, an African American man passes and looks sideways at the monument. He registers nothing, and does not stop like the White family whose greened-up little girl in a shamrock headband gaily prances up the steps of the monument under the words:

No nation ever rose so white
Nor fell so pure of crime

The little girl's parents quickly raise their cell phones to take a photo.

The statue was meant as a reminder of who runs this town. When African Americans marched down Broad Street in the 1870s, White Lost Causers of the city put up this gigantic statue of a Confederate soldier right in the middle of the street, so that if Black people were going to march in protest again, they'd have to go around the big White middle finger to them. On a nonsubtlety scale from one to ten, this one goes to eleven.

Down the street, a brass band is kicking ass in front of a flower shop. Dozens of folks have stopped to listen. One older, pot-bellied White man in a white cardigan and green leprechaun's hat sits through it all on a folding chair, clutching a koozied Silver Bullet, which he sets down on the sidewalk between songs to clap his hands enthusiastically. The all-Black band is mostly men and mostly trombones, one of which is played by a woman in jeans and Chuck Taylors. They are tight as an E-string. They each take turns leading. When I show up, a young man in denim shirt and blue jeans is out front on the trombone, a red-striped white towel in his right hand, Satchmo-style. A toddler bounces percussively on the sidewalk next to him, scratching on a tin grater with an afro pick.

During a break I ask the sousaphone player what their story is.

"We play at the United House of Prayer every Sunday. And right here every Friday night."

I was not expecting that. I've heard brass bands in church before in New Orleans, but I didn't see this coming in Augusta. I assume that it's one of those new-school churches that uses unconventional musical styles to draw in young people.

I am so wrong.

The House of Prayer has been around a hundred years, and by the time the Georgia WPA Guide was written in 1940, it was well established in Augusta, along with its house music: "The House of Prayer, 1269 Wrightsboro Road, is an unpainted, rough-board tabernacle in which Bishop Grace preaches a highly emotional religion to the accompaniment of much shouting, increased by the four brass bands that provide music for the services. At one end of the auditorium, decorated with streamers of crepe paper, is the "throne" of Daddy Grace, as the preacher is affectionately known. Worshippers sit on wooden benches arranged on the sawdust-covered dirt floor."[20]

The United House of Prayer for All People, as it is now known, is an unpainted, rough-board tabernacle no more. On the same Wrightsboro Road site is now a brightly colored brick and stucco building with three gabled and spired main portals, surrounded by a black aluminum fence. "Sweet Daddy," as he was affectionately known, was not the local pastor of the House of Prayer, but its founder, who established Houses of Prayer all over the country, the first of which was in West Wareham, Massachusetts. Born Marcelino Manuel da Graça, "Sweet Daddy" had come from the Cape Verde Islands in the early twentieth century, toured the country in a black cassock and pattypan squash hairdo. But he was a bishop, and like the cathedra in Catholic churches, the throne for Bishop Grace was usually empty, waiting for Sweet Daddy to come back from tending his many flocks around the states. Though he was not there much, they still called the place "Sweet Daddy's." I don't know if there is still a throne in the new building, or if it's occupied.

And I don't know what else James Brown took from Sweet Daddy Grace, but he walked out of the House of Prayer in Augusta one Sunday in 1941 with a future he'd seen and heard in there: the hairstyle and sass, the spirit-shake, the swagger and the bone-quaking brass. I am sure Sweet Daddy could shell down the corn like no man, but no one ever made a more persuasive on-film preacher than James Brown did in *The Blues Brothers*. Shameless and clichéd, yes, but slip-sliding and swing-kicking across the stage in a fuchsia gown that could barely keep up with him, calling us all back to the Old Landmark, his hair hilariously and uncharacteristically disheveled in a way only the Holy Spirit could get away with, James Brown could have made any damn body see the light.

On the Common, Augusta may look more like James Oglethorpe imagined it, but—today, at least—it sounds like James Brown.

Redcliffe Plantation, Beech Island, South Carolina. Photo by the author.

SOUTH CAROLINA I
Into the Mysticism of the Southern Road

A cross the Savannah River from Augusta, a row of mansions lines the South Carolina waterfront. Behind that row of homes sits a semi-private "golfers' paradise." It promises a "unique setting which includes ultradwarf bermuda greens, numerous lakes, wetlands, and dramatic bunkers." What it does not include is any trace of what used to be here.

Hamburg

Established in 1821, Hamburg took off when the train came to town in 1833. Forty years later, it came to be a thriving Reconstruction-era settlement built around the railroad, with a majority-Black population. Black people owned property in Hamburg, occupied important political offices, ran the local militia.

The year 1876 was centenary. Festivities for the hundredth anniversary of American Independence were a big deal around the nation. On the Fourth of July 1876 in Hamburg, Black residents including many Freedmen heard the words the Declaration of Independence read aloud in the town center: "We hold these truths to be self-evident, that all men are created equal, that they are endowed by their Creator with certain unalienable Rights, that among these are Life, Liberty and the pursuit of Happiness."

In 1876 those words rang with new promise, and it seemed for a moment as though the scope of those ideals might include Black men.

That afternoon in Hamburg, a Black militia unit on parade declined to yield to two White men passing down the street. The White men were incensed at this affront. A few days later, White paramilitary units of "Red Shirts" took their complaint to trial justice Prince Rivers and agitated against the Black soldiers. Born enslaved, a Union Army veteran, and former state legislator, Rivers represented everything the Red Shirts opposed. Matthew C. Butler, a planter from Edgefield, demanded the militia surrender its weapons. Refusing to do so, the militia holed up in the Sibley Building in Hamburg, and dug in. Butler and another Edgefield planter, named Benjamin Tillman, led an attack on the militia and opened fire on them.

By 4 AM the next morning, their bloodlust satiated, the mob released the remaining captives and dispersed. Six Black men were dead: Charles Attaway, Jim Cook, Alfred Minyard, Moses Parks, Dave Phillips, and Hamp Stevens. One white man was killed early in the conflict: Thomas McKie Meriwether. Hamburg magistrate Prince Rivers was forced to flee the town for safety. His house was attacked.[1]

Newspapers around the country condemned the actions of the White mob. The *New York Times* wrote that it "makes one blush for shame that the wretches who did the work should call themselves American citizens." Legendary cartoonist Thomas Nast drew at least two cartoons related to the massacre for *Harper's Weekly*. South Carolina's Congressman Robert Smalls, petitioned the US House to prohibit US troops from withdrawing from the state, to prevent the eruption of further outrages like those at Hamburg.[2] President Ulysses S. Grant condemned the "barbarous massacre of innocent men at Hamburg" as "cruel, bloodthirsty, wanton, unprovoked, and uncalled for," and worried aloud that "A Government that cannot give protection to life, property, and all guaranteed civil rights . . . to the citizen is . . . a failure."[3]

Prince Rivers issued arrest warrants for Butler and Tillman, and eighty-five other White men. A Congressional debate held in July 1876 and a subsequent Senate investigation into "the denial of the elective franchise in South Carolina" failed to hold anyone accountable, thanks in part to the unshakable skepticism of North Carolina's senator Augustus Merrimon toward the White mob's guilt, his badgering of Black witnesses, and his belief that the massacre was really the fault of "a vicious class of negroes" in Hamburg.[4]

The massacre was a stain on no White politician's career. On the contrary, its principal actors, Matthew C. Butler and Benjamin "Pitchfork" Tillman, would both be elected to the United States Senate. Tillman would become one of the most celebrated figures in South Carolina, with his own statue on the State House grounds. Wade Hampton III was elected governor in November 1876, thanks in large measure to the campaign of terror waged by Butler and Tillman's Red Shirts. At the height of his popularity, Tillman was a circuit-riding evangelist for "the gospel of white supremacy," and would later refer to the Hamburg "riot" as a "tragic episode in the struggle for white supremacy."[5]

Prince Rivers endured quite a different fate. No longer an ascending figure in state politics and a model of Reconstruction-era aspirations for "a new birth of freedom," he was reduced to driving a carriage for White people until his death in 1887.

Ultimately a flood took what was left of Hamburg. A regime of silence and forgetfulness took what was left of its memory.

But on major thoroughfares in Augusta and North Augusta, a different way of remembering dominates the view. On Broad Street in Augusta, the aforementioned seventy-six-foot-high monument celebrates the Confederacy in unambiguous terms. It was unveiled on Halloween 1878, two years after the massacre and a year after federal troops withdrew from Georgia. In attendance at the event were at least four detachments of the so-called "Red Shirt Democracy."

In north Augusta, a tall obelisk on the grounds of a prominent antebellum-style inn honors Thomas McKie Meriwether as "the young hero of the Hamburg Riot." The monument is not really about Meriwether, but about the "Cause" he represented. Whatever the precise nature of Meriwether's involvement in the massacre, his memory was quickly seized upon as that of a martyr who "gave his life that the civilization builded by his fathers might be preserved for their children's children unimpaired." The monument makes it unmistakably plain: "In life he exemplified the highest ideal of Anglo-Saxon civilization. By his death he assured to the children of his beloved land the supremacy of that ideal."

Just down the street, a Veterans memorial park is named in honor of Wade Hampton III. It features a granite marker for each of America's wars. The marker for the War of 1812 displays little confidence in what that war was about. There is no such uncertainty about the meaning of the Civil War: "Let their virtues plead for just judgment of the cause in which they perished."[6]

This may have something to do with the fact that the chairman of the Wade Hampton Veterans Park was also a life member of the Sons of Confederate Veterans. The park was constructed in 1993.

Today on either side of the Savannah River there is little evidence of the Black victims of the Hamburg Massacre. A devastating flood in 1929 forced remaining residents to relocate up the bluff. A small marker on a little-traveled dead-end road there commemorates the massacre and its victims.

Nor was Hamburg the last of it, as Robert Smalls feared. Two months after the massacre in Hamburg, a similar, and even deadlier massacre erupted twenty-four miles southeast in Ellenton, South Carolina.

Today the site is marked with a historical marker noteworthy for the spartan economy of its memory. It reads:

POST OFFICE EST. HERE 1873. TOWN CHARTERED 1880. ELLENTON
AND SURROUNDING AREA PURCHASED BY US GOVT IN EARLY
1950S FOR ESTABLISHMENT OF SAVANNAH RIVER PLANT.

This is how the town is remembered now—or at least was in 1993 by the Ellenton Reunion Organization which erected the historical marker. The 1941 WPA Guide was slightly more forthcoming, if decidedly less "objective":

In the environs of ELLENTON . . . occurred a riot on May 15, 1876, that, nonpolitical in the beginning, assumed major proportions because of the race hatred engendered by the times. It resulted from an attempt to arrest two Negroes who had beaten a white woman. Armed Negroes from miles around appeared in large numbers, and whites from adjacent sections took to their guns. In two days 15 Negroes and two whites were killed before State militia restored peace.[7]

The Hamburg Massacre barely gets any airtime in public consciousness; Ellenton even less, even though it was a much deadlier conflict. One possible reason is because accounts of the Ellenton massacre tend to diverge, often sharply, from one another, leading to a general uncertainty about what happened there, and when. This unclarity has given license to the identification of the Ellenton "race riot" as "nonpolitical" and arising from a generic "race hatred" engendered not by actual people and their regimes and policies, but by that useful abstraction, "the times." It is not that the WPA writers knew nothing about the Ellenton massacre; on the contrary—workers for the Federal Writers' Project in South Carolina recorded extensive interviews with survivors and witnesses, and filled boxes with oral history accounts of the episode. But in a curious and not at all isolated fashion, the misidentification of Ellenton as a "race riot" served to categorize it (along with Hamburg and countless similar episodes) in a class of nonessential historical marginalia.

The truth—now as then—is that "racial" and "political" conflicts are never so neatly differentiated from one another in American history, and certainly not in South Carolina in 1876, where all politics was emphatically racial. The year marked a violent overthrow of Reconstruction in the state, a violent backlash against Republican carpetbaggers and scalawags. And naturally party affiliation was highly racialized: the Republican Party attracted Black voters, while the Democratic Party became the citadel of White supremacy in the South. Reprisals against Black voters were also and at the same time reprisals against Republicans, and violence against Black men in 1876 in South Carolina simply cannot be understood solely as a "racial" matter, because the existence of enfranchised Black men who were likely to vote Republican if given the chance (a very big if) represented an imminent threat to Democratic rule. This is precisely why the Red Shirts and other White paramilitary organizations, such as the "rifle clubs" that operated in Ellenton, arose in the first place: as the martial arm of an explicit political strategy to intimidate, harass, or murder potential Black voters, in the confidence that doing so would incur precisely zero personal consequences.[8] Indeed, one White witness of the Ellenton massacre wrote at the time that the terrorist campaigns against local Black residents were part of an unmistakably political aim: "They intend to rule or kill the negroes."[9]

The drama in Ellenton began in an almost predictable way: in September 1876, two Black men were accused of attacking a White woman named Mrs. Alonzo Harley. The Black men fled when Mrs. Harley brandished a double-barreled shotgun, and before long, local White posses began searching the area for the perpetrators. According to the testimony of Phillis Jackson, Harley's son identified Peter Williams as the perpetrator. After Harley's husband hit Williams in the face three times, Williams tried to flee. As he was running away,

> the party fired on him, and he fell. He was not dead, but mortally wounded. They threw him on a wagon, and as his legs were hanging over the sides, one of the white men deliberately shot through one of his feet with his pistol . . . Soon after the wagon, with Peter Williams

lying on it, was brought up to Mr. Harley's door, and Mrs. Harley was called out to see him. Mr. Harley told Williams to rise up. The wounded man did so, and as Mrs. Harley looked at him she said: "Oh, you have shot the wrong nigger, you ought not to have shot him till you showed him to me. He is not the man who knocked me."[10]

Not that it mattered much to the mob, who were not interested in extralegal justice, but in bloody sacrifice, regardless of truth. A blood-lust borne of White fears demanded a scapegoat. What ensued after the alleged attack on Mrs. Hartley was an indiscriminate rampage against Black citizens for nearly a week. Hundreds of White members of "rifle clubs" from Georgia and South Carolina swarmed the countryside waging a bloody offensive against Black citizens. By the time it was over, at least one White man and as many as—possibly more than—one hundred Black men were dead.

During the rampage, Simon Coker, a Black representative for Barn-well in the South Carolina legislature, was captured by a rifle club under the leadership of A. P. Butler, who knew of Coker's status as an elected official. Butler addressed Coker, saying, "I am the nigger ruler, and you've got to go with me." Coker pleaded with Butler for time to pray, which Butler granted. But as Coker knelt to pray, Butler shot him in the back of the head, then ordered his men to fire upon him as well. As Coker lay dead, Butler's men stole Coker's watch and wallet, as well as the gold buttons from his jacket, "leaving the body to rot."[11]

Ben Tillman had made a reputation for himself at Hamburg; he burnished it in Ellenton. The future US senator was there at the time and loaned two of his own Red Shirts to Butler for the assassination of Coker. Tillman defended the killing, appealing to potential critics to "first put themselves in the places of the whites who had been trampled in the mire by the carpet-baggers and negroes for eight long years, and realize that the struggle in which we were engaged meant more than life or death. It involved everything we held dear, Anglo-Saxon civilization included."[12]

Not far from where Hamburg and Ellenton once were is the mansion of James Brown, and it's not as you might expect. It's easy enough to spot in the modest suburban neighborhood east of Beech Island where it sits somewhere beyond an empty and unguarded octagonal brick gatehouse and an unscalable brick and wrought-iron fence. The asphalt driveway slopes downward into the pine-dense distance. The house is not visible. Suburban Aiken County might not be where you would expect the Godfather of Soul to live out his days, but James was nothing if not unpredictable. He was born thirty-four miles to the west, in a one-room shack in Barnwell, and grew up in a Black neighborhood in Augusta known as the Terry, for "Negro Territory."

Brown's mansion in Beech Island could be a tourist destination, but it isn't. It lies in South Carolina's 2nd Congressional District, currently served by Joe Wilson of "You lie" fame, who is in a long line of South Carolina politicians who have used the Congress floor as their personal stage. (Most famously, Wilson's predecessor, Preston Brooks of Edgefield County, notoriously caned the abolitionist senator from Massachusetts Charles Sumner nearly to death on the House floor in 1856 for being critical of slaveholders, namely Brooks's first cousin, Andrew Butler.) James Brown was born and spent his final years in an area with a long history of proslavery sentiment, and the region has furnished the state with many of its elected officials who have been powerful if not the "best and the brightest," men who would have been horrified at the prospect of a powerful and influential Black man like Brown.

A little over three miles from Brown's home and about as off the beaten track is an antebellum mansion called Redcliffe, which was once home to a now-notorious US congressman, senator, and governor of South Carolina whose life reads like an allegory but is all too literal.

James, the Third

In the late afternoon, a thin almond-shaped oculus of light appears at the end of a dense and crowded lane of very old magnolias, which furnish a seasonal surface for the footpath. Rain-drenched and dried, the leathery brown leaves crackle under foot. On the other side of the dense line of trees, sunlight filtered through overcast skies plays upon generous pastures of uncut grass and bountiful quiet. But within the lane, there is only compression: the magnolias appear too big for the space, as if whoever designed this place never expected it to last this long. When the property's owner died, ninety-five carriages processed solemnly down this lane, but now you couldn't fit a Prius through it.

At the end of the lane, you emerge into a more or less open field scattered with old-growth trees. It is not quite the reveal you are expecting; a large, square plantation house emerges up to the right, offset from the main drive. A wide porch wraps around three sides of the home, a stair-case descends into the damp grass.

Redcliffe is elegant, of course: it exudes a life with room to breathe, that peculiar combination of misattributed toil and unearned leisure which defined the Southern planter class. The Master of Redcliffe spent his latter years overseeing agricultural operations in the morning and spending up to six hours laid out on the couch reading and writing.[13] Of course the reality of the place is quite different. Completed in 1859 for James Henry Hammond, United States Senator and governor of South Carolina who, the WPA Guide notes, "is credited with popularizing the phrase 'Cotton is king.'"[14] Today Hammond is credited with far more than the WPA writer was willing or able to say.

Hammond came by the 7,500-acre plot known as Sliver Bluff Plan-tation (along with 147 enslaved persons) through his 1831 marriage to seventeen-year-old Catherine Fitzsimons, a propertied young heiress from Charleston. Hammond clearly married Fitzsimons for her money and regarded wedlock as a burden. The marriage was an early indica-tion of what truly motivated Hammond: an inexhaustibly unscrupu-lous desire for power and access. The plantation that he developed at Silver Bluff served "as a foundation upon which to erect his ambitions in the wider world, a base from which to reach out to a more extensive domain of achievement and control."[15] Ownership of slaves was essential to Hammond's status, and he acquired a lot of them, owning over 320 human beings at the time of his death in 1864.

During his political life, Hammond justified his enslavement of Black people with astonishing—albeit not uncommon—forthrightness. He became one of the state's most vocal defenders of slavery as a necessity belonging to the very nature of things. Slavery, he argued in 1836, "can never be abolished. The doom of Ham has been branded on the form and features of his African descendants. The hand of fate has united his color and his destiny. Man cannot separate what God has joined."[16]

Racial subjugation was natural, according to Hammond, and enslave-ment was the logical condition of the African race.[17] He also appealed to a theological rationale for slavery that allegedly legitimated the prac-tice with Scripture. He famously claimed that "American Slavery is not only not a sin, but especially commanded by God through Moses, and approved by Christ through his Apostles."[18] In distended displays of high-minded, ham-fisted, and fantastically self-serving biblical exegesis,

Hammond railed against abolitionists as demonic and anti-Christian, and extolled the virtues of chattel slavery not just as a necessary evil but as a positive good. In a letter to a London magazine editor, he wrote, "Nowhere and at no time has the African ever attained so high a status as in the condition of American SLAVERY."[19]

He further warned that "It is the most fatal of all fallacies, to suppose that these two races can exist together, after any length of time, or any process of preparation, on terms at all approaching to equality."[20]

His position on slavery was not especially novel or unique; his idol John C. Calhoun much more famously made the same argument for slavery as a positive good and achieved the status Hammond always sought but never fully realized. Hammond died at Redcliffe on November 13, 1864, two days before General William T. Sherman began his march to the sea, as the specter of Confederate defeat ominously encroached. "When he called the slave children from the yard to sing him spirituals at his death bed, Hammond identified himself and his life with the myths of the Old South, even as it crumbled around him."[21]

A memorial essay to Hammond published in the *Edgefield Advertiser* in 1878 recalled the statesman as "affable and genial, warm in his friendships and devoted in his affections." "There was nothing negative about the man," the paper asserted.[22] The Southern press mourned Hammond as "a man of eminent genius and rare acquirements" and took the occasion of his death to indulge their most excitable rhetorical impulses: "Few who were admitted to his intimacy who did not feel the spell of his musical voice as he held them in the thrall of his glittering eye, like the Ancient Mariner or the wedding guest."[23] But Northern newspapers did not remember him that way. One could not resist pointing out the fact that one of South Carolina's most vocal Yankee baiters "was only one remove from being a Yankee, his father being a native of Massachusetts."[24]

For all its drooling praise of the long-late governor, Southern memory had softened the focus on Hammond, and came to brand him as an exemplary model of Southern virtue. A more categorical miscalculation—or deliberate untruth—is hard to imagine. To Louis D. Rubin, Jr.—a prolific literary critic and Charlestonian, and hardly an "outsider" to South Carolina—Hammond "seems to have resembled nothing less than a monster." He was "a driving fury of self-aggrandizement, a political ideologue, a highly indulgent sensualist, a tyrannizing father and domineering husband, and also a self-pitying man who flaunted his sensibility and throughout his days personified the deluded Romantic opportunist."[25]

By Rubin's time, Hammond's market value had tanked. The dramatic reversal of Hammond's reputation has everything to do with the publication in 1989 of his private diaries. Scholars of Hammond had, of course, known about the contents of those diaries, and knew as fact what others had only heard as salacious rumor. But when Hammond's "Secret and Sacred" diaries were finally released, it became plain to everyone just how much historical redaction and deliberate forgetfulness had been at work in the preservation of Hammond's legacy.

In his diaries Hammond confessed to a protracted, two-year sexual relationship with four young women whom he molested at his home in Columbia. He recorded it all in indulgent and painful detail:

> Here were four lovely creatures from the tender but precocious girl of 13 to the mature but fresh and blooming woman nearly 19 [in 1840–1] each contending for my love, claiming the greater share of it as due to her superior devotion to me, all of them rushing on every occasion into my arms and covering me with kisses, lolling on my lap, pressing their bodies almost into mine, wreathing their limbs with mine, encountering warmly every operation of my frame and permitting my hands to stray unchecked over every part of them and to rest without the slightest shrinking from it, in the most secret and sacred regions, and all this for a period of more than two years continuously.[26]

Which is bad enough. But to make matters even worse (if that is possible), the four girls were Hammond's nieces, the daughters of his brother-in-law, Wade Hampton II. Hampton was the son of a Revolutionary War general and the leader of one of South Carolina's most powerful families. His son Wade III—brother to the four girls—would become the most dominant force in state politics after Reconstruction, and the most widely memorialized and celebrated figure in South Carolina for generations.

Hampton II was incensed at Hammond's outrages of his daughters, and he engineered Hammond's removal from public life for a decade and a half. A permanent rift between Hampton and Hammond had opened up with the scandal, and never healed. Hammond remained far from penitent; on the contrary: at the very moment of his admission of his sins against Hampton's girls, he congratulated himself on his restraint and taunted Hampton as weak and cowardly, a "designing poltroon" and a "convicted dastard."[27] He accused him of "coarseness and fatuity,"[28] and mocked Hampton for not inquiring into the evils perpetrated against his own children.

Hammond knew that the "odium of revelation" of his wickedness would undo him politically and socially: "it is certain that few ladies would visit us for a long time," he admitted.[29] So in the interest of self-preservation, Hammond chose to pursue what would become a classically Southern strategy: "to bury the whole affair in oblivion as speedily as possible."[30]

It did not work out that way. Even if his sexual predation did not become public knowledge, he was a defeated man. "I am utterly broken down and prostrated forever," he wrote in 1850.[31] He indulged an especially Romantic sort of self-abnegation that he may or may not have really meant, simultaneously praising his own persistent striving and bitching about the weaknesses of others. He imagined himself as a sort of King Lear of the Sandhills, "a man more sinned against than sinning," a chronic victim of other men's tragic choices more than his own. Yes, he had wronged Hampton's daughters, he admitted, but only to return to his own favorite theme: his own importance. If, he wondered in 1850, "So[uth] Carolina refuses my services—drives me from public affairs—is it she or me that will suffer most in opinion, in fact, in the long run?"[32]

Hammond's sexual abuse did not cease after its exposure. In 1839, Hammond had bought an eighteen-year-old seamstress named Sally Johnson and her one-year-old daughter Louisa for $900. It wasn't long before Hammond took Sally as his mistress and impregnated her. When Louisa turned twelve, Hammond did the same with her, and fathered several more children with her.[33] When Catherine Hammond learned of her husband's sexual relationship with Louisa, she demanded her husband sell the Johnsons.[34] He refused to do so. Furious, she left Sliver Bluff for Charleston. James Hammond remained on the plantation, wallowing in "the utter annihilation of [his] political prospects," feeling "outlawed and abandoned," nursing resentment and scorn, which he heaped abundantly upon his estranged wife and her family:[35] "My God! What have I done or omitted to do to deserve this fate? I trace it all to the horrible connection which Satan seduced me into forming with the vulgar Fitzsimons family, whose low-Irish deceit and hypocrisy can only be compared with their low-Irish pride, selfishness, and utter want of refinement and tone. I feel deeply for my poor dear children, so deeply tainted with this blood. I trust mine, aided by my precepts, may master it in them."[36]

He admitted his own responsibility in his familiar way: "I am wholly to blame, not so much, as I view matters, for what I have done as for what I have left undone, for want of caution which led to discoveries."[37] It is a classic case of the political/psychological abuses of high Anglicanism in nineteenth-century South Carolina: the borrowing of the language of a confession from the *Book of Common Prayer* to cover a multitude of sins, without the spirit of contrition. In his own mind, Hammond's big mistake was not raping his slaves or his nieces but getting found out.

On Edge in Edgefield

Historically, all the wealth in South Carolina has been in Charleston, the power in Columbia, and the authority in Edgefield. Twenty-five miles north of Augusta, Edgefield is South Carolina's most storied political town. A mural in the town center proudly claims a number of important state politicians as local boys, including Andrew Pickens, Pierce Mason Butler, James Henry Hammond, Milledge Luke Bonham, Ben "Pitchfork" Tillman, John Gary Evans, and Strom Thurmond. Ten of South Carolina's governors have come from Edgefield, which is impressive considering the town is not even 5,000 strong. Many of these figures contributed directly to the establishment and maintenance of White supremacy in South Carolina, and built political careers on suppression of Black power, or outright violence against Black South Carolinians.

Today a tall obelisk to the memory of Confederate soldiers from the town dominates the small, unshaded town square. In front of it, a statue of Strom Thurmond, who was conceived shortly after the Confederate monument was erected. A blue bicycle, unlocked, one handle grip missing, its seat covered in a gray grocery bag, leans on its kickstand and casts an angular shadow against the wall in the long afternoon sun. It is quiet, apart from the loudspeakers on the square which bellow contemporary country music as if to embellish the area with an extra—if unnecessary—element of garishness. Otherwise the assessment of the WPA writers holds up: "The impression of peace that could never have been broken by anything more stirring than housewives' arguments across backyard fences belies the community's reputation as a source of constant upheaval when ante-bellum riots and hangings agitated the State."[38] On one side is the Edgefield County Courthouse, where ballots were forged and manipulated to guarantee Wade Hampton's gubernatorial victory in 1876. In a shady cemetery a few blocks from the square, the body of Matthew Butler lies beneath an obelisk proclaiming him "Knightliest of the Knightly Race." Martin Gary is here, too, along with the town's many political figures who helped to entrench the White supremacist establishment, like Preston Brooks and Thurmond.

Parked along a curb during our first visit here in 1998, a Chevy pickup truck with a homemade Rebel flag tailgate constructed out of plywood and painted. Beneath it, a bumper sticker reads: "BEEF IS BRAIN FOOD!! Don't Believe Me . . . Talk To A Vegetarian —" Nearby, a mural advises, rather differently:

> STOP
>
> VISIT &
>
> LINGER

Which we do, for a spell. Next to the mural a bank of newspaper machines hawks the news for August 18, 1998. The buzz about town—and around the country—is sex and scandal. The headline of the *State* proclaims, "Clinton Admits Lewinsky Relationship, Says, 'I Misled People, Even My Wife.'" It is an auspicious context in which to be in the Palmetto State's most notoriously scandal-rich town, whose reputation for political intrigue and incest is unmatched, maybe anywhere. Edgefield has not exactly been eager to shed its image; on the contrary, it has leaned into it, as they say. A law firm bearing the name Tillman operates a block off of Main. A marker in front of an attractive late-nineteenth century home on Columbia Road marks the birthplace of J. Strom Thurmond, the impossibly durable—and fertile—Senator who served longer than anyone else ever has or should. When the sign marking his birth home was erected, Strom was halfway into his eighth—and final term. He died in 2003, at one hundred years old.

Returning here in 2020, shortly after visiting Hamburg, Edgefield feels very different. The defiance I might have celebrated as a naïve twenty-something now seems as adolescent and unformed as my own sentiments about politics and the South were in 1998. At that time, "defiance"—especially of the Feddle Gubmint—was basically School

Spirit in Edgefield (as in the rest of the South, *mutatis mutandis*), the leit-motif of "Southern culture." "Ideas and opinions here are those of folk who live as individuals not dependent on group action," an anonymous WPA writer observed in 1930s. "This independent spirit has prevailed since the eighteenth century, when Edgefield was a courthouse district extending north to the Cherokee lands."[39] It was that way because it had always been that way and damn you if you question it. But now—in the context of chronic police brutality against Black men and women, a political party that makes puerile contrariness a condition of mem-bership, and an attempted insurrection at the US Capitol featuring con-temporary descendants of the Red Shirts, the up-yours-Yankee spirit doesn't feel so cool anymore. There is no pickup truck with a wooden Rebel flag on its tail this time, but that does not mean there's not one out there somewhere.

What is here, though, is Martin Gary's former home, called Oak-ley Park, which now contains a museum and shrine to the Red Shirts. From this site, Gary distributed copies of "the Edgefield Plan"—the literal battle strategy for the election of 1876, one executed with deadly precision at Hamburg, Ellenton, and elsewhere in the state. In it Gary encouraged White people to intimidate Black voters and remind them "that their natural position is that of subordination to the white man."[40] In many ways, the violence at Hamburg and Ellenton was incubated in Edgefield.

It was also celebrated here. While newspapers across the country—including Southern ones like the *Charleston News*—were almost unani-mous in condemning the Hamburg Massacre, the *Edgefield Advertiser* was carefully carving its niche, leaning into its White-people-are-the-real-victims angle on the news. The paper of record in Edgefield was nonplussed by the violence in Hamburg. The town had it coming, it implied. "For years past," the *Advertiser* claimed, "Hamburg has been the vilest and most pestilent hole in South Carolina," because it was ruled and dominated by Black people.[41] White people, the paper argued, were not even safe there, and were subjected to all manner of abuse. Contrary to overwhelming public opinion that held the massacre was unprovoked, the Edgefield paper claimed that it was "simply the climax of a wrath that had been long and wantonly provoked, and that could forbear no longer." But even that was not enough: "Hamburg is a very blot upon creation, and the life of every wretched negro in it—all of them politically poisoned, misguided, wrong-headed—is not worth that of young Meriwether who fell in the fray."[42]

Southeast of Edgefield on US 25, the tiny village of Trenton has cast its lot with hometown boy Benjamin Tillman. The home just north of Trenton, where Tillman spent the last twenty-four years of his life, no longer stands, but a historical marker on the site mentions his staunch defense of farmers, the cause which first led him into politics, and his role in establishing Clemson University, the state's agricultural school. There is a brief mention of Tillman's calling of the convention to rewrite the state constitution in 1895 but does not mention what that convention really meant to do. The current marker, erected in 2002, evidently replaced an older one that the WPA writers witnessed in the 1930s. That one extolled Tillman for introducing to the region the commercial cultivation of asparagus. But, the WPA Guide notes, in a moment poised at the precipice of truthfulness, Tillman is remembered for much more than asparagus.[43] The guide is much more forthcoming than either marker about Tillman's true notoriety, even if it does not take us all the way there. The overall gist of the current marker is a feel-good story of a big man who stood up for the little guy, a "spirited and controversial orator." There is no reference to Tillman's most enduring legacy, which he proudly touted in 1900: "I am only standing here to advertise the fact that the State of South Carolina has disfranchised all of the colored race that it could under the thirteenth, fourteenth, and fifteenth amendments. We have done our level best; we have scratched our heads to find out how we could eliminate the last one of them, and we would have done it if we could, but we could not under the thirteenth, fourteenth, and fifteenth amendments."[44] The "here" where Tillman stood to proclaim this great achievement was not a rural campaign stump; it was the floor of the US Senate.

In Trenton, a tiny cedar-shaked building houses the Ben Tillman Library, the local branch of the regional library system. Its front entrance bears the date of its establishment—1923—and a hand-painted pitchfork.

"The Castle" (Joseph Johnson House), Beaufort, South Carolina. Photo by the author.

SOUTH CAROLINA II
Descent into the Belowcountry

South of Barnwell County the landscape turns rectilinear. In the South Carolina sandhills, roadways straighten out through thinned-out forests of longleaf pine, where ample sunlight gilds the sandy forest floor, thick with wiregrass and broom sedge. Vegetation is otherwise slight in this agriculturally underperforming area. Along the roadside a white clapboard Black church sits in shade-dappled silence, as cars and trucks pass by hurriedly. It is an extraordinarily beautiful road, deceptive in its straight-as-an-arrow simplicity. For this region of South Carolina is a tortuous tangle of complexity, political deception, and intrigue. Even as we pass through it in July 2020, one scandal is unfolding just off the shoulder. The nearby home of Alex Murdaugh, a local lawyer and scion of a powerful family in the area, has become embroiled in one of the nation's most bizarre scandals that includes more twists and turns than you will find on sandhill roads. The short version is that—well, this is South Carolina. There is no short version.

But the lowlights are these: Murdaugh's housekeeper died at the family home in an unexplained "accident." His son Paul was somehow involved in the accidental death of Mallory Beach in an alcohol-fueled boating accident near Beaufort in 2019. Two years later, Paul and his mother (and Alex's wife) Maggie were found dead from gunshot wounds from two different firearms on their estate. Two months following, Murdaugh arranged to have himself murdered in order that his surviving son would receive a $10 million insurance payout. But the plot failed, and Murdaugh was left with minor wounds. He survived his botched attempt on his own life, but was faced with over seventy criminal charges, including fraud, embezzlement, and a lot more. The protections Murdaugh had enjoyed as a member of one of the Lowcountry's most powerful and established families had evaporated.

Hampton County Courthouse, Hampton, South Carolina. Photo by the author.

Murdaugh's father, grandfather, and great-grandfather had all served as solicitor for the 14th Circuit Court in South Carolina in unbroken succession from 1920 to 2006. Through their official position on the state court and their powerful law firm, the Murdaughs exercised legal dominion over a town and county named for another scion of a powerful South Carolina family, Wade Hampton III.

The Hampton County Courthouse sits one block away from Murdaugh's law firm, which was reorganized in 2022, without the founding family's name for the first time in 102 years. The county was created in 1878 out of Beaufort County, which had produced a powerful Black political class since the end of the Civil War. The lower part of that county was predominately Black, the upper section, mostly White.[1] The White residents who clamored for a new county resented the fact that, according to the WPA Guide, Beaufort County was "overrun with Northern soldiers, carpetbaggers, and scalawags," and "withdrew from the old district" to "escape subsequent indignities."[2] The courthouse itself was dedicated that October, just after the end of Reconstruction in the state. Governor Hampton, the White messiah who had "saved" the Palmetto State from Reconstruction, was on site for the opening, and laid the cornerstone himself. On the grounds adjacent to the courthouse, Hampton was fêted by the Red Shirts, whose violent campaigns of terror had secured his election two years earlier. They performed military drills on the lawn in "red blouses stitched about the collars, cuffs, and pockets with narrow black braid, with brass buttons down the front."[3]

Hampton County's other main town is thirteen miles away. Unlike the county seat, with its prominent central courthouse and main street, Estill is a railroad town. Like many of the surface roads in this part of the state, rail lines extend in a straight line into the distance in two directions. Along one side of the train tracks, a long brick warehouse bears a large mural for "Genuine" Bull Durham Tobacco on two sides. On one side, a black-and-white painting of the eponymous bull himself, which is definitely a bull.

As I am photographing this mural, a very put-together older white lady in a blue minivan pulls up alongside the road.

"Do you want to hear a good story about that mural?" she asks me.

"Standard of the World." Estill, South Carolina. Photo by the author.

She proceeds to relate—in a white-tablecloth accent that suggests deviled eggs and midmorning Chablis—how the original mural scandalized some other very put-together local ladies, who objected to the excessively realistic depiction of the bull's genitalia. After their protest, a fence was painted over the bull's nether region to discourage prurient desires. When the mural was restored years later, the added fence was removed and the bull was restored to its original, very virile, glory.

Old Sheldon

Southeast of Estill on SC 68, Yemassee is a terminus. By now you are firmly in the Lowcountry, a dense and lush range of live oak and palmettos. Yemassee is also a railroad town of barely a thousand people. In the tiny crossroads that form the town center, a railroad depot and a steam engine mural on a building now serving as the Holy Temple of the Lord Jesus Christ, Inc. of the Apostolic Faith celebrate the town's origins and source of subsistence. An odd proliferation of military imagery abounds here as well, which is explained by the fact that Yemassee was once the last onboarding site for US Marine recruits bound for training at Parris Island near Beaufort.

The Lowcountry gets lower by the mile from Yemassee, as Old Sheldon Church Road passes through a veritable thicket of live oaks interspersed with pines and palmettos. By the time you reach the site for which the road is named, the foliage is so thick that it seems to reach out and grab you as you emerge from climate-controlled comfort into a less controlled environment of dense and humid wildness. A wall of oaks serves as a kind of boundary to the site. At the entrance like a portal into an alternative universe, one tree is deeply scarred by an open wound, whether from rot or lightning, who knows. The massive scar has been repaired with bricklike masonry, in an extraordinary fusion of the natural and artificial. Like Japanese tea bowls mended with gold, it is a kintsugi sort of work, in a very Lowcountry style:[4] where there was a fracture there is a new creation. The remains of the church itself, however, are isolate and barren, a shell of a sanctuary surrounded by huge brick columns that support nothing. Instead, they seem only to aspire, either to a roof once more, or simply to sky.

The place is beautiful and gothic in all the clichéd sort of ways, but it is impossible to deny or resist the allure of what it all symbolizes, intentionally or not: decay, decline, a broken sort of permanence, the invincibility of time and nature. The WPA Guide describes it as an "eerie place in moonlight, the surrounding groves draped with swaying moss, it is scarcely less ghostly in the sun, when lizards scurry off among the graves."[5] The guide is not wrong. Eerie is definitely the vibe.

Originally constructed in 1753 as Prince William's Parish Church, Old Sheldon Church now typically serves as a set for glorified photo shoots also known as Southern weddings. The ruins do play host to an annual Easter mass on Low Sunday. But more than that, it services certain ways of remembering the Southern past. Conventional history holds that the church was burned twice: once by British forces in the American Revolution, and a second time by forces under General Sherman on his march from Savannah to Columbia. The narrative of Sheldon Church's burning served to further underline, for many Lowcountry White people, the identification of British tyranny with "Northern Aggression," and therefore the identification of the American Revolution with the Civil War as wars of independence. The ruins of Old Sheldon Church have certainly furnished visible evidence of Southern martyrdom in the cause of liberty, and in the mythologization of the American Civil War as the "Second American Revolution." The Colonial Dames of America made the connection explicit in a granite plaque they had affixed next to the main door of the church in 1937.

But it is not entirely so. Charles Edward Leverett, himself of New England, became the rector of Prince William's Parish in 1846, where he served until 1858. He was a priest, but also a member of the Beaufort County upper crust. He owned a beautiful, cozy Beaufort mansion, and a plantation near Sheldon called "Canaan," along with thirty-four enslaved people. After retiring from Sheldon Church, and dissatisfied with Northern contributions to the subject, he wrote a math textbook for Southern schools called *The Southern Confederacy Arithmetic*.[6]

Leverett wrote in 1865 that the church "was the place where was the worship of the better class of the people of the parish, who lived as in England after the style prevailing there."[7] It is not uncommon—if a bit precious—to find this sort of identification of Lowcountry White aristocrats with English nobility—especially those South of Broad in Charleston. (The Church Act of 1706 made the Church of England the official church of the colony, which it remained until 1778.) Perhaps most notably this is apparent in Charleston's particular form of Anglican polity, where some churches still visibly identify with the Church of England, even if they are formally affiliated with the Episcopal Church of the United States, whose first American bishop was ordained in 1784. Some churches, like Old Sheldon, predate that division, and stand for some South Carolinians as a visible, if tragically severed, connection with the Mother Country, if not the ancient faith.

As Sherman's troops were advancing toward Columbia in 1865, Charles Leverett wrote that Sheldon "was again reduced to ruin and there exists no probability of its being soon, if ever, restored."[8] The lugubrious pining for a lost world was already setting in in early 1865, even before the war ended. Leverett articulated a sentiment still present in the region over 165 years later, a sense of longing for a world stolen by force from Lowcountry White elites, a world they won't get back. A world given over, as Leverett says, to "strangers to the blood."

But Charles Leverett was not in Sheldon in 1865; he was in Columbia. He was not an eyewitness to the devastation he attributed—quite naturally, of course—to Sherman's forces. When his family returned to the area in 1866, Charles's son Milton wrote to his mother in February 1866 that "Sheldon Church is not burnt down. It has been torn up inside somewhat, but it could be repaired."[9]

The publication of the letters of the Leverett family in 2000 helped to shift blame for the demise of Old Sheldon away from General Sherman, everyone's favorite villain in the Lowcountry. A newer marker, erected in 2013, replaced a 1955 version that claimed simply that the church was "Burned 1865 by Federal Army." The new marker, while historically more accurate, shifts the guilt to another favorite villain in the Lowcountry: "It was actually dismantled by local freedmen ca. 1865–67." It's possible that both versions contain an element of truth. Either way, the revision owes a lot to Milton Leverett, who claimed that he saw repurposed pieces of the Old Sheldon Church cropping all over Beaufort.[10]

The local Anglican Church provided generously for the needs of its well-heeled parishioners. On the other side of Beaufort, on St. Helena Island, a Chapel of Ease was built for those unable or too put-out to make it to the parish church. When the chapel was built in the eighteenth century, the nearest parish was in Beaufort, which was not an easy journey along the rutted sandy roads of the rural Lowcountry. The chapel of ease that survives was built around 1740, and is today a rain-buffed and decaying tabby ruin. It is hard to fault one for wanting a wedding here:

there is a deep beauty in the relative humility of its architectural language. Unlike Sheldon Church, it makes no gestures to ancient Greece. The materials out of which it was constructed came from the fertile salt marshes that surround the island: sand, water, burnt oyster shells. It was most certainly built with slave labor, but was not built for them. It was meant to serve the planter class. Ease was not an option for St. Helena's Black population; and ease may have been a lot to hope for even for White people, since in 1739 the Security Act decreed that every White male in the area who owned ten or more slaves "to carry with him a Gun or pair of Pistols in good order and fit for Service, with at least six Charges of Gun and Powder and Ball" into any church or public house of worship, in order that "the Inhabitants of this Province may be better secured and provided against the Insurrections or other wicked Attempts of Negroes and other Slaves."[11]

Not quite three weeks before the act was signed, enslaved Africans on John's Island north of here raided a White store near the Stono River, beheading two men. The band of "rebels" wanted to make it to St. Augustine, to find freedom in the Spanish colony that had offered liberty to fugitive slaves since a royal decree in 1693. They burned homes and murdered White people, waving banners, beating drums, and chanting "Liberty!" But the band never made it past the Edisto River. They were met by an apparent personification of fate in the form of Governor William Bull, master of the Sheldon Plantation, the namesake of nearby Sheldon Church. Bull—whose own name adorns a major thoroughfare in Savannah, which he helped to plan for James Oglethorpe, and whose signature approved the Security Act—happened upon the group.

> I was returning from Granville County with four Gentlemen and met these Rebels at eleven o'clock in the forenoon and fortunately discerning the approaching danger time had time enough to avoid it, and to give notice to the militia, who on the occasion behaved with so much expedition and bravery, as by four o'clock the same day to come up with them and killed and took so many as put a stop to any further mischief at that time. Forty-four of them have been killed and executed. Some few yet remain concealed in the woods expecting the same fate, seem desperate. If such an attempt is made in a time of peace, what might be expected if an enemy should appear upon our frontier with a design to invade us.[12]

Vengeance was overwhelming, as was the White fear of an imminent Black uprising (a fear which would not abate for two centuries, at least). In order to ensure that such a thing never happened again, Bull's government issued another act "for the better ordering of Negroes and other Slaves" in May of 1740, requiring the return of fugitive slaves to the warden of the notoriously abusive Charleston Work-House. It forbade assemblies of slaves, penalized anyone who served alcoholic beverages to any slave without the consent of their owner, as well as anyone who taught a slave to read or write.[13] A simultaneous act mandated regular slave patrols, the ancestor of modern police forces.[14]

The Negro Act, among the first of many Slave Codes in the South, remained in force in South Carolina until the end of the Civil War and served as a forerunner to the Black Codes of the late nineteenth century. It also exhibited the paranoia of a minority ruling class in the state, which had been majority Black since at least 1710, and whose politics would attempt through every available means to shore up power for White people in a world where they were outnumbered for almost the entirety of the nineteenth century.

Today a historical marker stands on the northern side of US 17, a heavily trafficked four-lane divided highway east of Charleston. It is fitting, in a way: the disproportion between the importance of this episode in South Carolina's extremely tortured racial history and the way it is (barely) publicly recognized. There is little in the way of a shoulder, still less in the way of a turnout or other incentive to slow down and mark the largest slave uprising in colonial America. As with so much of American history, stopping to contemplate or otherwise mark the past is not encouraged.

Roads Not Taken: St. Helena Island

Elsewhere on St. Helena Island, one of a string of Atlantic barrier islands where Black residents outnumbered White ones for more than two centuries, a different form of ecclesiastical architecture dots the landscape, one that stands in stark contrast to the grand brick columns of Sheldon Church or the tabby ruins of the chapel of ease. "Praise Houses," tiny one-room wooden churches, originated as sites for enslaved people to gather to worship, sing, pray, and shout outside the control of slaveholders. At one time a dominant feature of the island, today only three remain, all of which were built around 1900.

Nostalgia is a certain longing for what once was, and a desire for return to that state of affairs. I do not know that the English language possesses a word for a similar form of recollection, namely a non-nostalgic desire to preserve tokens of the past not so that we might be enkindled with a desire to return to that past, but so that we might never do so. The preservation of places like Sheldon Church could originate from the former motive; that of Lowcountry praises houses out of the latter. The architecture of Sheldon Church is a gesture to antiquity, a visual claim of continuity with ancient civilization. Its ruined state further emphasizes the "lost" quality of that world and could serve to nourish the sentimental longing for that world to return. But praise houses represent the architecture of resistance, a deployment of limited available resources in the service of communal faith, a hope in the ever-receding reality of liberation, an apparently indomitable will to life even amidst the most horrific and brutal circumstances. Their survival evokes something quite different than that of Old Sheldon: not a nostalgia for a lost world, but, perhaps, an awe at such determination, and a kind of longing for the universalization of the desire for escape from the confinement of Christianity to a certain kind of cultural dominion.

While Charleston has made a career out of what once was, St. Helena Island to the south is a case study in what might have been. It is a monument to counterfactual history, a preserve of roads not taken, stories not quite told, heroes unpedestaled. The area fell to Union forces early in the Civil War, in November 1861, and remained under Union occupation for the duration of the war. In an early instance of White flight, local planters and aristocrats fled the tree-shaded mansions of Beaufort for Charleston or the upcountry, leaving Beaufort and St. Helena even more of a Black majority than it had been before the war. Many of their colonnaded homes were converted to hospitals.

Into the new environment entered Northern missionaries, who established a school on St. Helena Island for the formerly enslaved. Quakers and Unitarians built the Penn Normal School in 1862, the first school in the South for Black people.[15] The movement to educate newly freedmen and women on St. Helena was motivated in part by James Miller McKim, a Presbyterian pastor and abolitionist from Philadelphia who helped to form the Port Royal Relief Committee in 1861. Upon return to his hometown after a visit to the South Carolina Sea Islands, he gave a report of his findings on St. Helena to an audience in Sansom Street

Hall in July of 1862. His speech was more than just a recounting of a visit; he also recorded Gullah folkways, speech patterns, and music. But his main objective as an observer culminated in an approving report of the conditions of freedmen on St. Helena, and the success of the Penn School in proving that Black people were not "listless" and "unteachable." He also gave ample evidence against a Southern presumption that Black men and women would not work unless forced to. Under a new system of free labor, he reported, the formerly enslaved worked more industriously than they had under the yoke of chattel slavery. McKim had deconstructed a major myth of Southern culture. But he was not done; he moved on to another: "I have scraps of the private history of leading ladies and gentlemen in Beaufort and round about, with names and circumstances, which show that the airs of superiority assumed by these people are utterly unsupported by character, and indicate that their pretensions from beginning are a lie and a sham."[16]

Gullah culture was, for McKim, in many ways superior to the fraudulent culture of Charleston and Beaufort White residents. This assessment did not win McKim many fans among them. When McKim died in 1874, Southern newspapers had not buried the hatchet. "He had done some queer things in his day," read an obituary in the Columbia *Daily Phoenix* that reflects more upon the insecurities of the author and broader White resistance to Reconstruction than it does on the life of its subject. The writer of the obit used the occasion of McKim's death to what-about "sanctimonious Northern journals," and to insist that all slaveholders "asked was to be let alone."[17]

In 2003, the US House and Senate initiated studies of locations for a possible National Park Service site dedicated to the long-neglected Reconstruction era. They settled on Beaufort and Port Royal, but neo-Confederates promptly and predictably protested. They appealed to Joe "You Lie" Wilson, US congressman for the SC 2nd District, and a member of the Sons of Confederate Veterans. Led by SCV Commander-in-Chief Michael Givens, local members bombarded Wilson, who proposed the study, with letters in opposition to the project. Givens regarded the Reconstruction park as "an egregious affront to our Southern heritage."[18] Wilson, whose public support of the proposed site in his district was cool, "quietly told the National Park Service's higher-ups, 'Not this, not here, not now.'"[19] Jeff Antley, an SCV member from Charleston warned, "If the park service is talking about opening a site to celebrate Reconstruction, we're going to have a hard time with that."[20] Perhaps because of the opposition, Wilson failed to move the study through committee, and the bill died. The Reconstruction Park was dead in the water until it was picked up again during the Obama Administration in 2016, when Wilson's colleague from South Carolina, Jim Clyburn, introduced a bill to designate the Penn Center as a National Monument.[21]

In the meantime, something had changed. The SCV's opposition had softened, or at least been drowned out by more serious voices. The massacre of nine Black churchgoers in Charleston's most historic Black church in 2015 had drawn belated attention to the disproportionate power of the Lost Cause myth and the violence it has generated, and exposed national ignorance about the historical legacy of White supremacy. In one of his final acts as president, Barack Obama created the Reconstruction Era National Monument, which became the Reconstruction Era National Historical Park in 2019.

When we visit in 2021, baptismal rain drips from the tendrillike branches of Spanish moss. The gray sand of the barrier island darkens with moisture like the sea bottom that it once was millions of year ago. A return to origins. The Penn Center is a smattering of historic buildings of varying function. The Brick Church, built in 1855 by enslaved Africans, served for a time as the schoolhouse for the Penn Normal School. Inside, a second-story gallery accommodated Black churchgoers, and shielded them from the gaze of their White owners below. After the White evacuation of St. Helena in 1861, Black Christians repossessed the church from their former enslavers, and it became identified with Black Christian hope of liberation. It is still in use as a house of worship. Across the street, a long white tabby structure with a Spanish tile roof features a bronze bas-relief of Hollis Burke Frissell, one-time president of the Hampton Institute (now Hampton University). The building named for him served as a meeting site for members of the Southern Christian Leadership Conference (SCLC) during the 1960s, who came here regularly to retreat and to strategize. At the far edge of the Penn Center site, a small white cottage, shrouded by lanky arms of live oak hung with moss like the baggy flesh of old age, appears to retreat into a dense thicket of low brush. Gantt Cottage was Martin Luther King, Jr.'s personal retreat here. Local tradition holds that he wrote a draft of the "I Have a Dream" speech inside it.

Nearby, in a small swamp in the center of the town of Port Royal, thousands of waterbirds alight in the arms of bald cypress and on low bushes. Egrets fill the trees with white spots as if a bale of cotton has exploded beneath. In the late evening light, egrets, herons, wood storks, and anhingas squawk and cackle and soar into the rookery. Carolina wrens flit in the woods around the footpath that encircles the pond, where mergansers and moorhens swim with alligators. It is an unrestrained festival of life in an area that has produced more than its share of violence and death, a sign of an order of nature that will never fail to find a home, perhaps an image of the kind of freedom and vitality and homecoming that worshipers in the praise houses around here long for.

Along the shore of Port Royal, a wooden boardwalk traces the thin margin between land and water. It runs to a five-story observation tower, which watches over the Port Royal Reach and Battery Creek toward Parris Island, and westward over lush salt marshes around Archers Creek, where Mallory Beach was tragically killed in a boating accident involving an intoxicated Paul Murdaugh.

The town at twilight is empty, but along the water's edge locals and probably an overdose of tourists queue up outside the Fish Camp on 11th Street overlooking shrimp boat docks where fishermen mimic the roosting seabirds a few blocks away, keeping their daily ritual of outgoing and incoming, to feed and rest, feed and rest. But there will be no standing in line tonight. We pick up to-go boxes of Jamaican food at Jah'Nya's Caribbean Cuisine and cross the river back into Beaufort, where we set up on a cast-iron patio table on Bay Street to people-watch visitors to the annual Water Festival. We've taken the cue from two older ladies, who have brought folding chairs, a cooler, and huge Styrofoam cups of something they indicate by their knowing chuckles not to be sweet tea. They come here to just sit and watch people, every year.

Taking Beaufort Back

Beaufort is rightly prized: it is an extraordinarily beautiful port town whose architecture could feed years' worth of *Southern Living* covers. It elicits a probably perverse temptation to invoke the word "quaint," but Beaufort's charm belies a moral seriousness underneath. There is a reason a national park dedicated to the story of Reconstruction was put here. While it may seem to communicate ease to the average visitor, at the heart of Beaufort's past, and possibly its present, is conflict. That historical conflict expresses itself now in language. Beaufort is home to "Secession House," where the first conversations about secession took place in the 1850s. An American flag hangs ironically from the second story balcony. On the north side of the town center, Beaufort National Cemetery was established in 1863 for the burial of Union soldiers. In it are buried members of the First South Carolina Volunteer Infantry, the first Black unit in the US Army during the Civil War. What the marker in front of Secession House calls "Southern independence," a different one in the US cemetery names it more forcefully. An obelisk at the top of the fan-shaped burial ground proclaims

IMMORTALITY

TO HUNDREDS OF

THE DEFENDERS OF

AMERICAN LIBERTY

AGAINST THE GREAT

REBELLION

In Beaufort, historical preservation is something of a local religion. The powerful Historic Preservation Commission maintains the architectural integrity of Old Beaufort, and fortunately this seems to have been applied universally. One house, in particular, tells a story that is well-known in Beaufort, if not elsewhere.

A colonnaded two-level porch fronts the white clapboard home at 511 Prince Street. Branches of an ancient magnolia drawl across the brick walkway to the staircase, whose risers are thick with lush fig ivy. It exudes all the characteristics of an antebellum planter's town home and could serve as a poster house for prewar White wealth. But the house is famous because it was the home of freed slave, Union boat pilot, state senator and US Congressman Robert Smalls.

Smalls is the sort of person whose story you can't believe you never learned in school. Born into slavery in this house at 511 Prince Street, Smalls was put to work behind the wheel of a Confederate steamer named *Planter*. In the early morning of May 13, 1862, Smalls commandeered the *Planter*—with his wife and family on board—and piloted it past five Confederate fortresses, beyond Union naval lines in Charleston Harbor, where he surrendered the ship to the United States, and won freedom for himself and his family.

Within months, Smalls was a national hero—at least in the North. A free Black Union regiment in Pittsburgh built an earthwork fort named for him in 1863. After the war's end, Smalls resettled in Beaufort. He bought 511 Prince Street. Smalls had reappropriated the site of his bondage as his own property.

Elected to the South Carolina State House of Representatives and then Senate, to the US Congress in 1874, Smalls's career as a legislator follows the trajectory of White rule in post-Reconstruction South Carolina. After the Red Shirt–engineered election of Wade Hampton III in 1876, Redeemers and Bourbon Democrats regained power of the state amidst a culture of newly energized White supremacy. Smalls lost the 1878 and 1880 elections to the House to George D. Tillman, brother of "Pitchfork" Ben, and lost a contest for a Senate seat in 1884 to Hampton himself. In 1884, he was back in Congress, but this time as a representative for a different district. He served as a delegate to the 1895 South Carolina Constitutional Convention, in which the state formally and unambiguously committed itself to White supremacy. The 1895 Convention represented the formal codification of two decades of anti-Black politics, and the elevation of Tillmanism to a national stage, as "Pitchfork" Ben graduated from governor to US senator. Although Smalls retained a position of power and influence in Beaufort until his death in 1915, he experienced the rise and fall of hope-stripped Black political power. Upon his death, he was remembered as a hero in northern newspapers. But in his home state, the *Sumter Daily Item* called him "one of the most notorious figures of the negro regime which was overthrown by the Hampton revolution of 1876" and "the last of the ring of looters who grew fat from the spoils of the most corrupt government which any American state ever suffered."[22] A small marker in Joe Riley Waterfront Park—named for Charleston's long-serving progressive White mayor, who served the city for over forty years—sits near the site where Smalls delivered the *Planter*, and himself.

Smalls was baptized at the First African Baptist Church in Beaufort in 1905. His funeral was here ten years later. On the day we visit, the Reverend Alexander McBride is sweeping the floor of the sanctuary. McBride has been here twenty-two years as pastor. He shoulders the broom for a few moments and shows us around the house of God. The present church was built by freed slaves in 1865, on the site of a praise house. A few blocks away, a striking bronze bust of Smalls by Marion Ethredge stands alongside the brick sidewalk, in the courtyard of Tabernacle

Baptist Church in Beaufort where Smalls worshipped and is buried. It has been there since 1976 and is notable not least for its rarity; in a sane country, there would be more monuments to Robert Smalls than there are to John C. Calhoun, Nathan Bedford Forrest, or Ben Tillman.

Nearby, a new monument is planned for Harriet Tubman, who in June of 1863 led a twenty-five-mile steamboat raid on nine rice plantations along the Combahee River, destroying bridges and railroads, and liberating over 700 enslaved men and women. Tubman was the only woman to lead a military operation in the Civil War, and arguably "the most successful uprising against slavery in the U.S."[23] An uprising I am only just now learning about.

Charleston Is America

En route to Charleston on US 17, we pass by the Stono Rebellion marker, so inconspicuous we don't even notice it. We cross the Ashley River south of The Citadel, Charleston's elite military school. Charleston's scrupulously protected skyline betrays the architecture of noncompliance: a refusal to let Charleston become one more homogeneous American megalopolis, a cityscape which seems to utter a great "no, thank you" to modernity. Its zoning ordinances preserve the profile of Charleston as the South's "city of dreaming spires," and prevent it from being modified, ever. It is elegantly and refreshingly retrograde. There are, thankfully, no glass-faced skyscrapers in Charleston to repeat one another ad nauseam. But there is also little here to reflect the city to itself. In this beautifully insular place the sun-glistened air is humid with a creeping paranoia. One senses it crossing the Ashley River: a feeling that you are entering not just a place but an agreement, to not say too much, not ask too many questions, not to scuff the polished veneer of Charleston's incontestably gorgeous surface.

Pat Conroy, a native of the South Carolina Lowcountry, described Charleston as a "city distorted by its own self-worship."

> The city, river-girt, has a tyrannical need for order and symmetry. It is not a city of outlaws, not a landscape for renegades. There is no ambience of hazard here, but something so tightly repressed, so rigidly ordered, so consecrated to the adoration of restraint that you sometimes want to scream out for excess, for a single knee bent toward bad taste, for the cleansing roar of pandemonium to establish

a foothold somewhere in the city. But, of course, the charm of the city lies in this adherence to a severity of form. Entering Charleston is like walking through the brilliant carbon forest of a diamond with the light dazzling you in a thousand ways, an assault of light and shadow caused by light. The sun and the city have struck up an irreversible alliance. The city turns inward upon itself, faces away from visitors, alluringly contained in its own mystery. The city has a smell, a fecund musk of aristocracy, with the wine and the history of the lowcountry aging beneath the verandahs, the sweetly decadent odors of lost causes.[24]

This extraordinary depiction of Charleston echoes a passage at the beginning of Honoré de Balzac's *Père Goriot*, which describes a city built upon a kind of duplicity. Balzac's Paris is a valley "of joys that often turn out to be false."[25] Charleston has more than once been described as "The Paris of the South," but when refracted through Balzac, Conroy's description of "the Holy City" is less than flattering.

It was no accident that underneath the posh heart of Balzac's Paris lay vast catacombs of dried skulls, the inner life of the city a desiccated heart, its citizens walking cadavers. Like Balzac's *Père Goriot*, Conroy's *Lords of Discipline* portrays a character trapped in an apparently inviolable contract with the city itself, who must make a decision ultimately to submit to the terms of that contract or refuse them.

The reality of Charleston is far more interesting than its self-presentation as a *Garden & Gun* feature spread would suggest. Along the Battery at dusk, Black and White locals and tourists mingle beneath a full moon overlooking the Ashley towards James Island. Further out in the harbor, Fort Sumter recedes into deepening night.

You should see Charleston, I had said to the Canadian linguist all those years ago. Now I was seeing it, really for the first time.

Standing on the brow of Charleston Harbor in 2021, I am aware of how I was encouraging more or less complete strangers to see a place that I am only now, this beautifully sun-washed evening, beginning to see for myself, even though I have been here many times. I become aware of an old and irresistible urge to prove that the South isn't *like that*, that it has antiquity and elegance and paved roads, too. The suggestion emerged out of defensiveness, a genteel remonstration that we are not as backward as you might think. I was, naturally, fabulously wrong.

I hadn't really *seen* Charleston the first time we visited, on our second trip together, in 1998. The aggressive power of "Southern charm" is difficult to break, even for one who aspires to intellectual sobriety. It exerts its force nowhere so seductively as in Charleston. Which makes sense, because no city has as much to hide.

I have only lately—very lately—come to see Charleston differently. In 1998, I saw the Battery, the lush and voluptuous mansions South of Broad, their august and palmetto-garlanded defiance of hurricanes and modernity. They were signs of an alternative order. What I did not see was the real alternative order in Charleston, the history of brutal enslavement, oppressed rebellion, the mythologizing of heroes of White supremacy; but also the story of Black Charlestonians who—as is the way of it in America—only entered the collective national conscience after the Mother Emanuel massacre in 2015. Of course, many of the sites of this history remain unmarked even today. The movement to remove the monuments to the old Confederacy has largely been subtractive, but what is still lacking in their absence is a full restoration to public memory of the storied human lives that people like John C. Calhoun and his legions of spiritual descendants wanted to remain unheard. But in Charleston—in which historic preservation is practically the orthodox faith—there remain traces of that as yet (to most White people) undiscovered history.

The Pillar and the Witness Tree

Today in Charleston you will not see John C. Calhoun towering over Marion Square. You might see this as a victory. It could be, but only if his absence diverts your attention to a deeper truth. Maybe you will stand at the convergence of two diagonal sandy footpaths in the center of Marion Square (which, from above, bears a striking resemblance to the Confederate battle flag) and contemplate what it means that he is no longer there on this particular plot of manicured barrenness that is not so easily divested of a tainted history. If you turn to the north, you will see a military garrison, surmounted with battlements and parapets, now disguised as an Embassy Suites Hotel. Inside, the vast, once open-air courtyard has been roofed over and submitted to the imaginations of corporate interior designers, who have proven unable to give the inside a warm, welcoming feel. Its remodeling into a John Portman–esque atrium hotel is uneasy: the furniture is much too small for the space, even if it does communicate the same sense of alienation one feels in the cavernous lobby of a Marriott Marquis. There is something entirely fitting about this sense, in this particular place.

The current hotel served as the city of Charleston's arsenal, established in 1822 following an attempted slave revolt allegedly led by Denmark Vesey, a Black pastor who reputedly incited his parishioners to kill every White man in Charleston. The choice of the site of the arsenal is no accident: Vesey was admitted to first communion directly across Meeting Street at Second Presbyterian Church, and in 1818 helped to form a new congregation that would eventually settle a block away, named Emanuel African Methodist Episcopal Church.

In retaliation for Vesey's crime, furious White Charlestonians burned his church to the ground. Following a show trial in the summer of 1822, Vesey and other conspirators were hanged from a tree on Ashley Avenue. The current structure of the hotel was built in 1829. The ground you are standing on once served as the parade grounds for cadets stationed at the military academy formally established there in 1842 and now known as The Citadel, an institution whose existence is the direct outgrowth of native White fears of an imminent Black insurrection.

As you face the hotel's main entrance as it fronts Marion Square, you may not sense the alienation from the site's history, which does not announce itself. But wander around for a few minutes and you can begin to feel the proximity of American history, as close as the weather: Charleston's most prominent Black church, Mother Emanuel AME, was born on Boundary Street. The Citadel was born four years later, on the next block. Boundary Street was renamed for John C. Calhoun. The grounds where White cadets prepared for a race war was ornamented with two monuments to Calhoun. None of that is an accident.

The density of this history and the connections it is built upon cannot really be felt in a book; it can only really be experienced on foot. I certainly did not feel it in 1995, when insisting to my international peers that they should really see Charleston. I hadn't really been able to see it myself. It only began to emerge slowly, when, nearly two centuries later after the Vesey uprising, Vesey's successor as pastor of Mother Emanuel AME, Clementa Pinckney, was murdered by a white nationalist who hoped to incite a race war. As manic as it may seem on paper, there was a perverse logic to all this that does not make it into the travel brochures.

The example of Charleston is just one of many that repeats itself over and over again across the region. Arguably the South's most romanticized city, Charleston also owns the South's most vigilantly protected mythology, which is defended with a fervor and religious conviction that borders on paranoid cult worship. This is entirely reasonable, because it is also the city with the most condensed intersections of privilege and poverty, where the prodigiously dark undercurrents of racism, White supremacy, and treason to the national cause are pleasantly masked in Instagram-ready scenery. Charleston is a particularly rich and intense example of these largely unnoticed convergences, where shadows and light seem to flit playfully with one another in off-limits back alleys. Charleston aside, the rest of the South is rife with instances where the viaduct of contemporary human life rubs up against the rough shoulder of American history, for those who pause long enough to confront it.

One such convergence is just to the southeast of the current site of The Citadel, where Ashley Avenue inexplicably circumnavigates a small island in the middle of the road between Fishburne and Nunan Streets. There is no readily apparent logic to the preservation of the spot. It has little practical advantage other than to slow traffic, but that is not why it is there. In the middle of the island stands a not-especially ancient oak. If this had been Atlanta, the tree, no matter its vintage or significance, would have been summarily hacked down, its roots ground to dust, and paved over. Charleston is fanatical about historic preservation, but this is not a *oh-how-cute* instance of making cars yield to nature. Oral tradition holds that from a previous tree on this spot, Denmark Vesey was hanged in 1822. Whether it is true or not, the place has been preserved by a more-or-less silent compact to remember without naming.

It is uncertain where Vesey was born—possibly St. Thomas, possibly in Africa—but what is certain is that he was purchased by Joseph Vesey in 1781. The fourteen-year-old who would eventually be known as Denmark Vesey was known as Telemaque to his enslavers. On September 30, 1799, he purchased a lottery ticket. When the lottery results were announced in November, Telemaque was holding the winning ticket, number 1884, worth $1,500. For $600 Telemaque bought his freedom from Joseph Vesey and his wife. By New Year's Day, 1800, he was a free man. He soon chose a new name and borrowed the surname of his former enslaver as his own. In an act not unlike that of Robert Smalls's purchase of his former master's home, Vesey's "taking of a surname reversed the process of his family's enslavement."[26]

Vesey believed that racial equality should extend to all things, and flouted Charleston conventions by dressing like a gentleman. He used his towering stature to often intimidating effect and presented himself on the streets of Charleston as a free Black man who refused to be cowed by the pressures exerted by a minority but dominant White culture to "know his place." Vesey was a sort of proto-James Brown, Black and proud and not afraid to say it loud. His "physical demeanor and habitual immaculacy of wardrobe indicated his defiance of Charleston's racialist code of appropriate deportment."[27] The Negro Act of 1740 had forbidden slaves to wear any clothing "of greater value [than coarse] negro cloth."[28] But Vesey did not abide. He dressed and comported himself in a manner that demonstrated that he did not accept the terms of the agreement with Charleston that, as a Black man, he was expected to submit to.

Vesey received first communion at Second Presbyterian Church in Charleston and was later a founding member of the African Methodist Episcopal Church in Cow Alley. The AME Church in Charleston originated with the exodus of several prominent Black clergymen, including Morris Brown, who tired of the persistent proslavery theology preached from the pulpits of mainline Protestant churches like Second Presbyterian. The final straw had been when Bethel Methodist decided to build a hearse house on top of a Black cemetery in their churchyard. They formed a branch of the Philadelphia-based AME Church in Anson Street, and a second one in Cow Alley.[29]

In June 1818, in the days of the Cow Alley church's infancy, the city of Charleston abruptly chose to enforce early-century laws requiring Black worship services to be held only in daylight and demanding a majority of every congregation to be White. Armed city guardsmen stormed the Cow Alley congregation and arrested 140 people, presumably including Vesey.[30] Over the next several years, Charleston law enforcement repeatedly harassed the two Black congregations with surprise raids.

Denmark Vesey could hardly be said to have "enjoyed" the freedom he won with his lucky ticket. He had been unable to secure the liberation of his wife and family, who remained enslaved. He was forced to visit his second wife—another man's property—at another man's house, rather than at his own home at 20 Bull Street.[31] In 1820, evidently partly in response to the rise of the African Church in Charleston, the South

Carolina State Assembly passed "An Act to Restrain the Emancipation of Slaves," which forbade the importation of free Black people into the state, and empowered White citizens with the authority to arrest any such individual and remand them to the local court. Violators of the act were subject to a fine, and liable to be resold into slavery.[32]

Vesey had reached a breaking point. Beyond frustrated, and with little hope in the power of mere words to change the status quo, he began plotting a revolt in the streets of Charleston founded on a theology of revolution grounded in the Hebrew Scriptures' stories of liberation from bondage, most especially the Exodus.

The planned uprising failed before it ever got off the ground. Reprisal against Vesey and his conspirators was as swift as it was ruthless. Suspects were tried in secret courts, where they were unable to defend themselves against their accusers. The city of Charleston hanged thirty-seven men. Vesey was hanged in what was then known as Blake's Lands. His body was sent to surgeons to be dissected.

White mobs destroyed the AME Church, and church trustees advertised an estate sale on August 16, 1822, for the remaining lumber.[33] Like Vesey's own body, the broken and dismembered body of the church was distributed, but not for the building up of the faithful. One block away and seven years later, Charleston built a two-story fortification and arsenal for its city guard for the prevention of further Black insurrection. A direct result of the Vesey uprising, the battlemented ramparts of the new structure faced Second Presbyterian Church, where Vesey received first communion. Charleston had constructed both an unwitting memorial to Vesey, and an explicit monument to White fears of Black power that he elicited. In 1842, the fortress became home to the first twenty cadets of the Military College of South Carolina, known as The Citadel.

As if to emphasize the otherwise discreet history of the elite military academy, the parade grounds in front of the original Citadel became the site for two successive monuments to John C. Calhoun, the state's most prominent advocate of slavery.

While The Citadel has been slow to acknowledge its roots in White people's fears of Black liberation, the City of Charleston has not entirely avoided the Vesey legacy. A house at 56 Bull Street is designated as Vesey's home, but it is not likely accurate. In 1976, the city commissioned a portrait of Vesey for the Gaillard Memorial Auditorium.[34] The portrait was stolen a few weeks later, but eventually returned. After twenty years of planning, a statue of Vesey was ultimately unveiled in a park in 2014 named for Wade Hampton III adjacent, appropriately, to The Citadel, the institution Vesey helped to inspire.

To many Black Charlestonians, Vesey was a hero; to many White people, a terrorist. The Vesey conspiracy, however, illustrates the limits of Black patience, the extremes to which a Black man can be pushed, and the extent to which he will tolerate the conditions of his existence, and the disingenuous language of "freedom" in White Christianity. Vesey may have sought violent means to challenge that order of things, but his courage cannot be gainsaid. He had nothing left to lose, and wagered everything he had against a White supremacist dominion hell-bent on keeping Vesey and men like him in a corner.

As for the church, congregants worshiped in a rebuilt AME church until 1834, when Charleston prohibited all-Black churches. The AME congregation went underground, worshipping in secret until 1865, when they built a new church on Calhoun Street. The new structure was designed by Denmark Vesey's son, Robert. The revived congregation adopted the name Emanuel AME, popularly known as "Mother Emanuel."

Its new pastor, Richard A. "Daddy" Cain, served as a delegate to the South Carolina Constitutional Convention. An 1876 photomontage of "Radical Members of the First Legislature after the War" printed in 1876 pictures Cain next to John's ancestor, Eben Hayes. Also pictured: Prince Rivers and Benjamin Franklin Randolph.

Rivers I know from Hamburg. I will know Randolph by suppertime.

Rivers in Columbia

Upon our return to Columbia, on a moderately substantiated hunch we seek out the grave of Rivers, who is supposedly buried somewhere in the capital city. A small cemetery adjacent to Trinity Episcopal Cathedral across the street holds the gravesites of Wade Hamptons I, II, and III, and that of the only-in-South-Carolina named States Rights Gist, a Confederate General whose father went to unusual lengths to prove himself John C. Calhoun's Number One Fan.

It is over twenty years since we were last here in 1998, when the Confederate flag flew from the cupola. It was moved from the dome in 2001 to a Confederate monument in front of the State House, which was an improvement, if only because it made it easier for Bree Newsome to shimmy up the pole in 2015 and remove it. Not that climbing a thirty-foot pole is especially easy, but it was less of a logistical challenge than climbing a flagpole on top of the state house, as Thomas Reed had attempted to do in Montgomery twenty-seven years earlier.

Like many people, I watched on live television on July 10, 2015, when, in the aftermath of the horrific murders of nine parishioners at Mother Emanuel AME at the hands of an avowed White supremacist, the flag was deposed once again. A White member of the South Carolina Highway Patrol honor guard passed the Confederate flag to Lieutenant Derrick Gamble, a Black man and the most senior member of the guard. It was a moment pregnant with symbolism. President Barack Obama said at the time that the removal was "a signal of good will and healing, and a meaningful step towards a better future." It certainly *felt* meaningful. But walking the grounds of the statehouse in 2021, it feels less so.

When the state of South Carolina removed the Confederate flag from the grounds of the state house in Columbia in 2015, they left behind some conspicuous monuments to the state's White supremacist past:

1. Ben "Pitchfork" Tillman, governor and US senator, who led the Red Shirts in a massacre of nine Black men in Hamburg in 1876, just for starters;
2. Wade Hampton III, governor and US senator who rose to power on a tide of White violence instigated by the Red Shirts;
3. Strom Thurmond, governor and segregationist and so much more;
4. Marion Sims, "father of modern gynecology" who experimented on enslaved Black women without the use of anesthesia;
5. A monument to Confederate soldiers, unveiled three years after Wade Hampton's election as governor. Erected in 1879, the monument was struck by lightning in 1882, which decapitated the Carrara marble statue of a Confederate soldier. It destroyed the statue almost completely, leaving only a section of the left leg up to the ankle.[35]

Tillman, who was elected governor in 1890, proclaimed in his inaugural speech a month later inside this very building: "In our own State, the triumph of Democracy and white supremacy over mongrelism and anarchy, of civilization over barbarism, has been most complete."

He reminded the Black man in South Carolina "that his best friends and safest advisers are the white men who own the land and give him employment."[36]

Tillman began to make a political name for himself though his advocacy of farmers, but by the time he was elected governor, he had found his true voice, which he used to appeal to both White farmers and White aristocrats. He said:

> The whites have absolute control of the State Government, and we intend at any and all hazards to retain it. The intelligent exercise of the right of suffrage, at once the highest privilege and most sacred duty of the citizen, is as yet beyond the capacity of the vast majority of colored men. We deny, without regard to color, that "all men are created equal"; it is not true now and was not true when Jefferson wrote it, but we cannot deny, and it is our duty as the governing power in South Carolina to insure, to every individual, black and white, the "right to life, liberty, and the pursuit of happiness."[37]

Tillman could hardly deny that Black people had rights according to the law; but, more importantly for him, they had a place. When the Confederate battle flag was put atop the State House in 1962, in the midst of not only the Civil War Centennial, but also the burgeoning civil rights movement, it was specifically to remind Black South Carolinians of that place. Years of political wrangling over the flag finally came to a halt after the Mother Emanuel Massacre. The flag is gone, but it is worth remembering that it took the slaughter of nine Black Charlestonians for the state legislature to summon the "good will" to remove it.

On the other side of the building, the monument to Strom Thurmond went up in 1999. It lists his many positions in public service, including "Father of Four Children," with their names below. Four years later, a few months after Thurmond's death, Essie Mae Washington-Williams, a Black educator in Columbia, announced in a press conference that she was the child of Senator Thurmond. Her mother, Carrie, was a teenager working for Strom's parents in Edgefield when she became pregnant with his child.

After the revelation, the monument was revised. "Father of Five Children," it now reads. The new letters are rough and irregular; despite every effort to disguise the "Four," its shadow is still visible, the residue of a long-held secret. Essie Mae's name has been etched in below those of Thurmond's other four children, a fitting irony for the first write-in candidate ever to win an election to the Senate.

Not far from Thurmond, a massive bronze statue of Wade Hampton III on horseback stands in front of the building that bears his name. A 1970 guide to the state house credits Hampton with leading the state out of "the terrors of the Reconstruction decade." Without a trace of irony nor bashfulness, the guide indulges the messianic cult of Hampton, the "Savior of South Carolina" who "guided so wisely the course of the incredible Red Shirts campaign of 1876."[38]

On the east side of the State House, a monument to African American history tells the story of Black South Carolinians from the seventeenth century to the present. It is powerful in its way, but its real power lies in its surrounding context here. It reads like an afterthought, a concession. It's the idea of "African American History" and "Black History Month" represented in space: an optional, elective detour from the main thoroughfare of American history. It represents the logic of White American culture laid out on a site plan: if you enter the main door of the State House from Gervais Street, you have no choice but to pass by the Confederate monument (and through the field of vision of Ben Tillman); the story of Black Americans remains off to the side, sequestered, nonnecessary.

Indeed, the monument is the fruit of a compromise. In 1994, state legislators agreed to the construction of a memorial to African American history on the grounds of the State House, but with a few caveats: no public funds would be used, and the monuments to Hampton, Tillman, and others would stay. Black people would get their monument, but White people would get to keep their flag. In 2000, the state assembly agreed to take the flag down from the cupola, but it didn't go away. A compromise allowed the flag to remain, on a thirty-foot flagpole next to the Confederate monument in front of the main entrance of the State House. If anything, the move made the flag even more prominent and even less distant than before, as one could not enter the state's most important and powerful official building without passing it.

After an extended wander around the grounds of the South Carolina State House, we light out north on Assembly in search of one of the reputed burial places of Prince Rivers, like Randolph a delegate to the state Constitutional Convention in 1868, later a lawyer in Aiken

County, and a trial justice and mediator in the 1876 Hamburg Massacre that determined the course of state politics for generations. Rivers had served in the First South Carolina, and like his contemporary, Robert Smalls, had escaped to freedom by subterfuge in 1862, when Rivers allegedly stole his enslaver's horse and fled to freedom. The order of Major General David Hunter declared Rivers and his wife and children "free forever."[39]

In May 1864 in Beaufort, Rivers was elected as a delegate to the Republican National Convention alongside Smalls but seemed destined for even bigger things. Rivers's superior in the First South Carolina, Thomas Wentworth Higginson, said that "if there should ever be a black monarchy in South Carolina, he will be its king."[40]

There would not only be no throne to Rivers, but no rest. After the Ellenton massacre, Rivers's home was burned, and he died penniless in 1887. Rivers represented one possible trajectory of Reconstruction: he was an empowered Black man who became disempowered, his life an anti-Bildungsroman, an inversion of the Horatio Alger myth whose precipitous rise is followed by a dramatic fall occasioned by a fatal vice not his own. A new attempt to incorporate Black men into full membership into American society crumbled, and its failure initiated a new pattern of dissection, whereby the humanity of Black men and women was systematically dismembered, assigned to explicit and sharply delimited roles within a minority-rule power structure. At the same time, the protracted dismembering of Black lives—often literally but more often figuratively—is instructive for what it might mean to "remember" those lives: not simply recall them to memory but to restore their memory, insofar as we are able, to wholeness.

Rivers's story traces the outlines of the increasingly compressed expectations of what a Black person in America was allowed to be: no longer a war hero, a minister of the law, or a free man, but an elected witness to a state- and region-wide covenant between White men and the principles and policies of White supremacy. Of Randolph, Rivers, and Smalls, only Smalls lived enough to see the protracted dissolution of Black humanity written into law at the 1895 Constitutional Convention. Smalls, the Ur-Black-and-Proud statesman and war hero, was utterly powerless to challenge his state's new constitution, and had been made a marginal character once again. For Randolph and Rivers, that perverse opportunity was stolen from them by White terrorists and an invidious reentrenchment of prewar social order. As James Henry Hammond died clinging to the consoling fables of the *ancien regime* as it went up in flames around him, Rivers saw first-hand the old ways return with a vengeance. After Reconstruction came to a violent and bloody end in 1876, Rivers subsisted by painting houses and driving a carriage for White people.

A first unsuccessful attempt to locate him not far from the state house turns up nothing, except for the accidental discovery of the state hospital, established in 1821 as the South Carolina Lunatic Asylum. Unlike its counterpart in Milledgeville, it is apparently a work in progress. Surrounded by chain-link fence, the Babcock Building is fronted with a columned portico. But the rest of it looks like Central Hospital in Milledgeville: a testament to an outdated mode of psychiatric treatment. But unlike Georgia's state sanatorium, South Carolina's is apparently amid rehab: construction trucks and heavy equipment imply a different future. This would seem to be the appropriate place for the obligatory citation of James Petigru's quip that "South Carolina is too small for a republic, but too large for an insane asylum."[41]

But even more poignant is what is next door to the old hospital: a new baseball park for the Single-A Columbia Fireflies. There is something fitting about the proximity of baseball to insanity, about how close the national game is to madness. I've seen this sort of thing before: in Bostwick, Georgia, there is a cemetery along the first base line of the local baseball diamond. In the face of dissolution—of mind, of body—we defiantly assert our humanity in play. *Homo ludens* at the edge of the abyss.

In any event the state asylum is not the place we are looking for. The prolific fencing around the property signals to us that we won't be tramping around here the way we did in Milledgeville anyway. Everywhere we are surrounded by the buzz of corporate interests and liability insurance.

The real object is further west on Elmwood Avenue. A rumor has led us to seek out Randolph Cemetery—Rivers could be there. The site is so tucked away as to appear deliberate, like the urban planning equivalent of the far corner of the attic. It is reachable from only one direction, a dead-end access road that passes another burial ground before terminating in Randolph Cemetery. Beyond the dead end are a railroad, an interstate, and a river.

We park and begin the search for Rivers, who may or may not be buried here. If he is, we probably won't find any sort of marker to indicate it.

But what we do find is another story, hinted at on a sizable monument at the far end of the cemetery, almost to the river. An obelisk, maybe ten feet high, sits at the side of the cemetery road. It reads:

> B. F. RANDOLPH
>
> LATE STATE SENATOR
>
> FOR ORANGEBURG COUNTY
>
> AND CHAIRMAN REPUBLICAN
>
> STATE CENTRAL COMMITTEE,
>
> WHO DIED AT HODGES' STATION
>
> ABBEVILLE COUNTY
>
> AT THE HANDS OF ASSASSINS
>
> ON FRIDAY OCT$^{r.}$16TH
>
> A.D. 1868.

At the Hands of Assassins? Did not see that coming.

I am no historian, and I have never heard of B. F. Randolph, but I recognize what the date 1868 means in South Carolina. This is an unexpected connection I must pursue, a story I have to hear.

En route back to North Carolina on US 25, a sign for Hodges in two miles. I veer off onto County Road 246 toward the tiny upcountry village, one block long. There is little to it. The station where Randolph was murdered by members of the Klan is no longer there, but shadows of the old railings are still visible, like a levee in a dry land.

Benjamin Franklin Randolph was born in Kentucky and served as a chaplain to the 26th Colored Troops during the Civil War. In early 1868 Randolph served as a delegate to the state Constitutional Convention in Charleston, which allowed the state to rejoin the Union in July. But for many White people, the price of readmission was far too high. The editor of the *Charleston Mercury* was stark in his assessment of the new "policy of negro rule." He prophesied that the new conditions would lead to one of two possible outcomes, either "civil equality but political inferiority" for Black people, or the extermination of "the negro race."[42] White paranoia over Black suffrage and empowerment was so acute that the very existence of a figure like Randolph evoked for them the terrifying specter of genocide.

Randolph so triggered White audiences that he stretched the *Charleston Mercury*'s powers of description to their limit. Frantically grasping for words, the state's most pro-secession newspaper called Randolph "huge of mouth," "the saddle-colored delegate,"[43] "molasses-colored carpetbagger,"[44] "phlegmatic and not particularly brilliant,"[45] "gingerbread colored, large, kinky-headed, lethargie [*sic*]."[46] "Very mouthy and boastful, and forsooth, thought the people in his country owed him debt of gratitude for not having advised his more ignorant brethren to rapine, arson and blood." The otherwise anonymous "Caucasian" who attached his name to one piece claimed, with an especially coded turn of phrase, that Randolph had "done more to demoralize and disorganize the labor system of this State than any other dozen of his brother emissaries."[47]

D. Wyatt Aiken, former Confederate colonel and future US congressman, took special pains to drum up White fears about Randolph. In early October, after a speech by Randolph, Aiken publicly daydreamed about the murder of "the hyena Randolph."[48] Aiken urged attendants at a speech in Anderson in 1868 "never to suffer this man Randolph to come into your midst; if he does, give him four feet by six."[49]

On October 15, 1868, Aiken confronted Randolph on the train platform in Hodges. "You damned black son of a bitch," he shouted at him, "you have no business here."[50]

As Randolph changed trains in Hodges the following day, William K. Tolbert and two other men shot Randolph in the head and fled the scene on horseback, unpursued, unmolested. Tolbert was a member of a local Democratic Club in Hodges, established to limit the power of the Republican vote, and especially to oppose the mostly Black Union Leagues. Their instructions were "to break them up, kill the leaders, fire into them, and kill the leaders if they could."[51] Tolbert was eventually arrested and imprisoned in the State Penitentiary, but escaped in August 1869. A $1,000 bounty was placed on his head by the local constable, but apparently it was never paid. The constable himself killed Tolbert at a house party. In May 1869, the South Carolina House of Representatives formally investigated the "disordered state of affairs" in the upstate, and questioned witnesses to Randolph's murder. One of the members of the investigating committee was Robert Smalls, and Prince Rivers testified. Despite Tolbert's testimony directly implicating the involvement of several other men, no one was ever tried for the assassination of a Black state senator.

The original railroad depot was moved three-quarters of a mile away in 1975. In its second act it became "Jackson Station," a popular live music venue ~~called~~ owned by two gay men, not a small achievement in the upstate in the 1970s.[52] The depot's former site is now a blank space. The railbeds and their memory have long since retreated into the soil, beneath an expanse of rough-cut crabgrass. Fronting the old rail line, a lone brick warehouse overwhelmed with vines is the only building of significant age. An overgrown shrub crowds the padlocked front door, which does not look as if it has been opened in a while. It may have been here in 1868, but maybe not. It may or may not be the last remaining witness to the world of Wyatt Aiken and Benjamin Franklin Randolph, a wordless sign of another age that this state has worked very hard not to remember. "Inconspicuous" is an understatement. There is no marker of any kind to indicate what happened here, and my encounter with it is entirely the function of a series of accidents or coincidences.

I cannot name the precise causes of these accidents, if there are any. I can only assume there must be one or more, since these convergences present themselves too frequently to be accounted merely to chance or dumb luck. Instead they may be akin to some sort of epiphanic apparitions of the local genie-soul, as Walker Percy named it. I do not know if I mean by the term the same thing Percy meant by it, and I am not even entirely sure I know what Percy meant by it, but I do know that it is a name for some quality of personality that is particular to every locality. And I know that a name is needed, especially in a place like Hodges on a day like this one, in which the convergences of history and experience seem so willful. Whatever the genie-soul or souls is or are or may be, it or they seem to relish a sort of enforced collision of pasts into a single, unrepeatable present. They tend to reward openness to the unexpected, but often with a blindside to the back of the head. They seem to appear when you are not in any special hurry to get somewhere, apart perhaps from a new condition of knowledge about the world and your tiny but not irrelevant place within it. Yes, I visit the site of the death of Benjamin Franklin Randolph at the hands of assassins, but the place itself becomes the scene of a visitation of another persona who seems to want to show me something. Something is being offered here that cannot be refused nor simply tucked away as a trinket of information. That weird quality for which I have no other name than genie-soul seems to demand a new disposition of spirit, an enlargement of memory, a will to testify. I came into Hodges on County Road 246. I leave on the *via peregrinorum*, initiated into the mysticism of the Southern road.

Gee's Bend, Alabama. Photo by the author.

ALABAMA
Stranger than a Strange Land

When the gold-seeking Spaniard Hernando de Soto rolled into Mobile Bay in 1540, he came at it in reverse—from the north, and not from the Gulf of Mexico, as one might expect. It was certainly not the last time in Alabama's storied history that someone there did something so monumentally counter-intuitive, or—in the local parlance—bass-ackwards. Hernando imagined the future Alabama to be a gold-laden El Dorado, and while he did not find what he was looking for, he may well have planted the seeds of Alabama's deeply rooted reputation for backwardness. *Qué extraño*, de Soto must have thought as he left Alabama, or—again in local vernacular—"Well, that was weird."

In any event, de Soto was not the first *extrañero* to come to Alabama—and to the South more generally—with preconceptions that had to be revised in the wake of personal experience with the place. Accounts of Alabama have long acknowledged, if only implicitly, the deep prejudices against the state that obtain even still, on into the age of Bible-waving district attorneys prowling suburban shopping malls for young girls and a seemingly endless lineage of not-ready-for-primetime politicians who provide more than ample confirmation of every stereotype of the state. Even the WPA writers could not escape this: the very first words of 1941 WPA Guide to Alabama are "Too often vaguely thought of as," etc. *The state is complex, OK?* basically goes the rest. And yet everywhere there are—for those with eyes to see—*sed contras* to confound received impressions. "All that is gold does not glitter," Gandalf wrote to Bilbo Baggins in *The Lord of the Rings*, and while he was not talking specifically about Alabama, he might as well have been. There is gold to be found here, but not the kind de Soto was after.

Near the Georgia state line, in the town of Seale, a rusted-roofed, weathered-pine structure looks as if it could have been in Evans & Agee, but for the huge letters in highway-stripe yellow on the roof that read TRUMP. So far, so Alabama.

Built in 1868 and newly fitted with an elevator in 2016, the Old Russell County Courthouse from the time when Seale was the county seat is disproportionately well-preserved. A row of shops along Glenville Street is abandoned, widening fissures the sidewalk in front sprouting with weeds. Starke's Farm Supplies no longer sells the Purina Chows that an embossed-tin sign advertises. Next door, dried leaves cover the floor of an empty store. The windows all deglazed, panes denuded. Shelving units face the back wall, the ceiling, the floor. A vinyl-covered chair, stained with bird shit, sits alone in front of a battered upright piano, its keys all wildly out of line, as if suspended in the middle of some rowdy dance-hall ragtime. Two doors down, the letters naming the defunct SEALE ALABAMA post office are two As short, their familiar typeface pointing to a Futura never realized. The storefronts seem to merge together into a common hue of rust and sand. Trumpet vine reaches over and around them like a giant green hand pulling it back into the woods behind.

A few miles north, across from the Dollar General at the junction of US 431 and Silver Run Drive, painted shipping containers stacked like the tail end of an oversized Jenga match. A gas station marquis just like the one in front of Billy Carter's gas station announces

WORLDS FIRST

DRIVE THRU ART

AND ANTIQUE GALLERY

AND MUSEUM

We park and walk through it instead. The shipping containers have been fitted with picture windows on one side repurposed into galleries like shadow boxes in a combination of circus freak show, taxidermist, curiosity shop, and folk-art museum. The brainchild of Butch Anthony, the museum features a lot of his own mixed-media form of art that he calls "Intertwangleism."

Seale is the first interruption, a kind of generous corrective to what you thought you knew about Alabama. By the time we get to the Black

Belt almost every prejudice I have harbored against the state (mainly in the service of seasonal, football-related antagonisms) will be overturned. Along this relatively uninteresting stretch of four-lane US highway, a moment of undeserved and improbable beauty, an act of cultural intervention, a moment of grace, tinged with melancholic humor. One of Anthony's paintings features a 1970s family portrait, overpainted with white outlines of stylized skeletons. Above them, in what looks like red lipstick: "She Got the Money."

It's a welcome reprieve, before the road leads to a different kind of confrontation.

What I Did Not See in Tuskegee

Forty miles west of Seale in Tuskegee, distances begin to open up, between a preconception of this state, my region, and its actual history.

In 1997, we stopped in Tuskegee long enough to eat lunch at Thomas Reed's Chitlin' House Chicken Coop, and visit Booker T. Washington's grave and the "Lifting the Veil" statue on the campus of the university. But that was about it. The town center of Tuskegee is barely a mile away from the campus. We missed it entirely.

This time is different. We come at it from another angle.

We park the car across from the First Methodist Church to take pictures of the foliage growing out of the brick spire. One block up, past the beauty shops, cell phone stores, and the *Tuskegee News*, the Confederate monument on the town square is not "partly hidden by thick elms and magnolias" like the WPA Guide says it was in 1940. A few magnolias remain, but the elms have presumably long since succumbed to the blight like they have everywhere in America. The monument is in full sun now. Like a redacted document, the inscription is blacked out. Someone has taken a can of black spray paint and a blunt object to the base.

I get the sense this is not the first time.

The Tuskegee Normal School for Colored Teachers (and later, Tuskegee Institute, and ultimately Tuskegee University) was established in 1881, and would eventually become one of the country's most important institutions for higher learning for African Americans. The Confederate monument in Tuskegee was erected in 1906. Two months after the school—and many around the nation—celebrated its twenty-fifth anniversary, the White-controlled city of Tuskegee gave the town square to the United Daughters of the Confederacy as a "park for white people."

Twenty years ago, I wasn't wise to the ways the legacy of White supremacy is written into the landscape of places like Tuskegee, how monuments to Confederate soldiers were put up in public places like the town square here as reminders to African Americans of their place in an overtly racist regime, and as a warning to them not to forget it. I might have been able to believe then that the monuments were pretty banal, just part of the landscape, but exceptions to America's story of itself. I failed to ask some pretty basic questions.

We ate in Thomas Reed's restaurant in 1997, but I did not think then to ask about who Thomas Reed was.

But now I know that Thomas Reed once vowed to climb up the State House in Montgomery and personally remove the Confederate battle flag flying atop the white dome. Apparently, the flag went mysteriously missing the night before the planned coup and was moved to the Confederate memorial on the north side of the Capitol. The episode landed Reed both in jail and in the *New York Times.*

On February 3, 1988, Reed and thirteen others attempted to scale an eight-foot chain-link fence around the Capitol and purloin the flag. They were arrested, briefly held, and later released on $300 bond. Reed had made the removal of the flag a personal mission. "This is just the beginning," he said at the time. Five years later, the flag was taken down from the cupola of the Capitol. "But," a write-up in the *Chicago Tribune* concluded, "the flag's supporters argue that removing the flag is tantamount to erasing history."[1] In the thirty years since Reed's mission to depose the Confederate flag in Montgomery, it seems that no new arguments for preserving Confederate flags and monuments have presented themselves. "Leave it, as a reminder," used to be the final word on the subject, and where most White people were keen to leave the matter. It's probably where, if pressed in 1988, I would have left it, too.

But not Thomas Reed. In 1988, Reed was president of the Alabama NAACP, and had been involved in state politics for over twenty years. In 1970, he and Fred Gray, the pioneering civil rights attorney from Montgomery, became the first African Americans since Reconstruction to serve in the state legislature. Photographs of Reed in the Alabama State Archives show him on the edge of the town square in Tuskegee in 1966, campaigning to a small crowd of mostly African American men in fedoras, hands crossed, on hips, in pockets. He stands on the tailgate of a

station wagon emblazoned with signs that say, THOMAS REED, THE MAN
WE NEED.

The image does not show what Thomas Reed can presumably see
from the tailgate of the station wagon: the Confederate monument in
Blackface. The marble soldier is covered in black paint after a march
earlier that year protesting the murder of Samuel L. Younge, a Tuskegee student and Navy man shot by a gas station owner in Tuskegee for
attempting to use the White restroom.

In 1965, Sammy Younge, local field secretary for the Student Nonviolent Coordinating Committee, had been involved in setting up "Tent
City" along US 80 in Lowndes County, which provided temporary homes
for African American sharecroppers and tenant farmers kicked out of
their homes by White landlords for trying to register to vote. That summer, he had led a movement to integrate the local swimming pool. On
May 31, 1965, Younge and about twenty-five students from the Tuskegee
Advancement League arrived at the municipal pool to swim. The next
day, twice as many African American students showed up. Each time,
all the White swimmers left the pool, toweled off, grumbled, and hurled
insults. The city promptly closed the facility because local authorities
allegedly found "quantities of rubbish" in the pool.[2] Not coincidentally,
Alabama newspapers soon began regularly running advertisements for
planned communities featuring private swimming pools.

In early January 1966, Younge was at the courthouse in Tuskegee
helping Black citizens register to vote. That night, he attempted to use
the White restroom nearby at Marvin Segrest's Standard Oil gas station.
After an altercation, Segrest, 68, fatally shot Younge in the face, twice.
His body was found the next morning on a rain-dampened driveway.
Later that day, Segrest was arrested and released on $20,000 bond. Ulti-
mately indicted for second-degree murder, Segrest's trial was postponed
for months and relocated to Opelika, where he was supposed to have a
greater chance at a "fair" hearing than in mostly-Black Tuskegee. An
all-White jury heard arguments in the case for two days in early December 1966. After deliberating for a little over an hour, the jury acquitted
Segrest. He died in 1986.[3]

When Thomas Reed looked across the city park towards the Confederate monument, he saw the legacy of Samuel Younge. Reed's Chicken
Coop is one instance of a larger phenomenon that becomes more and

more apparent: the way in which the world presents itself to us at face value, but if you simply take it that way, you will miss a lot. The encoded histories of the American South only make themselves available if you care to examine them. Thomas Reed is clearly a household name in Tuskegee, and his coop serves up some damn fine chicken, but it is a moment in a history that is not self-evident to visitors like us.

Across the street, we seek out the grave of Booker T. Had I known who Charles Keck was, I might have sought out his grave, too, in Fish-kill, New York, when I happened to pass by it on a family road trip to Canada. I had seen his work, regularly walked past his statue of James B. Duke, the tobacco magnate and founder of Duke University, during my days in Durham. On the second tour, in 1998, I would take an under-exposed image of his statue of Stonewall Jackson in Charlottesville, with no inkling that twenty years in the future, it would be shrouded under a black tarpaulin for five months because of the symbolic bloodguilt it would bear for the murder of Heather Heyer by a White nationalist dur-ing violent orgy of White resentment in 2017. But in 1997, I stood in front of his statue of Booker T. Washington, unaware of the ways in which these disparate figures had a connection to one another in Charles Keck.

Keck was a famous sculptor from New York, responsible for at least one of the most controversial public monuments in the country in the 2010s. His image of Washington, called "Lifting the Veil of Ignorance," is a visual expression of the title of Washington's most famous work, *Up from Slavery*. It shows a vested and bow-tied Washington standing upright, his left hand extended demonstratively. With his right, he is rais-ing the veil from a shirtless slave, whose own left hand clutches a book. On the pediment beneath them both, the inscription:

BOOKER T WASHINGTON

1856 1915

HE LIFTED THE VEIL OF IGNORANCE

FROM HIS PEOPLE AND POINTED

THE WAY TO PROGRESS THROUGH

EDUCATION AND INDUSTRY

It is a powerful image, but it is not uncomplicated. The narrator of Ralph Ellison's 1953 novel *Invisible Man* attends a fictional version of

Tuskegee. Ellison was himself a student at Tuskegee in the 1930s, a trumpet major with ambitions of becoming a classical composer. Early in the novel, he recalls, across the distance of time, the sight of a statue that is clearly Peck's "Lifting the Veil:"

It's so long ago and far away that here in my invisibility I wonder if it happened at all. Then in my mind's eye I see the bronze statue of the college Founder, the cold Father symbol, his hands outstretched in the breathtaking gesture of lifting a veil that flutters in hard, metallic folds above the face of a kneeling slave; and I am standing puzzled, unable to decide whether the veil is really being lifted, or lowered more firmly in place; whether I am witnessing a revelation or a more efficient blinding. And as I gaze, there is a rustle of wings and I see a flock of starlings flighting before me and, when I look again, the bronze face, whose empty eyes look upon a world I have never seen, runs with liquid chalk—creating another ambiguity to puzzle in my groping mind: Why is a bird-soiled statue more commanding than one that is clean?[4]

What is it that the Founder sees, and the invisible man does not? The statue is no less soiled now, no less commanding, and probably no less complicated. Whatever Booker T. is meant to see, his face is set directly toward the Kellogg Hotel & Conference Center, named for the foundation established by the Michigan-based cereal magnate. It is one example of the contradictions at the heart of *Invisible Man*: the vision of an elite educational institution for young Black men, endowed and underwritten by wealthy White philanthropists.

I first encountered Ellison in the early 1990s during a freshman English Lit class from which I took nothing except a deep impression left by *Invisible Man*. To me, Ellison seemed like the closest thing to Dostoevsky that America had ever produced: a philosophical novelist with an eye for the dissonance between high ideals and the lived experience of human existence, a musician's ear for the fierce and subtle power of language. He had honed that ear in the 1930s, when on a much-needed reprieve from Tuskegee. In 1936 he went to New York to scrape up enough cash to finish his music degree. A new friend and mentor, Richard Wright, got Ellison a job with the Federal Writers' Project interviewing people on the streets of New York, recording their stories. It took. Ellison was now a writer. He never returned to Tuskegee.

In meeting the Invisible Man I had once again the feeling of having been cheated out of something great, something incomparable that I wish I had been exposed to earlier. It was an adolescent kind of resentment, as I would later understand. An education cannot give you everything; the best it can do is make you wise enough to locate the great chasms in your own knowledge, and some idea about how to fill them.

Ellison's prose could communicate, better than any theory, the sense of distance between the invisible man, the beneficiary of the Founder's vision, and the Founder's vision itself. How much greater must the distance be between either vision and my own?

This time, Tuskegee is a case study in what we White people often come to expect from Black history. We often expect it to look and sound one way, to be easily categorizable under the all-encompassing label of "struggle" or "protest" or "uplift." We may tacitly expect Black literature to sound like a series of variations on a basically homiletical theme. Many of the heroes of Black history White people come to celebrate—if at all—are confirmatory of this perception, which often shapes and determines white experience of African American history *in situ*. For example, the White person curious enough about that history might be disappointed, on attending Sixteenth Street Baptist Church in Birmingham, to hear a rousing sermon not about justice rolling down like rivers but about the more prosaic challenges of domestic life. This was my experience, and while maybe it was a rookie error, it was also illustrative of what I as a White male have been trained to expect out of Black church culture. Whatever I expected the church that Sunday to be for me, it may have been untutored but it was not innocent. It is the other side of Black history as spectacle, analogous to the disappointment a German tourist may find on looking for Tara that it just ain't there.

On the other hand, the upsetting of expectations can be enormously life-giving, as it was for me when I was first introduced to Ellison. Same with Murray. Both Tuskegee men who did not at all just take the "Lifting the Veil" motif at the heart of Tuskegee's campus and simply parrot it. In one respect, *Invisible Man* showed Ellison both drawing on and pushing back against the Tuskegee mythology. And it is not Buka T. who haunts the halls of Albert Murray's recollection about Tuskegee but

Ellison. Murray's *South to a Very Old Place* is an exercise in respectful demystification of the "shadowy figure of legend," too—his own form of lifting the veil for the rest of us on the way Tuskegee men actually relate to their "tuskegeeness," as he calls it. In Murray's day, the "noble inscription" on the "the Monument" had become

> "Hey lift the veil, man. Hey, man, lift the goddam veil." Had become: "Hey, horse, you know what the man said; Unka Buka say lift that shit, man, goddam!"[5]

We visit the Ford Motor Company Library where, as a student, Murray could not find the books he was looking for—James Joyce, T. S. Eliot, William Faulkner—because they had been checked out by Ralph Ellison. Far less spectacular than the Monument, but a structure of far more consequence for all our histories.

From Tuskegee, we wander northward toward Tallassee, at one time home of the only Confederate Armory not to be leveled during the war. Time and gravity and have done what Union armies neglected to do, however. The structure is a collapsed, empty shell, but still a source of pride for the local chapter of the SCV, who have—fittingly—borrowed their name from the Armory and confidently announce their presence across the town. The SCV, which sponsors an annual reenactment of the "Battles for the Armory," are now headquartered in a building they call "Fort Talisi," which once served as the city's welcome center. In front of the building, the SCV erected a monument to the Confederacy featuring a copious display of Confederate flags. The group insists that the display is in the name of "heritage," which is difficult to square with the chapter's sponsorship of a failed attempt to erect a fifty-foot-high pole with a gigantic Rebel flag across the street from the campus of Alabama State University in Montgomery, one of the oldest historically Black colleges and universities in the country.[6]

Along with nearby Wetumpka, it is a region of bridges and high crossings. In the latter town, a 1931 bridge that looks like a cousin of the Edmund Pettus Bridge in Selma crosses the Coosa River. It is the fourth bridge on this site, and now named for Bibb Graves, who was both a member of the Klan and a two-time governor of Alabama who abolished the convict leasing system. He's progressive as Alabama governors go in the 1930s, but even so the Graves name covers over another one.

The second bridge on this site was designed by Horace King, an African American architect who was born enslaved in South Carolina and practiced as an architect while being the property of John Godwin of Columbus, Georgia. King was successful enough in his design practice that he purchased his freedom in 1846, and eventually became the most prominent bridge builder in the South, designing bridges all over the region. Out of gratitude to his former enslaver for training him in bridge construction, King donated a small funerary obelisk to John Godwin for his gravesite in Phenix City, Alabama. Horace King eventually served in the Alabama legislature during Reconstruction.

From Wetumpka we arc northward around Montgomery via Millbrook, where a surreal fake town sits in the middle of a small island. Once the set for the film *Big Fish*, the fictional town of Spectre is composed of wooden shell-houses along a center lane that terminates at one end in a wood-framed church, and at the other end in a sort of trellis of dozens of laced-together sneakers flung over a high wire. In between, a bevy of overly friendly goats have colonized the property and polices the visitors with nudges to the thigh and the occasional nibble on the ankle.

Montgomery

We pass through the industrial northern side of Montgomery into its seemingly ancient heart, which has all the antiquity of the Old South that Atlanta lacks. At the center of it all is the storied State Capitol, the site of so much of consequence. Next to the building in 1997, the displaced Confederate battle flag flies atop the eighty-eight-foot-high Confederate Memorial on the state house, relocated here from the capitol dome thanks in part to Thomas Reed, the Man We Need. It is 111 years now since white-bearded and comfortably retired septuagenarian Jefferson Davis laid the cornerstone in 1886. He has a statue of his own in front of the Capitol, erected much later. His Civil War residence, "The First White House of the Confederacy," a beautiful wood-frame Italianate structure, is a regular field trip site for Montgomery school kids. They will learn there that:

> Davis was a Jeffersonian Democrat dedicated to the principle of State
> Rights under the Constitution. He had inherited his ideas on politics and slavery from his father and George Washington. They felt

that in giving Christianity to the Africans and submitting them to Anglo-Saxon culture, the Americans were preparing them for eventual citizenship. Jefferson Davis believed "the peculiar institution" a temporary necessity in developing the cotton economy of the South on which New England textile industry depended, and that gradual emancipation would come as the Africans were prepared to meet the responsibilities of freedom. The more intelligent of "his people" were educated and served as his plantation overseers and secretaries. Jefferson Davis was held by his Africans in genuine affection as well as highest esteem.[7]

A marker on the steps of the Capitol—oddly, in the shape of a Star of David—marks the spot where Jeff Davis was inaugurated as president of the Confederate States of America on February 18, 1861. "The audience was large and brilliant," Davis wrote to his wife Varina two days later. It was the biggest thing that had ever happened in Montgomery, or ever would.

Until, that is, early January almost ninety-two years later. Jefferson Davis was big in Alabama, but he was no Hank Williams. Hank's funeral on January 4, 1953, drew thousands to mourn Luke the Drifter's sudden and mysterious death. From the stage of the Montgomery Auditorium to standing-room-only congregation, Roy Acuff led Ernest Tubb, Bill Monroe, Jimmie Dickens, Webb Pierce, and all God's children in singing "as Hank would want it done."

"Goodbye, neighbors," Acuff said, dismissing the faithful.

Hank Williams's alcohol- and morphine-induced death remains shrouded in intrigue, controversy, and contradiction. The short version is this: Hank and his driver Charles Carr left the Andrew Johnson Hotel in Knoxville in a Carolina blue 1952 drop-top Cadillac for a New Year's Day show in Canton, Ohio. Williams had been administered morphine and vitamin B-12 by a local doctor and slept much of the trip. When Carr stopped for gas in Oak Hill, West Virginia, he found Williams already stiff from rigor mortis. He was twenty-nine.

None of the above details are really certain.

According to legend, Hank had some premonition of his own death in the days before. But his music had always had a sense of dark foreboding, especially in the haunting "Alone and Forsaken," written in 1949 but released after his death:

The darkness is falling, the sky has turned gray
A hound in the distance is starting to bay
I wonder, I wonder, what she's thinking of
Forsaken, forgotten, without any love.

It might be the saddest and most ominous song in the country music tradition. It's a dense, two-minute religious lament in a minor key, but its chorus seems to resolve, paradoxically, momentarily, to a major chord, and then back to minor again:

Alone and forsaken by fate and by man
Oh, Lord, if You hear me please hold to my hand
Oh, please understand.[8]

As much as contemporary mainstream country music claims, or would like to claim, Hank Williams as a, if not the, seminal influence, it goes nowhere near the bleak despair of "Alone and Forsaken." That song seems to arise directly from the soil of Alabama's Black Belt, of a piece with the spiritual agony and occasional but always provisional release that Black blues music from the region has generated. There is something here that is almost too painful to approach too closely, a voice that like that in the epistle to the Hebrews, which contemporary country music has, heard once, and then begged never to hear again, for it could not endure it.[9]

The State Capitol is famous as the terminus of the Selma-to-Montgomery march in March 1965, and as the backdrop for Dr. King's "how long, not long" speech. From his spot on the dais in front of the capitol, King could see his former church, Dexter Avenue Baptist, a block away from Governor Wallace's office on the hill. Dexter has come to represent a kind of countercultural vision of Christian teaching and practice, swimming upstream of the main arteries of White Protestant Christianity in the South. The religious vision of the civil rights movement was rooted in the Black church, but it also found nourishment from Jewish and Catholic traditions. One of the most improbable, and inspiring, religious institutions in the overwhelmingly Baptist South served as a campground for demonstrators on the final night of the march to Montgomery from Selma.

In 1934, Father Harold Purcell was a Passionist priest from Pennsylvania, who was scandalized by the treatment of African Americans in the South. He imagined a "city" within Montgomery, Alabama, that could provide medical care, education, and spiritual aid to the poor and oppressed Black community in Montgomery. He appealed to the superior of his order for help implementing his bold vision but was denied. Purcell forsook his vows to the Passionist order and became a priest of the Diocese of Mobile. His archbishop, Thomas J. Toolen, provided the funding for Purcell to procure fifty-six acres of land on Fairview Avenue, in the heart of Washington Park, a historically African American district.

The City of St. Jude is a kind of miniature civilization built on the principle of Christian charity, and includes a parish church, an assisted living facility, a pediatric nursing home for developmentally disabled children, a food pantry, and a soup kitchen. Due to declining enrollment, the school closed in 2014.

As part of a long Catholic tradition of hospitality to strangers and neighbors, St. Jude sees its mission as a response to the words of Jesus in the Gospel of Matthew: "For I was hungry and you gave me something to eat, I was thirsty and you gave me something to drink, I was a stranger and you invited me in, I needed clothes and you clothed me, I was sick and you looked after me, I was in prison and you came to visit me."[10] On the rainy final night of the Selma-to-Montgomery march, Father Paul J. Mullaney, director of the City of St. Jude, had a unique opportunity to exercise this mission when the city offered to over 25,000 dog-tired and rain-soaked marchers sanctuary and rest in the shade of tall pines scattered around the spacious grounds, where they might enjoy the blessing of St. Jude Thaddeus, the "patron saint of hopeless cases and champion of impossible causes."[11]

The thousands were fed with a program scraped together by Harry Belafonte that featured an A-list of Hollywood celebrities taking turns on the makeshift stage: Leonard Bernstein, James Baldwin, Floyd Patterson, Tony Perkins, Sammy Davis, Jr., Pete Seeger, Nipsy Russell, Mike Nichols, and Odetta and Nina Simone. It was a feast of entertainment and a powerful expression of the Catholic tradition of hospitality to wayfarers. But it was not met with approval from Grover Cleveland Hall, Jr., editor of the local paper of record, who urged citizens to keep it all under their hats, not to give the protestors any attention, just get through the final day of the march and let the marchers "move on to afflict other regions." He likened the demonstrators to the Union "occupiers" who came into Montgomery via the same direction in 1865 and dismissed "the folly of this bizarre procession" as "a costly indulgence in wild self-righteousness."[12] The impact of the march was not as evanescent as Hall fantasized: In response to the marches, the Voting Rights Act of 1965 was passed five months later.

Monuments, anthropologists sometimes tell us, are public expressions of what a society holds to be ideal and worth remembering, and the marker to the City of St. Jude is one instance where the Alabama Historical Commission has rightfully restored to memory an important institution with or without the addition of name-dropped celebrities. In an important 1983 article on the place of Confederate monuments in the South, John Winberry describes a monument as "the creation of a people, and as a symbol it 'encapsulates and nurtures an idea or a set of ideas' that incorporate certain values and ideals of that society."[13] But you don't have to walk two blocks on Commerce Street in Montgomery to find out that this is not quite right. In that space between Bibb and Water Streets, fronting the Alabama River where steamboats unloaded thousands of Africans for the American slave market, there is a memorial marker to the "Indian village of Encanchata," the future site of Montgomery. At the other end of the block, a life-sized Hank Williams looks up Commerce toward the fountain on Court Square, once the South's most active slave-trading center. A few paces away, a marker commemorates—for some reason—the building program of Montgomery Freemasons. Around the corner, a marble slab inlaid into the red-brick sidewalk marks the site of the first offices of the Confederate government.

Each of these monuments was put there not by a "society" but by a particular group of people with the desire and the funds to commemorate a representation of some ideal worth hanging on to. In the first case, it was the local chapter of the Sons of the American Revolution. Hank's statue was commissioned by Hank, Jr. The one to the Freemasons was put up by the Freemasons. And the Confederate slab was put there by the Sophie Bibb Chapter of the United Daughters of the Confederacy in June 1911.

Montgomery is in many ways the anti-Atlanta: while the latter is famously indifferent to its past, Alabama's capital city is scrupulously clued-in to its own history. Historical markers proliferate in downtown Montgomery. There are at least a half a dozen just surrounding Court Square, a roundabout between the state capitol and the Alabama river-front. At the intersection of Commerce Street and Dexter Avenue, Court Square is the crossroads of Southern and American history. In the center of the roundabout is a nineteenth-century iron fountain atop an artesian well, the site of an ancient water source that has nourished the people of this area for hundreds of years. The fountain is crowned with a statue of Hebe, goddess of eternal youth. From an upturned pitcher she dispenses an endless stream of chlorinated nondrinking water into a large basin surrounded by an ironwork fence. It is an ironic, but auspicious landmark in a city so deeply identified with a movement in which access to water fountains became a site of contest for equal rights. It is possibly contradictory, too: Court Square was once the center of Montgomery's prolific slave trade, the most active in the South. More enslaved men and women lived in or were sold in Montgomery than anywhere else, including Charleston, New Orleans, Natchez, and Mobile. At the same time, and not by accident, Court Square is in some ways the wellspring of the first mass countermovement to the legacy of slavery. On this site in 1955, Rosa Parks boarded a city bus and refused to yield her seat to a White passenger, prompting the first direct action campaign of the civil rights movement.

Contradictory historical and personal forces seem to collide at this intersection, where the city seems intent upon establishing bulwarks against forgetfulness. The implication of the vexed and multilayered image of the goddess Hebe seems to be that eternal youth—or at least a more promising temporal future—is to be found in the confrontation with difficult history, at that point where public and personal memories clash. Collective memory must be constantly renewed by perpetual vigilance, the fountain seems to imply.

The National Memorial for Peace and Justice, which commemorates African American victims of lynching from 1877 to 1950, is the most extraordinary and promising national memorial in a generation or more. But it is not just a memorial; it is a confrontation. Four blocks from Court Square, the exhibit partakes of Montgomery's history of nonviolent protest. In this case the protest is not for rights but for memory. It elicits a reckoning with the horrors of an essential part of American history that has effectively been evacuated—a history that is just too shameful for many people to talk about, if it is remembered at all.

The memorial opened in 2018, along with the nearby Legacy Museum. Both are projects of the Equal Justice Initiative (EJI), an organization founded in 1989 by Bryan Stevenson, who is part of a distinguished tradition of Montgomery attorneys devoted to civil rights. In addition to its legal activities, the EJI serves the work of vigilant memory: it recalls the atrocities committed against a people who have been "kidnapped, terrorized, segregated, and incarcerated." These four themes form the framework of the story told by the museum, which is situated in a former warehouse on Commerce Street once used for holding enslaved people, along with the livestock from whom they were legally indistinguishable. The aim of the museum is not just to carry a candle into a dark and unvisited chamber of American history but to flood it with stadium-grade light.

The memorial focuses that unsparing light on one aspect of the museum's larger narrative: lynching. Designed by Michael Murphy and his team at the MASS Design Group of Boston, it is the architectural embodiment of EJI's unprecedented six-year research project to document and memorialize the African American victims of lynching in twelve southern states. It grows from the same conceptual soil broken by Maya Lin's Vietnam Veterans Memorial in Washington, DC, which soberly presents the names of the war dead with no other identifying information. For their families and survivors, who frequently make charcoal rubbings of names onto paper, this has proven to be a powerfully tactile way of connecting to their loved ones. Like the Vietnam Memorial, the National Memorial for Peace and Justice represents a watershed moment in the idea and practice of what a public memorial can be and do and how visitors engage with it.

The confrontation in Montgomery does not come at you all at once, but by way of a slow initiation into a subject that everyone and no one knows about, that is rarely explored in depth and at best tacitly taken for granted. The confidence, authority, and incontrovertible evidence with which the memorial presents itself means that the subject can be ignored no longer, not without a grave cost to American—and especially Southern—self-understanding.

The site is a grassy six-acre knoll overlooking downtown Montgomery. Newness is everywhere: across the street, aluminum frames on a new building await drywall. Newly paved roads are still tar black. Workers paint metal braces on a fence. In the memorial garden in front of the main entrance, recently planted azaleas, hydrangeas, and pansies are still pushing out their roots into new soil.

You enter through a small portal, past a quote from Martin Luther King, Jr.—"True peace is not merely the absence of tension: it is the presence of justice"—and along an angular gravel path lined with dark concrete walls textured with the shadowy impressions of rough-cut lumber. A series of placards along the way narrows your focus from the museum's "From Enslavement to Mass Incarceration" narrative to the particular: lynching as the ultimate expression of a White supremacist regime of terror. A sculpture by Ghanaian artist Kwame Akoto-Bamfo depicts African men and women bound together in chains around the neck, wrists, and ankles, striped with worming trails of rusty tears and blood, the vestiges of corrosion.

The memorial itself is a cloister-shaped, open-air canopy, with a mounded green space in the center. As you enter from one corner, six-foot rectangular boxes hang from the ceiling like suspended, upturned iron caskets. They appear to float just above the pale wood floor. There is one box for each county in which a lynching is known to have been committed, and on each box are the names of that county's known victims. Sometimes there is only one name per county; for others there are dozens. The marker for Phillips County, Arkansas, includes fifteen individual names, as well as a sentence collectively remembering the 229 African Americans slaughtered in the Elaine Massacre, one of the deadliest racial conflicts in American history.

There are more than 4,000 names on 800 individual monuments, each one made of Alabama-forged weathering steel. As the steel weathers, it oxidizes and becomes discolored like rust. Each one has a unique personality of its own in hues—cocoa, chestnut, burnt umber, ochre—as varied as the skin tones of the victims it represents. On many of them, the discoloration runs down the steel surface like a trail of blood. Over time, as they are exposed to the elements, the individual county memorials will bleed onto the oak floor and down the ramp that descends deeper into the memorial.

Each name, in a dignified font, has been cut through steel with a high-powered water-jet cutter. When the guide tells me this, I recall the fire hoses of Bull Connor. The names are not engraved the way they are on the Vietnam Memorial but cut out of the steel, creating a negative space that makes the named person present and absent at the same time.

Past the first corner, the floor seems almost imperceptibly to drop out from under you. It slowly slopes downward, so that by the next corner you are standing underneath the monuments, in the position of the spectators for whom lynchings were postcard material. You can look up at them but cannot touch them—they are now out of your reach. When you get to the third side, you are entirely underneath steel avatars of Black bodies dangling over your head, the floor still descending. In the staggering abundance of names above me, I feel a need to incarnate them into human flesh, to remember that for each name there is a story. I turn back and seek out the few with whose stories I was somewhat familiar before coming here: Jesse Washington, Joe Spinner Johnson, Wiley Webb, Mary Turner, Sam Hose.

As if anticipating this sensation, the designers have placed markers along both sides of the third leg that tell one-sentence stories of some of the victims. At the far end, water cascades down the surface of a one hundred–foot wall in memory of all the undocumented victims of lynching, the number of which is impossible to calculate.

The waterfall is the only audible feature of the memorial. It is reminiscent of the 9/11 Memorial in New York, and of King's favorite passage from the prophet Amos: "Let justice roll down like waters, and righteousness like a mighty stream." Or of the waters of baptism, which is what it begins to feel like by the final leg: not a sprinkling but full-on bodily immersion into a legacy of torturous violence. The memorial invites you to participate in the resurrection of forgotten names but not without first being drawn into an overpowering spectacle of brutal and grotesque death.

At the end of the last leg, a path leads up into a memorial square suggestive of the public squares in which so many of these men and women were mutilated and brutalized. The exit to the building leads you past a quote from Toni Morrison's *Beloved*:

> And O my people, out yonder, hear me, they do not love your neck unnoosed and straight. So love your neck; put a hand on it, grace it, stroke it and hold it up. And all your inside parts that they'd just as soon slop for hogs, you got to love them. The dark, dark liver—love it, love it, and the beat and beating heart, love that too. More than eyes or feet. More than lungs that have yet to draw free air. More than

your life-holding womb and your life-giving private parts, hear me now, love your heart. For this is the prize.

Across a newly sodded lawn, workers are still shoveling gravel into steel-bordered pathways, laying sod onto the red soil. They aren't done with the memorial yet, and neither are you.

The memorial has been designed to grow and transform over time, like the newly planted saplings lining its perimeter. Outside the main building, in row upon row, duplicates of the individual monuments hanging inside are laid out on their backs, like shipping containers in a boatyard. Brought here as cargo, the dead leave it the same way. There is strange relief in this arrangement, though: the same names that were previously inaccessible to you are right in front of you, to touch, to run your fingers across the weathered steel and feel their coarse absence. The container-like boxes lie supine in purgatorial suspension—in hope that each one will eventually be placed in the county it represents.

Beyond the 800 casket-like monuments, a reflection garden dedicated to Ida B. Wells offers a welcome opportunity to catch your balance and your breath, and to cry your eyes out.

This is not a feel-good story. But the aim of the memorial is ultimately hope: a clear-eyed and unromantic hope, grounded in honesty about the harsh reality of White supremacy and its relentless stranglehold on Black lives. The overall effect of the memorial is immense sorrow but oriented toward the regeneration that comes only from genuine confrontation with horrific injustice, from the recognition that there is no reconciliation without truth.

Visitors respond to the memorial in different ways. For some, it is a corrective to received histories taught in school. William, an African American guide, tells me that growing up in Pittsburgh, his takeaway from Black History Month was slim. "King carried some signs, Rosa Parks sat down, and that was pretty much it," he tells me. His version is not substantially different from what I grew up with in Atlanta.

For others, it is a wakeup call. William tells me about some Germans who visited a few days before and had been completely unaware of this aspect of American history. I suspect the revelation will come as just as big a surprise to many American visitors who have grown up believing that slavery simply ended with the Emancipation Proclamation—visitors who, if they encountered the subject of lynching at all, did so only under the aegis of Black history, a subject presumed to be important for some people, but not all.

For yet others—most profoundly—the memorial is the cemetery that the descendants of lynching victims never had. The biggest gift the memorial gives them is the public restoration of their memory, the return of their names—names no longer fettered by either iron chains or oblivion.

For me, the effect is awe—at the ingenious beauty of the memorial's design, at the unspeakable cruelty of human beings, and at the lengths to which we White people go to maintain our cherished delusions. The scale of savagery of the collective campaign of lynching in America is frankly not something I was fully prepared for. But to be presented with it, so silently, so unflinchingly, is a gift. Because confrontation with truth—like the lifted burden of a secret, no matter how disorientingly painful—is always a gift.

I try to take the names in, one at a time, until I cannot compass them anymore. I weep in the shipyard. I say "Jesus" a lot. I leave through the same small portal through which I entered, but I am not the same.

There is no gift shop.

After I leave, I walk a circuit around the outside of the memorial. New saplings—pecan, poplar, pine—have been planted around the grounds, signs of new life. On the southwest corner of the site, a lone pecan is the only established tree on the site. It is not that old, but old enough to serve as a jarring reminder of the favored instrument of white mob terrorism. West from Montgomery toward Mississippi, great southern trees crowd the margins of Highway 82 as if for some parade procession or protest march. They all look different now. Shortleaf pine, yellow poplar, live oak, shagbark hickory, Southern magnolia—their arms seem to reach toward the blacktop with heavy menace.

~

US 82 will take you to Tuscaloosa, and then—if you so choose—all the way to Alamogordo, New Mexico. US 80 will take you to Selma. West from the state capital, the route traversed by thousands of marchers from Selma to Montgomery in 1965 dips south below the Alabama river through one of the most fertile stretches of soil in the nation. A layer of rich, coffee-black loam running atop the Selma chalk formation gives the region its name: the Black Belt. At one time it was the wealthiest part of the state, home to rich planters sitting on sprawling cotton plantations. The WPA Guide said in 1941:

> The pattern of life, with its stratified society, rests on the twin pillars of a Negro's strong shoulders and a bale of cotton. Only in recent years has there been recovery from the economic stress left by low cotton prices. Under the brilliant red-bud trees in many pastures are large herds of fine cattle, fattening on Johnson grass, and great Poland China hogs rooting through deep stands of cover crops—crimson clover, vetch, and lespedeza. Big, rambling mansions along the road are the visible reminders of the region's historic and romantic past.[14]

Before the Civil War, the Black Belt was the center of political power in Alabama, driven by the massive wealth generated on the backs of slave labor. By the twentieth century, the term "Black Belt" came to be associated with the skin color of the majority of its residents. Currently the population of the region is over 50 percent African American; in Greene County it is over 80 percent.

Whatever the origins of the term, the area is now indissociable from the legacy of slavery and has become identical with the civil rights movement. Outside of Montgomery, US 80 passes into Lowndes County. After Reconstruction, White reprisals against African Americans were frequent here. The "slaveholder mentality" persisted long after Emancipation, and into the 1960s. Violence was so regular a feature of life here that the county came to be known as "Bloody Lowndes." Historical markers put up in recent years—to Elmore Bolling, Jonathan Daniels, and Viola Liuzzo—show that the violence is not limited to the distant past. Together they tell a story of violent White resistance to the ideas at the heart of the civil rights movement: some White people did not like that Elmore Bolling was a successful Black businessman, so they shot him 150 yards from his store near Lowndesboro; a White special deputy in Hayneville shot Reverend Daniels, a White Episcopal priest from New Hampshire, for entering Varner's Cash Store with Black patrons; and Viola Liuzzo, a White civil rights worker born in Pennsylvania, was shot twice in the head by Klansmen while shuttling marchers from Montgomery back to Selma after the end of the march.

Selma

The weight of all that history concentrates on a single symbol on US 80, the Edmund Pettus Bridge. It is strangely artful and leaden: its repeating concrete arches under the deck echoed by the huge, latticed steel arch spanning the width of the Alabama River. Its now iconic central arch has been declared "functionally obsolete," and while it still carries traffic in and out of Selma, the heavy load it bears now is metaphorical.

Here is what the official version of Selma sounds like, when written in 1940 by White writers:

> Selma is like an old-fashioned gentlewoman, proud and patrician, but never unfriendly . . . On the broad streets, shiny new automobiles honk impatiently while a cotton-laden cart, drawn by a plodding ox, pulls slowly aside, and the aged Negro driver smilingly tips his battered hat . . . Since Reconstruction days, Selma's Negro and white citizens have lived in an atmosphere of sympathetic understanding, tinged by a friendly paternalism on the part of the whites. Many of these Negroes are descendants of slaves who, after emancipation, chose to remain and work on the plantations where they had always lived.[15]

This was basically the version of race relations as many White Southerners narrated it to themselves: Black slaves were happy on plantations, so they stayed there once they were freed. They smile from their plodding, ox-driven carts, so they must be content. (But they are also slow.)

As another example, a local resident whose house at 722 Alabama Avenue is worth a look, "entered Confederate service as a private and was mustered out as a brigadier general. He served United States Senator for 12 years and had been reelected when he died in 1907."[16]

Thirty-three years after his death, a year before the WPA Guide to Alabama was published, they named a bridge across the Alabama River for him. His name is not on a plaque on the land side like most bridges' namesakes but emblazoned in large black capitals on the bridge itself, so that when you cross it, you pass under his name.

The WPA Guide does not tell you that Edmund Wilson Pettus was also Grand Dragon of the Alabama Ku Klux Klan from 1877 on. You can do the math yourself: when the bridge in Selma was named for Pettus in 1940—thirty-three years after his death—it was not just for his political accomplishments. It was meant as a message. And it is no accident that on March 7, 1965, when John Lewis led marchers out of Selma over the bridge named for the former head of "the most notorious white terrorist group in Alabama probably up until the civil rights movement,"[17] they were sending a message too. Their heroic stand on the bridge was a reappropriation, a taking back of a site named for someone whose name was a monument to Jim Crow.

Crossing the river under Pettus's name, African American visitors to Selma in 1940 may not have found the place as gentlewomanly as the WPA Guide promised it would be. If a Black family, cruising up US 80 in 1941, the far side of the Edmund Pettus Bridge invisible behind its whale-back crest in the middle, the rider in the passenger's seat directing the driver with *The Green Book*, they would have found no listings for Black-friendly hotels in Selma.

Joe Spinner Johnson did not find Selma so friendly in 1935. Johnson was a leader of the Alabama Sharecroppers Union and an outspoken critic of "exploitative and racially discriminatory practices of wealthy white planters and landowners."[18] On July 11, Johnson was called out of the field into Selma, where a white landlord mob seized him and beat him to death in the Dallas County Jail, then dumped his body in a field forty-five miles away near Greensboro.

Johnson wasn't the only one. The Selma jail had been the site of several notorious lynchings in the 1890s—Willy Webb in 1892, and Daniel Edwards in 1893—when Edmund Pettus was Grand Dragon of the state Klan. He would be elected to the United States Senate in 1896.

From another perspective, when John Lewis and his fellow marchers like Amelia Boynton Robinson were savagely beaten by Alabama State Troopers, the bridge was fulfilling its own destiny, continuous with a long legacy of oppression, intimidation, and abuse of Black people for which its namesake stood. *Nomen est omen.*

Crossing the Edmund Pettus Bridge again in 2018, for the first time in over two decades, I wish that I had had more of a moment with John Lewis thirty years ago, had the guts to go down front and shake his hand, ask him to tell me more, to teach me, point me where to go to learn. But that's not what happened; he was off and we were soon backpack-laden again and shuffling off to geometry class or PE, resuming grade-school gossip and maybe pretending not to have been too shaken by what we had just heard because that would not have been cool.

Turning left after crossing the Edmund Pettus Bridge, we make the Live Oak Cemetery our first stop in Selma. The site sits behind a low wall on Alabama SR 22 that takes you on to Beloit, Orrville, Safford. Live Oak is that familiar, haunting Southern mis-en-scène overhung with gnarled, knotty, Spanish moss-draped live oak branches older than the republic itself, where the air seems darker and rife with either mystery or menace, or both. In other words, a book cover.

Clichéd, maybe, but it's also real, and like everything Southern, a cocktail of living myth and misremembered history. Established in 1829 and expanded in 1877, Live Oak is Southern-old, not English-old, a plot of antebellum antiquity where light perpetual dances with mortal shadow over the bodies of the dead, while rumors about them still flit about like foraging nuthatch in search of something, someone to give them life. To rest in peace here seems a lot to ask for. The cemetery is named for the grandest, most sentimentalized of Southern trees, whose contorted, knobby, skeletonic branches draped with moss like the discarded skins of fugitive ghosts, resemble the contorted, haunted, and very old history of the South itself. Their incredibly strong heartwood is the stuff from which American ships and American myths are made, sometimes—as with "Old Ironsides"—both at the same time. But also: each branch a minor ecosystem of its own playing host to who knows how many forms of vegetal and animal life—ferns, mosses, bugs, birds. As with the contradictions of history, those contortions can be life-giving. Those organisms wise and fortunate enough to root themselves into the clefts and branches of *Quercus virginiana* and feed on the impossibly stout verdure of their over-generous host may hope for a long and healthy life. It is no accident that one of those organisms is a fern named "resurrection." If you would live, they seem to say, you must first mingle with the dead. The live oak has been witness to and sometimes victim of American Sin: greed, war lust, slavery, lynching, violence, waste. In the indomitable tree marrow that courses from its hair-like outer roots to its waxy evergreen leaves run our darkest collective secrets; but its own are even greater, more mysterious, and maybe more full of promise. These trees are older than anything most non-Native peoples in the New World will ever know, a living connection to a time before all of us, before America, before slavery. And if the order of the cosmos is just, the live oaks will outlive us all.

But in the meantime, we park the Odyssey at the first logical place, off to the side of a crushed cinder circular driveway in the newer part of the cemetery. There's not a living soul around. In the center of the circle, a small clapboard springhouse with a wraparound porch gives the requisite plantation aura to the circle next to which it sits: Confederate Circle.

In the middle of the circle, surrounded by the graves of unknown Confederate dead and cannon to defend them, a thirty-eight-foot monument topped with a downcast, caped soldier, his hands on the butt of his rifle, which is pointed to the ground. On either side, the national flag of the Confederate States of America, and the Confederate battle flag. On the pediment, an inscription so loaded with theological freight it would take a dissertation to unpack it:

> THERE IS GRANDEUR IN THE GRAVES
> THERE IS GLORY IN GLOOM.

For all its attention-grabbing height and bluster, the official Confederate monument is not the most startling thing about Confederate Circle. Almost as soon as we step out of the climate-controlled comfort of the Honda into the swampy shade of Confederate Circle, we are struck by it, and without a word we both walk around it, taking it in, as if it were a beached megalodon.

At least this much can be said of the old, off-the-shelf Confederate monuments: even when they were mass-produced in Ohio, they had a certain artistic panache to them, an attention to typography that, while sometimes amateurish, reflect a time when carving things out of stone was actually something people did with their hands. They seemed often to rely on a tacit agreement about symbols, motifs, turns of phrase, even verses of poetry.

So when you see one that works with a different set of visual markers, you notice. And that's what hit us at the edge of Confederate Circle. Its clearly new—brand new, in historical monument terms—and the tell is that it's flanked by not one but two not-at-all-concise explanatory plaques, surrounded by dime-store Rebel flags stabbed into the grass, and emblazoned on the front side with a two-color Confederate battle flag. Atop it, a slightly crazed likeness of Nathan Bedford Forrest. Below it, in all caps—curiously similar to the typeface used on Crimson Tide jerseys—an inscription proclaims:

DEFENDER OF SELMA
WIZARD OF THE SADDLE
UNTUTORED GENIUS
THE FIRST WITH THE MOST

Below which is more obligatory dedicatory text, ending with the national motto of the Confederate States of America (CSA):

DEO VINDICE (WITH GOD AS OUR DEFENDER).

It has been sponsored by the usual suspects—SCV, UDC, and "those who love the South."

The monument was put there in 2000.

The tone of the monument is belligerent, like its honoree, and seems eager to start a fight. Almost every line contains something to designed to provoke. A not-very-subtle double-entendre, the use of the term "Wizard of the Saddle" seems especially calculated, given the timing of the monument. Forrest earned the moniker in his own day for his pro-digious military prowess—which was not enough to defend Selma from a Union raid in April 1865—but there is a subtext at work that does not seem accidental. Forrest is well-known as an accomplished general, but he is better known as the first Grand Wizard of the Ku Klux Klan.

The plaques have even more to say, but right from the start something is different about them.

Whether put up by a state historical commission or tourism office or the Freemasons, American historical markers have a certain uniform look to them. They trade in a visual currency of historical trustworthi-ness: they come in recognizable shapes and often share the same letter-form (Most historical markers in the country are the work of a single studio—Sewah Studios in Marietta, Ohio, the largest historical marker foundry in the country—which created the familiar style in the late 1920s.)

When you see a historical marker in the familiar Sewah serif letter-form (the upward axis of the lowercase "e" is the giveaway), you know—or at least assume—that they contain a certain amount of reliability, that what they say wasn't cast in aluminum without at least some element of peer review. So when you see not one but two historical markers right next to one another, both of irregular dimensions, in Helvetica knock-off typeface, you can bet that what you are about to read is going to be a breathless, wordy attempt to correct one received account with the "true" story. And you can also be sure that the version you are about to read will be shamelessly one-sided and contrarian. You are presented with a tableau not in the visual language of historical authority but of sectarian reactionism. The typeface prepares you for it, if you have seen enough of the sorts of markers, when you read that "Forrest's memory has been gained by the accusation, started by a Northern newspaper during the War, that he had ordered the execution of black troops captured at Fort Pillow in Tennessee." The tone of the whole of four sides of historical markers is not of a complicated figure with some real virtues and some real vices but a defiant defense of a man of unimpeachable virtue. It presents a message for which there is no possible response, nothing left to interrogate, because it concludes with the most classic conversation stopper imaginable:

HAVING ACCEPTED JESUS CHRIST AS HIS LORD AND SAVIOR
IN 1875, HE WAS CALLED HOME OCTOBER 29, 1877.

Now that is not the sort of thing you will read on a state historical marker, for good reason. It's not only goofy and sentimental; it is problematized by the inscription directly under it:

PLAQUE DONATED BY THE ORDER OF THE SOUTHERN CROSS

Founded in 1863 by Leonidas Polk—the famous "fighting bishop" of Sewanee—and others, the Order of the Southern Cross (OSC) is a fraternal organization devoted to "helping to preserve Southern heritage and its history," and not for a moment to be confused with the Brazilian chivalric order who claims among its honored members both Her Royal Highness Elizabeth II, Che Guevara, and the king of Norway. The admission requirements of the American version are both more populist and far more limited. The OSC is open to anyone to join—as long as

he is
~~they are~~ "a male descendant of an honorably serving Confederate soldier, sailor, marine, or member of the civil government." In other words, you are entitled publicly to claim, represent, and celebrate "southern heritage" only if you are a pedigreed White male.

So when the OSC tells you that Nathan Forrest gave his last breath to Jesus, then you would not be wrong to wonder whose Jesus they are referring to. There are—according to the 1860 United States Census—roughly four million good reasons to be highly skeptical of a Jesus under whose cross that number of men and women created in his divine image were sold and traded as chattel, a savior who provides religious cover for a culture war in defense of ideals that nakedly subject one race of people to another.

After John does a dramatic reading of the second plaque in his seersucker planter voice, we wander the circle, stepping over Confederate flags that pepper the weed-whacked lawn. In the shade of a magnolia at the circle's edge I park myself on a bench to marvel at the wonder of this garish new monument. Midmorning sun dapples the granite pediment beneath Forrest's bronze bust. His hair is swept back wildly, eyes deepset in heavy shadow under his furrowed brow. An empirical gaze. From this angle, he is the picture of calculated madness, analytical savagery. It's a powerful depiction of the tactical detachment of a veteran slave seller not above flouting the law, but I am not sure that is what the monument as a whole is going for.

On the grass below the bench, among upturned fallen magnolia leaves like suede slippers and patchy, thinned out crabgrass, a white piece of paper. I turn it over. It is in good condition for a bit of looseleaf in Alabama in July, unweathered, as if some immediately prior visitor left it behind unawares. It reads:

YOU ARE CORDIALLY INVITED TO ATTEND

CONFEDERATE MEMORIAL DAY

COMMEMORATION

AT

CONFEDERATE MEMORIAL CIRCLE

HISTORIC LIVE OAK CEMETERY

SELMA, ALABAMA

THURSDAY 26 APRIL 2018

6:00 PM

The flyer has been edited: the original name and hometown of the guest speaker crossed out and replaced with his substitute. It concludes with a few imperatives:

BE PROUD OF YOUR SOUTHERN HERITAGE!
HONOR YOUR CONFEDERATE ANCESTORS!
BRING YOUR LAWNCHAIRS AND A FRIEND!

I have heard about Confederate Memorial Day, and that in places like Georgia and Alabama it's still a thing. Hell, in Mississippi, Alabama, and South Carolina, it's still an official holiday. So if you are an employee of the state, you can have a state-sponsored day off to HONOR YOUR CONFEDERATE ANCESTORS!

I used to think of groups like the UDC, SCV, and other sponsors of the celebration in the cemetery as Southern versions of the Freemasons: shadowy, even shady, secret society sorts of organizations that may or may not have any actual members.

At least I had never met one. And here in my hand I have evidence that they not only still exist but do get together with lawn chairs every April in the old graveyard in Selma in order, I presume, to sip sweet tea, nibble on pimiento cheese sandwiches, and be proud of their heritage together. It is intriguing, a little exciting, even, to think that we have only narrowly missed these weird revelers performing whatever esoteric annual rites and oblations they come here to supplicate whatever god it is whose protection they claim for themselves. But on closer inspection, maybe even this piece of paper is insufficient proof of their existence. The flyer is dated April 26, 2018. Today is July 11. Is it plausible that this piece of 8.5- × 11-inch Staples copy paper has survived on the ground for three months with nary a tear, ink splotch, or footprint? Or could it have been planted there as evidence that, despite all the commie naysayers and politically correct mafiosi, the UDC is still here? Was one name scratched out and another added simply to indicate that there are more of them than just the people on the program?

While I am still rapt in contemplation at the prospect of a counter-intelligence wing of the UDC, a Lincoln Town Car pulls into the circle driveway. The car is a fleshy hue of pink—Caucasian flesh in January, I mean. The driver, an older woman, rolls down the passenger window and says something to John.

I do not know what she says, but she wheels the big Lincoln behind the minivan, throws it into park, and is soon in deep with John. They are soon walking away and talking, in the direction of the tomb of Edmund Pettus, the two-term US Senator and former Grand Dragon of the Ku Klux Klan, for whom the famous bridge in Selma is named. And William Rufus King, briefly vice president of the United States under the spectacularly incompetent Franklin Pierce. And John Tyler Morgan, a CSA general and later US senator who argued for the repeal of the Fifteenth Amendment, for the deportation of freed slaves to Africa, and the legalization of lynching, and who preceded Edmund Pettus as head of the Klan in Alabama.

I do not know if she is telling John about when an all-White private school was established in Selma in 1965—just a few months after the voting rights marches—it was named for John Tyler Morgan. In 2007, a young African American girl named Shania was admitted, the first nonwhite student in the school's history. Some members of the Morgan community were outraged. One board member quit.

Shania was not personally bullied, but older siblings of her friends were beat up and called "nigger lovers." She couldn't sleep over at her White friends' houses, and nobody from her school would come to her birthday parties. Graffiti on the back of Walmart depicted Shania being lynched. "Nigger" it said, pointing to her head. "Hang the bitches," it said below, next to "MLK is a homosexual" and a drawing of a swastika. Shania spent two unhappy years at Morgan before leaving for the public elementary school.

Morgan Academy is one of a slew of private schools that broke ground after the 1954 US Supreme Court ruling *Brown v. Board of Education of Topeka*, which overturned nearly sixty years of legal segregation. In its decision, Chief Justice Earl Warren wrote that "in the field of public education, the doctrine of 'separate but equal' has no place. Separate educational facilities are inherently unequal."

The ruling set in motion a wave of tactical responses by White citizens opposed to integration. One popular reaction to Brown was the establishment of "segregation academies": private schools not held to the same legal requirements as publicly funded ones. Many segregation academies were established in the mid-sixties, like Lowndes Academy in Lowndesboro, Alabama. Many also adopted the mascot "Rebel," using variations on the familiar, prodigiously mustachioed "Colonel Reb" White planter image borrowed from Ole Miss.

Morgan Academy is still around and is still named after the former Grand Dragon. Nonwhite students are conspicuous by their rarity in photos on the school's website. The school raises funds for itself by host-ing an annual deer hunt and a gun raffle, in which one firearm is raffled off each day for the month of December. I do not know any of this in July of 2018, but if I had I might not have been so surprised to find race rela-tions in Selma as retrograde as they appear today. I will learn much of this later, but today, I am beginning to wonder what has become of John when I wander over in the direction of the Pettus tomb in search of him and his new tour guide.

I intercept them as they are walking back toward Confederate Circle. She asks John what we are doing here. He tells her the basics, mentions that I am working on a book about the South.

"Oh everybody is writing a book these days," she says with a well-practiced eye roll, "especially about the South."

We meet midway between Nathan Forrest and Edmund Pettus on a footpath in-between knee-high marble gravestones. I introduce myself.

She does not ask me what I do, because she has been forewarned.

"My name is Pat Godwin, and I am the president of Chapter Fifty-Three of the United Daughters of the Confederacy."

I can only imagine what sorts of tales she has been telling John for the last fifteen minutes. It is not long before she starts telling me a few, too, but only after she has performed the apparently obligatory UDC back-ground check on my Southern credentials.

"Are you from the South?" she asks.

I tell her that I am from Atlanta, but this does not seem to answer her question.

"Born and raised?"

"Yes," I say.

"Born and raised?" she repeats, as if I have misunderstood or she is unconvinced.

I have never been subjected to two-factor authentication about my own Southernness and feel no urgency to display it. At this particular moment, it is not something I am feeling especially proud of. But I feel unexpectedly placed on the defensive, and quickly summon to mind a snapshot genealogical record, but fortunately she has moved on to something else before it needs to be deployed.

It isn't long before the subject of the Forrest monument comes up. Pat knows the whole story of the project, because it was all her idea. Initially, she seems upbeat, riding high on the news that the city has finally, after a long legal struggle, deeded Confederate Circle and the Forrest monument to the UDC to do with it what they like.

But glee about a legal victory soon yields to bitterness. She relays the story of how the monument was originally erected in the middle of Selma, with money from the City Council—specifically, the discretionary funds of five White members, including the former mayor, Joe Smitherman—but that apparently wasn't good enough for some folks.

The monument was initially unveiled in October 2000 in front of the Joseph T. Smitherman Historic Building, a Greek Revival structure on Alabama Avenue that housed a museum devoted to Selma's history. Built by the Masons in 1847, it has served a school, Confederate hospital, Freedman's Bureau Hospital. During its tenure as the Dallas County Courthouse, on at least two occasions while Pettus and Morgan were Alabama's representatives in the US Senate, Black men being held in the jail were forcibly removed from the building and lynched.

The 2000 placement of the monument on public property in the heart of a city identical with the civil rights movement was met with a collective *Oh hell no* on the part of members of the local African American community. Alternately garlanded with greenery and rope, the monument has been the site of an ongoing contest over the legacy of White supremacy. In January 2001 opponents tried to pull the thing down by tying rope around it—"not around the neck! That's what they did to us," one participant urged. A month later, it was surrounded by evergreen wreaths and cut flower. It was eventually relocated, and Forrest's legacy was adjudicated by a public mock trial in February of the following year. In March 2012, Forrest's bust went mysteriously missing. And despite a $20,000 reward for the head of the Confederacy's most controversial general, it never turned up.

Pat is still sore about the episode. She begins an unsolicited tirade against a woman she calls Rose Sanders, her apparent nemesis. "It's all her doing," she says. Sanders is the founder of the National Voting Rights Museum and Institute, a private organization on the southern side of the

Alabama River, at the foot of the Edmund Pettus Bridge. The first African American woman judge in Alabama, Sanders changed her name to Faya Ora Rose Touré in 2003. But Pat still calls her Rose Sanders.

"She gets on the radio and talks about how horrible White people are. Channel One-Oh-Five. We call it Hate One-Oh-Five. She gets on there and just spews her hatred of White people."

In Pat's telling, Rose is responsible for the fuss about the monument. It was a much-needed tribute to a much-maligned and virtuous warrior, she says, but Rose could not understand any of that. Selma was just fine until Rose and her cronies started agitating. Just look at downtown, she says.

"Plywood City, I call it."

To Pat, Rose is an "outside agitator," a familiar character type here in Selma who came from way up north (North Carolina) just to stir up trouble. She's been doing it a long time, she says. In 1987, Norward Roussell was appointed the first Black superintendent of city schools. When his three-year contract was not renewed by the mostly White school board, Sanders was quick to object. It was "the unfinished business of the 1960s," she said. She helped to make the story national news.[19]

Some in town did not welcome the agitation and blamed it on forces external to Selma. At the time, a former city councilman said that "Rose Sanders is not a Selma native. She has never quite fit in with the White community in Selma."

Nathan Forrest is not a Selma native either, but he seems to have fit in with at least one segment of the White community in Selma just fine.

"What is it that you like so much about Nathan Forrest?" I ask her.

She repeats many of the qualities listed on his monument. "He was an untutored genius," she says, extolling Forrest's military resumé despite his utter lack of book learning. She becomes especially animated in response to a question neither of us asks, about Forrest's involvement with the Klan.

"I am interested in truth, and if Forrest had founded the Klan, I would have no problem admitting to that. But he did not found the Klan. The Klan was not then what it later became, but either way Forrest did not start it."

The first Klan was established in Pulaski, Tennessee, in 1865, and died out in the early 1870s after federal legislation banned the group.

Forrest led the Klan during a period when it was described by a federal grand jury as a "white terrorist" organization instrumental in intimidating newly empowered Black people and preventing them, under the threat of violence, from voting in elections during Reconstruction. Never mind that no one here is arguing that Forrest founded the Klan. That he was asked to be its first Grand Wizard is, however, not really contestable. That part somehow escapes Pat's truth obsession.

It's not the only thing.

Walking back toward Confederate Circle, she expresses an unexpected disdain for Supreme Court Justice John Roberts. What did he do?

"He screwed up the oath of office when Obama was sworn in."

This is the first I have heard of this.

"Yes, Obama was sworn in twice. Did you not know that?" she asks with an expression of what I think is supposed to be surprise, and mutters under hear breath some rhetorical question about what they teach kids these days.

"Help me out," I say. I am not familiar with this particular theory.

"Yes, it's true. Justice Roberts—I liked him until he went and did this—he messed up the words of the oath of office, so they had to do it again. It's the law—you have to do it exactly right, and if you don't do it the way it's supposed to be done, you have to do it over again. So they had to do it a second time, in private."

"So what do you think went down the second time?" I ask.

"Well I don't know. Nobody knows, do they? It was all in secret."

"What do you think might have happened, then?" I ask.

"He could have been sworn in on the Holy Koran, who knows?"

As it is becoming increasingly challenging to accept as gospel truth the account of Nathan Bedford Forrest from a person who still believes that Barack Obama is a secret Muslim, John and I make a move to part ways with our overgenerous hostess.

I take my iPhone out of my back pocket to take a photo. Pat recoils.

"Whoa! Hold on a second—have you been recording me all this time?"

I shouldn't be taken aback at this outburst of suspicion, but I am.

"No," I say. "I just wanted to see if you wouldn't mind if I take your picture next to the Forrest monument."

Her tone shifts dramatically. She is more than happy to oblige a Kodak moment with her pride and joy. I thank her for the opportunity, and for sharing so much unsolicited information with us. We shake hands and start toward the minivan.

The sound of a big diesel tour bus heaving into the cemetery driveway, scraping the low-hanging live oak limbs, stops us short. Pat is frozen in place, staring at the tour bus.

"Well here they come," she says. "Rose's people."

John and I freeze, too. We aren't going anywhere.

Slowly, thirty or so high school kids, mostly Black, alight from the bus and make their way to the Forrest monument. Leading them is an African American woman in middle age. She looks serious. I've heard it said that Selma "goes in for pain": White people regularly reenact the failed Battle of Selma, which no living person remembers; for Black people, Bloody Sunday marks the most searing moment in collective memory, which is living history for many in Selma. Maybe this woman, too. She walks slowly, as if bearing the pain of that history. A history that had to be endured, that maybe she endured. She is in no hurry to greet Pat.

"Oh hello, JoAnne," Pat calls out.

"Hello, Pat," JoAnne says. They do not make eye contact.

The group of students eventually gathers in a loose arc in front of Forrest. Pat does not forfeit the opportunity to introduce herself, with the same line she uses on me.

"My name is Pat Godwin, and I am the president of Chapter Fifty-three of the United Daughters of the Confederacy. I welcome you to Confederate Circle."

The students do not seem to take the hospitality in the way she seems to expect them to.

"So where are y'all from?" Pat asks.

"Washington, DC," one student says from the back row.

"Ohhhh," Pat says. "Trumptown!"

An audible groan, like a rumble of the collective stomach of the group. They are not taking the bait.

For a moment it appears as if it's going to be the Pat Godwin Show. She has taken over as emcee, confidently presenting herself as if the students have come there to see her. I begin to wonder whether the timing of her arrival in advance of "Rose's people" is really such a coincidence.

Pat is into her Forrest routine, dishing out bullet points about who Forrest "really was" and how he's been given a really bad rap lately. And with a sudden flourish she takes awkward leave of the group, apparently reluctant and none too hasty to hand things over to JoAnne, whose account of Forrest is not Pat's.

As Pat sinks into the plush, squishy comfort of the Town Car and fires up the hefty eight-cylinder engine, I wonder if it irks her that she drives a car that shares a name with the Great Emancipator. Does she pine for an alternative history, imagine a world in which things turned out differently and South had won the war, and she would be driving not a Lincoln but a Davis?

When JoAnne takes over, there is a palpable sense of relief, but when she begins talking it's clear that she is not at all interested in who Forrest really was, or whether the Klan was really as bad in 1868 as it was in 1920. She talks to the students with a confident indifference about all that, as if she might even be willing to grant that yeah, Forrest is misunderstood by almost everybody who does not care to read about him. Instead, the theme of JoAnne's Forrest-side chat is about what this particular statue of him means, here, in Selma, at this moment in its history. She points out that the monument was put up in 2000, just months after Selma's first African American mayor, James Perkins, Jr., took office.

"You do the math," JoAnne says.

Perkins replaced Joe Smitherman, who until 2000 had been mayor of Selma since 1964. That's thirty-six years, nearly half of Joe's life. His long tenure is often characterized as politically moderate, enjoying the support of both Black and White people, and like his political godfather, George Wallace, Smitherman changed his segregationist ways when they became unpopular. But early on Smitherman played the "both sides" rhetoric somewhat skillfully, conspicuously bitching on national television in 1965 about the nefarious subjection of Selma to "outside agitation groups," including the Nazi Party and the States' Rights Party, as well as the man he infamously called "Martin Luther Coon." Smitherman later claimed that it was a "slip of the tongue," an attempt at self-defense convincing to absolutely no one.

Whatever else the Forrest monument is, it is a memento to a political status quo its supporters were not pleased to see yield to a new order. Pat sees that order represented in the boarded-up stores along Water Street and Alabama Avenue. Some in Selma blame the *ancien régime* for the fact that the city has lost a third of its population since 1965, when White folks began to flee the downtown and start new schools for their own kind, like John Tyler Morgan Academy. Today, enrollment at public

Selma High is 100 percent non-white. A de facto segregation has been revived in Selma, which is now hemorrhaging its population faster than anywhere else in the state.

A sudden pop like a firecracker goes off to our left. Most of the students do not even flinch, but I exchange a *what-was-that* look with one of them and turn to look behind me towards the low stone wall running along the backside of the cemetery. It is low enough for someone to hide behind and hurl lit Black Cats over just to startle or distract people from, say, a conspiratorial account of Nathan Bedford Forrest. Is this where Pat ran off to? Maybe the UDC Counterintelligence Squad has a tactical munitions wing. I look around for the roof of her Town Car peeking out above the cemetery wall, but seeing nothing, I turn back to JoAnne.

Her tone is steady, even, nonplussed. She's given this speech before. If she has an "agenda," as Pat has it, it sure doesn't sound like it. She does not tell the students what to think, but it's clear where she stands. Where Pat wanted to talk about a few suppressed aspects of the man on the monument, JoAnne is interested in what the act of erecting this monument in Selma in 2000 means.

By the time the stark contrast between the two perspectives fully develops, John and I are aware that we are witnessing the confrontation of the two antipodes of racial discourse in the United States: the clash of an ideology with historical context, the encounter of the mythological nostalgia of a graying generation with a younger group who not only has no interest in that version of the past, but is wise to its lack of innocence.

We also become aware that the two of us—balding, middle-aged White men with graying beards, in a minivan, hanging around Confederate Circle in Selma with cameras—probably do not look that innocent to the students, either. Some of them occasionally shoot glances our way. *Who are those dudes?* they seem to ask. While we are beholding the spectacle of the phenomenon of American race relations being crystallized into a single moment of conflict around a single contested monument, we realize that we are part of that spectacle, too. It becomes apparent that we are not the only ones to get a load of the bizarre, that among the first things the students see upon alighting from the tour bus are three White people hanging out with Nathan Bedford Forrest. Only then does it become thinkable that this group of young adults may have had to steel themselves for an encounter with us, to prepare themselves for the possibility that we would not exactly welcome them warmly.

Out of a desire to respect the students' space, and not to come across as emissaries for the UDC, we quietly return to the minivan. Back in the driver's seat, I am grateful for a moment that we aren't driving John's 1977 Ford pickup that we took on the first few tours and am happy to embrace the prejudice against minivan drivers over the prejudice against drivers of pickup trucks. For one thing, the Ford might only have confirmed suspicions that we were there as Forrest admirers. For another, unlike the pickup, the minivan has air conditioning. It's barely 10:00 in the morning, but it's already sweltering. Slowly—reluctantly, even— I pull the Honda into the circular driveway.

Near the edge of Confederate Circle, a young African American man is looking down at the graves at his feet. He is wearing a black T-shirt with first names printed in white: Emmett, Amadou, Trayvon, Eric, Mike.

John rolls down the passenger-side window and calls out to him. He remarks about his T-shirt, asks him about his tour group.

They are on a civil rights bus trip from DC. They have already hit Greensboro, Atlanta, and Birmingham. They've just come from Montgomery and are on their way to Jackson. We have a lot to talk about.

I throw the car into park and we get out. We stand next to the idling minivan and talk about places we've both seen in the last few days, about the coincidence of our itineraries. He's actually interested in what we are doing, and he's excited about being on this trip. I sense a tinge of unfamiliarity—and maybe jealousy—arising within my gut: I never went on any school field trip that aroused that kind of existential attention, that was both intriguing and vitally important. I tell him I am really glad he is getting the opportunity to do it, but I don't know whether or not the sincerity I say it with really lands with him.

In a few moments, three other students come over from Confederate Circle. We realize how weird and discomforting the scene must look from a distance: these two bearded white dudes in a Confederate cemetery who not five minutes earlier were apparently hanging out with the president of the UDC are now talking to a young Black man in a T-shirt, listing names of Black victims of White violence. They size us up—not suspiciously, but definitely with caution.

"Oh we aren't with her," John says. "We were just looking at the Forrest monument—kind of baffled that it's even here at all, frankly— and she came up to us."

"Oh," a young African American woman says, with relief. "'Cause we were wondering."

We tell the new arrivals what we're doing, too, talk about how we're driving around to many of the same places they are visiting, shooting photographs, films, writing about it. About how we never did this when we were their age, and how we regret that now. They seem genuinely interested.

Another group—much larger this time, a half-dozen or more strong— wanders over. It's clear now that they aren't coming over because they want to hear what we have to say. They are coming in for their friends' moral support. As backup. I'm struck by how much these young people look out for each other, how protective they seem to be of one another.

One member of the first group turns to one of the new arrivals.

"Oh it's okay," she says. "They're woke."

The last group comes over, and in their midst, walking slowly but with deep intent, is JoAnne.

I expect to meet with open suspicion from her, and by now I wouldn't blame her. It seems only natural and just that her beef with Pat might rub off on us a little. The whole student group has gathered around the idling Odyssey, windows rolled down and A/C blasting. JoAnne moves into the crowd and is quickly brought up to speed about what in the world we are doing there. She seems to be relieved too, as if for once she doesn't have to argue with White folks.

"Move out the way," she says. "I got to get some of that air conditioning."

JoAnne leans up against the minivan in heavy shade under a high-branched live oak. Cooled air spills out of the passenger window, hot exhaust from the tailpipe. She lets out a deep breath like an unleashed spirit.

Leaving the cemetery, we stop at the Coffee Shoppe on Broad. It's an unpretentious one-level structure that could pass for a barber shop. Now owned by Our Lady Queen of Peace Catholic Church, the building used to be home to the Thirsty Boy, a Selma institution opened by John E. Warren in 1962 that served foot-long hot dogs, ice cream, and apple tarts to White customers in the dining room where African Americans were not allowed.

On Independence Day 1964, Silas Norman and three other African American SNCC workers attempting to eat at the Thirsty Boy were refused service and told to leave by the owner. When they tried a second time, Selma's notorious Sheriff Jim Clark chased them out of the entrance with a cattle prod and arrested them. The following year, the Thirsty Boy was found to have violated the 1964 Civil Rights Act and was ordered by a federal judge to comply with the law. Unlike Georgia's Lester Maddox, Warren adapted, and kept the Thirsty Boy open and on the level with the federal government, but not without a fight. John Warren died in 1977, and the Thirsty Boy passed down to his son Billy.

The Thirsty Boy closed in 1985. When Billy Warren sold the place to pursue other interests in Jacksonville, Florida, he reminisced with pride about the tumultuous days of its past. Billy proudly thought of the Thirsty Boy as a pioneer, a site of firsts. "We were the first place hit by civil rights demonstrators," he told a reporter in 1985. "We were the first to hire a black waitress."[20] The Coffee Shoppe is a Black-owned business now. Staff feed lattes and pastries through the walk-up window that used to be for "colored" folk. Inside, towards the back, a man on headphones works on a laptop. He does not register our entry. While the barista brews an espresso, I notice a flyer next to the register advertising a group that meets twice a month at the cafe. They call it "Chat n' Chew," but the fare is meatier than the name suggests. Sponsored by a local organization called the Selma Center for Nonviolence, Truth and Reconciliation—a group committed to "building the beloved community"—the biweekly sessions are meant to be a chance for local people to talk openly about hard subjects, with a view toward healing. The sponsoring group is led by one of the daughters of Rose Sanders.

I ask the non-barista about the Chat n' Chew.

They still meet, she says. "It's usually just a few of them now, if any. At first it was packed. People showed up, and it was really good. But after a while people just stopped coming."

A year later, we return to Selma. In the meantime I have learned that the JoAnne we met a year earlier is JoAnne Bland, a native Selmian.

JoAnne was at the Edmund Pettus Bridge on March 7, 1965, "Bloody Sunday." She stood on the Selma Side of the bridge as the front line of marchers was confronted by state troopers on the far side of the bridge. She was eleven years old and had already been arrested at least a dozen times. JoAnne's story is one I missed, too, even though it was right in front of me fifteen years earlier, when, during my first month as an assistant professor at Baylor University, her story was published in the university's magazine. It's taken me at least that long to pay attention.

"I saw this horse running full speed," she said of Bloody Sunday. "I don't know why this woman didn't hear it. The sound of his hooves on that bridge was awful. She stepped right in front of it, and this horse ran right over her. The sound of her head hitting that pavement was the last thing I remember. I fainted."[21]

Something dripping on her skin brought JoAnne around in the backseat of a car. When she woke up, she saw her sister Linda was leaning through the car window. *Linda's tears*, she thought. "When I came fully awake, I realized what was falling on me was not her tears, it was her blood. She had been beaten. She had a wound on her head. Her whole face was covered with blood; it was dripping into her blouse and soaking everything. And she was only fourteen."

Before we arrive in Selma, we meet up with my cousin Bruce and his friend Chip Brantley, cohost of *White Lies*, a podcast about the culture of silence around the murder of Unitarian minister James Reeb in Selma in 1965. Chip—like almost everyone who pauses for long enough in this town—has a Pat Godwin story. Over a barbecue lunch in Birmingham, we find our Pat tales follow a familiar script. Chip gives us JoAnne's phone number, and suggests we contact her.

A few days later, John calls JoAnne and arranges for us to meet at the Coffee Shoppe on Broad. She is clearly a legend around here, but unlike her counterpart in the Confederate Cemetery, she seems to carry a manifest indifference to celebrity. She is an almost intimidating force, a bearer of personal and national history in a way that I will probably never understand.

She is sitting at the back table when we approach, a little sheepishly. *You may not remember us*, John tells her. But she does.

"Oh yeah," she says. "Y'all were the ones in that ugly-ass minivan."

This time it is as if we all exhale together, a sort of sigh of collective relief that we don't have to go through the small talk. We have a common, if brief, history. It's often a shock for sheltered, private school White boys like me to come across a Pat Godwin, as if all our habituation in the American idea of inevitable forward progress has inculcated in us a naïve sense of surprise that someone in the twenty-first century could hold such views. At the mention of Pat, JoAnne groans.

She has seen all this shit before. She and Pat have such a long history that when outsiders enter into it, it can feel like this confrontation is happening for the first time, in real time. Pat, JoAnne tells us, has got her encampment outside Selma called Fort Dixie. She lives there, behind a huge, gated entrance featuring every version of the Confederate flag there is. Ultimately what seems so intransigent to JoAnne is not Pat's prodigious racism but her seemingly insatiable need to insert herself at the center of the story. Pat Godwin is an interesting character, that's for sure. But it says something about a city with such a deep, rich, complicated past and present—a city that could exist nowhere else in the world but in the American South—that so many of those who stop here for long enough come away from this place with a Pat Godwin story.

While we were witnessing the Pat Godwin Show in Confederate Circle, JoAnne just held back, standing in the center of the group of students. She did not interrupt her or call out her convenient untruths. Her patient waiting a kind of expression of realist hope that this old-school blather will go on for—*How long? Not long*—and that this distended filibuster on "Southern culture" that has been going on for over a century and a half will eventually exhaust itself, tire out, and have nothing left; it will soon be no more threatening than spent shells in an Alabama quail field, a reminder of a violent force that has blown its wad.

Gee's Bend

Alabama SR 22 takes you on to Beloit, Orrville, Safford. When it ends, we pick up SR 5 and follow it as far as Alberta and turn south for the tiny hamlet of Boykin. You've got to want to go there: like a giant cul-de-sac on an inland peninsula, it's not on the way to anywhere. It sits on a bend in the Alabama River, across from the town of Camden. Boykin is its official name, but it is still known as Gee's Bend, after the cotton plantation established here by Joseph Gee in 1816. Gee came here from Halifax County, in northeastern North Carolina, with eighteen enslaved men and women. When he died, he had three times as many, which he willed to his nephews. In 1840 they sold the property to Mark Pettway, a relative back in Halifax County. When Pettway relocated from North Carolina, he made his one hundred slaves walk the 700-mile journey to Alabama on foot.

Today the population of Gee's Bend is roughly 750—entirely Black, and mostly descendants of enslaved people on Gee's and Pettway's plantation.

Many of the residents still carry the Pettway name, a vestige of a time when neither their identity nor their work was their own.

Arlonzia Pettway's great-grandmother was enslaved here. She clutched her mother's quilt in her thirteen-year-old hands when she was lured aboard a slave ship with red ribbons and lights and kidnapped from Africa. Descendants of that quilt and others were often burned for heat in cold seasons, later descendants brought not warmth but fame, and consolation.

All around Gee's Bend are painted murals depicting designs for quilts created by the women of the town, who have been making quilts in a distinctive style for generations. This is not your grandmother's patchwork. The quilts from here are highly stylized works of abstract textile art. Frequently highly improvisational and personal pieces, they are jazz in cotton. Reappropriations of the raw materials of their oppressors' cash crops, new orchestrations of old tunes.

When we arrive at the nondescript white cinderblock building that houses the Gee's Bend Quilters' Collective, we are unsure if we are in the right place. We ring the doorbell and are greeted inside. The workshop is a low-ceilinged, fluorescently lit studio filled with sewing stations, bolts of fabric and stacks of batting, spools and spools of thread. One elderly woman is at work on a richly colored, extraordinarily patterned quilt. In the next room is a shop/gallery of quilts. Larger quilts sell for thousands of dollars.

I cannot afford anything more than a few coasters, but it feels like justice. Exploited for their free labor for generations, the residents of Gee's Bend haven't just turned the tables now. They are doing something far more radical than simply selling their wares, earning their own profits rather than someone else's. Rather, they are—here in the heart of the Black Belt, a place that White America tried to forget, performing an ongoing act of cultural generosity, creating objects that have no real purpose other than that they are beautiful in the deepest sense of the term: they are challenging manipulations of texture and color that reward attention, open up imaginative possibilities, reorient vision. They are wholly indigenous and unrepeatable.

"I never thought I would be lifted up and feel so great because of what I made," Pettway told Wes Smith of the *Orlando Sentinel*.[22] "I didn't think nothing of those quilts. I thought of them as common quilts." But Michael Kimmelman of the *New York Times* did not think of them as common.

He described them as "some of the most miraculous works of modern art America has produced. Imagine Matisse and Klee (if you think I'm wildly exaggerating, see the show) arising not from rarefied Europe, but from the caramel soil of the rural South in the form of women, descendants of slaves when Gee's Bend was a plantation."[23]

I do not think Kimmelman was exaggerating.

The "show" he refers to is a pioneering exhibition at the Whitney Museum in New York in 2002, which introduced the Benders to the world, and brought them wholly unexpected attention.[24] The attention was not at all ephemeral, either. In 2006, The United States Postal Service released a series of stamps featuring the Quilters of Gee's Bend.

The attention directed to Gee's Bend is largely the fruit of the interventions of William Arnett, a sometimes-controversial art collector from Columbus, Georgia. In 2010, after years of supporting and publicizing the work of African artists and outsider artists from the South, Arnett founded the Souls Grown Deep Foundation to advocate "the inclusion of Black artists from the South in the canon of American art history and [to foster] economic empowerment, racial and social justice, and educational advancement in the communities that gave rise to these artists."[25]

Arnett was a passionate, if sometimes avuncular, apologist for Black folk art, sometimes to his own misfortune. He rubbed a lot of people the wrong way, especially sectors of the museum and media establishment that were not ready to acknowledge artists like Thornton Dial and Lonnie Holley as belonging in the same authorized space as Thomas Eakins and Edward Hopper. A 1995 episode of 60 Minutes entitled "Tin Man" traded upon well-trodden stereotypes to cast the story in terms of the illiterate minority artist manipulated and exploited by an educated, rich, White opportunist masquerading as a liberator. The episode was deeply damaging to Arnett's reputation, and probably says as much, if not more, about the television news market than it does about Arnett. He had done something akin to what Paul Simon had done with the African artists who contributed to Graceland, by bringing them attention. But Arnett's foundation has aimed even higher, by ensuring a livelihood to Black artists and an investment in the cultures and communities that have produced them.

Arnett didn't come to Gee's Bend until the 1980s, but Mary Lee Bendolph was here in 1965 on the day King came. He preached at the Pleasant Grove Baptist Church and urged the people of Gee's Bend to register to vote. Many of them took him up on it. But in order to do so, they had to cross to the other side of the Alabama River, to the much larger city of Camden, the seat of Wilcox County. The only way to get there was by a ferry. Until the civil rights movement, no Black person was registered to vote in Wilcox County. When citizens of Gee's Bend took the ferry to Camden to register to vote, "the ferry nearly capsized as Benders swarmed into Camden, clapping hands, singing," as J. R. Moehringer put it.[26] The elation in evidence on that ferry ride makes sense on its own, but even more so considering the backstory.

Sherriff Lummie Jenkins, who ran Wilcox County from 1939 to 1971, and the ruling powers in Camden discontinued the ferry service in 1962, forcing the people of Gee's Bend to make a two-hour drive to Camden. Lummie said, "We didn't close the ferry because they were black. We closed it because they forgot they were black."

That's what one might expect of Alabama in 1962. But this place is nothing if not a landscape of left turns. The Gee's Bend ferry is running again, but not on diesel like it used to. Now powered by rechargeable lithium-ion batteries, it is the first electric passenger ferry in the nation.

The Night the Lights Went Out in Marion

While Selma is known for the famous marches that began there in 1965, those marches actually began forty-six miles north of Gee's Bend in Marion, the Perry County seat. More specifically, the marches originated in February 1965 a few hundred feet away from Zion United Methodist Church in a second-story cell at the Perry County Jail on the corner of Pickens and Greene Streets, where Billie Jean Young, a poet, playwright, and professor at nearby Judson College, tells me the story.

"Dr. King sent people like James Orange and others here to the Black Belt to work with the youth, and that was the game changer," Young says. Marion had long been a center of education in the Black Belt. In 1867, the American Missionary Association, along with the Freedmen's Bureau, chartered the Lincoln Normal School in Marion for formerly enslaved African American students. Lincoln educated generations of Black Alabamians, including Coretta Scott King and Jean Childs Young, for over a century until its last class graduated in 1969. In the 1960s, it was fertile ground for recruiting Black students to the movement. Young explains: "James would come here from Greene County and Hale County, and he would go to those schools earlier, and get to Lincoln before noon, and those kids would be waiting for him. Sometimes they'd have demonstrations, march to some of the eateries that didn't allow Black people to eat there, march downtown, or just march for the heck of it because they were mad that day, you know, about the conditions under which they lived."

Agents from the FBI and local law enforcement had been monitoring the movements in Marion and had targeted Orange for his civil rights work. On February 18, 1965, Orange led a march from Mount Zion United Methodist Church across the street to the county courthouse. Among the protestors were students from Lincoln. Orange was arrested for "disorderly conduct" and "contributing to the delinquency of minors," and held in the Perry County Jail. On February 18, 1965, James Lee Orange was arrested and held in this building for allegedly inducing local schoolchildren to stay out of school in protest of local voting practices. In protest of Orange's detention, local civil rights leaders organized a march from Zion Methodist Church to the jail. Among the marchers: Jimmie Lee Jackson, a twenty-six-year-old local deacon in St. James Baptist Church, and his eighty-two-year-old grandfather, Cager Lee.

Albert ("Big Al") Turner, a Marion native and civil rights leader, Reverend James Dobynes, a local minister, and C. T. Vivian of Atlanta led the march out of Zion at 9:15 PM. About 500 peaceful protestors turned out of the church onto a Pickens Street lined on both sides with law enforcement officers, including Alabama State Troopers, Marion Police and Perry County deputies. The marchers began to process down the block to the jail, singing and praying peacefully. Not fifty feet away from Zion, the marchers were confronted by state troopers, who ordered them to disperse. As planned, Reverend Dobynes knelt to pray before returning into the church. A state trooper clubbed him in the head and dragged him to the jail where Orange was being held.

Suddenly, the streetlights were turned off. In the darkness, Alabama state troopers, Marion police, and Perry County deputies began to billy club and pistol-whip protestors.

They arrested some marchers and pressed others to return to the church, where police had blocked the front entrance. Forced to go around back, the protesters were met with more violence. During the chaos, in a cafe behind Zion, local Baptist deacon Jimmie Lee Jackson was shot in the stomach by trooper James Bonard Fowler.

Albert Turner, Sr. saw it happen:

In the melee in back of the church, Jimmy's grandfather was hit in the back of the head with a billy club and his skull was bust. He left the church and went down to the café to have Jimmy carry him to the hospital. Jimmy immediately tried to rush out, forgetting about what was going on, to take his grandfather to the hospital. As he attempted to go out of the door, these troopers met him and forced them back into the building. Of course, Jimmy kind of insisted that he wanted to carry his grandfather to the doctor and they insisted that he did not go. From that they ganged him, physically subdued him and put him on the floor of the café. There they started to whip him up pretty bad. His mother was in the café also. She had come down with her daddy. She just couldn't stand it no longer, so she took a drink bottle and tried to knock people off her son because they was going to kill him right there on the floor, it appeared. When she hit them, they knocked her out. And then they took Jimmy and pinned him against the walls of the building and at close range they shot him in the side. After shooting him, they ran him out of the door of the café. Some of the remaining troopers was lined up on the sidewalk, back towards the church. He had to run through a cordon of policemen, then, with billy sticks, and as he ran down, they simply kept hitting him. He made it back to the door of the church, and just beyond the church, he fell.

Young tells me how some people in Marion say that after he was shot, Jackson was brought to the Perry County Jail to be booked. Jimmie Lee died at Good Samaritan Hospital in Selma eight days later. Founded just a year earlier by the Fathers of St. Edmund and staffed by nuns of the Sisters of St. Joseph, Good Samaritan was the only hospital in nine counties that would take Jackson, who was refused treatment everywhere else because he was Black.[27]

Outrage over Jackson's murder propelled the Selma-to-Montgomery marches the month after Jackson's death. An elderly local activist named Lucy Foster first proposed the idea of carrying Jackson's body all the way to Montgomery and laying it at the doorstep of Governor George Wallace. Eleven days after Jackson's death, marchers, led by John Lewis, Hosea Williams, and Albert Turner, were met with a reprise of the state-sponsored violence at the Marion march, but on a much larger scale. A second march took place two days later, on "Turnaround Tuesday," but did not proceed past the Edmund Pettus Bridge. On March 21, 1965, two weeks after Bloody Sunday, approximately 4,000 marchers crossed the Pettus Bridge under federal protection.

Cager Lee, Jackson's grandfather, was on the front line in Selma that day, alongside Martin Luther King Jr. The March was "like nothing Selma had ever seen before or dreamed of," Paul Good wrote in the *Washington Post* in March 1965.[28] And Cager Lee "knew better what it was like than anyone else. For him, it was loss and gain to the roots of his soul."[29]

To Lee, the march from Selma to Montgomery was what his grandson had lived and died for.

"Yes, it was worth the boy's dyin'," Lee said. "And he was a sweet boy. Not pushy, not rowdy. He took me to church every Sunday. worked hard. But he had to die for somethin'. And thank God it was for this."

A 1965 grand jury in Perry County declined to indict the trooper who shot Jackson. He was never questioned by local law enforcement or the FBI, whose agents were present in Marion on February 18th, 1965. For many years the identity of the state trooper who shot Jackson was not publicly known, until a 2005 profile in the *Anniston Star* revealed him to be James Bonard Fowler.[30] In 2007, Fowler was indicted for second-degree murder. After years of delays, he pled guilty to second-degree manslaughter in 2010. He served five months of a six-month sentence.

Billie Jean Young stands in the corner of the jail, next to the cell where Orange was held. Her hands hang through the slim panes of a jalousie window. Peeling paint curls up from the wall. Prisoners used to hang their hands out like this, she tells me. "From outside, all you could see were hands."

The jail has long been abandoned and is showing it. The building has a story to tell, and Dr. Young wants to make sure it is passed on.

At the time, Young was two counties away in Choctaw County. Despite its proximity to Marion and Selma, Choctaw felt like a world away. "We had one TV station, and it was coming out of Mississippi. They would 'snow' the TV when news of the movement came on. Somehow, it just miraculously got snowed, so we didn't hear too much about that was happening up right here, and I lived sixty-seven miles from Selma. There was no cable, there were few telephones, there was no internet." Young continues:

From Choctaw County, Young landed in Selma shortly after the height of the marches. "I was working for one of the antipoverty programs of

President Johnson, working for a farmers' co-op." In 1965, leaders for
the Student Nonviolent Coordinating Committee in Selma—including
Marion's Albert Turner—proposed the idea of a farmers' cooperative,
which led in 1967 to the establishment of Southwest Alabama Farmers
Cooperative Association (SWAFCA). Facing displacement and migration to northern cities, Black farmers found in SWAFCA a way to com-
bine resources to keep their farms and assert their economic power.
But it was not without resistance: when the Federal Office of Economic
Opportunity awarded SWAFCA a substantial federal grant, the funding was blocked by Selma mayor Joe Smitherman and Alabama governor Lurleen Wallace, who tried to argue that the co-op was linked with
Stokely Carmichael and "Black Power" movements in Alabama. Office
of Economic Opportunity (OEO) director R. Sargent Shriver overruled
the governor, and SWAFCA became a model for Black economic development. It was also a turning point for Young. "It was the economic
development aspect following the civil rights and voting rights protests
of 1965, so I was working with many of the people at SWAFCA in Selma
who had been directly involved in the movement. I caught the fire."

Foot soldiers in Selma weren't Young's only encounter with the movement's leadership. She says, "I met Dr. King when he came to Selma on
the way to the Poor People's Campaign. He came back to Selma just
before he was killed." King visited Young's church, Tabernacle Baptist,
in Selma in February 1968. "I didn't wash my hand for the next day.
We knew that we were in the presence of greatness. He didn't have to
die for us to know that. Dr. King walked in, it was like Christ." Two
months later, Young was in Atlanta for King's funeral. "And that's what
hecklers were actually saying to us on the sidewalk: 'Your Black Jesus
gone.' In Atlanta, there were people there selling us Dr. King—selling
us books and magazines, glossies had been created. And I learned that
if you don't chronicle your history, somebody else would do it for you,
and do it quickly."

Young's time in the northeast opened her eyes to other disparities she
hadn't known in the South: "I found after the movement that Whites in
the South were more willing to listen to my complaints about their racism than they were in the North. Because the northerners didn't understand it. Matter of fact, most northerners think all southerners are dumb,
not just Black folks. I found that out when I went north." One White
southern law student at Boston College told Young that his experience in

the North was the first time he felt equal to Black people. Northerners, he told her "don't think I'm smart, either."

In 1972, Young ended up in Marion as a student at Judson, and spent thirty years as an attorney, community organizer, poet, and playwright. In 2006, she returned to Judson, where she serves as associate professor of fine and performing arts and artist-in-residence. She has written three books and plays about Fannie Lou Hamer and Jimmie Lee Jackson. The sense that many visitors have—that there is something different about Marion—drew Young back and keeps her here. "If you've been told that you're better than other people all your life," she says, "you're likely to believe it. And if you have been taught, by the same token, that you are less than, you're going to believe that. And so there's a lot of unlearning to go on."

The restoration of the Perry County Jail can, Young believes, facilitate that unlearning. "One of the purposes of this museum is to chronicle history here, so that a thinking person, a person with some analytical powers, will be able to come in here and see what life was like, to make their own decisions about whether a movement was needed, and whether or not it has helped us. I think the movement has helped us all in the sense that it has brought [this history] to the fore. It is out."[31]

Professor Young's big vision for the site led to a $500,000 grant from the National Park Service in March 2018, intended to fund the rehabilitation of the jail into a voting rights museum and theater space where plays about the movement, some written by young and aspiring playwrights, can be performed for visitors. Marion's children, Young hopes, will have not just a place to call home, but a story to inhabit for themselves. "[I]f we can leave the story here for future generations, maybe they won't have to cross this path again. We need to chronicle all of our history. You don't write it down . . . it gets lost."

The Perry County Jail's story is a somber one, "but it is a history worth telling. A history worth preserving. And it is a precious history, and this jail is precious to me for that reason because it was a place of infamy, and we can make it into a place of knowledge and understanding and hopefully some reconciliation."

Young died in 2021. The future of the jail is uncertain.

West of Marion on US 80, the Marengo County seat of Demopolis is the last town of any seize until Meridian, Mississippi. The WPA Guide to Alabama describes Demopolis as a "quiet, leisurely town, built about a grassy, deeply shaded square."[32] The town is so quiet and leisurely that in the wee hours of a Saturday in July 2016, a Demopolis police officer patrolling a decidedly uneventful city center fell asleep at the wheel and crashed his squad car into the Confederate monument just off the town square, sending Johnny Reb tumbling from his pedestal.

By morning, rumors were already swirling. "There was jubilation on the African American side of town," a Black pastor told the *Washington Post*. On the White side, there was anguished head scratching, along with speculation that it was part of a plot, a local version of the George Soros–funded "agitation" strategy. "He hit the statue on purpose," one local White man suggested. "Ain't no way to tell what they paid him."[33]

No sooner had the sun risen on Demopolis than were folks campaigning for either its restoration or to leave it just the way it was. *We need to unite together*, some said. Others got in on the act too, including no less than Pat Godwin, who urged White people in Demopolis to "Be proud of your history."

The felling of the Confederate statue became another opportunity for Demopolis to live into the idealism of its name, or not. The city decided to do something unusual in our day: to talk about it. White people told of how little they ever thought about the statue, despite driving past it daily. It had become a part of the shrubbery. They were surprised to learn that African Americans didn't see it that way. The White residents also began to learn why they never said anything about it, either. The City Council voted in 2017 not to return the Confederate soldier and approved a plan to replace it with an obelisk in memory of "all the fallen war dead." In December 2018, the new version of the memorial was completed. Like the top of the new obelisk, the promise of the exercise in democracy that led to it was blunted. Members of the SCV, the UDC, and other neo-Confederate organizations were quietly proclaiming the new monument as a victory. On a stop here in 2018, the pedestal remains vacant.

Demopolis was established in 1817 by members of the "Association of French Emigrants for the Cultivation of the Vine and Olive,"[34] a group of "fugitive French comrades of the exiled Napoleon,"[35] and given a name with all the dignified air and high ideals of Greek civilization. "No stranger colonists ever penetrated a wilderness. They were cultured people from the heroic battlefields in Europe, and the glittering drawing rooms of the old French aristocracy. None had ever set foot in a plowed field."

The attempt to grow grapes and olives was not a success, but local Choctaw taught them how to raise corn and beans. They did not lose heart: "They hired German redemptioners to do the harder labor, but the Germans were arrogant and unwilling."[36] Despite attempting something authentically American by making a "lesser" race of people do all the hard work, misfortune and poor executive function dogged the settlement, and the French could never quite get handle on Alabama. So they eventually left, and in came the rich descendants of English settlers, who built "fine old mansions" with the wealth that they accumulated through cotton and slave labor.

But in the twentieth century, in many ways, the town has tried to be true to its name as "The City of the People." Unlike Selma and other towns in the Black Belt, desegregation proved successful in Demopolis, whose public schools are representative of the town's fifty–fifty racial makeup. As David Montgomery writes,

> Progress in Demopolis has been complicated, though: As recently as 2003, students at the high school attended separate proms. Black students would go to the sanctioned school prom; White students would be invited to a private spring formal. Yet current students can't imagine such a practice. Instead, together they dance the night away—at Gaineswood plantation, where the big house looks exquisitely Old South in prom pictures.[37]

One all-White segregation academy was established in Demopolis, but it didn't take. Demopolis Academy—later renamed West Alabama Preparatory School, whose acronym is one rearranged letter away from WASP—is no longer in existence. In nearby Linden, where Ralph David Abernathy was born and later led school desegregation campaigns, White people took flight. As in Selma, the student body of the public high school is entirely African American. Two miles away, there is not a single Black student at the all-White Marengo Academy when we pass through the county in 2018.[38] The local football field has become a battleground for White control under the aegis of the state's favorite pastime.[39]

The local newspaper in Linden, the *Democrat-Reporter*, had been in the Sutton family since 1917. Its editor until 2019, Goodloe Sutton, watched subscriptions dwindle to the low thousands. But declining readership wasn't all he was upset about. In 2019, he fumed that "Democrats

in the Republican Party and Democrats are plotting to raise taxes in Alabama." Enough of the "socialist-communist idealogy [sic]," Sutton wrote.
"Time for the Ku Klux Klan to night ride again."[40]

The paper didn't survive the inevitable national backlash. The
Democrat-Reporter was not unlike the private paper bullhorns that
Thomas Watson and John Addison Turner ran in the nineteenth century. *The Democrat-Reporter* was a good example of what happens when a
single demagogue controls the local newspaper, which Sutton apparently
tried to do even after he was forced to yield his editorship and allegedly
sold the paper to a new owner. The paper never published another issue
after 2019.

At lunchtime in Mobile in 1997, something shifts. A twist in understanding, a new turn in perception—it throws my understanding of the South
off balance.

There's a version of American history that we all learned in school:
before it was a nation, the patchwork collection of English colonies began
in New England and Virginia, and then gradually spread west and south.
America was a porous, fibrous sheet of paper, the first settlements like
inkblots that slowly bled out towards the edges of the blank white page.
Expansion moved right to left: first Georgia, then Alabama, then Mississippi, and so on.

But Mobile is a whole new inkblot.

The first clue that there's something different about it is in the way
you say its name. If it were in Italy, it would be pronounced *MO-bee-lay*,
in Georgia *MOW-bile*, and anywhere else just like the phones, to rhyme
with "global," which is how I imagine it sounds in the mouths of the
few Idahoans or Canadian linguists who come here. But the French
pronunciation lingers on, a trace of an alternative origin story.

At lunchtime, dozens of locals cross Cathedral Square for a midday
mass at the Cathedral Basilica of the Immaculate Conception. The building is huge: the six Doric columns on the portico are more what you'd
expect from a Federal Building than a church, but twin gold-domed
towers on either side give it away. The Basilica is assertive in a way that
Catholic churches in the South usually aren't. It is grand, confident,
and—in the middle of the day in August—packed.

Everywhere in the South you regularly encounter the visual idiom of Southern Protestantism: wreathed and silk-flowered roadside crosses *marking the sites of fatal road accidents, mostly unsteepled one-room white clapboard church buildings punctuating the landscape with regular judgment and occasional grace, tacked up on telephone poles, hand-scrawled signs exhorting the wayfarer to GET RIGHT WITH GOD. If you ask a New Yorker or a German—or even an Alabamian, for that matter—to sketch the religious landscape of the state, they might give you something like this.

But Mobile is more crucifix than bare cross, more Martin of Tours than Martin Luther. Catholicism is front-and-center here and is written into the cityscape. Streets are named for Saints Francis, Louis, Michael, Anthony, and the Immaculate Conception. The cathedral bell marks the time according to a different, more ancient order that has roots here older than Alabama, older even than Protestantism. By the time the Waldsee-müller Map was printed in 1507, the Spaniards had already named the bay for the Holy Spirit. Mobile is old, but not as old as the native tribes who have been mostly displaced from here, who still lend their names to counties in the region. Nor is the Basilica a dead monument, but—to judge at least by its appearance at lunchtime in 1997—home to a living tradition.

The current Cathedral Basilica was built in 1850, but the parish was established in 1703, by Jean-Baptiste de la Croix de Chevrière de St. Val-lier, the bishop of Quebec. And almost immediately, the parties began. That same year, Nicholas Langlois inaugurated the Mardi Gras celebra-tions that have been going on longer in Mobile than in New Orleans. And Nicholas wasn't the only member of the Langlois family to leave a lasting legacy to the spiritual life of Alabama. His son, Fifise, is alleged to have introduced in 1754 another object of religious devotion revered in virtu-ally every Alabama home, regardless of denomination: *Rhododendron pentanthera*. As in Rome the Basilica of St Peter was built on top of the bones of the Apostle to the Gentiles, in Alabama the Basilica is built on top of the holy relics of the great missionary Apostle of the Azalea.

A few blocks away, the azaleas in Bienville Square—maybe distant descendants of Fifise's, but probably not—have long lost their blooms, and the park is shrouded in thick shade of arching live oaks. In the cen-ter of the square, local physician George Ketchum, who lobbied to bring fresh drinking water to Mobile, is memorialized by a five-tiered fountain that you are not supposed to drink from.

Catholic tradition is strong here but Mobile is still Alabama, and the old-time religion of the rest of the state is never far off. By the Ketchum fountain, a clean-shaven White man in crimson polo shirt, almost-white jeans, and sneakers, clutches a Bible in his right hand. With his left index finger, he jabs at something or someone, possibly the woman with a leather purse and hospital ID card attached to her waist, lit cigarette casually perched in her right hand. Looking only at the ground in front of her feet, and paying the park preacher no mind, she seems to project a uniquely Southern Catholic indifference to Proddy hellfire.

On cast iron benches lining the walkways that fan out from the fountain, Black and White men linger in dappled shade. One has his shoes off. They are only slightly less indifferent to the preacher, who is pointing to the sky and declaiming loudly about debauchery or the waywardness of the age or something. To the men on the benches, he is not especially compelling entertainment.

North of here runs a major thoroughfare that, according to the WPA Guide to Alabama, "is for the Negroes of Mobile what Eighteenth Street is to Birmingham" (i.e., a thriving African American business district). And then, without a wisp of irony, the guide notes that the street is named for "President Jefferson Davis of the Confederacy." In a characteristically condescending tone, the guide describes the street scene: "Department stores, specialty shops, motion picture houses, Pike Hall, a social center, drugstores, offices, and even a wholesale establishment or two cater to the Negro population on a scale and with prices to which their limited economy is adjusted."[41]

Davis Avenue was known locally as "the Avenue," for obvious reasons. African Americans could do without a daily reference to Jeff Davis, a regular reminder that however successful and thriving their businesses along the Avenue might be, they were still on the White man's turf, on his terms, on his street. (The Avenue was eventually renamed—not merely as a formality—for Martin Luther King, Jr.)

We hit the road south out of Mobile on the west side of the Bay for Dauphin Island. We are led here by the WPA Guide, which tells us that it was originally called Massacre Island when the French landed on it in 1699. They found sun-bleached bones all over the place, which led them to think some horrible slaughter had taken place there (always thinking the worst, the French). They built an installation there anyway, because a few hundred corpses and the ghosts of a massacre should never get in the way of an advantageously situated military garrison. Either way, they were mistaken: Massacre Island was in fact an ancient burial site that had been turned up by a hurricane, which strewed the newly unburied across the sands. Despite the appealingly forbidding name, it was changed to honor the heir of Louis XIV, the dauphin who would become Louis XV.

The far less intimidatingly named Dauphin Island changed hands many times, and the English built a fortress on the end of the island in 1822 to guard the entrance to Mobile Bay. It was last held by the Confederacy, until August 8, 1864.

Dauphin Island is one of two halves of a pincerlike formation framing the entrance to Mobile Bay, each one tipped with nineteenth-century pentagonal brick fortresses—Fort Gaines on the west side, Fort Morgan on the east—that now guard little more than the memory of Mobile's strategic location. Between these pincer points, under cover of night in July 1860, a small steam ship crept into Mobile Bay. In tow: a twin-masted, copper-hulled schooner named for a fifth-century Frankish saint venerated as patroness of brides, sons, and exiles. Sails and part of its foremast removed, the *Clotilda* was traveling incognito to avoid both capture by Portuguese men-of-war in hot pursuit and a run-in with federal authorities. Sneaking past Dauphin Island, the ship's captain, William Foster of Mobile, was fidgety, anxious to avoid being caught importing illegal contraband into the United States. Chained and silent below deck on the *Clotilda*: over a hundred West Africans to be sold into slavery.

The United States had outlawed the transatlantic slave trade in 1808, and if Foster was caught, he could be hanged just like Nathaniel Gordon of Maine, who would later be caught doing the same thing. Foster landed the *Clotilda* on Twelve Mile Island north of Mobile. "I transferred my slaves to a river steamboat," he wrote, "and sent them up into the canebrake to hide them until further disposal. I then burned my Sch[ooner] to the water's edge and sunk her."[42]

The *Clotilda* was the last known slave ship to enter the United States. Foster was caught, but unlike Nathaniel Gordon, he never faced more than a slap on the hand. Thirty-two of the men that he bought from the King of Dahomey (present-day Benin) were sold to Timothy Meaher,

Foster's business partner. After the end of the Civil War, the enslaved men and women on Meaher's plantation began their own settlement just north of Mobile, which became known as Africatown.

Africatown is the fruit of African American resilience and self-determination, but also of a White man's hubris: Foster's entire venture to smuggle African slaves into the United States in contravention of federal law arose out of a bet between Foster and Meaher and a group of New Englanders who didn't think that they could pull it off. A plot hatched in the smoky haze of some Alabama alehouse, perhaps, ended up trading in the lives of over a hundred human beings. The irony is that Foster's wager led to consequences neither he nor Meaher could ever have imagined: the establishment of a colony of free Black families in the heart of Mobile. Nor could they have imagined that one day a grand-daughter of enslaved people would come out of Alabama a celebrated American novelist. They could not have imagined Zora Neale Hurston, who would tell the story of the survivors of the *Clotilda* based upon her 1927 interviews with the last remaining survivor of the ship, Cudjoe Kazoola Lewis, in *Barracoon*, a book that would finally be published in 2018, almost sixty years after its author's death.[43]

A whole new inkblot, but in familiar colors.

Clarksdale, Mississippi. Photo by the author.

MISSISSIPPI I
The Delta Influences Everything

The Mississippi Delta is where America bottoms out. A sparsely populated, almond-shaped depression tipped on either end by the relatively prosperous cities of Vicksburg and suburban Memphis, its distended middle is one of the most economically impoverished parts of the country. The site of intense racial violence during Jim Crow and up to the civil rights movement, the Delta is the other of the American Dream: the question mark to every high-minded claim America likes to make for itself. It is the provenance of "the shifting unappeasable god of the country, feared and loved, the Mississippi."[1]

This region, almost like an inland tidal marsh, has been nourished for millennia by alluvial deposits from The River, whose myth and mass are equally beyond human comprehension. The Big Muddy is identical with the paradox that is America: capricious, self-serving, generous; it flows where it wants to, is no respecter of human boundaries, and its overflowing has been both destructive and life giving. It bears within itself traditions and voices it does not give a name to, its merciless indifference to human well-being a bringer of death and new birth.

Only a massive civil engineering project begun in earnest after a devastating flood in 1927 has managed somewhat to control the Mississippi's regular superabundance. But even these the River—which has given human history many good reasons to anthropomorphize it—clearly feels no compulsion to respect. "Every few years," wrote William Alexander Percy, "it rises like a monster from its bed and pushes over its banks to vex and sweeten the land it has made."[2] The Delta is the product of residue, and as such is one of the most fertile ecological zones on the planet.

And one of the most violent. Before there was "the Wild West" of celluloid romances, there was the Mississippi Delta. On the lawless "Old Southwest" frontier before the Civil War, petty disputes frequently led to murder. When such disagreements were settled more formally, White men dueled it out in the streets, until the late nineteenth century, when Black men became the target of choice for White violence. This dark legacy of bloodshed is written into the language of the soil: when dry, the ubiquitous and fertile vertisols across the Delta form aggregated clay pellets known locally as "buckshot." *Buckshot is not good row crop land.*

In the Delta you are forced to give up your pretense to purity: everything here is complicated. And also unimaginably beautiful. Flatlands stretch out fore and aft towards seemingly unreachable horizons. The soil is black as night, the sun as white as the sumptuous plantations that once dominated the landscape here. High-definition contrast is everywhere: fabulous cotton-borne wealth enjoyed by powerful White planters and produced by the broken bodies of Black men and women, whose legacy now dominates this region.

The plantations are gone now, but the poverty left behind by a century of sharecropping, disfranchisement, and other forces remains. The Delta is both bisected and bounded on either side by thoroughfares: to the east and west, the Mississippi and Yazoo Rivers flow, ultimately, to the Gulf. Right up the middle, a different, man-made route leads, in one direction, to New Orleans. But it's the other way that these routes are famous for. Those Black Americans who were well-off enough to own a car in the first half of the twentieth century and had a mind to get the hell out of Mississippi, caught US 61 North, to look for work in St. Louis and Chicago, where they took their music, their food, their Delta-born hopes and nightmares. Others followed a similar northbound route on the rails, escaping oppression on Illinois Central's *Panama Limited* to Chicago, now known as Amtrak's *City of New Orleans.*

Everything in the Delta seems to be oriented elsewhere.

Which is where many African Americans in the Delta wanted to be, and where, from 1915 on, many of them went. White rule had been so firmly reestablished in Mississippi that just about anywhere but the Delta seemed like a potential paradise. Thanks to the promise of employment and the lure of affordable new homes, the Great Migration was "the first mass act of independence by a people who were in bondage in this country for far longer than they have been free."[3] Some of those promises were less than bankable, including Robert Abbott's "exaggerated claims of factories willing to dispense free train tickets to new black workers (this almost never happened) . . . for groups of black families who could pool their money."[4] As the famous editor of Chicago's famous and influential Black newspaper, *The Chicago Defender*, Abbott—born on St. Simon's Island, Georgia and himself a migrant to Chicago—used his paper's power to lure countless Black families out of despair.

When we first passed through the Delta in 1999, we carried with us a version of the region that we received through two main sources: William Alexander Percy and Robert Johnson. They represent two polar artistic responses to Delta life. Percy's is that of the bookish landed gentry, Johnson's of the hellhound-haunted Black *Faust*. I encountered both in the early 1990s: Percy's *Lanterns on the Levee* through a college literature and theology course, and Johnson through Eric Clapton, repeating a decades-old tradition of White Americans being introduced to Black blues music through very White English musicians. It's shocking, I know, but true: most White folks in America did not learn about the blues from juke joints in the Mississippi Delta, nor even from Alan Lomax's field recordings in the 1930s. They began to learn of it through what could have been called, but were not, musical "outside agitators:" White boys in Manchester and Liverpool and Brighton who were listening to Lomax and reminding Americans of their own music.

Like most things, it's complicated. Here is one example. I and other well-off White kids in 1986 did not learn about apartheid in South Africa because we read the *New York Times*. I learned about it because of Paul Simon's *Graceland*. Simon took a lot of flak for "appropriating" the music of South Africa, but in truth he drew our attention not just to their music but to the political context in which it was being made. I don't know if something similar happened in the 1960s when White kids discovered the blues and the horrors of the Delta at the same time, but it's entirely possible.

The Delta Blues are still alive in 2018, but in revived juke joints and music venues like Morgan Freeman's Ground Zero club in Clarksdale, it is mostly White folks who are filling the seats.

Our first time here, we were looking for juke joints like those we had seen in photographs by Birney Imes.[5] We didn't find many. By then most African American kids weren't listening to the blues and shooting pool, we were told. We found more juke joints in 2018 than in 1999, though, not least because we knew where to look but also because original sin is real and most human beings don't give a shit about things of value until they are critically endangered. Founded in the 1960s, Po' Monkey's

Lounge near Merigold is archetypal; its lines are distorted and exaggerated, as if it was drawn onto the landscape freehand. It is closed when we arrive, as is the Blue Front Cafe in Bentonia, the longest-running juke joint still in existence, a living relic in a region once rife with roadside music halls. It's technically not in the Delta, but just south of it.

We are sent there on a tip from Ann, my neighbor in Asheville, who had been a few months earlier. The Blue Front's long-reigning patriarch is Jimmy "Duck" Holmes, a bluesman himself. Anne and her crew stopped in the Blue Front one afternoon looking for live music, but didn't find any. But they did find Duck Holmes, who offered to give the ladies a guitar lesson, which he did for an hour. Duck's parents opened the joint in 1948, and he took over in 1970. He has been playing there since, in the same room where Skip James, Sonny Boy Williamson (no. 2) and Son Thomas played. When Ann was there, Duck gave her friend a guitar lesson. She gave me Duck's phone number.

The day before, we angle into a parking spot along the main square in Demopolis, Alabama, and make tomato sandwiches in the back of the minivan. In a gazebo on a plot of land officially known as Confederate Park until 1975 and which forbade Black kids from playing on the merry-go-round, we eat lunch. In the gazebo, wiping a liquor of tomato juice and Duke's mayonnaise from my chin, I call Duck Holmes.

I do not expect him to answer, but he does. I ask him if they will be having live music tomorrow night, or soon.

"No, man. I'm in Vancouver," he says. Holmes is about to go on stage at the Vancouver Folk Festival, but he took a call from some random white dude anyway. He is surprisingly chatty for a man on a tight schedule.

Maybe we can connect on the way back, I don't want you to keep Vancouver waiting, I say. "Thank you, brother," he says. We hope it works out.

But for now, Duck Holmes has got to go on stage.

We pull up to the Blue Front the next day. Not only is there no Duck; the joint is jam-up and jelly-tight. We get out to take a few stills of the front of the Blue Front for good measure, if only to prove to Ann that I was there. The sign above the door is familiar one across the South: a white banner with a red Coca-Cola logo on either side. In this case, it's not just *de rigueur*; it's a trophy. During Jim Crow the Blue Front was not allowed to serve Coke to its Black patrons, so customers had to endure

Nehi and Double Cola instead. After segregation was outlawed, the Blue Front got its Coke sign.

While setting up the tripod, a sedan pulls right into the viewfinder and throws it into park. *Well damn*, I think.

The driver hops out of the car and goes in through the front door, leaves it open. John and I exchange could-do glances.

We pop our heads in through the doorway and ask if we can come in to take some pictures. She thinks about it, says *ok but you gotta be quick*. Gray-painted bead-board walls are hung with guitars and lined with concert posters featuring Bobby Rush and Duck Holmes. (A curious harbinger in poster form: three years in the future, in 2021, both Bobby Rush and Duck Holmes will be nominated for the Grammy for Best Traditional Blues Album; Rush will prevail over Duck.) A drum kit and mic, two acoustic guitars in stands, and amps. At one table, a cigarette butt poised on the edge of an ashtray, almost as if it's just gone out, gives the sense of some sudden departure, or the rapture.

About thirty miles north of Jackson on US 49, Bentonia is just outside the Delta proper. But further north in Yazoo City, the Delta begins. Approaching from this way—unlike through other ports of entry we have accessed in the past—gives a sense of the dramatic difference from the rest of Mississippi, and therefore America. From the south side of Yazoo City, a steep hill on East Broadway Street descends down a bluff into Yazoo. From here you can see it stretch out before you, a vast and seemingly endless plain of cotton fields, the source of so much American wealth and hardship. Once, you would have seen from this vantage a primeval forest, but the ancient hardwoods have long been emptied out. And so it goes.

At the bottom of East Broadway, suddenly you are in it. The Delta. Yazoo City is a border town: on one side the hill country of gently rolling swales of earth; on the other, uninterrupted flatness. The town center is mostly vacant on a blistering August afternoon. Men in suits and women in cocktail dresses disappear, somewhat bizarrely, into an unmarked storefront. No one else is going anywhere. But music pipes out onto the streets from speakers mounted on lampposts. The second-story level of the stores along Main Street have all been painted in bright colors—chartreuse, hot pink, pool table green. The one exception is the Black & White Store, painted up in the historically dominant colors of the Delta.

These turn out to be preliminary examples of this region's insatiable need to express itself.

Mound Bayou

Following the Civil War, the US government laid down the conditions for the readmission of secessionist states in the Reconstruction Act of 1867. Section 5 of that act required each of those states to draft "a constitution of government in conformity with the Constitution of the United States in all respects, framed by a convention of delegates elected by the male citizens of said State, twenty-one years old and upward, of whatever race, color, or previous condition, who have been resident in said State for one year previous to the day of such election."[6] In 1868, like other Southern states, Mississippi wrote a new constitution that affirmed in law the Fourteenth Amendment to the US Constitution, which granted full citizenship and equal protection to the formerly enslaved. The Constitution was ratified by the people of Mississippi in December 1869, but it did not hold sway for very long.

Suddenly an entirely new voting bloc had emerged in Mississippi: African Americans constituted over 58 percent of the electorate. Within a little over twenty years, White resentment at Republican carpetbaggers and the new legal and political enfranchisement of a race still firmly held to be inferior had grown so intense that a new convention was called. Black people had gotten too much power, White Democrats argued. The 1890 convention was called for a single purpose: to reestablish White supremacy.

> "Let us tell the truth if it bursts the bottom of the Universe," declared [Constitutional Convention] President S.S. Calhoon. "We came here to exclude the negro. Nothing short of this will answer." Indeed, so single-minded were the framers that Judge Chrisman was said to cry "My God! My God! Is there to be no higher ambition for the young white men of the south than that of keeping the Negro down?"[7]

Among the more consequential of the new constitution's provisions was the introduction of literacy tests and poll taxes at the voting booth, which effectively made it impossible for Black men to exercise their constitutional right to vote. It was a clever tactic, designed to restore White power entirely within the law, and it totally worked. Mississippi's new refounding document became a model for other states, like Alabama.

One hundred and thirty-four men sat in deliberation over the state's new, overtly White supremacist constitutional convention. One of them was Isaiah T. Montgomery. The only African American at the convention, Montgomery was truly extraordinary.

Born to enslaved parents on Hurricane Plantation on a peninsula sticking out into Mississippi, at age twelve Isaiah became the personal secretary of the plantation's master, Joseph Emory Davis, the older brother of Jefferson. Like the eccentric geography of the plantation itself, the elder Davis had tried to develop an unusual system for a plantation at the time: he raised not just highly profitable cotton, but also Indian corn and sweet potatoes. He raised hogs, sheep, and cattle. Davis bucked other trends, too: under the influence of the British utopian socialist, Robert Owen, he wanted Hurricane to be a model of humanistic labor in which the enslaved were given a highly atypical amount of autonomy, and he believed that his workers were best motivated by positive incentive rather than the lash. Davis established a court on the property, "eventually held every Sunday in a small building called the Hall of Justice, where a slave jury heard complaints of slave misconduct and the testimony of the accused in their own defense. No slave was punished except by a jury of his own peers."[8] Moreover, the plantation's overseers were not allowed to punish a slave without the consent of the court. It did not always work out. When punishments were administered, they often resembled those one might find on any other plantation in the South.

But it was an undeniably radical vision of plantation management in its day, and clearly left a mark on the young Isaiah Montgomery. His father, Benjamin, ran the dry goods store at Hurricane. When Joseph Davis fled the plantation as Union naval boats moved up the Mississippi from New Orleans in 1862, Benjamin Montgomery took over operation of the plantation until Union soldiers took the Montgomerys to Cincinnati.[9] By 1865 they had all returned to Davis Bend, where they operated something even more radical than Joseph Davis could have imagined: a thriving cotton plantation on the Mississippi River run entirely by African Americans.

Though by 1865 he could no longer be considered Joseph Davis's property, he still did not own the land he managed—until Davis sold it

to him. After Benjamin died in 1877, Isaiah took ownership of the plantation, but after the collapse of the cotton market the project at Davis Bend
become no longer feasible.[10] In 1887, Isaiah Montgomery and two other
African Americans from Hurricane Plantation left Davis Bend for Boli-
var County in the western Delta, where they implemented a kind of self-
sustaining, Owenite community for African Americans, called Mound
Bayou. It soon became one of the most thriving Black-only towns in the
country, and home for Black desire so alluring that even white artists
were taken in by it.

> Mound Bayou, I feel blue and all in,
> Mound Bayou, I can hear you callin'!
> All my friends are lucky to be way back there,
> If they knew what I've been through, they'd stay back there!
> Mound Bayou, got to cover ground for
> Mound Bayou, that's the town I'm bound for!
> Wish my arms were long enough, here's what I'd do,
> I'd reach and wrap them gently round my Mound Bayou.[11]

Mound Bayou was the subject of a popular song written by Leonard
Feather, a noted music critic and composer born into a well-to-do Jewish
family in London. In 1942, backed by the British-born trumpeter Henry
Levine and his Strictly from Dixie Jazz Band, a white woman from Mississippi named Linda Keene cut a record of the song for RCA Victor. In a
classic move now well-known in the history of American music, her version takes the story of an extraordinary town created entirely by African
Americans and turns it into a sentimental cliché about a quaint Southern
town. The cover art for the album that Levine made for Victor, *Strictly
from Dixie*, features a stylized image of a Black boy eating a watermelon.

That October Keene was playing the Patio in Cincinnati, singing
"Mound Bayou" and evoking a wistful, ice-tinkling-in-the-gin-glass
nostalgia of the Old South. The *Enquirer* described the subject of her
"special song" as "One of those Shangri-la places where there are no
jails, everyone sits around in the sun, and there's always fried chicken
on the table."[12] It's safe to assume that most of the clientele in the Patio
would have been surprised what they'd have found in the actual Mound
Bayou. It is possible that Feather had seen as much about the real Mound
Bayou as Stephen Foster had of the Suwannee River.

The actual Mound Bayou has diminished somewhat since its heyday; if someone were to write a song about the place today, it might not evoke the kind of longing for welcome that Feather's song did.

We first came here in 1999. I am struck then by the extraordinary hand-painted signage that adorns almost every storefront. I shoot stills of Ray's Bargain Spot, which advertises T-shirts, caps, stockings, snacks, and haircuts. A metal sign hanging out over the sidewalk, suspended by guy wires attached to the roof, calls the place "The Crowe's Nest." I try to capture the artful signage, but I do not really know what I am looking at. One poster in the window features the apparently immortal Bobby Rush.

The Crowe's Nest was started by Milburn Crowe, a local activist and historian who devoted his life to preserving the story of Mound Bayou. His father, Henry, was one of the first settlers here. In the 1960s the Crowe's Nest became a meeting spot for civil rights activists traveling through Mississippi, who would often stop in to talk with Crowe, eat some ribs, play a little poker, and drink some whiskey.[13]

In 2018, I am looking for the Crowe's Nest again, not because I know about the history of the place yet, but because of the signs. I remember it from a series of photographs from almost twenty years earlier, which I use as a cue. The building is still there, but all the old signs have been painted over, including the one for the "Crowe's Nest," which has been crudely scrawled with a can of spray paint.

Meanwhile, the home of Isaiah T. Montgomery is surrounded on Main Avenue is less decrepit than it once was. Signs out front and orange fencing around betoken its forthcoming restoration, thanks to the National Trust for Historic Preservation.

Montgomery's vision for racial uplift in Mound Bayou shared a lot in common with the ideals of Booker T. Washington, who visited the town, wrote about it as a model of the classically Washingtonian values of "thrift and self-government." Through the Tuskegee Institute Washington secured investments from White northerners in the settlement.[14] Mound Bayou had effectively hitched its fledgling wagon to the Booker T. Washington express train.

Montgomery himself also seems to have had Washington's pragmatic but limited aspirations for African Americans in a largely White supremacist culture. In his profile of Mound Bayou, Washington quotes Montgomery: "What we need . . . is an agricultural school, something that will teach the young men to be better farmers than their fathers have been. But, more than that, we need here a system of education that will teach our young men and women the underlying meaning of the work that is being done here."[15]

Like Washington, Montgomery was learned, eloquent, and inspiring, and regarded by many African Americans as a model for what a self-determined Black life could be. To many White people, on the other hand, he was proof of the aspiring, up-by-your-bootstraps ideology that simultaneously exalted people like Montgomery and ensured that their bootstraps not pull them up too far.

For all the exemplarity of the self-governed community at Mound Bayou, Isaiah Montgomery seems to have accepted the White terms of Black political life. He was held up as a hero to White folks because he was a successful Black man who knew his place.

That may not be how Montgomery himself saw it, but it was certainly one of the reasons why he was elected to serve as a delegate to the 1890 constitutional convention, which would prove the most consequential moment of his life. He delivered a "remarkable speech" to the convention, which drew comparisons between the power of Montgomery's oratory, and that of Frederick Douglass. He conceded that Black folks had helped to build "the proudest aristocracy that ever graced the Western hemisphere," but also wondered what it cost:

> Sometimes, Mr. President, as I gaze over our broad acres, my heart would rejoice in the progress and glory of Mississippi, but a feeling of sadness represses my exultation, as the unanswerable question arises, How much of life, how much of privation, sorrow and toil has it cost my people? Perchance every acre represents a grave and every furrow a tear. And what have they by recompense?[16]

Montgomery was no radical; he paid dutiful obeisance to the primacy of White culture and offered little legal objection to it. On the contrary, Montgomery described the Franchise Committee's proposal to levy a poll tax, require a literacy test for voters as "adequate to restore purity to the ballot-box, and render it what the genius of our institutions demand that it should be, a free and untrammeled expression of the popular will."[17]

Montgomery knew that this would effectively disfranchise thousands of Black voters. He cited an illuminating statistic that plainly exposed the anticipated outcome of the new law:

```
Present voters, white . . . . . . . . . . . 118,890
This bill will restrict . . . . . . . . . . . . 11,889
And leave a net white vote of . . . . 107,001
Present voters, negroes . . . . . . . . . 189,884
This bill will restrict . . . . . . . . . . . 123,334
And leave a net negro vote . . . . . . . 66,550
Giving a white majority of . . . . . . . 48,451
```

If there was ever a moment when Mississippi state politics was on the edge of its seat, this was it. It could go either way. On the one hand, Montgomery could press the case against the "unquestioned white supremacy" of the convention and protest the move, stalling the whole convention and frustrating the white consensus. At this point delegates W. S. Farish, George Dillard, and P. Henry, who had contested the legitimacy of Montgomery's election as a delegate and proposed that he be unseated,[18] were surely squirming in their seats, their worst fears confirmed. On the other hand, Montgomery could yield, and confirm to all the rest of the delegates that in Montgomery's election the convention had gotten its perfect poster child: a dutiful and submissive Black person.

It soon became clear which party was going to get their "I-told-you-so" moment. In the interest of "purity," Montgomery entrusted the ballot to "the virtuous and intelligent voters of the State," and waxed floridly on the promises of the franchisement clause for a restoration of order: "the grave dangers which called this body into being will be dispelled as the dewy mist of the morning by the rising sunburst of political liberty, which shall bring into renewed life the dormant energies of a new South and inaugurate an era of progress that shall rapidly bring our State abreast of any section in this broad land."[19]

With that, Montgomery threw his meager political weight but powerful consent—and with it, the symbolic consent of Mississippi's Black voters—"to lay the suffrage of 123,000 of my fellow-men at the feet of the Convention."[20]

It wasn't even a consent made in protest; Montgomery offered "a fearful sacrifice laid on the altar of liberty" in the belief that it would "restore confidence, the great missing link between the two races." He could have stopped there, but he didn't. He concluded his speech with a final gesture:

> The greatness and chivalry exhibited by your race in springing from the lowest depths of barbarism to the position of dominators of the civilized world needs no commendation at my hands.
>
> To them the world is indebted for the great triumphs of architecture, mechanism, art, literature and science, and for the perpetuation and dissemination of the ennobling principles of morality, Christianity and immortality.[21]

One can only imagine how this must have swollen the hearts of Mississippi's White delegates on the convention floor, but the *New York World* detected "a deep sense of relief and surprised wonder" among the audience at the "burning words" of the "dusky orator." "That which the culture and the polish of Mississippi's proudest had vainly tried to effect had been accomplished by this once slave—the exponent of a despised race."[22]

The gaslit parlors and breezy front porches of the White delegates that evening must have radiated with self-congratulatory giddiness at their triumph. For here in the flesh was all the proof that they needed for their own program of White supremacy: an industrious and eloquent Black man just educated enough to know his own place, exactly the kind of Black person a White planter or politician in Mississippi in 1890 could imagine living in racial harmony with, so long as he never forgot or tried to rise above his own station. While Jackson throbbed in the aftermath of Montgomery's "noble speech," it did not play as well in DC. Less than a month after Montgomery's speech in the Mississippi capital city, Frederick Douglass delivered one of his own in the Metropolitan AME Church six blocks north of the White House. He was unsparing in his rebuke of Montgomery, arguing that he "has surrendered to a disloyal State a great franchise given to himself and his people by the loyal nation." And that was just the beginning. He condemned Montgomery's assimilationist attempt to kowtow to the White principalities and powers and was complicit in the national backtracking on the promises of Reconstruction. For all his criticism of Montgomery, he reserved his judgment for his act, not the man himself. "Yet I have no denunciation for the man Montgomery," Douglass said. "He is not a conscious traitor though his act is treason: treason to the cause of the colored people, not only of his own State, but of the United States."[23]

For Douglass, the consequences of Montgomery's concession speech would be wide ranging. He feared that the Mississippian's gesture would be repeated across the South. But most revealing is the concession Douglass made to Montgomery, and his attempt to empathize with the circumstances that led to his great betrayal:

> I hear in the plaintive eloquence of his marvelous address a groan of bitter anguish born of oppression and despair. It is the voice of a soul from which all hope has vanished. His deed kindles indignation to be sure, but his condition awakens pity. He had called to the nation for help—help which it ought to have rendered and could have rendered but it did not—and in a moment of impatience and despair he has thought to make terms with the enemy, an enemy with whom no colored man can make terms but by a sacrifice of his manhood.[24]

Montgomery had, unwittingly, perhaps, and unavoidably, abetted the White supremacist revival in late-nineteenth-century Mississippi, and became a kind of prototype for later Black politicians (or aspiring politicians) who, for one reason or another, prove useful to the White status quo, who are celebrated by White Americans as a testament to a post-racial society and are tolerated as agents within the White establishment so long as they don't say anything or advocate any policy that would mitigate against it.

We pull the car onto the capacious shoulder of Mississippi State Highway 32 east of Mound Bayou. A crop duster swoops low past the tree line and hovers a few feet above the cotton fields, letting loose a trail of pesticide. At the near end of the field it rises and loops back, and repeats the process. It's what passes for free roadside entertainment in the Delta, but it is genuinely engrossing, this underappreciated feat of aeronautic gymnastics that happens on the daily here. It's also archaeology in the air, and a reminder of a connection to our hometown.

Delta Airlines, currently the world's largest airline in terms of annual revenue and one of the anchors of Atlanta's New South economy, was founded in Atlanta in 1925, shortly after Asa G. Candler, Jr., offered the

City of Atlanta a former racetrack south of downtown for use as an air-
field. The forward-thinking and commercially minded Alderman William B. Hartsfield saw the potential in the plan, and the site eventually
became Hartsfield-Jackson International Airport, the main hub for
Delta Airlines. But it didn't get to Atlanta until 1941. Originally called
Delta Air Service, the future passenger airline behemoth started out as
a crop-dusting operation built to combat the boll weevil, the nemesis of
long-staple cotton. The Air Service's most significant early client was the
Delta Pine and Land Company, based in the heart of the region whence
the airline derived its name.[25]

The slogan du jour in my hometown is "Atlanta Influences Everything," the latest in a long line of boosterish catchphrases going back at
least to Hartsfield himself. But I am not sure it isn't more accurate to say
that the Delta influences everything.

Parchman

If the Delta is America's bottomland, the lowest point in the Delta itself
is in Parchman. The WPA Guide calls the farm here "a typical Delta
plantation, consisting of 15,497 acres planted in cotton, corn, and truck,"
and while at first blush it might seem that there is nothing typical about
Parchman, it's Mississippi's history condensed into a sparse twenty-
eight square miles of cotton fields.

We pull into an empty gravel lot across from the main gate to the Mississippi State Penitentiary, better known as Parchman Farm. The main
road into the site stretches first along "Guard Row" lined with trees and
small, identical houses built by the WPA for prison staff. Beyond that,
the shade ends and the road seems to extend into the treeless distance
like a life sentence. I stand across the street from the gate, and take a bad
photograph of the entrance, until a prison guard emerges—reluctantly, it
seems—from her climate-controlled hut, and shouts across US 49 to urge
me to stop what I am doing.

I've heard about Parchman, and nothing I know about it is good.
But what I learn about it is even worse. Parchman is the state's penitentiary penal farm, and the site of death row. Its history goes back to late
Reconstruction, when county jails leased out prisoners to planters looking for cheap labor. The system was simply "slavery by another name,"
as Douglas Blackmon's book on the subject calls it.[26]

It all started with Edmund Richardson, a North Carolinian who moved to Mississippi and built a cotton empire out of an inheritance of "2,800 and a few slaves." In 1868:

> he struck a bargain with the federal authorities in Mississippi. Richardson needed cheap labor to work some land he had bought in the sparsely settled Yazoo Delta; the state had a gutted penitentiary overflowing with ex-slaves. The result was a contract that allowed Richardson to work those felons outside prison walls. He promised to feed them, clothe them, guard them, and treat them well. The state agreed to pay him $18,000 a year for their maintenance and an additional sum for their transportation to and from his primitive Delta camps.[27]

The voracious hunger for cheap labor among Mississippi's capitalist class led to an explosion in convictions. Suddenly men—mostly Black men—could be hauled in on the most specious of charges, and subjected to penalties that could be paid off by hard labor for a private company. Except few leased convicts ever actually succeeded in paying off their debts to the state: many died under the merciless conditions of the new system in which convicts as young as eight years old were held in cages and forced to work inhuman hours, punished severely for almost anything, fed worm-infested meals and, when they fell over dead in the middle of their work, were often buried on the spot while work continued uninterrupted.

Men like Richardson and many others—including General Nathan Bedford Forrest and Colonel Jones S. Hamilton—fattened their coffers on the backs of cheap workforce and even cheaper lives. When Hamilton was publicly criticized by *Sword and Shield* editor Roderick Gambrell for his involvement in the leasing system, he challenged Gambrell to a duel on the Capitol Street Bridge in Jackson. Gambrell died on the spot, but Hamilton survived with a bullet wound in his chest and was acquitted of Gambrell's murder after the jury deliberated for the whole of fifteen minutes.[28]

Meanwhile, in the Mississippi hill country, James Vardaman boiled with resentment at the ability of rich planters to live lives of luxury off of the system, while poor white people were still struggling in a sharecropping system that kept them indebted to rich white people. Vardaman—a flamboyantly camp and outspoken racist and ardent defender of lynch mobs—was no friend of African Americans; his opposition to convict leasing was grounded on the conviction that no White man should be doing work that only a Black person should do.

Vardaman's opposition to convict leasing ultimately led to the establishment of Parchman Farm in 1901, which opened for business in 1905 during his tenure as governor. The system at Parchman was not intended to reform wayward Black people; it was meant to put them to work, and to teach them their place. Moreover, it would have another effect Vardaman sought: to take some of the fabulous wealth generated by convict leasing for White elites and redirect it to the state's accounts. In its first year of operation, "Parchman had turned a profit of $185,000."[29]

Parchman was just a plantation by another name: it operated on similar principles to the antebellum cotton estates, and its goal was the generation of White wealth through the use and abuse of Black bodies.

The property doesn't have a fence; it doesn't need one. For miles and miles there is no cover in which an escapee could hide. They could be easily tracked down at a relatively leisurely pace by horse-mounted guards and a pack of the most elite bloodhounds in the South, who could "follow a scent without difficulty on a five hour lead."[30]

Parchman Farm was not an outlier. Starry-eyed legislators in Mississippi apparently saw the immense financial potential for financial gain in the Parchman model. The rapidly swelling incarcerated population at the turn of the century provided a ready-made workforce that was not limited to criminals. In 1904, Parchman's first year of operation, a motion in the Mississippi House of Representatives proposed that the increasingly overcrowded state Insane Hospital be transferred to one of the state's farm properties. The motion's sponsor, J. C. Kyle, argued that "there are now several hundred patients in said institution who are mentally and physically capable of doing outdoor work, and to some extent perform manual about, for whom such outdoor work, etc., both to their physical condition and mental restoration would be helpful." He proposed that the new farm be "set apart for the use of the State as a home for this class of patients, and to be used as a farm for agricultural and horticultural purposes."[31]

We get back into the van and circle through the gravel parking lot towards Highway 32 toward Webb, US 49 toward Glendora, and then south on the Money Road.

Money: Memories Full of Bullet Holes

The South is torn between at least two (and probably many more) versions of history: on the one hand, the view expressed by the passage from William Faulkner's *Requiem for a Nun*—"The past is never dead; it's not even past"—a text cited with such frequency that it's become almost as clichéd as a kudzu metaphor. On the other hand, there is the view expressed by an anonymous North Carolinian in the late V. S. Naipaul's travel memoir, *A Turn in the South*: "We have had too much of the past." Sometimes these two conflicting attitudes co-exist in the same town, the same neighborhood, or the same person.

They do in what little is left of Money now. The remains of two stores illustrate these two dispositions toward the past. Done up in fresh white paint, Ben Roy's Service Station looks like it could be a movie set from *American Graffiti*. It projects a kind of 1950's nostalgia ready-made to confirm *those were the days*–seeking tourists. As a historical restoration, it's impeccably well-done.

Next door, it's a different story: a building of consequence, with its own bespoke historical marker, is a crumbling ruin, overrun with invasive vine, surrounded by barbed wire, and flimsy orange fencing. Barely visible through a tangle of Virginia Creeper and English ivy is a sign on what remains of the front door that reads,

PRIVATE PROPERTY.
NO ONE ALLOWED ON PROPERTY
VIOLATORS WILL BE PROSECUTED

It's an ironically principled sign for Bryant's Grocery and Meat Market, considering its history. On August 24, 1955, a young teenager from Chicago, in town to visit his Mississippi cousins, entered the store and left with a price on his head. Emmett Till was—in the minds of Carolyn Bryant, her husband, Roy, and half-brother-in-law J. W. Milam—a violator who must be prosecuted. Whatever Till actually said to Carolyn Bryant that day (it is still not entirely clear), he had crossed the same line we will later see etched in stone in Meridian. Put simply, he had dared, as a Black man, to speak to a White woman in a way that was not allowed.

The details of Emmett Till's lynching four days later have been thoroughly treated elsewhere, canonically by Devery Anderson in 2015 and most recently in Tim Tyson's 2017 book, *The Blood of Emmett Till*. In

"Violators Will Be Prosecuted." Bryant's Grocery Store, Money, Mississippi. Photo by the author.

Why do people nowadays seem to feel obligated to use that word?

his research for the book, Tyson interviewed Carolyn Bryant Donham, who, according to Tyson, admitted that she had exaggerated the details of what Till did and said in the grocery store. Her testimony at trial, she confessed, was not true. Unfortunately, at the precise moment when Bryant Donham allegedly confessed to perjury, Tyson was changing the tape on his audio recorder. All we have to go on are Tyson's handwritten notes that "that pt. wasn't true." (And the choice to use an analog recorder would have been antiquated, even in 2008.) Whether or not she actually confessed to making the story up, Tyson's failure to get her on the record is a fuck-up of the first order. The FBI took the allegation seriously but concluded that Tyson's evidence that Bryant Donham recanted was "insufficient to establish beyond a reasonable doubt" that she had perjured herself. This was arguably one of the most high-profile criminal confessions of the century, and Tyson blew it (if it ever happened at all).[32]

Bryant's Grocery is a monument—for now—to the "let the dead bury their dead" school of Southern memory. A stark contrast to the sanitized history of Ben Roy's gas station, it seems destined to submit to its

Bryant's Grocery, Money, Mississippi. Photo by the author.

owners' stubborn insistence that that was all in the past. *Time to move on.* Unless, of course, someone is ready to pony up the $10 million that they are asking for the building.

The current owners are the descendants of Ray Tribble, who bought the property in the 1980s. At one point, Tribble wanted $40 million for the site. They have left the property to rot, in the apparent hopes that the sordid memory of this tainted place will sink back into the ground along with what is left of the structure. It's not that the Tribble family doesn't know how to conduct a restoration: on the contrary—they've shown they can do it with the Ben Roy Gas Station next door, which they also own. To make matters even weirder, Ray Tribble, at one time the president of the Tallahatchie County Board of Supervisors, was the foreman of the jury that acquitted J. W. Milam and Roy Bryant of the murder of Emmett Till.

Up the road a few yards, a one-story white cinder-block building with a single window. Iron bars cover the glass. Above the window, a tin sign with raised metal letters reads MONEY ___ CO. The letters for the middle word are missing, but an inverse shadow reveals the absent letters: GIN. A spectral palimpsest of an ominous and not-at-all innocent history.

The WPA Guide to Mississippi describes the violent nature of the modern cotton gin:

> The modern gin operates on the "saw" principle of the Whitney gin but is a far cry from the original model. The whole process of ginning has been perfected to expedite labor. Suction pipes, which had the appearance of large stove pipes, draw the cotton from the wagon. An elevator from the suction pipe to the second story transports the cotton to shoots leading to the gin saws. These saws pull the cotton apart, separating it from the seeds. The lint is removed by air blasts, going into a condenser where it receives a final beating and cleaning, and there it becomes glorified, snowy-white drifts.[33]

It's impossible to read this simple description without hearing in it unintended but perverse prefigurations of Emmett Till and the violent culture that abetted his murder: "wagon," "shoots," "pull apart," "blasts," "final beating," "glorified, snowy-white." These words are now doing more than the writer could have ever asked of them, but they cannot do otherwise.

With barbed wire like that which enwraps the decaying meat market, Till's body was bound to a seventy-pound suction fan possibly taken from a gin across the county line near Glendora and tossed into the Tallahatchie River. Looking across from the front of Bryant's Grocery to the Money Gin Company is to traverse in images the fate of Emmett Till. And it is no accident that his brutalized body was laden with machinery of mechanized cotton, the physical and material grammar of the cash crop that enriched generations of "glorified, snowy-white" enslavers in the Delta and elsewhere. When Mamie Till insisted on an open casket for her son's funeral in Chicago, and that pictures of his bloated, beaten, and unrecognizable face be published widely, it did not just bluntly illustrate the reality of white terrorism. It also symbolically demonstrated the long and deadly historical reach of servitude to King Cotton.

In 1955, two months after Bryant and Milam were acquitted by an all-white jury for the murder of Emmett Till, another young Black man was dead in Glendora. Clinton Melton, a twenty-year-old father of four, was filling up his gas tank at a service station in Glendora when he was shot twice with a shotgun by Elmore Otis Kimbrell, operator of the Glendora cotton gin. Kimbrell claimed that Melton wanted two dollars' worth of gas, but went on to fill up his entire tank, and for some reason shot at Kimbrell three times (although Kimbrell testified he did not know if it was really Melton who allegedly fired upon him). When local marshall D. O. Rogers went to question Kimbrell about what happened, he found him at the home of his friend, J. W. Milam.[34] At least one witness testified in September 1955 that Kimbrell was with Milam and Bryant when they brought Till to Bryant's Grocery in Money on the morning of Till's death.[35]

Despite Kimbrell's allegation that Melton shot first, witnesses said that Melton was unarmed. And even though finding a gun to plant on a Black male was rarely a problem in Mississippi in 1955, no weapon ever turned up. "We haven't been able to find the negro's gun yet," Sheriff H. C. Strider told the press. "This case is a real puzzle."[36]

Like his buddies, Kimbrell was acquitted by an all-white jury in the Tallahatchie County Courthouse in Sumner, upon which he demanded that the court give him back his shotgun.

Just north of Glendora—where the cotton gin still stands from which Milam and Bryant likely stole the fan—we turn off Sharkey Road onto the River Road and pull off onto the shoulder to look at a roadside marker.

Across the street, a Black man smokes a cigarette in front of a ranch house. In the front yard, a satellite dish angles up toward the sky. In the back, a huge antenna. He calls out to us, and approaches.

His name is Terrell. The house belongs to his mother, he tells us.

"Everybody knows what happened to Emmett Till in nineteen fifty-five," Terrell tells us on the lawn.

He gestures down the unpaved River Road. Down there, around several bends and through a patch of woods is the muddy riverbank where Robert Hodges, seventeen years old, checking trot lines from the water's edge, first saw Emmett's feet break the surface of the Talla-hatchie River. The rest of Till's waterlogged, mutilated body remained submerged from the weight of a cotton gin fan tied around his neck, hung up on the river bottom. Terrell points to a roadside sign marking the area. It's painted bright purple, labeled "The River Site."

It is riddled with bullet holes.

I am not sure if Terrell is right. I don't know if everyone knows what happened to Emmett Till, but around here they do. This corner of the Mississippi Delta has become a sort of crossroads of memory, where at least two currents of American culture intersect: the vigilant who want to keep alive the memory of Till's violent lynching, and those who don't. Despite its local significance here, "crossroads" may not be the best metaphor; a "roundabout" might be more apt, since the cycle of remembrance-oblivion seems to go around and around from everlasting to everlasting. Almost as soon as the Emmett Till Interpretive Center puts up a sign, it is shot up.

"This sign right here," Terrell says, "it's been here maybe eight years. Guys come here, you know, they catch people not at home, they shoot up the sign, out of anger and frustration. And nothing is done about it. No investigation or anything."

Maybe Terrell is being too charitable. The guys who regularly fire rounds outside Terrell's mother's house certainly know what happened to Emmett Till. They're definitely angry and frustrated and probably more than a little resentful that this bit of Delta history keeps getting attention. Maybe they think Till had it coming, he got what he deserved, serves him right talking to a White woman like that. Maybe they'd do it just like Bryant and Milam if given the chance. The holes in the sign aren't pellet-sized. They're not from a shotgun or a .22, but clearly from something more aggressive, more deadly, more demonstrative. They're from a .45, probably not unlike the one J. W. Milam and Roy Bryant pistol-whipped and shot Emmett Till with before they dumped his fan-laden body into the Tallahatchie River.

We say nothing as we drive the winding River Road south from Terrell's place, the sound of coarse gravel beating the steel belly of the minivan punctuating the silence. To the left, soybean fields stretch themselves out to receive the Delta sun. To the right, a line of hardwoods, heavily laden with vines and crowded by thick undergrowth, borders the river. I pull off into a small driveway at the River Site marker, switch off the engine to the always-already sound of crickets intoning a late afternoon orison.

A new marker stands at the edge of the River Road. The old one has been cut off at the knees, and relocated to a vacant store in Sumner. Two, thick steel legs from the former marker jut up from the ground, coarsely sawed off just above a flanged-out exit wound. Left, maybe, as a reminder that nothing ever really changes. Two weeks after we visit here, the sign will be shot up for a third time, just thirty-five days after being re-erected. When it was replaced again in 2019, the sign was made of steel and weighed 500 pounds. The hope is that this fourth marker will prove bulletproof.[37]

I'm no student of numerology, and I am not—I don't think—natively superstitious. But lately the number 828 has been popping up with strange frequency.

Emmett Till was lynched on August 28, 1955 (8/28). He was fourteen. In 1961, A. Philip Randolph and Bayard Rustin began planning for the March on Washington for Jobs and Freedom to take place two years later. They eventually settled on the date: August 28, 1963. It was no coincidence that eight years to the day from Till's murder, Martin Luther King, Jr., stood on the steps of the Lincoln Memorial in Washington and proclaimed that, one hundred years after the Emancipation Proclamation, "the Negro is still not free."

August 28 is also the feast day of St. Augustine of Hippo, a bishop and theologian from north Africa, one of the four great "Doctors" of the early Latin church. Augustine died on August 28, 430, and his legacy remains wider, deeper, and more contested than perhaps that of any other figure in church history. He was an unusually prolific and imaginative thinker and writer. His first complete masterpiece, *The Confessions*, is by some accounts an early landmark in the genre of memoir. The book is a work of memory, but it is also a treatise about memory. After retracing the story of his life—or rather the story of God's grace through Augustine's life—for nine books, Augustine suddenly takes what seems to many to be a sudden turn, an optional detour from juicy autobiographical narrative into a highly abstract mini-treatise on the nature of memory.

This is the point at which many people stop reading *The Confessions*. The first nine books are well-trod, but the final four are like unpaved road into a dense forest of metaphysical speculation. "Proceed at your own risk," seems to be most teachers' advice. But avoid at your own risk, too, because you'll miss out on lines like: "Late have I loved you, beauty so old and so new."

In Book Ten, Augustine pauses to reflect on what he has just done, to ask: what is this capacity that we have to recall—and forget—our own past? A student and teacher of rhetoric, Augustine used classical images of memory as a "great cavern" or a "vast hall" or "stomach of the mind," all common tropes in the ancient (and very popular) "art of memory" in the Latin West. For Augustine, memory was one of the most essential, and most mysterious, faculties of the human soul. "This power of memory is great, very great, my God," he writes. "It is a vast and infinite profundity. Who has plumbed its bottom?"[38]

We are all sites of carefully curated memories, which often serve something less than a full and honest picture of ourselves. "I myself cannot grasp the totality of what I am," Augustine writes. We are unfathomable, sometimes terrible, mysteries to ourselves: "The human mind, so blind and languid, shamefully and dishonorably wishes to hide, and yet does not wish anything to be concealed from itself. But it is repaid on the principle that while the human mind lies open to the truth, truth remains hidden from it. Yet even thus, in its miserable condition, it prefers to find joy in true rather than in false things."

It's almost as if Augustine is talking about Emmett Till, and the way we (mis)remember him, or do not remember him at all: Till did not figure once in my own education, and only later did I come to learn the details about his killing. It seems easier to hide from the truth about what happened to him, and the conditions that brought about his murder and led to his killers' acquittal, and how those conditions still benefit some and harm others. The good news, for Augustine, is that we all naturally desire truth, even if it brings pain, because falsehood and deception are their own sorts of bondage. There is freedom—and joy—only in truth.

Salvation—literally, "well-being" in Augustine's language—consists, at least in part, in a healed memory, a restored, unvarnished, fearless account of oneself. Salvation, in other words, subsists in truth.

So Augustine's *Confessions* are an exercise in recollection and remembrance, gathering and putting back together the pieces of a fractured existence and offering them as a prayer to God, a confession both of waywardness and of gratitude. Because regions are comprised of human beings, public memory in the South is always conflicted, too. Sometimes it is a confusing mixture of affirmation and inaction.

The number 828 is also my area code.

It's come—strangely—to be shorthand for where I am these days, for the weird convergence of places and stories that now constitute my life.

When I was first really exposed to *The Confessions*, I had this sense: "Where has this been all my life?" Lately, I am experiencing a similar sense about other figures and episodes in my city's—and my own family's—history. I seem to keep circling back on a question that I pass by over and over again like a signpost on a roundabout (Big Ben, Parliament): "why am I just learning about this now?"

There was a time in my own life, not so long ago, when I tried to help young people try to make sense of Augustine's words, and maybe—of their own lives. Now, I find myself trying to do as he did: putting the shards of a dismembered self back together again, attempting to recover the unremembered pieces of a life that seem so eager to speed away from me, to get off the roundabout, onto a different road.

Augustine was after something similar: a whole and full self that included the memory of both regretful faults and great joys, and the conflict between them. "Which side has the victory," he said, "I do not know."

So 828 is a kind of sign for all that: the convergence of these stories, in this particular place, this area code, this moment in my own history, a shorthand for an urgent need to tell a fuller story of myself. It's yet another draft, another revision, but one that includes Emmett Till and other people and truths that previous versions of myself left out, a reminder of all the signs I might have missed, ignored, built up or shot down.

Terror so old, and so new.

Clarksdale: The Brick Man

On a Sunday night at Red's Lounge, one of Clarksdale's legendary juke joints, a portly White dude in combat boots, jeans, and a camouflage trucker hat is sitting on a stool with a Stratocaster in his lap. It's the kind of scene that invokes the suspicion that maybe the blues is dead after all, that White people did like we did with just about everything else: we took it over, and in the process made something that wasn't ours—something beautiful and terrifying—and totally ruined it.

But at Red's, a Black-owned business, the dude with the guitar is singing the blues not all that seriously, taking breaks and talking and cutting jokes in the middle of songs, chuckling and talking to folks at the bar. It becomes clear that what he is engaged in is not really a performance at all, not a spectacle for the consumption of paying customers, but something more like an act of communal memory and culture making, a quasi-religious ceremony of healing or something that doesn't require that you get it exactly right. Because it turns out he's earned his chops. During one interlude he tells us how he went to Parchman at age eighteen.

Red scolds me for taking video inside the club, because that's what everyone with a camera does now. It doesn't feel like the right time to nitpick that I am using film and shooting stills, so I concede, but pay the price for my semi-transgression by opening the camera back with the film still in it. The negatives come back even redder than the inside of Red's, an intensification of color in an already color-saturated place.

Later, we take lunch at Abe's BBQ on the corner of the fabled crossroads of US 61 and US 49, where Robert Johnson according to legend but not according to history sold his soul to the devil in exchange for ungodly guitar playing ability. Abe's is old enough to have been written up in the WPA Guide, but those books didn't include eateries. It would have made for an appropriately unpredictable entry: founded as the Bungalow Inn in 1924 by Abraham Davis, a Lebanese immigrant born in Beirut who settled in Clarksdale in 1915, Abe's has been serving hot tamales since at least 1934—Robert Johnson's time—when most restaurants around here were segregated. But Davis, an immigrant from a

Muslim country, had no truck with the prejudices of local White people. He served anyone, no matter their race, from the beginning. It is one of the few restaurants in Mississippi never to need to integrate, because it never segregated in the first place.

Like the hot tamales Abe's serves, this story is not the kind of thing you would expect from the Mississippi Delta. But the Delta is nothing if not a confounder of preconceptions.

We sit in the dining room. I have—for reasons that defy logic—sworn off meat for the second time on one of these trips, and due to some unexpected spasm of self-discipline I refrain from ordering the tamales I so badly want and go for the only vegetarian option on the menu, the $1.99 grilled cheese.

After ordering I get a message from Patrick Weems down in Sumner, who has figured out that I am in the area. Whatever barely laid plans we had for the afternoon are quickly scrapped, and we arrange to meet up with Patrick after lunch.

But in the meantime, we have some time to kill in Clarksdale, which is as photogenic as it gets. Shooting in front of the New Roxy Theater, which I have photographed on every trip here, a white pickup truck pulls up and pauses in the middle of the road. Behind the wheel is a large Black man in a Stetson and overalls, white button-down and bow tie.

"How y'all like my beautiful town?" he asks.

He introduces himself as the Brick Man of Clarksdale, shows us his business card with an image of MLK in brick, which he's done in town.

We talk about Clarksdale, but he talks about giving back. He talks with deliberation, and what comes out is oracular. *You got to give back to the place that birthed you*, he says. *We all got to stick together. When we are together, nothing can stop us.*

He throws the pickup into park. The engine revs higher, to keep the A/C pumping.

He stays inside the air-conditioned cab for a spell because he is no fool. *We need to go back to basics*, he says. *Being kind to your neighbor.* Eventually he pulls out of the middle of the street, parks and hops out of the truck. It's an impromptu sermon at the New Roxy, on the need for kindness and gratitude, and I am not unaware of the irony.

Indirectly, it's a running-board homily on a fundamental paradox of American life: that portion of the American population who has the most reason to give up on the whole American promise, the ideal and the dream, keeps calling the rest of us back to it. The community in America that is most justified in its skepticism of American words has typically been the one most diligently holding American culture and politics to them, calling America, as Dr. King said in his pointed, almost-final words to the country, "be true to what you said on paper." *The Brick Man* is living proof of what Ralph Ellison wrote in 1970, that "it is the black American who puts pressure upon the nation to live up to its ideals."[39]

So on Issaquena Avenue in Clarksdale, the Brick Man preaches an improbable humanity, a refusal to yield to the kind of cynicism and/or despair that has become the lifeblood of the politics of White grievance of late. He radiates a cheerfulness that frankly feels otherworldly, especially in this place, which has known White exploitation, abuse, and terror more than most.

What reason does a Black man in Clarksdale have to encourage two middle-aged White dudes in a minivan with a message of hope and unity? He also seems to be pointing a way ahead, a forerunner presaging some further encounter down the road, a John the Baptist in overalls.

Sumner

Wordless, we return to the minivan and point its nose southward on US 49 for Sumner.

When we arrive, Patrick is in the spacious offices of the Emmett Till Interpretive Center, which he cofounded and currently directs. The goal of the center at the moment is to preserve the lived geography of the Emmett Till story in Mississippi and Chicago for posterity as part of a proposed National Park Service site. The project is near fruition, we learn, but it's not quite there yet.

We walk across the street to the Tallahatchie County Courthouse, where the trial of Till's accused murderers was held in September 1955. We climb the stairs to the upper room where the trial took place. It has been restored to its 1955 appearance. We take a seat in the jury box, where twelve all-White jurors acquitted J. W. Milam and Roy Bryant of Till's lynching, to which they later rather gleefully confessed in an interview for *Look* magazine. I don't know if Patrick does this with all his White visitors to the courthouse, but the poignancy of the seating arrangement is palpable. We three White men are sitting in the very spot where White men before us participated in one of our country's most egregious and obscene miscarriages of justice. We are seeing the court

It really was.

from their perspective. And the dimensions are almost overwhelming in their power. Against the far wall opposite, the Black press stood in an atmosphere of unimaginable tension. Knowing that at any minute, violence could break out, the Black press had devised a contingency plan whereby Mamie Till, Emmett's mother, would be dropped from the second-story window into the arms of awaiting rescuers below. From along that wall, Ernest Withers (whose Beale Street studio we had been in a day earlier) shot his famous, iconic photograph of 64-year-old Black sharecropper Mose Wright at "the decisive moment" when he pointed a burden-bent finger at Milam and Bryant and publicly identified them as the two men who had kidnapped his grand-nephew. The stakes could not have been higher, nor the risk greater for Wright.

Sitting in the jury box, the dimensions of Wright's courage stand out in sharp relief. Right in front of us to the right, the table where the defendants and their counsel sat. The two White men Mose Wright accused— who had the entire state, county, and their legal apparatus on their side—were barely ten feet from the witness stand where Wright hung out a finger of judgment at them. It is not apparent from the published version of the photo, which is tightly cropped, just how small is the distance between them.

As the story is usually told, Mose Wright is cast as something of a country bumpkin, an uneducated and naive farmhand. During Wright's testimony, the judge asked Wright if he could identify the two men who kidnapped Till. According to the standard version, Wright replied, in a country dialect, "Dar he." But as Patrick tells us, Wright was a conscientious objector during World War One. He was no bumpkin. And contrary to received tradition, he did not say "Dar he" from the stand, but in slow, deliberate, carefully articulated words, "There. He. Is."

About this time the door to the courtroom swings slowly open. There are not supposed to be any visitors today; the building is not open to the public. But through the door walks a middle-aged Black man in a red plaid button-down and navy trousers, an ID tag hitched to his belt. He looks as if he has just stopped in after lunch. Slim, hair close-shaven, almost bald, he bears a striking resemblance to Mose Wright. He enters silently; the three White men keep talking. He wanders around the courtroom, looking. We register his presence with a silent nod but carry on talking amongst ourselves.

"I don't mean to bother you gentlemen," he says. "But I wonder if you could answer a question for me."

It is July 25, 2022: Emmett Till's birthday. A few weeks earlier, news broke nationally about the discovery in the Leflore County Courthouse of an unserved 1955 arrest warrant for Carolyn Bryant. It's been sitting in a box in the basement in Leflore County for sixty-plus years. What will be done about it remains an open question but it is a very live one for the man who has just walked in the door. He asks a series of highly detailed questions about what went on in the courthouse, who stood where, what the judge's name was.

Here we are in the upper room, three White men in Emmett Till's jury box, being interrogated by a Black man who has just entered through locked doors. Patrick answers each question and is met with another. What happened here is not just a historical curiosity for him: his questions arrive with urgent necessity.

"You know, I once met Carolyn Bryant," he says.

I beg your pardon, none of us says aloud, it's clearly legible in the startled expressions on our three White faces.

He proceeds to tell a story about how one time he was working for a health care agency, paying visits to individuals in a nursing home. One lady in particular proved especially elusive. He was never able to get a meeting with her when he went through the regular receptionist at the front desk. But one day the regular receptionist was not there, and a different person at the front desk who either did or did not know better let him back to meet this mysterious lady. He engaged her in conversation for an hour or more. She was polite, very kind, he says. *Name is Carolyn Bryant,* she said to him. Only later did it dawn on him which Carolyn Bryant this actually was: the very woman at the center of the Emmett Till story, in an assisted living facility in Mississippi.

After he relays this story to us, silence hangs over the courtroom, whose dimensions seem to contract around us. This still nameless visitor an unexpected mediator, the three of us in the jury box now one degree of separation from the woman upon whose testimony pivots, I do not think it is an exaggeration to say, the history of American civil rights in the twentieth century.

We talk about what should happen to her. Should the warrant be served? Should she go to jail? Is it worth the effort? What if the system fails? What if it works?

He seems to need something to happen, whether it means a nearly ninety-year-old woman getting locked up or letting her off for whatever thinning days remain for her. Either way, he wants to see the American legal industry actually going to the effort to make good on its word, whatever the outcome.

"People have got to know our justice system works," he urges. "Serve the warrant."

He thanks us all—somewhat backwardly—and exits the same way he came in. Not for the last time today, we sit together in stunned silence.

"I am not sure that wasn't Jesus," I tell Patrick.

This all seems more than enough to process for one day. Ready to call it, I shake hands with Patrick and fiddle with the car key.

"What do y'all have planned for the rest of the day?" he asks.

Patrick already seems to know the answer.

"Do y'all want to go to the barn?'

I both do and do not want to go. The barn is not on any map. It is not marked, and until today it has never entered my understanding of the geography of the Emmett Till story. It is outside the small town of Drew, which is also a name I've never heard mentioned in the context of this story. Almost no one seems to know about it.

Patrick hops into the driver's seat of his white Forerunner and pulls the door to. "His name is Matt," he says. "I got his email." We ease back into the courthouse square and then forward over the railroad tracks, drive the long road from Sumner out to the property in neighboring Sunflower County where the barn sits. If it's not a gravel road, it might as well be. What asphalt remains is pocked and rutted like a lava field. En route, Patrick tells us the story of the barn—"Ground Zero," he calls it—which has long remained off the main drag of the standard version of the Till story, on which I thought I had a decent grasp. He tells us about the seminal article about the barn by Wright Thompson for *The Atlantic*, which we will read on our way back east from Sumner. The road there is as flat as it is possible for a road to be, but it feels like a descent. Westward from Sumner the towns decline—in infrastructure, in weed control, in visible human life. But as we drive out beyond Drew—where "run-down" is not adequate to describe the empty shell of the now-abandoned public high school—I can sense the shifts in the geography of my understanding. Even now the map of the landscape of my mind is being redrawn.

"The Barn." Drew, Mississippi. Photo by the author.

What I thought I knew is gathering up behind me like the prodigious clouds of road-dust turned up by the Forerunner.

We turn into a driveway that divides a small pond rife with swamp cypress in two. Beyond the handsome country house open fields or row crops stretch almost to infinity. The only signage here reminds us that we are on private property. The lawn around the barn is close-cropped like a Citadel haircut. A crape myrtle in pink flower frames one end; the other is partially shaded by a hardwood that is neither young nor old. The barn is well-preserved and clearly still used. Emmett Till, fourteen, died in this barn.

At the far end, Till was tortured and shot in the head. Today the family uses that section of the barn to store Christmas ornaments. In 1955 the property, part of Sturdivant Planation, was managed by Leslie Milam, J.W.'s brother. Leslie was here when his brother and Roy Bryant—and as many as five other men, maybe more—showed up to the place in the early morning of August 28, 1955, like a perverse unholy family, looking not for shelter in which to give life but for secrecy in which to take it.

It is nearly impossible to take in the weight of what I am looking at. The barn has survived not because of memory but because of use. Its current owner apparently had no idea what happened here when he bought the place, and neither would you if you were to drive by it today. Sometimes a detour off the main road of American memory is not enough to cure your ignorance; you need someone like Patrick to lead you by the hand.

Driving back along the Drew-Ruleville Road in the kind of awestruck loss for words that has become the rule of the day, I am struck by the distance from Money to Drew, from Mose Wright's home to this grim death house. It is way the hell out there today, and even longer in 1955 terms, when roads were even worse and less paved. The drive was long enough for any one of the men in the cab of the truck to think about what they were doing, so many opportunities to turn back. But they didn't, and driving on this same road that they did reinforces the cold deliberateness of it all, the sheer incomprehensible evil that I don't want to write about anymore.

The genie-souls of this region are invisible on the surface, but they are spry and almost hyper-active. The convergences are coming so hot and fast I can barely keep up with them. It is like being caught in rough surf—just when you find your feet and catch your breath, here comes another massive wave.

On the way back to Sumner, we take a detour south towards Ruleville, past North Sunflower County Academy, a private school (a.k.a. a "seg academy") established in 1970, at the same time the State of Mississippi desegregated its public schools. They no longer quite so openly display the Confederate flag, but their mascot is the white "Rebel," poached from Ole Miss. As we pass by, the school is gated up, out of session. When the new school year begins in a few weeks, the student body will be 98% White in a county that is 75% Black.

When I first started writing about the Till trial a few years ago (long after many, many others had done so), several people my parents' age told me they had never heard about it growing up. They were shocked both at the horrific nature of the crime itself, and at the fact that they never really learned about it. For them and for me, the Till case had been an optional item in a White education, a nonessential episode from American history.

But as Matt's comments reveal, the case is far more of a litmus test of American justice for Black people than for White people, and the imbalance is as revealing as it is damning. Even now, on the day when Emmett Till should have turned eighty-one, some are still searching for some measure of accountability for his death sixty-seven years go. There is so much riding on it, as if what happens to Carolyn Bryant Donham, the only remaining witness and potential accomplice to Till's kidnapping and murder, will decide the trustworthiness of the American legal system. In a hot Mississippi summer, two years after George Floyd and Ahmaud Arbery, America needs a win from its courts. In a summer of discontent, following a session of a newly aggressive Supreme Court, Black Americans in particular need to know whether the courts will have their back, and if anything has fundamentally changed since Till's confessed lynchers got off scot-free. If you are White and old enough, the system seems to imply, you are off-limits. If you are no longer a threat to anyone, then the legal system seems to have abandoned interest in you. American justice, it seems, has a definite sell-by date. No one really wants to believe this, but it is true that most White people could take it or leave it; it may be true, but so what? At the end of the day White Americans will be able to trust that the system will work for them, or at the very least not against them simply because they—we—are White.

The case for prosecuting Bryant Donham is riding on this razor's edge: serve the warrant and trust the legal apparatus to do its job, let the chips fall; or don't even bother, and nothing changes, no one ever goes to jail. The latter is certainly a possible outcome of a trial, too: the risk is that if the warrant is served, she goes to trial, she is acquitted for lack of evidence, and therefore we are back where we started, the only difference being that the status quo now has the imprimatur of due process. It is a risk Matt is willing to take.

On the way back from Drew, Patrick, John, and I talk about the warrant. Matt's words still ringing in the ears as the gravel road passes through the harsh and fertile Delta landscape.

"I don't know," Patrick says. "Maybe Matt is right."

In 2004, the Federal Bureau of Investigation reopened the case, and assigned Oxford, Mississippi-based Special Agent Dale Killinger as lead investigator. He had Till's body exhumed and tested for DNA evidence, and conclusively proved that the body was his (contrary to what the counsel for the defense, as well as Tallahatchie County Sherriff H. C. Strider, had attempted to argue at trial). Killinger amassed a mountain of evidence, but when the grand jury met in 2007 to decide how to proceed, they only drew on a tiny percentage of that evidence. The case died without anyone paying a price, again. Killinger was thorough, unsentimental, and did not suffer fools. But this career federal agent could not compete with the will-to-inertia of the members of the local community who comprised the grand jury.

Maybe this time will be different, a new opening. In 2007, Tallahatchie County had made a go of it, and even held a powerful public ceremony at the courthouse and issued a formal apology for the trial in the presence of the Till family. It was restorative in many ways, but retributive justice still proved elusive. Maybe Leflore County would put an end to that.

In August 2022 a grand jury in Leflore County decided not to indict Bryant Donham. In a statement made shortly after, Till's cousin Wheeler Parker—who was with Emmett when he was kidnapped in Money—said, "The prosecutor tried his best, and we appreciate his efforts, but he alone cannot undo hundreds of years of anti-Black systems that guaranteed those who killed Emmett Till would go unpunished, to this day."

I wonder what Matt thinks. I send him an email. Within minutes he writes back:

> It grieves my heart to hear the grand jury decided to not take action. There has to be some accountability, this is unfathomable. I believe justice delayed is justice denied. In order for us to move on there is a need to hold people accountable for their actions, during and after.
> This is a sad day for all.

While two major federal acts now bear Emmett Till's name—the 2007 Emmett Till Unsolved Civil Rights Crime Act, sponsored by the late representative John Lewis, and the 2022 Emmett Till Antilynching Act, introduced by Representative Bobby Rush of Illinois—it is finished; no one will ever be disciplined in any way for Till's lynching.

Leaving Sumner, we stop in Tutwiler. The last time we were here, the funeral home where Till's body was embalmed and prepared for burial was a crumbling ruin. A purple historical marker now stands in front of an empty lot, but the funeral business still operates next door. I go around the back side of the short row of shops to photograph the rail line along which Till's body was carried back home to Chicago. A series of murals adorn the back wall. One features two Black men sitting on a bench. One, his hat in his lap, is listening to the other man, in a hat and sunglasses, playing slide guitar. The painting commemorates the site nearby where W. C. Handy reportedly first met the blues while waiting for a train along these tracks in 1903. As Handy described the moment, "A lean, loose-jointed Negro had commenced plunking a guitar beside me while a slept. His cloths were rags; his feet peeped out of his shoes. His face had on it some of the sadness of the ages. As he played, he pressed a knife on the strings of the guitar . . . the effect was unforgettable."[40]

A local policeman pulls up in a Ford Explorer. I'm prepared for him to ask me what the hell I'm doing here, but when he rolls down the passenger window to talk to me, that's not what he says. He points me to the map on one of the murals that identifies the location of the final resting place of Sonny Boy Williamson II, a famous blues harmonica player from here. He points down the road ahead, gives me verbal directions how to get there. *We'll head there straight away, check it out,* I tell him in my speaking-to-a-police-officer voice. He pulls away between the building with the murals and the rail line and then abruptly stops his car, honks at me, and calls out the window one more time.

I don't know how he knows that I'm interested in the Emmett Till story. I never mention it to him. But through the open window he says to me, "You know, the undertaker who dressed up Till's body back in nineteen fifty-five—his wife is still alive. She lives right over there," he says, pointing over my shoulder behind me. "If you ever want to talk to her, just give me a call and let me know," he says, handing me his business card. "I'll set it up."

On the way out of Tutwiler, a now-familiar floored sort of silence descends once more. This time, its source is the generosity of a local Black police officer and his unsolicited offer to connect me with another person here, perhaps unwittingly acknowledging the ubiquity and inescapability of convergence in this part of the world, a tacit recognition that if you plant your feet here for a few minutes, before long the connective tissue of this area will absorb you, too. The gratuitous meeting W. C. Handy experienced here is totally in character. Beneath the deep black, nutrient-rich soil of the Mississippi Delta, there is far more life than just roots and worms. There are words—millions and millions of them—which have yet to come to the surface. This place has already given us so many, but there are so many more that have yet to find the breath to carry them forth. Listen up, now—the Delta wants to talk.

Beale Street, Memphis, Tennessee. Photo by the author.

MEMPHIS
America's Only Medieval City

ocal lore holds that the Delta begins in the lobby of the Peabody Hotel in Memphis.[1] The current hotel was built in 1925, so where the Delta began before that is unclear.

The Peabody is now known chiefly for its famous ducks, who are escorted twice a day by a red-coated, cane-toting hotel porter from the central Travertine marble fountain down a flight of steps to march into a waiting elevator along a red carpet laid out just for them. It is perfectly adorable and eccentric, and a little absurd. But it is absurdity of a particularly Memphian order, a gesture of sublime ridiculousness in a world whose priorities are already wholly out of joint. There is an air of the Feast of Epiphany to it, a daily crowning of the Lord of Misrule, an upturning of worldly order in which the red carpet is rolled out not for kings and senators, but for waterfowl.

Transgressing the normal order of things is practically a Memphis habit—sometimes in innocuous fashion, sometimes in a more apocalyptic way.

In October 1931, a band of African American jazz musicians stopped in Memphis en route to a gig in Little Rock, Arkansas. The band's manager had left for New York, leaving his wife, Mary Collins, a White woman, in charge of arrangements. After a disagreement between Mrs. Collins and the bus company, Memphis police were summoned to the scene, and arrived to find the bandleader chatting with Mrs. Collins. Furious with this act of social and racial transgression, they arrested the entire group, including Mrs. Collins, and threw them in the slammer. According to one of those arrested, the cops said, "All right, you niggers . . . You're in Memphis now, and we need some cotton pickers, too."[2] The next day, the *Memphis Commercial-Appeal* listed the names of the performers:

Z. T. Randolph, 32; Fred Hall, 35; Sherman Cook, 39; Preston Jackson, 29; A. Washington, 29; Charles Alexander, 44; George James, 25; Paula Moore, 23; Lester Boone, 27, and Louis Armstrong, 31, all of Chicago.

The judge attributed the whole thing to a "misunderstanding,"[3] and released the members of the band "on condition that they return the next day to play a benefit concert."[4] They were free to go, but they would have to pay their dues to the principalities and powers. The next day, the group played a matinée for an all-white audience at the Peabody. In what is surely one of the gutsiest gestures in the history of American music, Satchmo played the song, "I'll Be Glad When You're Dead" and dedicated it to the Memphis Police, many of whom were Klansmen. A different kind of misunderstanding ensued. Not wise to Armstrong's diss, and apparently unable to make clear sense of the words of the tune directed at them, members of the Memphis police force approached Armstrong and Jackson after the performance. "No other band coming through town has ever honored them like this, they tell him."[5]

My first entrée into Memphis was via US 61 from Mississippi. The sense of emerging from the Mississippi bottomlands is palpable: the road begins gently to rise and fall, and Memphis emerges gradually as you slowly ascend to the "Bluff City." When Memphis began to experience White flight and urban sprawl, the city expanded mostly to the east, not south along 61. North on Interstate 55 from Hernando, Mississippi, the porosity of Memphis's borders—and those of Mississippi and Tennessee—is evident. The usual signs of expressway-centric growth proliferate: Tanger Outlets, a Walmart Supercenter. But on 61, there is little sign that you are about to enter the third largest city on the Mississippi River. Suddenly you are just there, in the thick of it all.

Memphis is named for an ancient city in Egypt that sits on the Nile, which I suppose is the rationale behind the existence of a gargantuan glass pyramid on the eastern bank of the Mississippi. It is in many ways the apotheosis of late 1980s architecture and poor planning. It was designed to serve as an arena, but things got weird from the beginning. The pyramid was originally capped with an inexplicable crystal skull at the top, in keeping with Memphis's seemingly inexhaustible capacity for inexplicability. On opening night in 1989, the toilets flooded. One thing city planners did not appear to take into account in their architectural paean to Memphis's namesake was the fact that ancient Egyptians did not use pyramids for arenas. Anyone with a basic understanding of geometry can see how the interior of a pyramid makes for some complications when used as a basketball arena or performance venue. The stands were unusually steep to accommodate the inward-sloping lines of the roof. Locker rooms were situated at an unusually long distance from the playing surface. At 535,000 square feet, utility bills ran upward of $700,000 a year. Penny Hardaway, a Memphis native and NBA legend who now coaches the University of Memphis basketball team, played in the building as a student at what was then called Memphis State University. "As a basketball arena," he said, "the Pyramid was out of this world. It wasn't natural. It wasn't normal." It lasted for just over fifteen years as an arena. It is now a Bass Pro Shops.

How it got that way is a story as weird and unlikely as Memphis itself. It all came about on a bet between Johnny Morris, owner of Bass Pro Shops, and Bill Dance, a legendary fisherman whose television show, *Bill Dance Outdoors*, has had a run on TV almost as long as the Nile itself. Since 1968, Bill—a native Memphian who has a University of Tennessee ball cap apparently permanently affixed to his skull—has taught viewers how to catch bass while cracking jokes and hosting guest stars (one episode with Terry Bradshaw remains one of the funniest things I have ever seen on television).

In 2005, Dance hosted Morris for a catfishing trip on the Mississippi. Morris was mulling over the idea of turning the Pyramid into his flagship store. The two men tossed the decision up to fate and made a bet: if they caught a big catfish on their outing, then Morris would close the deal. The first day of the trip turned up nothing. The second day didn't look much more promising. By that afternoon, it was looking like the Bass Pro Shops megastore was dead in the water. Morris was getting increasingly anxious calls from another executive, Jim Hagle, asking whether they were going to go through with it or not. Ten minutes before Hagle was scheduled to hold a press conference with an announcement about the company's plans, Jack Emmitt hooked a thirty-four-pound catfish. The deal was on.[6]

The pyramid now includes a 103-room hotel, a bowling alley, restaurants, a spa, and an indoor cypress swamp. The Peabody notwithstanding, by the time you are inside the Pyramid, you are definitely not in the Delta anymore.

You may not even be in Memphis, either, which is increasingly becoming a city designed for tourists more than for residents. Nowhere is this as visible as on the city's most famous thoroughfare, Beale Street.

The current version of Beale Street is an imitation of sorts. Once the center of Black Memphis, Beale is now an officially designated "entertainment district." Its history follows a familiar trajectory in American cities: a blighted urban core by the 1970s, real estate developers seized upon Beale Street as a potentially profit-rich tourist destination and began a redevelopment program that both injected new life into the ailing street and drew the old life out of it.

In its youth, Beale grew into one of the nation's most prominent Black business and residential districts, thanks in very large part to Robert Reed Church, born into slavery and ultimately the unofficial mayor of Beale Street.[7] Church built a fortune off of the libidinous urges of White Memphians with money and lust to burn in houses of ill repute, which he owned but did not operate, on nearby Gayoso Street, and turned his profits into political and economic power. He established businesses, community centers, parks, and a bank. He was Memphis's richest and most powerful Black man. So when the Memphis Fire Department intentionally set fire to Church's mansion at 384 South Lauderdale to demonstrate its new fire hose in 1953, it was displaying not just the power of new technology, but just how high Black people were permitted to rise under the iron hand of Memphis's de facto dictator, Edward Hull "Boss" Crump.[8]

The burning of the Church home was in many ways the apotheosis of the Crump regime, whose lasting legacy to the city he effectively commanded for half a century is expressed most visibly in the decimation of Beale Street and its surroundings, the federal housing projects that were made possible by Crump's "slum clearance" campaigns, and the evisceration of the city's Black power structure: once one of the most well-established in the country, and even now still struggling to overcome the legacy of Boss Crump.

The Beale Street of today is not at all the Beale Street of the 1939 WPA Guide to Tennessee, when the thoroughfare was "crowded with pawnshops, clothing stores, fruit stands, restaurants, doctors' office, and photographic studios." The WPA Guide was composed just before the Memphis Housing Authority began bulldozing Black neighborhoods to make way for federal housing projects. Little to nothing remains of the "'conjure' doctors and medicine men" who practiced on East Beale, offering "luck bags to wear around the neck, containing strange mixtures to cure diseases and drive away trouble." To be sure, Beale offered White visitors in the 1940s a spectacle of supposed Black exoticism, as if to confirm White prejudices of Black superstition. Today you will not likely find "Love powders, packets of 'goober' or graveyard dust, and black and white cat bones."[9] But you will find a Hard Rock Cafe and Coyote Ugly.

People of every color seem to come here for an uncomplicated good time. But for Black residents and visitors, Beale represents something more:

"Music for good times earned in adversity. A sound track for an affirmative life-style riffed in resilient blue steel from the least congenial of all American circumstances."[10]

That is how Albert Murray imagined the lure of the place prior to 1971, when even a beleaguered Beale still radiated, however dimly, some glimmer of an older, still-green vigor. Before real estate developers saw profit and promise in a revived Beale Street, purged of its voodoo and jive, before urban renewal and gentrification and the FedEx Arena inched Memphis that much closer to Anywhere, USA.

In 1977, the US Senate resolved that Memphis henceforth be known as "the Home of the Blues." The motion—Senate Resolution 335—was introduced by Samuel Ichiye Hayakawa, a Vancouver-born former teacher of semantics and university professor with a penchant for old-school jazz. Hayakawa simultaneously submitted a resolution declaring Memphis Slim as official "Ambassador At-Large of Good Will of the United States."[11] Hayakawa's interest in Memphis did not play well in his home state of California, however. During his bid for reelection to the Senate in 1982, he was called to the carpet by opponents in the Progressive Political Action Committee in northern California, who ran a full-page ad pillorying him for directing his attention elsewhere. The ad cited the Memphis resolutions as evidence of the Senator's ineffectiveness and busyness with fluff.[12] He dropped out of the race in early 1982, but the "Home of the Blues" moniker stuck.

The new trademark was especially serviceable as a kind of federal imprimatur on the city's new self-image as a tourist destination. Memphis exudes both modernity and antiquity, particularly the form that passes for antiquity in the South, where White memory tends not to venture beyond the boundary of 1861. Like many Southern cities, Memphis is an incarnate paradox. Its most famous street, once the epicenter of Black life in the city, is now a Disneyesque tourist destination.

For good or ill, Memphis has become congenial. Today it represents "the Home of the Blues," but Beale Street is the site of an ongoing contest for the American soul. What is lost in all of this neon newness is some experience of proximity to those adverse circumstances that birthed the music for which Memphis is so rightly famous. Of course, White visitors can never *know* that adversity in the same way that Black visitors can, and tourists typically don't book hotels and Airbnbs in search of adversity. But the redevelopment of Beale Street has served more or less to render those "least congenial of all American circumstances" opaque to the average visitor, Black or White. What remains is "music for good times," but without the adversity and the hard-earning, a "sound track for an affirmative life-style," but without all the negations of humanity that life-style defiantly repudiates.

By the time Elvis died in 1977, Beale Street had become like the city's most famous resident: used up, worn-out, bloated and spent—but not without the occasional glint of old life. In images of a vacant Beale from the 1970s, the street is still photogenic: fading street signs in script and neon for non-tourist-oriented shops next to rubble-strewn lots. Even an abandoned Beale is richly textured. The building that housed pawnbrokers at the corner of Second and Main is now home to Blues City Cafe, where I took in fried catfish on our first visit here in 1999. It claims to serve the "Best Meal on Beale," but I am not qualified to verify this claim. Nighttime on Beale is not at all unenjoyable, even if it is something of a simulacrum of Old Beale sanitized largely for White tourists. Nonetheless, there is legitimate bone-shaking music made here in the prolific blues clubs and out on the street.

Beale Street—even as Elvis knew it, as the place where he learned how to shake his hips from watching Calvin Newborn at the Flamingo Room[13]—was once raunchy and fierce, but not so much these days. Put it this way: music used to come *out of* Beale Street. Whole strands of American popular music originated there, between the Mississippi River and Sun Studios, at the far end of Beale. Today, much of the music heard in the truncated, two-block "entertainment district" is designed to evoke nostalgic longing for a time now lost, for a past that may or may not have lived. Like the name of Memphis's professional basketball team—the Grizzlies—the music now mostly comes from somewhere else.

Beale today is cut from the same cloth as contemporary Salem, Massachusetts (which abounds in witch-related retail), and to some extent Bourbon Street in New Orleans. They seem designed not to disappoint the hordes of tourists who venture to these places in search of what they already expect to find—the blues, witchcraft, and debauchery, respectively. But there is genuine vitality—and racial diversity—at night on Beale Street. It is reasonable to suppose that Black and White visitors come here for different reasons. All of them seek the blues, perhaps, but from different angles.

Few around here seem to care much about history, which may be just fine for tonight. At some level Beale Street offers everyone enduring an uptight age a session of unabashed therapy in psychiatric ass shaking. The institutions along Beale may be somewhat more buttoned up these days, but to judge by the scene out on the sidewalks and in the pedestrian zones, the people—even some of the tourists—have still got it.

We stumble back to the state park to sleep, and despite the immeasurable wideness of God's mercy, do not feel presentable for church at Al Green's parish the following morning.

Albert Leornes Green was born in Forrest City, Arkansas, forty-seven miles east of Memphis. Just nine years old in Forrest City (named for Confederate general Nathan Bedford Forrest who made his fortune in Memphis by selling Black bodies), Green formed his first band, a gospel group called the Green Brothers. After his family relocated to Grand Rapids, Michigan, Green's father kicked young Albert out of the group when the elder Green discovered his son had been listening to Jackie Wilson records.

Eventually, Green returned to Memphis, and from 1970 on began recording secular R & B music, with increasing success. In 1971 he recorded his most famous tune, "Let's Stay Together," a number one single on the pop charts in 1972. A couple of years later, Green's former girlfriend poured a pot of boiling grits on Green, and then committed suicide. Green was hospitalized with second-degree burns. He took the episode as a sign from God to change his life, and in 1976 he established the Full Gospel Tabernacle church in Memphis, a little over two miles from Graceland, where the Reverend Al Green still preaches regularly.

If this fitting juxtaposition of two of Memphis's most indelible stars weren't enough, Aretha Franklin was born a few miles to the north, very close to where in 1960 a former movie theater became Stax Records.

Much of this landscape is well-known, and is part of the reason tourists flock here. But less known—even to many Memphians—is the darker story of how Beale Street, and the flourishing Black community around it, grew and was beaten back over and over again. Beale is supposed to be Fun Central in Memphis, but it is the site of a series of genuinely American traumas that are not at all apparent on the surface, even after several visits here. What is even more striking than these histories is their connection to contemporary Memphis, which become inescapable once you find the key to unlocking them.

There are plenty of episodes in Memphis's history that city movers and shakers would not like to draw attention to. Even the memory of King's assassination has been avoided for decades. It wasn't until 2012 that the city named a street in his honor, long after almost every other village and hamlet in the nation had an MLK Boulevard. By contrast, other figures whom Memphis was quick to memorialize and celebrate are now being belatedly scrutinized, their roles in collective memory being duked out in very public ways.

In the heart of Memphis, on a bluff overlooking the Mississippi River, the public space once known as Confederate Park was renamed Memphis Park in 2013, and later renamed Fourth Bluff Park. Jefferson Davis lived in Memphis for only a few years, but the city happily adopted him as a native. The erection of a monument to him was largely predicated on the fact that every other city in the South had one, but Memphis did not. So it put one up in 1964, the year the Civil Rights Act was signed. When it was unveiled, the subtext of the ceremony was made plain in the *Commercial-Appeal*, which proclaimed, "Confederate Park was no place for Yankees when the Old South came alive for an hour yesterday afternoon."[14]

In December 2017, the City of Memphis sold the park to a private nonprofit organization for $1,000. The new owners promptly removed the statue of Jefferson Davis. They did the same with a park named for Nathan Bedford Forrest, which featured a huge statue of him on horseback erected in 1904, when the remains of General Forrest—along with those of his wife—were reinterred beneath the monument. In 2021, the Forrests' remains were dug up and taken out of the city altogether.

We first visit Confederate Park in 1999, when I am too naive to ask questions about the Davis statue. I photograph it at dusk, the stark silhouette of Davis, palm upraised against a cottony August sky. Nearly twenty years later, on a return visit to the park in 2018, Davis is gone. Only the pediment remains, surrounded by a chain-link fence. The empty pediment reads, "He was a true American patriot."

But Nathan Bedford Forrest, who was born in central Tennessee but moved to Memphis in 1852, did far more to shape the city than almost anyone in the mid-nineteenth century. In Memphis, Forrest himself is the subject of conflicting accounts of his history, reflected by conflicting styles of historical marker. One, erected by the Tennessee Historical Commission in 1955 in an older black-on-silver form, marks the site where Forrest lived before the war. It states simply that after he married in 1845, "he came to Memphis, where his business enterprises made him wealthy." In its concision it leaves you with the impression of a man whose rise-from-poverty story is simple to relate, and morally uncomplicated.

On the same corner, a newer sign entitled "Forrest and the Memphis Slave Trade"—in the same Sewah typeface, but in gold-on-green, like a colorized photo negative of its monochrome counterpart—tries to fill in some of the blanks left by the first sign. In compressed, two-sided text it corrects the received account of Forrest beloved of some White folks as much as it possibly can in the space of a historical marker. For example, Forrest's "business enterprises" were not just boilerplate hardscrabble American go-getter. Forrest made a fortune as a slave trader along Adams Avenue. He had competition, it's true, which he presumably tried to outdo and undercut by—in defiance of federal law—trafficking enslaved men across the Atlantic, "directly from the Congo." Even after Emancipation and abolition, Forrest was still advocating for the importation of cheap labor from Africa.

Both of these markers fail to mention two other episodes. In 1864, Forrest oversaw and possibly ordered the wholesale indiscriminate slaughter of Black soldiers at Fort Pillow, forty miles north of Memphis. And after the end of the Civil War, Nathan Forrest became the first Grand Wizard of the Ku Klux Klan. Monuments (like the one in Selma) have been erected to the "Wizard of the Saddle" not in spite of these chapters in his biography, but because of them.

From a second-story patio at the corner of Front and Adams overlooking the Mississippi in one direction, the iconic neon sign atop the Peabody in another, John points out how much of Southern memory—and what often passes for "Southern culture"—is popularly defined by a mere four-year span between 1861 and 1865. Twentieth-century memorials have often done much to reinforce this. Take, for instance, the monument to Jefferson Davis erected in the same the year the Civil Rights Act of 1964 was passed. Public memory in the South has no official organ, or organizer, but in Memphis John helps me see how much this short half-decade disproportionately dominates the collective conscience in the South, as if there were no South before and not much of one after. Such an exercise in protracted and selective nostalgia cannot help but be melancholic, a longing for a past that was not and a future that never will be. But in this city—where Black life has fought harder for itself than in perhaps any other place in America—there is so much to celebrate and hold alive in the memory that does not belong to the Civil War. Besides, one of the most important episodes in Memphis's history belongs entirely to the Civil War and its legacy, and yet there was no marker to it for a century and a half.

Exactly one year after General Lee's surrender at Appomattox, the Congress of the United States formally enacted the Civil Rights Act of 1866, which granted citizenship to all people born in the United States "without regard to any previous condition of slavery or involuntary servitude." Andrew Johnson, a Tennessean from the opposite side of the state, vetoed the Act, but for the first time in history, Congress overrode a presidential veto. In a rhetorical move that would become part of a long-running historical pattern, Johnson claimed that the act established "for the security of the colored, and against the white race."[15] For Johnson, Black citizenship and civil rights meant a diminution of the power of White people, who he believed would be victimized by the new statute. In a telling—if not representative—response, the editor of the *Daily Appeal* leaned into the theme of White suffering, encouraging readers to "abide with patient endurance and dignified submission the trial" of the new legislation. He turned the attention of readers away from the denial of civil rights to Black Americans, and instead pointed to the ways in which White Southerners were "[s]tripped of suffrage, denied representation."[16]

Less than a month after the act was passed, forty-six Black soldiers and civilians were killed in an orgy of White violence known as the "Memphis Massacre." The origins of the violence began on May 1, 1866, as Black soldiers stationed at Fort Pickering, just outside the city, fired shots into the air in a spontaneous celebration. When ordered to disperse by local police officers, gunfire broke out. One White officer accidentally shot himself in the leg while unholstering his pistol. Naturally this was blamed on Black people. But in the melee another White officer was shot and killed. Reprisals were swift and bloody. White mobs attacked Black Memphians, including women and children. A subsequent Congressional investigation reported forty-six African Americans and two White people killed, seventy-five people injured, five Black women raped, and numerous homes, schools, and churches destroyed.[17] But when the WPA Guide to Tennessee was published in 1939, it was silent on the subject.

In 1870 a different kind of violence was visited on Memphis. A devastating epidemic of Yellow Fever ravaged the population and emptied the city of over half of its living population. Of those who remained, largely White immigrants and Black residents who could not afford to flee, over 5,000 died.[18]

The epidemic known locally as Black Vomit claimed the lives of the parents of Ida B. Wells. In 1889, Wells returned to Memphis to work at the *Free Speech*, a newspaper based in Beale Street Baptist Church. She also owned a one-third stake in the paper. In 1892, her career shifted when a personal friend of Wells—Thomas Moss—along with Will Stewart and Calvin McDowell, proprietors of the Black-owned People's Grocery, were lynched by a White mob at a railyard in Memphis. The People's Grocery lynching was the apparent result of White commercial resentment when White shop owner William Barrett found his monopoly on groceries challenged. The *Appeal-Avalanche* applauded the work of the lynchers, claiming: "Never were the plans of a mob more carefully and skillfully executed."[19] White dailies hastily pinned blame squarely on the shoulders of Black citizens; they "wrote up the murders in such harrowing detail that it was clear the reporters had been called in advance to witness the lynching."[20]

On a Sunday in 2022, we take in a heaping plate of fried catfish, collards, a generous slice of cornbread, and peach cobbler at the Four Way at the intersection of Walker Avenue and Mississippi Boulevard. We arrive just after doors open at 11 AM, and just before the church crowd. The Four Way was opened in 1946 by Irene and Clint Leaves, who had been the chauffeur for Boss Crump. I do not know if the Cleaves chose the site intentionally, but the location of Memphis's most famous "soul food" joint seems to take the role of "restaurant" literally: it is a site of communion of sorts at the intersection of African American foodways and White violence, across the street from where the Peoples' Grocery once stood.

A historical marker stands on the corner of Mississippi and Walker to mark the spot. On this day, the marker is a headless, mute silver post: the aluminum plaque has been lopped off and the post that held it a metal stalk growing up from a patch of crabgrass and asphalt. Back in the parking lot next to the Four Way, a new mural honors the Cleaves and their legacy. An older one across the lot reproduces the missing marker, next to the likeness of Ida B. Wells.

Wells excoriated the practice of lynching and the system that tacitly or openly endorsed it in a May 21, 1892 editorial for *Free Speech*, the newspaper she worked for based in Beale Street Baptist Church. "Nobody in this section of the country," she wrote, "believes the old thread-bare lies that Negro men rape white women. If Southern white men are not careful they will over-reach themselves and public sentiment will have a reaction, or a conclusion will be reached which will be very damaging to the moral reputation of their women."[21]

It was so incendiary that Wells was forced to stay away from Memphis for her own safety. Edward Ward Carmack, newly hired editor of the *Memphis Commercial*, responded with unrestrained vitriol: "The fact that a black scoundrel is allowed to live and utter such loathsome and repulsive calumnies is a volume of evidence to the wonderful patience of white Southerners. But we have had enough of it. There are some things that the Southern white man will not tolerate, and the obscene intimations of the foregoing have brought the writer to the very outermost limit of public patience."[22] The editor of the *Scimitar*, unaware of Wells's identity, went even further, implying that readers "tie the author to a stake, brand him on the forehead, and perform a surgical operation on him with a pair of shears."[23]

Wells was in Philadelphia when the *Free Speech* editorial appeared. While in the northeast, she learned that her home was being surveilled. She was warned that "the trains were being watched, that I was to be dumped into the river and beaten, if not killed; it had been learned that I wrote the editorial and I was to be hanged in front of the court-house and my face bled if I returned, and I was implored by my friends to remain away."[24]

Fearing for her safety, she stayed away from her former home, and encouraged her fellow Black Memphians to follow suit, and abandon the city. Within the week, angry White mobs comprehensively destroyed the vacated offices of the *Free Speech*. To this day, not a single copy of the *Free Speech* has survived.[25] But months later, Carmack was still incensed. He held nothing back in a scathing rebuke of both Wells and Boston in a frothy and vengeful editorial that the "effete civilization of that city of thin-legged scholars and glass-eyed females finds pleasant mental diversion in worshiping at the large flat feet of Ida B. Wells, and in crowning her kinks with flowers from the conservatories of the elite."[26]

Laid bare for readers—although not at all obvious to White ones in 1892—was the distorted logic of the defense of Southern womanhood that Wells had the audacity to expose. Outraged at Wells's "gross and scandalous libel upon the virtue of Southern womanhood," calling her a "wretch" and a "black harlot,"[27] Carmack's solicitude for "Southern womanhood" extended only so far. The piece made it entirely clear whom the delicate abstraction "Southern womanhood" covered, and that it could just as easily be violated by "Black brutes," as well as educated Black women with a pen. Southern womanhood obviously did not include Black women like Wells, whom the *Commercial* editor likened to a figurative rapist for her literary outrages against the virtue of Southern ladydom.

As usual, White outrage was directed not against extrajudicial murder in the form of lynching, but against those who dared to call it out. For one thing, lynching was highly popular. Newspapers like the *Commercial* carried articles about lynchings daily, usually on their front pages. With its headline the day after the People's Grocery lynching, the *Memphis Appeal-Avalanche* indulged the expectant bloodlust of its White readers with a sensational headline that read "LYNCHED!"[28] Grammatically, it differed little from the kind of headline one sees now after the local football team wins a championship. While feeding readers' appetites for lynching news, the paper also stoked fears of an imminent Black uprising. In October of that year, the *Commercial* ran a front-page story on an alleged "Black Mafia" which, the paper claimed, "An Oath-Bound Gang of Assassins" were organizing in Mississippi to "Murder White Citizens" and to carry local elections "by force of arms." The newspaper ran a copy of one of the flyers published by the National Citizens' Rights

Association, claiming to expose the nefarious conspiracy being perpetrated by malicious Black people in the name of civil rights.[29]

The author of the flyer and president of the National Citizens Rights Association (NCRA), Albion W. Tourgee, was a White "carpetbagger" and Union Army veteran from Ohio. Possibly "the most vocal advocate of African American rights in the post-bellum period,"[30] Tourgee was hardly a militant by later standards. The NCRA was arguably "the most direct ancestor of the N.A.A.C.P.,"[31] which, in the 1954 Brown decision, succeeded where the NCRA failed, namely, as Homer Plessy's lead attorney in the landmark Supreme Court case in 1896, *Plessy v. Ferguson*. In our time, the aspirations of the National Citizens' Rights Association do not read as a radical manifesto for Black power, but at the time they clearly gave White Southerners more than a little to worry about, and a putative excuse to exact payback against a rising Black populace.

This was the atmosphere in Memphis after the Peoples' Grocery lynching, and after the departure of Ida B. Wells. Over 6,000 other Black Memphians followed Wells in vacating Memphis, mostly for the western territories.

No one was ever punished for the murders of Moss, McDowell, and Stewart. On the contrary, while Wells was under threat of vengeance, the prolynching Carmack enjoyed the fruits of his vitriol, being subsequently elected to the US House of Representatives in 1896, and to the US Senate in 1901. Tennessee rewarded Wells's most prominent antagonist in the state with a bronze statue, unveiled on June 6, 1925, erected on a not-at-all subtle site on the steps of the Tennessee State Capitol in Nashville overlooking a vast public square called Legislative Plaza. It stood until the summer of 2020, when it was toppled by protestors who informally renamed the site "Ida B. Wells Plaza." It would not be until 2021 that Wells was commemorated with a statue of her own, located adjacent to the Beale Street Baptist Church where she worked until 1892.

In late March, 1968, Beale Street was the site of wreckage. A march in support of Black sanitation workers—who had endured inhumane working conditions, low pay, and persistent discrimination—began at Clayborn Temple on Hernando Street, a block south of where the FedEx Forum now looms behind the brick rooflines of Beale Street. Dr. King had just arrived on a flight from Atlanta to find the crowd of as many as 20,000 tense and on edge, already bristling from a postponed start time. By the time King joined the head of the march, the crowd was so pressurized that "King could have lifted both feet and been propelled by the great momentum behind him."[32]

[T]urmoil erupted at the rear of the march, several blocks back, where some long wooden sticks that had originally held placards were thrown through the plate-glass windows of two Beale Street businesses. Within seconds, the disruption spread, with more sticks being used to break store windows. Some of the youngsters, plus a handful of street people, started looting goods from the shattered storefronts, and onlooking policemen called for more officers.[33]

It escalated quickly. But municipal leaders had in some way enabled the melee, choosing not to protect Beale Street with law enforcement officers, who were instead concentrated in the White business district.[34] The sticks that were used to vandalize businesses and attack police officers were a kind of irony. They were intended to support the now-iconic "I AM A MAN" signs carried by striking sanitation workers and their allies, a proclamation of inherent human dignity. It was "the first time in the six-week-old sanitation stretch that demonstrators would carry mounted picket signs—a minor change that would have dire consequences." The sticks were the brainchild of Ernest Withers, a veteran—and legendary—Black photographer based on Beale Street who had first photographed King and Abernathy together on the first integrated bus in Montgomery, and who had taken the iconic photograph of Mose Wright at the trial of Emmett Till's lynchers in 1955. But by 1968, Withers was working as an informant for the FBI. His involvement with the march has led to speculation that his role as an informant may have contributed to the disaster that erupted.[35]

Police officers turned on peaceful protesters as well as looters. The *Memphis Commercial-Appeal* was more than happy to pin responsibility for the riot on King, whose reputation was badly damaged by the display of violence. In a characteristic instance of convenient amnesia, the front-page story described it, as if unleashing a deep-rooted urge to employ the term, as the city's "first full-scale race riot."

Fearing an intensification of violence, King was removed from the scene. When it was over, sixteen-year-old Larry Payne was dead, shot in the stomach with a sawed-off shotgun. According to some witnesses, Payne, who was Black and unarmed, was raising his arms in the air when he was killed by a police officer at the Fowler Homes housing project across the street from Mason Temple. (Fowler Homes were demolished in 2004; in 2018, in partnership with the City of Memphis, the Church of God in Christ cut the ribbon on Mason Homes, a seventy-seven-unit affordable housing project on the site.)

Internally, leaders of the march blamed the outbursts on the Invaders, a group of militant student activists. King himself admitted that he had "miscalculated," and failed adequately to prepare for the realties on the ground in Memphis. Distraught and despondent, King returned to Atlanta, and privately cussed out the Southern Christian Leadership Conference's (SCLC) staff for not supporting his mission to Memphis. He planned a return for the following week.

King's colleagues did not want to go to Memphis at all. When SCLC organizer Xernona Clayton went to pick up King at his home on Sunset Avenue to take him to the airport, his children pleaded with him not to go, climbing on the hood of Xernona's car, begging him to stay home.[36] But King came back to Memphis for a second attempt at a march, this time with a supportive team more fully prepared for infiltrators and for a deliberate show of nonviolence.

In words that eerily presaged the *hands-up-don't-shoot* chants of protestors after the shooting of Michael Brown fifty years later, the Reverend James Lawson invoked the murder of Larry Payne in his remarks at Mason Temple: "If their job requires that they stick a shotgun in the midsection of a seventeen-year old boy who has his hands over his head and is saying, 'don't shoot, then we need . . .'"[37] Whatever he meant to say next, it was drowned out in a passionate chorus of cheers from the audience. Ralph David Abernathy was supposed to be the headliner that night, but he knew whom the crowd really wanted.

Abernathy stepped away from the stage and called King, already in bed at the Lorraine, pleading with him to come to Mason Temple to share some words. He reluctantly roused himself and dressed and made it in the lashing rain to Mason Street. King delivered a simultaneously inspiring and foreboding speech at Mason Temple. Surely no one in the audience that night in the mother church of the Church of God in Christ had any idea what they were experiencing, or what portents were pouring forth from the microphone:

We've got some difficult days ahead. But it really doesn't matter with me now . . .

King never made it back to Beale Street. Less than twenty-four hours later, he was shot in the neck on the balcony of the Lorraine Motel. The same Memphis Fire Department that, years before, had set fire to Robert Church's home on Beale Street billed Coretta Scott King for the cost of the ambulance ride to take her slain husband from the Lorraine to St. Joseph's Hospital.

The thin concrete balcony of the Lorraine seems incongruously inadequate to bear the tremendous weight of such incomprehensible sadness and tragedy. It is arguably America's most weighted corner, where the realities of American history—especially its remembrance and forgetfulness—converge.

One hundred and two years before, almost on the very same spot, White mobs began attacking Black citizens in the Memphis Massacre of 1866. Two blocks away from the Lorraine, at the corner of Second Street and what is now G. E. Patterson Avenue, a historical marker now stands. It is fair to say that even—perhaps especially—in Memphis, few were aware of this historical trauma, and the wounds it left on the city. Many still are. It would take 150 years for the City of Memphis to mark this episode publicly with a historical marker. So for the *Commercial-Appeal* to proclaim the March 28, 1968, riots on Beale as the city's "first full-scale race riot" reveals how deep the regime of collective forgetfulness runs, and how long it has taken for cracks in that regime to emerge.

As with so many places in this book, the proximity of contingent historical episodes only becomes really apparent on foot. The deadliest massacre in Memphis's history, which was waged in direct response to new legal rights for Black people, is roughly 400 footsteps away from Memphis's most notorious killing 102 years later. The long struggle for Black rights had made substantial progress in one hundred years, but at street-level, it doesn't seem to have made it very far at all. Where the Memphis Massacre began is almost identical with the spot where the civil rights movement's most powerful and prophetic spokesman was slain.

Heading south out of Memphis along Lamar Avenue, one of the most mural-rich environments I've ever seen. Even in a busy thoroughfare through a depressed part of town, Memphis remains a sprawling eruption of artistry, uncontained creativity and drive toward beauty and dignity. I don't know of any other American city that has so vigilantly fought for itself—speaking specifically of its now majority Black population—as Memphis. Memphis was saved once by the Black men and women who stayed behind, to face plague and disease to nurse the city back to health, and have saved it again and again, and repeatedly have been beaten down for it. Nowhere, in my experience, is the human demand to be treated with dignity so persistent and so funky, and nowhere is what King called "creative maladjustment" so prevalent and rife with promise. Memphis is, to me anyway, the epiphanic city, where a kind of generous anarchy reigns, constantly challenging the order of things, calling them into question, turning them upside down. Memphis is arguably America's only medieval city, in the fullest range of meanings of that word. Backward, imaginative, corrupt, vivacious, synthetic: a kind of divine unreason seems to rule here, ordered not by conventional rationality but by a more ludic, more human spirit. Play in Memphis is serious. Maybe only Memphis could birth "an affirmative life-style riffed in resilient blue steel from the least congenial of all American circumstances."[38] Heading southeast out of town on Lamar, evidence is everywhere that not even urban dereliction is enough to overcome the insistent echo of a modest but radical claim from an earlier time, which reverberates visually from the prolific and prodigious public artworks along the roadside. With slight, more inclusive revisions, it is the same message, in new materials, new colors, on old surfaces: I AM A MAN.

"The galaxy's number one Elvis fan." Holly Springs, Mississippi. Photo by the author.

MISSISSIPPI II
How Far? Not Far

Memphis is as tempting to linger in as it is to write about, but we move south, following Ida B. Wells's route back to her home. Wells grew up in Holly Springs, as did Boss Crump. The two could hardly be more different.

We approach from the north, through the Memphis suburbs, then along MS 178 through Byhalia. North of Holly Springs, we pass the campus of Rust College, where Wells was once a student. Founded in 1866, Rust—known as Shaw University during Wells's time, is one of the oldest historically Black colleges and universities in the country. Across the street, the decaying campus of Mississippi Industrial College. Established in 1905 by the Colored Methodist Episcopal Church, the school closed in 1982.

Long, skeletal green vines of ivy like bony arms reach up and around the stately brick buildings. The tidily maintained grounds—on this day recently mown, scattered with drying green piles and towy streaks of dried grass clippings—contrast starkly with the abandoned structures. Exposed beams on the roof of the 2,000-seat auditorium appear blown-out like war wounds. The site exudes stately vulnerability. The roof of adjacent Catherine Hall has fallen inward, dormers now pointing skyward like eyes lifted to the heavens asking, *From whence cometh my help?*

But if Holly Springs is famous now, it's not because of Rust College. It's because of Elvis. Sort of.

Two blocks from the Marshall County Courthouse, we park alongside a two-story white house that is doing its damndest to look stately. Next to the house, a sign on an unwired and bulbless electric marquis on wheels reads "THE UNIVERES [sic] THE GALAXYS THE PLANET THE WORLDS ULTIMATE1ELVIS FANS PAUL AN ELVIS AARON

PRESLEY MAC LEOD TAKEN CARE OF BUSINESS IN A FLASH AT GRACELAND TOO."

Paul MacLeod claims to be the "galaxy's number one Elvis fan," and has dedicated his life and property to proving it. Every inch of his house in Holly Springs is given over to the King. It is part shrine, part database: ceilings are covered with newspaper clippings that mentioned Elvis; walls and hallways lined with photos, concert posters, magazine covers, stacks and stacks of *TV Guides*. Anything and everything that might have a reference to Elvis, Paul MacLeod put it in Graceland Too. With his son, Elvis Aaron Presley MacLeod, he oversees what he claims to be the world's largest (and most valuable) collection of Elvis memorabilia. He estimates its value to be in the millions. For twenty bucks MacLeod, paunchy as Vegas-era Elvis, with grayer sideburns, shows us around the place, along with a curious and keyed-up German gentleman. Elvis Too shows off Elvis One–related swag, whose authenticity can only be described as suspect. He holds up a leather jacket whose significance is unclear, except that Elvis also wore a leather jacket. He hoists a T-shirt from Sun Studios that looks right off the merch rack at Sun Studios. As a final act, he croons "Love Me Tender" into a plastic toy microphone with an undersized internal speaker like a walkie-talkie. The likeness to Elvis's golden voice is not uncanny.

The house is supposed to look like the original Graceland in Memphis, with the columns on the front porch and a pair of white lions guarding the entrance. It became a sort of obligatory destination for night-tripping Ole Miss students who probably shouldn't have been on the road to begin with but were up for more of an adventure than the Oxford Waffle House. Like the Waffle House, Graceland Too was open 24/7.

When we visit in 1999, the house is painted white. Behind the white fence, fake plastic Christmas trees emerge from a mound of white-painted stones piled inside white-painted tractor tires. In later years, MacLeod would occasionally make dramatic changes to the exterior, spray-painting the entire house and surrounding walls in dark blue, then in hot pink, and finally in a beige-ish tone that was presumably intended to make the house more closely resemble its namesake. But the beige paint job was never finished.

On July 15, 2014, Dwight David Taylor, Jr., allegedly tried to break into MacLeod's home. Taylor, a twenty-eight-year-old Black man who

"Graceland Too," Holly Springs, Mississippi. Photo by the author.

was working for MacLeod, was after ten dollars MacLeod owed him. They got into it. MacLeod shot and killed Taylor inside the front door of Graceland Too. Two days later, MacLeod himself was found dead in his rocking chair on the front porch. The following January, the entire collection of Elvis memorabilia was sold at auction to Marie and Jeffrey Underwood, a couple from Illinois, for $5,500, a fraction of what MacLeod assessed his collection to be worth.

When we return to Graceland Too in 2018, the house has been repainted white, but is still a work in progress. A porta-potty stands along the curb in front. A handwritten sign on the front door lets it be known that the owners have gone to Home Depot and will be back in a few minutes. Around the back of the house, Elvis is playing from an unseen loudspeaker. Behind the windows, posters of the King still hang taped to the inside glass. The house is in new hands, but Elvis has not left the building.

A maroon Lincoln pulls up as we stand by the car, preparing to leave. The driver and passenger—presumably the Underwoods—slow in front of us and roll down the window. *Hang on just one second,* they plead. They have just gotten back from the Depot with fat-boy Styrofoam cups of Coke and supplies for what appears to be an interminable DIY restoration. With an air of frantic desperation, they beg us to come inside. *We'll unlock the door for you,* they said. If they ever do, I don't know. By the time their Lincoln is parked, we are gone, in a flash.[1]

The Dixie Limited

Thirty miles south of Holly Springs, Oxford is and is not like the rest of Mississippi. Named for "the city of dreaming spires" in England, it's a university town that makes its living off of education, football, and William Faulkner. Oxford is what my friend Scott calls "a professional town," which means it spends most of its time trying to be what everyone expects of Oxford, Mississippi.

"I lived a hundred miles from William Faulkner but he meant less to me than Albert Camus," Walker Percy once said. "I may have been lucky that way."[2] Lucky or not, I lived a lot farther from Bill than Percy did, and I wasn't clued in enough to know whether that made me lucky or not. Faulkner didn't make an impact until I was even farther away from him.

My high school education could have been anywhere; when I was in the tenth grade, there was no sense that I was in the tenth grade in a particular place. Sure, we knew we were all in forward-looking Atlanta, but the idea that our city had a past that had something to do with us was not a hot topic. We read what tenth graders everywhere, I assumed, were supposed to read: Emerson, Hemingway, Salinger. The idea that there was this thing called "Southern literature" did not dawn on me until I was in college. In high school, those omissions were standard fare.

Maybe my ignorance of that stuff was not unique, but by the time I got to college it became culpable ignorance. Along with my freshman English professor's name, I have forgotten everything I was supposed to have read that semester, with two exceptions. Because I had my head up my ass, I regarded freshman English as a hoop to jump through, and I definitely did not "apply myself." Each act of literary knowledge attempted upon my life failed, but sometimes books can transcend both a professor's good intentions and an incorrigible student's resistance.

Years before, I had first seen a high-powered hydraulic tree shaker in South Georgia grip the trunk of a pecan tree and rattle the living bejeezus out of it, and make it turn loose of its nuts, which showered down on the bare ground below. That was the effect Ralph Ellison's *Invisible Man* had on me. It totally challenged what I thought a novel could do and renewed a kind of literary faith in the power of fiction, which despite my embarrassing noninterest had still managed to survive, barely, into college. I tried to return the favor by assigning *Invisible Man* years later as a college professor myself, but I don't know if it took for my students the way it did for me.

Ellison took, but Faulkner did not. My freshman professor—bless her heart—tried to expose me to *Light in August* and possibly *Absalom, Absalom*, but my only takeaway was a sense that these were important books. Flannery O'Connor once wrote that "The presence alone of Faulkner in our midst makes a great difference in what the writer can and cannot permit himself to do. Nobody wants his mule and wagon stalled on the same track the Dixie Limited is roaring down."[3] O'Connor was talking about the gigantic shadow cast by Faulkner over later writers of fiction; but he also came with the heavy freight of an overloaded reputation—for influence, for difficulty, for an aversion to punctuation—that probably scared off a lot of readers like me. Within a decade, as a graduate student in a foreign country, I had reached a point where I needed some avatar of home, some way of return to what I thought was "my" region. A friend of mine—from Nebraska—had told me one night at a dinner in St. Edmund's College that he had once spent an entire summer reading everything Faulkner wrote. I felt ashamed—here I was supposedly a literate Southerner, but ignorant of all of it. It was time to stop getting out of the way of the Dixie Limited.

So not long afterwards, I bought a copy of *Light in August* in Heffers Bookshop in Cambridge, which I read a little of in a pub one afternoon, but it still didn't sink in. A bookmark revealed how far I did not get; but I needed the book less for what Faulkner wrote than to mark where I was, where I had been, and—oddly, because I didn't know it then—where I would go. *Light in August* itself became a sort of bookmark: a physical object to draw me back to a region I had left behind, and really hadn't even known that well at all. It was a momentary comfort in a place where I did not know any other people from my part of the world, where if I couldn't be with people with whom I shared a history and a place, at least I could be with Lena Grove, who at the beginning of the novel is, like I was, farther away from home than she has ever been.

Buying books is inherently pleasurable, but there are some books that bring you such pleasure, or represent such important interventions in your life that, as if to pay them back for what they have given you, or to reawaken the experience of newness and discovery they gave you the first time, you feel a desire to buy a new copy every so often. The desire may be impractical, but it is not irrational. With some books— *The Hobbit* is one—I can easily summon up what seem like legitimate reasons for buying a new edition, even though I may already have several at home. A new hand-drawn cover, perhaps. Or the fact that I am 4,000 miles from my main copy. I have several different copies of both Flannery O'Connor's *A Good Man Is Hard to Find* that are symptoms of this syndrome (one of which I also bought in Heffers). I have at least three copies of *Light in August*, the most recent of which I bought at Square Books in Oxford in 2018, as one does.

When you are in Oxford, you go to Square Books, and you buy a Faulkner. That's just the way it is. It does not matter if you already own every Faulkner there is. It's like going to Pisa and having your picture taken pretending to hold up the Leaning Tower. It may be clichéd, but it's what you do.

In my case, I wasn't ready for *Light in August* until 2018. In 1990 and again in 1998 I was not yet really in a position to understand what Faulkner meant in a famous passage in the novel:

> Memory believes before knowing remembers. Believes longer than recollects, longer than knowing even wonders. Knows remembers believes a corridor in a big long garbled cold echoing building of dark red brick sootbleakened by more chimneys than its own, set in a grassless cinder-strewnpacked compound surrounded by smoking factory purlieus and enclosed by a ten foot steel-and-wire fence like a penitentiary or a zoo, where in random erratic surges, with sparrow like childtrebling, orphans in identical and uniform blue denim in and out of remembering but in knowing constant as the bleak walls,

the bleak windows where in rain soot from the yearly adjacenting chimneys streaked like black tears.[4]

I am still in no position to understand that extraordinary tidal wave of a sentence, but at least I can make a little more sense of the idea of memory as a kind of "belief." I am more attuned, maybe, to the ways in which memory tends to be self-serving or self-preserving, tends to edit out the unpleasant or unflattering. We all have parts of our own past that we hope never make it into a rehearsal dinner speech or funeral sermon. For Faulkner, though, memory is a high-stakes game. Memory and knowledge are intimately related to one another, but the desire to remember the past in a certain way can often overwhelm the truths of history. Knowledge can often be a kind of exercise in historical archaeology, uncovering the reality of the past from the encrustations of self-preservation.

Years of compulsory summer reading lists had felt designed to breed out of every red-blooded schoolchild the idea that one could read for pleasure, an idea reinforced by decades spent in higher education as a graduate student and then college professor, which can tend to induce in one a sense of pathological guilt that one is actually getting paid to read books but not necessarily enjoy them. *Do this because it is good for you, dammit,* like eating peas or calf liver (debatable) or strenuous exercise.

John and I visited Faulkner's home, Rowan Oak, and his grave in 1997, and I have returned multiple times since. I have tended to keep my distance from the cult of Old Count No 'Count, lest my profound admiration turn into fawning imitation. Faulkner's style is inimitable, but it's also nearly impossible to read him at his best and not think, *Damn, I wish I could write like that,* and then, like an overeager night tripper to Graceland Too, attempt to do something really foolish and ultimately unrewarding. In truth I probably avoided Faulkner out of a certain kind of fear that doing so will change everything I think about everything. In even more truth, there is just a whole lot of Faulkner that for the life of me I just can't make heads or tails of. He's just difficult to understand sometimes. But the allure or terror of literature is not that it is difficult, but that it will provoke an existential confrontation with yourself and the world you think you live in, and with the "you" who is doing the living. (James Baldwin, for example, was so sequestered from my education as to be neither feared nor alluring.) I feared, I suppose, being seen by

Faulkner in the way that Rainer Maria Rilke felt seen by the fragmented torso of Apollo in the Louvre. His 1908 ekphrastic poem unfolds the experience, with its inevitable oracular consequence: "You must change your life."

Flannery O'Connor was the first writer I ever read as an adult who had this effect on me, and her own sense of intimidation by Faulkner may have passed on to me. The anticipation of that life-altering effect may also help explain why we were not told to read James Baldwin in an expensive private school in Atlanta in the 1980s—*Do this because it is good for you, dammit*—because it would have meant we would have had to be changed.

Oxford

In front of the courthouse in Oxford, a marble monument—one of many such produced by the Columbus Marble Works nearby—blindingly white in the hot August sun, is almost too hot to look at directly, which may help explain why it is still there. It is the old soldier in the familiar pose: standing, relaxed, his hands around the barrel of a rifle, whose muzzle is just below his own. It looks like a microphone in his hands, as if he is about to give a speech. Beneath him, on the pediment, the inscription:

IN MEMORY OF
THE PATRIOTISM OF THE
CONFEDERATE SOLDIERS
OF LAFAYETTE COUNTY, MISSISSIPPI.
THEY GAVE THEIR LIVES
IN A JUST AND HOLY CAUSE

The Lafayette County Courthouse is the model for the fictional version in Faulkner's Yoknapatawpha County. The fictional Jefferson is virtually identical to Faulkner's Oxford. When he describes, in *Intruder in the Dust*, the courthouse square in Jefferson, I see Oxford: "The amphitheatric lightless stores, the slender white pencil of the Confederate monument against the mass of the courthouse looming in columned uproar to the dim quadruple face of the clock lighted each by a single faint bulb with a quality as intransigeant against those four fixed mechanical shouts of adjuration and warning as the glow of a firefly."[5]

In 1997, the "slender white pencil" does not strike me as anything especially peculiar. Versions of this scene are ubiquitous in the South, and so familiar as to be innocuous. It does not occur to me at the time to ask why that statue was put there, because it seems a simply de rigueur feature of southern courthouse squares. A better question to ask would have been *when*? It is a more basic question with a more definitive answer. Had I asked it, I would have broached the *why* question at the same time. The rationale for the erection of the Lafayette County monument, and so many like it, has everything to do with its timing. When I first see it, it has been standing for ninety years, but it might as well have been a hundred and thirty. None of the intrigue of its placement there is self-evident. That part takes work.

But when Faulkner sets the Yoknapatawpha County Courthouse at the center of the action in *Intruder in the Dust*, it is not an accident. In the novel, Lucas Beauchamp, an older Black man falsely accused of murdering a local White man from the impoverished hills of Beat Four, is being held in the jail inside the courthouse. He's waiting there, not for justice, but for the inevitable lynching that awaits him from the crowd outside, who had come "not to see what they called justice done nor even retribution exacted but to see that Beat Four should not fail its white man's high estate."[6]

The courthouse bears the symbolic weight of the "white man's high estate," an architectural representation of who Yoknapatawpha County— and by extension, Mississippi, the South, America—is really for:

It existed only by their sufferance and support to contain their jail and their courthouse, to crowd and jam and block its streets too if they saw fit: patient biding and unpitying, neither to be hurried nor checked nor dispersed nor denied since theirs was the murdered and the murderer too; theirs the affronted and the principle affronted: the white man and the bereavement of his vacancy, theirs the right not just to mere justice but vengeance too to allot or withhold.[7]

Taken by themselves, most of the monuments that punctuate the South are not very interesting, and often not especially good. Many of the monuments to both Union and Confederate soldiers were made by the same company, the Monumental Bronze Company on Howard Avenue in Bridgeport, Connecticut. Monumental was proud of its "white

bronze" (cast zinc) and touted it in its promotional materials as superior
to either marble or antique bronze. In 1882, the company offered Product
No. 220, "The American Soldier," six feet, one-and-a-half inches high,
for $450.[8] Monumental sold hundreds of both Union and Confederate
versions of it, which began to crop up in both Northern and Southern
small towns whose budgets did not allow for custom-made bronze sculptures by Italian artisans. The same prefab soldier statue is sometimes
used to represent Confederate and Union soldiers in different places, a
fitting sort of irony in a culture of mass-produced public memory.[9]

The year 1900 marks an uptick in new Confederate monuments,
but 1907—the year the Lafayette County statue in Oxford was raised—
marks the beginning of a boom that did not level off until the end of the
First World War. The timing of the move is illustrative of a larger cultural shift in the South. The 1880s and 1890s had produced new, explicitly White supremacist state constitutions in Florida, South Carolina,
and Mississippi, new Black Codes all over the country, and the *Plessy v.
Ferguson* decision. The wave of monument building in this new context
of unrepentant White supremacy is less like an outpouring of collective
grief over war dead than a public victory celebration, a planting a flag in
the ground, a marking of space.

The courthouse statues stake a claim to territory—in this case juridi-
cal territory—as White space. They began to pop up in the Jim Crow
era, the period when lynchings proliferated and legal disenfranchisement
intensified. The courthouse statues are a reminder to African Americans that the rule of law in a place like Lafayette County means the
White rule of law. "When placed in the center of town," Sarah Beetham
writes, "Confederate soldier monuments explicitly claimed civic spaces
for white Southerners and discouraged black celebrations and political
involvement."[10]

In his speech at the dedication of the 1906 Confederate monument on
the campus of Ole Miss, Charles Scott, a Rosedale attorney and veteran
of the 28th Regiment of the Mississippi Cavalry, described the response
to "Dixie" he heard while in the rotunda of the Grand Hotel in Paris:

Why is Dixie so honored in the far-off land of the French lilies? The
cause is not far to seek. It is the involuntary homage paid by the civilized world to the memory of the old South, once radiant with all the
glory that was Greece and the grandeur that was Rome.

"No nation rose so white and fair
None fell so pure of crime."
And the world is beginning to recognize this fact, and we are now, in part at least, understood.

Prose rarely gets more gratuitously self-serving than this, but it does in the next paragraph of Scott's speech:

The Southern soldier, whether officer or private, fought neither by vengeance nor hatred. No unholy lust for conquest nor consuming love of martial glory summoned them from their peaceful homes to the tented fields. These men battled for a principle, in which each believed with all his heart, soul, and mind. Overwhelmed at last by countless numbers and the boundless resources of a hostile world (for the South fought the whole world), the soldiers returned to their desolate homes and devastated fields; but they promptly assumed and faithfully discharged the duties of American citizens. All this was done with a Southern grace and courtesy and good humor which in the course of time disarmed enmity and criticism and brought peace and good will to the whole country.[11]

"The South fought the whole world": a good example of the grade-inflation style of Lost Cause memory. It is not hard to imagine that there were a few eye-rollers in the audience on the "red-letter day" of May 10, 1906: jaded and wounded Confederate veterans and amputees who were less sanguine than Scott about the realities of war and its specific motives, who were left to interpret for themselves what the unspecified "principle" was for which they fought, who may have returned to the "devastated fields" to ask what the hell it was all for, this allegedly valiant and glorious battle in defense of a "principle." If Scott sounds as though he were running for office, he was, though despite campaigning across the state on horseback and in his Confederate States of America uniform to adoring crowds, he lost in the 1907 gubernatorial primary.[12]

The glut of new Confederate monuments celebrating the Lost Cause began to taper off around 1915, not because of a loss of interest, but because that year marks one terminus of the Jim Crow era. By 1915 White people had won their campaign to disenfranchise African Americans. In that year, D. W. Griffith's notorious film, *The Birth of a Nation*, premiered in Los Angeles; Jess Willard, "The Great White Hope," took twenty-six rounds to defeat Jack Johnson in Havana; Jewish factory superintendent Leo Frank was lynched in Marietta, Georgia; and the Great Migration began to lead millions of Black Southerners out of the South. Statues "To The Confederate Dead" that were now everywhere in the South were received in precisely the way they were intended by the United Daughters of the Confederacy and other groups who put them there: as a message to African Americans in the South that they were welcome only so long as they submitted to the terms establishing their place in society. Many of them got the message and got the hell out of there. It is no mere coincidence that the monuments boom accompanies a massive wave of lynchings from the 1890s until 1920.

Oxford, Mississippi, has not one Confederate monument, but two. In addition to the one in front of the county courthouse, there is another on the campus of the University of Mississippi. The former was put there partly through the insistence of William Faulkner's grandmother, who thought the first memorial did not do justice to all the fallen of Lafayette County.[13] Both were erected within a year of one another, in 1906 and 1907.

In 2020, the state of Mississippi finally removed the Confederate battle emblem from the state flag. Two weeks later, the state's flagship university relocated the Confederate monument from a prominent spot on campus to a Confederate cemetery in a less prominent spot on campus. To the student body and faculty, who had voted unanimously in 2019 to relocate the 40,000-pound monument, it seemed like a victory. That sensation lasted until artist's renderings for the new setting for the old monument were revealed about a month before it was moved. The monument was getting moved from The Circle at the heart of the campus to a less heavily trafficked site, but it was going to get an upgrade in the process. As with the removal of the Confederate flag from atop the State House in Columbia, South Carolina, the plans for the Ole Miss statue were the result of a *quid pro quo* that benefited the defenders of the monument more than the student body. Critics feared that the relocation would be an opportunity to enhance the monument with new landscaping and lighting and create a sort of shrine to the Lost Cause, much like Confederate Circle in Selma had become. Professor Anne Twitty, a scholar of antebellum social and cultural history at Ole Miss, said that the renderings suggested "a kind of Confederate-palooza that the university wants to establish in its back forty and it just means that they're replacing one site for Lost Cause nostalgia . . . with another one."[14] Twitty, along with thirteen of her colleagues in the History Department, cosigned a statement urging the university to scrap the proposed redesign, which would, they argued, "create a new destination for neoconfederate and other extremist groups on campus" and endanger the well-being of the university community.[15] It was followed by another letter from faculty all across campus, authored by Kiese Laymon and published in *Vanity Fair*.[16]

The fear of such groups was real: a monument to James Meredith, who integrated the campus in 1962, has been vandalized numerous times since it was erected in 2006. In 2014, three members of the Sigma Phi Epsilon fraternity placed a noose around the statue's neck, and covered its face with an old version of the Georgia flag that contained the Confederate battle flag. (The episode repeated itself in 2019, when three Kappa Alpha members at Ole Miss shot up a marker at the site where Emmett Till's body was recovered in 1955, and posed for a photo-op). The Sig Ep chapter was permanently shut down, while the Kappa Alphas suspended their members and escaped discipline from either the university or the national order.

In Faulkner's *Go Down, Moses*, the young Issac McCaslin is a boy to whom "old times would cease to be old times and would become a part of the boy's present, not only as if they had happened yesterday but as if they were still happening, the men who walked through them actually walking in breath and air and casting an actual shadow on the earth they had not quitted."[17] In Oxford, Faulkner is never past; he is not even dead.

Meridian

If Oxford is a professional town, Meridian is currently looking for a job. What there is of a skyline in Meridian is dominated by the seventeen-story Threefoot Building, an imposing art-deco skyscraper, its upper floors set back from the street and adorned with richly colored enameled tile friezes. It's the kind of thing you would expect to see in Manhattan, not Mississippi. It was built by a family of German Jewish immigrants called "Dreyfus," but who changed their name to "Threefoot" in the New World. But for now, its upper windows are busted out, the sidewalk at its foot lined with porta-potties, a green dumpster positioned to receive the deposits from an aluminum garbage chute clinging to the side of the structure.[18]

"Laid out with a singular lack of design," Meridian is, in the words of the WPA Guide to Mississippi, "like a vast spiderweb with a multitude of streets intersecting at curious angles and coming to abrupt endings."[19] But Meridian has a history of another kind of abrupt endings.

In 1871, Republican rule of the state had bred tensions among White Democrats, who resented their own alienation from government, and the rising status of African Americans. It came to a head in March of that year, when a fire destroyed two thirds of the city. Local White residents pinned it on three African American Republicans, J. Aaron Moore, William Clopton, and Warren Tyler. During their trial in Con Sheehan Hall—two blocks from the Threefoot Building—someone opened fire in the courtroom, killing the presiding judge. The WPA Guide unsurprisingly blames "one of several Negroes on trial" for instigating the shootout, but it remains unclear who shot first.[20] The guide simply repeats a long history of loose editorial judgment in absence of hard evidence, always in favor of White people. The *Hinds County Gazette* claimed that "Meridian has been cursed for a year or two with one or more very bad public officers, and with a gang of base and infamous negroes who have been used by very corrupt men for the worst of purposes."[21] The papers regularly attributed the chaos to "incendiaries" and "Mongrels." In its final issue of the year, the *Atlanta Constitution* listed in the calendar of an "eventful" 1871 "the "Great negro riot at Meridian, Miss."[22] Nourished by popular belief in Black people's *a priori* guilt, local Klansmen went on a retaliatory rampage, killing dozens of African Americans, and effectively ending Reconstruction in Meridian.[23]

The three Black men who had been on trial in Con Sheehan Hall were not random scapegoats: they were singled out because they were public officials who represented White people's worst fears. In a public rally on the steps of the Lauderdale County Courthouse just hours before the conflagration that would be blamed on them, they gave speeches in support of the embattled, Connecticut-born Republican mayor, calling for an end to mob violence. "Ku Kluxing has got to be stopped," Clopton urged.[24]

It wasn't, of course. On Confederate Memorial Day, 1913, White rule was celebrated in stone with the erection a monument to the Confederacy in front of the same Lauderdale County Courthouse where Moore, Clop-ton, and Tyler had delivered speeches they were later punished for.

The courthouse today is different from the one that stood here in 1871, but the monument is the same. Confederate monuments often repeat themselves, and there is little variation in what they say. But this one has an angle that we haven't seen before.

IT WAS THE TEACHING OF THE SOUTHERN HOME WHICH
PRODUCED THE SOUTHERN SOLDIER; THE DEEP FOUNDATION
OF WHOSE CHARACTER WAS DEVOTION TO DUTY AND RELIANCE
ON GOD. BY THE SIDE OF EVERY MARCHING SOUTHERN SOLDIER
THERE MARCHED UNSEEN A SOUTHERN WOMAN.

In the revisionist narrative of the Lost Cause, the Confederacy stood for the defense not of the institution of slavery but of home, embodied in the virginal feminine purity of the Southern Woman. This retroactively redefined holy war in defense of White women's virtue, carved into the base of the Lauderdale County monument, became a pretext for the fever of lynching African Americans from 1880 to 1940 and even later. It gave a kind of official imprimatur to the enactment of White terrorism on behalf of the state. It wasn't just a memorial to the Confederate dead: it served as a license to exact revenge against violators of "Southern womanhood," who it hardly needs to be stated were naturally presumed to be Black.

What happened in Meridian "set the stage for a full-blown epi-demic of racial violence in the South," David Oshinsky writes.[25] When Emmett Till was lynched in the Delta in 1955, it was, in the minds of his murderers, due to an unforgivable breach of the code of Southern conduct enshrined on the monument in front of the Lauderdale County Courthouse.

In 1964, Andrew Goodman, Michael Schwerner, and James Chaney were in Meridian for Mississippi Freedom Summer. On June 21 they were on their way back from Longdale, where they had been visiting with the African American community at Mount Zion Methodist Church, which the Klan had burned to the ground five days earlier. Goodman, Schwerner, and Chaney had been working with the Congress of Racial Equality (CORE) to educate the local community in Longdale about voting rights. On their return to Meridian, the car suffered a flat tire just outside of Philadelphia, not quite forty miles northwest of Meridian.

They were arrested for speeding by Neshoba County Sheriff Lawrence Rainey and his "baby-faced deputy," Cecil Ray Price, both members of the White Knights of the KKK. Meanwhile, other Klan members scurried to plan an ambush. After their release from the jail in Philadelphia, the three men were chased down onto a dark country road by Klansmen from Neshoba County and Meridian, including Deputy Price, and murdered.

We came through Philadelphia on an earlier trip, stopping in at a local café for lunch. It was a forgettable meal, shaded by negative associations with the town I brought into it. The faces of some of the older white men in the café seemed—unfairly, perhaps; perhaps not—still to communicate the timbre of suspicion of outsiders that Goodman and Schwerner must have read on the faces of the sheriff of Neshoba County. What intense hatred James Chaney, as a Black man, must have seen, I can scarcely imagine.

Then, there was no marker to indicate the site where Goodman, Schwerner, and Chaney became the victims of a complex conspiracy between the Ku Klux Klan and local authorities to murder them. That has since changd: a marker erected in 2013 by the state's Department of Archives and History today stands near the site.

It is understandable why markers like this are often late to the scene. Individuals, communities, nations—we are all loathe to bring to the fore of memory the darker and regrettable instances of our personal or collective failure, hatred, or indifference.

Chemirocha

No one really wants to broadcast to the world that their town was popular with the Klan, for example. But lots of places, it seems, want to claim Jimmie Rodgers.

Asheville, North Carolina, has a marker to him on Haywood Street downtown, near where he "began his music career" playing on local radio station WWNC. Bristol, Tennessee has several mentioning his 1927 recording sessions there as the origin story of recorded country music. There are no less than three Jimmie Rodgers markers in Meridian, which has a legitimate claim as the birthplace of "The Singing Brakeman."

His influence shows up everywhere—from Hank Williams to Bob Dylan to the Kipsigis tribe in the highlands of the Rift Valley in western Kenya.

The story goes that sometime around the Second World War, Christian missionaries traveled from England to Kenya to evangelize the native Kipsigi people, bringing with them the gospel of Jesus Christ, a gramophone and a seventy-eight-rpm vinyl pressing of Jimmie Rodgers. Christianity didn't seem to stick the way the missionaries may have hoped, but Jimmie Rodgers took.

Years later, a British ethnomusicologist called Hugh Tracey came to Kenya to record indigenous tribal music he believed was an endangered cultural treasure. Among the Kipsigi he encountered an unusual tune called "Chemirocha." He recorded three versions of it, but the Kipsigi didn't know it. Rodger's name—along with his identity—became transformed in the local tongue into "Chemirocha," "a half-man-half-beast creature whose origins are mysterious," but grew out of colonial missionaries' celebration of the Eucharist in which the faithful eat and drink the body and blood of Jesus Christ, combined with "how, during World War II, the Kipsigis were rounded up to give blood for wounded soldiers," says Josiah Arapsang, whose father coordinated the recording sessions for Hugh Tracey. "Man-eaters—half-man, half-beast chemirochas, comments Ryan Kailath. "The irony is delicious: the Africans thought the Europeans were savages."[26]

Tracey's recordings of "Chemirocha," are haunting, elemental, and plaintive, not unlike Jimmie Rodgers's own. But through an almost impossibly complicated and circuitous itinerary of cultural transmission, "a record of mid-century African field recordings made by a British folklorist contains a Kenyan folk song inspired by an early country singer from Meridian, Mississippi, himself supposedly inspirited by Swiss yodellers and Celtic hymns and African American gandy dancers, themselves the descendants of slaves brought to America from Africa,"[27] yielded something totally unexpected: whole new item in a living tradition. The life of "Chemirocha" began in a context of British imperialism but has continued to expand and yield new fruit thanks to digital technology. New versions of the song—for example, the bottom-heavy 2014 version by the Johannesburg-based "eclectic dream-pop" trio Bye Beneco—further hybridize a song of an already highly mixed ancestry.

For decades the Kipsigi had no idea they had been recorded, and even played on radio in the United Kingdom. In 2015, a team from the International Library of African Music, founded by Hugh Tracey, returned to

Kenya "to repatriate Tracey's recordings."[28] They presented "Chemiro-cha" back to the people who had not really meant to give it to them in the first place.

How Far? Not Far

To really get anywhere in the South you have to take the long way. The old joke about going to heaven but having to change planes in Atlanta first is revealing of our transportation networks but more revealing of Atlanta's sense of importance, which although exaggerated, is not wholly false. The gnosis that is so useful a tool to the resident of Atlanta is pretty unhelpful in Mississippi, where it is especially profitable to get lost a little bit, to detour. Not knowing where you are going could be your most valuable intellectual asset.

The road back to Georgia for me passes through northeastern Mississippi. It's a kind of signal in its way of both the interconnectedness of the South, and the inescapability of fate, destiny, the persistence of genie-souls, whatever it's called.

On our first tour in 1997, we hit Corinth, Mississippi, because of its importance in the Civil War. Like Atlanta, Corinth was established as a railroad junction. And like my hometown, someone with my last name served as its mayor at one point. You have to go up and over several branches of the family tree to get from me to him, but he's there.

Ezekiel Samuel Candler was the second son of Samuel Candler and Old Hardshell. He was Uncle Milton's younger brother, and older brother to Asa, the Bishop, and the Judge. In 1870 he moved to Tishomingo County, Mississippi with wife Julia and two boys. Their firstborn, Ezekiel, Jr., went over to Ole Miss to study law, opened his legal practice in Iuka in 1881, and represented the Mississippi 1st Congressional District in the US House of Representatives for ten consecutive terms from 1901 to 1921.   Corinth?

Even here in the Mississippi Delta, I cannot seem to escape the relentless ability of my family's history to show up everywhere.[29]

His peer in the other house of Congress, John Sharp Williams, unseated the notorious race baiter, James Kimble Vardaman, from the Senate in 1911, but the Great White Chief found his way to Washington in 1913 when he succeeded Le Roy Percy—great-uncle of Walker—as the junior senator from Mississippi. The two rivals, Percy and Vardaman, frequently sparred publicly, accusing one another of almost everything.

In the campaign for the House in 1907, their first contest against one another, Vardaman played the fearmongering hand he had become so adept at, vowing to rescind the Fifteenth Amendment to the Constitution, arguing in his campaign speeches that "the negro will within the next ten years outvote the white population, which would be detrimental to the welfare and happiness of our fair sons and daughters of the South." For Vardaman—much of whose political rhetoric would be unprintable nowadays—it was an uncharacteristically measured remark.

In an April 1907 speech in Poplarville during that campaign, Vardaman was more on-brand:

> How is the white man going to control the government? The way we do it now is to pass laws to fit the white man, and make the others come to them. There are 50,000 more negroes than whites of voting age in the state of Mississippi. If the fourteenth and fifteenth amendments were enforced to the strict spirit in Mississippi every office in the state government and in more than half the counties would be filled with negroes. But the white man is going to rule in this state as in every other state, and if it is necessary every negro in the state will be lynched in order to maintain white supremacy. The fifteenth amendment ought to be wiped out. We all agree on that. Then why don't we do it?[30]

Williams and others—including the *Yazoo Herald*—weren't taking the bait. However, they didn't object to Vardaman because he seemed to be advocating lynching or anti-Black racism, but because he was just exaggerating. "The negroes will never again outnumber the whites at the polls in Mississippi," the *Herald* offered, "for the simple reason that they are making no attempt to do so, and if they did they know their efforts would be futile."[31]

Williams had studied in Europe and was positively cosmopolitan compared with the parochial Vardaman, whose view of the world remained largely determined by the boundaries of white resentment towards the planter class. Unlike Vardaman, Williams did not treat "this negro question" as a personal hobby, and disliked Vardaman's relentless stoking of the fires of race hatred. But it wasn't because Williams was not a white supremacist; he simply viewed the "negro question" as settled. By 1907 White people in Mississippi had little to fear from African Americans at the voting booth. Vardaman's regime—along with the culture of Jim Crow and the dominion of White terror in Mississippi—had effectively put the "Negro" in his "place." So if Williams chose not to indulge in the kind of overt racism that was Vardaman's bailiwick, it was simply because he didn't need to.

So in 1915, to aggravate Williams, Vardaman reprised one of his favorite targets: Black postmasters. Earlier, in 1903, then-Governor Vardaman had managed to intimidate Minnie Cox, the first African American postmaster in Indianola, into resigning from her office. Since the position of postmaster was a federal appointment, approved by the president of the United States himself, Vardaman persuaded crowds that nosy Yankees were trying to force what he called "Roosevelt's criminal policy of social and political equality" down the throats of Mississippians by putting Black people in federal offices. Vardaman shouted, "We are not going to let niggers hold office in Mississippi!" Cox appealed to President Theodore Roosevelt, who ultimately accepted her resignation on the grounds that it would be unsafe for her to continue in that office.

In 1915, Vardaman alleged that Williams's people had managed to install a Black man as postmaster in Muldrow, near Starkville. Williams's response was telling. He did not defend the practice, even if he had been responsible for it; and he certainly did not call out Vardaman for his racism. Instead, he accepted the terms on which Vardaman made the accusation into a slur, and, with Ezekiel Candler's help, shifted the blame.

Muldrow was in Zeke Candler's district. He wrote to Williams explaining that indeed there was a Black postmaster in Muldrow, but only because there weren't any White people in town. Neither Williams nor Candler wanted a Black person in that position, but there was little they could do about it. "While Candler was seeing a 'cause' for the Negro's removal he urged Williams to get the postmaster-general to write letters to their constituents explaining that they were not responsible for the Negro's appointment or retention."[32]

In response to public outrage over the Black postmaster, Candler issued a statement in August 1916 insisting he was in no way responsible for the appointment. "I am for white supremacy," he insisted publicly. "This is a white man's country and ought to be managed and controlled and all the offices should be filled by white men."[33] But in private correspondence, he was blunter: "I hope to get the nigger out,' wrote Candler, 'and give the place to a white man.'"[34]

The Williams–Candler counteroffensive against Vardaman and his political machine shows how one could despise a notorious race baiter and still be as much of a White supremacist as the White Chief.

On our first trip here, Walker Percy's *Signposts in a Strange Land* lay on the bench seat, open to an essay called "Going Back to Georgia." In it, Percy projected—this was 1978—what the South might look like in the year 2000. His projections were characteristically melancholic and dour, not without glimmers of hope but also not without a somewhat jaded wit that—in all of Percy's wit—always seems just on the verge of exhausting itself. He predicted that the "race question" that had so preoccupied politicians and writers up to and including Percy's generation would finally be behind the nation, and that writers like him could at last get about the business of making fun of what we have in common, which in Percy's view was something like an inexhaustible capacity to disappoint one another.

I do not think Percy was wholly wrong, all requisite caveats being made for anyone's ability to predict the future. If, however, there is something that Percy was—atypically—too optimistic about, it was that the issue of race would have finally been confronted. There is an argument to be made that constantly talking about how "haunted" the South is by its history on race is a way of sustaining a habit of avoidance of the subject. So long as you believe that there is a monster lying in wait for you under your bed, you are unlikely to get down on the floor, yank up the bed skirt, and shine a light on what, if anything, is under there. In my case, it turns out that the answer is quite a lot, and that nothing is gained by continuing to remain snugly tucked into in a state of what can now only be called deliberate amnesia. The only thing one really risks losing by confronting those ghosts is one's self-deception.

Those ghosts await me in Georgia, and still orbit around my hometown like washed out satellites in the noonday sky. In Okolona, south of Corinth, we come upon the intersection of US 45 and US278. The latter road lads all the way across the Deep South to Atlanta and Decatur, and Avondale Estates, where it passes by the front door of the home where The Judge once lived. It is a concrete vein connecting the heart of my own history with its extremities, out in the Mississippi hill country. So at the corner of Church Street and Monroe Avenue in Okolona, we make the turn for the heart.

Iron grave markers, Cedar Lane Cemetery, Central State Hospital, Milledgeville, Georgia. Photo by the author.

SATELLITES
You Can Go Back, But You Can't Go Back All the Way

Marietta was supposed to have been Atlanta. Established as a White settlement on Cherokee land in the 1830s, the seat of Cobb County was originally intended to be a hub for the Western & Atlantic Railroad. But a political dispute led to the construction of a major terminus twenty miles to the south and to the invention of Atlanta. Hidden away for years in a downtown garage, the Zeromile marker that once defined the city of Atlanta is a museum piece now, an orphaned origin story in marble in a city pathologically unfascinated with its own origins. Atlanta no longer possesses any single identifiable benchmark for distance, but Marietta does, in the form of a fifty-six-foot high, eye-rolling mechanical steel hen known locally as "the Big Chicken."

It is what the Zeromile Post in downtown Atlanta once was: a sign to measure space with, a roadside way-marker by which to orient travelers (and even pilots). Distances were measured from the Zeromile marker the way directions are now issued with reference to the giant metal bird: "Turn left at the Big Chicken," "Go three miles past the Big Chicken," and so on. In an expression that could almost describe the city today, the WPA writers described Atlanta in 1940 as a "lusty offspring of railroads—restless, assertive, sprawling in all directions and taking in smaller towns in its incessant push toward greater growth."[1] Marietta is one of those towns.

Atlanta is less libidinous about its railroads these days, but since 1940 Marietta has been absorbed into the sprawling Atlanta metroplex and the rapidly metastasizing amnesia that goes along with it. Since White folks began fleeing the city of Atlanta following the *Brown v. Board* decision in 1954, Atlanta has outsourced to Marietta a good portion of its workforce, its baseball team, a share of its living memory, and one of its most notorious crimes.

Though it now serves a Kentucky Fried Chicken, the Big Chicken was built in 1963 for Johnny Reb's Chick-Chuck-N-Shake, an indication of the way in which the conflicted language and history of the Confederacy is written onto the landscape here.

Across the ten lanes of Interstate 75, a much less eye-catching historical marker stands in the middle of a concrete walkway next to a Mexican restaurant. It marks the spot where Leo Frank, a Jewish superintendent of the National Pencil Company warehouse in Atlanta, was lynched by a mob of White men in 1915. A small, black granite monument erected by Jewish organizations puts Frank's killing in the context of the roughly 570 mostly Black Georgians lynched between 1880 and 1946, and "the thousands across America, denied justice by lynching; victims of hatred, prejudice, and ignorance."

Frank was tried and convicted of the murder of Mary Phagan, a thirteen-year-old girl whose body was discovered in the basement of the National Pencil Company on April 27, 1913. She had come to collect $1.20 in pay, and never left the warehouse. Someone had strangled and apparently sexually assaulted her.

The Leo Frank case was one of the most sensational in Atlanta's history and became fodder for the city's three major newspapers—the *Atlanta Journal*, the *Atlanta Constitution*, and William Randolph Hearst's *Georgian*—which waged daily battles for readers with increasingly attention-grabbing headlines. Reporters made names for themselves during the coverage, including the *Journal*'s Harold Ross, who later founded the *New Yorker*.

Frank, whose death sentence was commuted to life imprisonment in 1915 by outgoing Governor John Slaton, was vilified by populist politician Thomas E. Watson, who used his own rag, *Thomas Watson's Magazine*, to press the case against Frank. In issue after issue, Watson exploited familiar racist tropes in order to stoke the fires of White outrage: "Leo Frank was a typical young Jewish man of business who loves pleasure, *and runs after Gentile girls*. Every student of Sociology knows that the black man's lust after the white woman, *is not much fiercer than the lust of the licentious Jew for the Gentile.*"[2]

Two months after Slaton's commutation, spurred on by rhetoric like Watson's, a mob of white men called the Knights of Mary Phagan kidnapped Frank from his cell at the state prison in Milledgeville, and drove him to Marietta, where they planned to murder him on Mary Phagan's grave. He was instead hanged in a field next to where the Big Chicken now stands. Postcards of his lynching were sold for twenty-five cents, and portions of the rope used to hang him sold as souvenirs.

In reading Steve Oney's outstanding and thorough account of the Frank case, *And the Dead Shall Rise,* I was struck by how many names I recognized. I had never heard a word about Leo Frank as a kid, but I went to school with people with the same names as some of the central figures in the trial of Leo Frank: Selig, Dorsey, Hopkins, Elsas, Frank.

I am even closer to this history than my education or family lore let on: when Governor John Slaton commuted Frank's sentence, some responded with threats against his life. To protect him from a potential mob, a detachment of the Georgia National Guard was sent to his home, led by Major Asa Warren Candler, my great-grandfather.

Shadowed by overt antisemitism in the press and in the popular culture, Frank's trial was a total mess. The trial judge, Leonard Roan, was not convinced of Frank's guilt, but sided with the jury's guilty verdict. Without pronouncing on his guilt or innocence, Governor Joe Frank Harris pardoned Frank in 1986. The case remains both controversial and painful: over a hundred years later, some are still pressing the state for an official exoneration, despite the Phagan family's insistence upon Frank's guilt.

From the beginning, though, Mary Phagan's murder was colored by the mythology of the Lost Cause. Her life was quickly turned into a symbol, and her death quickly became a *cause célèbre* of neo-Confederate propaganda. Her grave in Marietta City Cemetery features a headstone erected by the United Confederate Veterans. Her body lies under a slab whose text remembers Mary for her "heroism," and treats her tragic death as a commentary on "this day of fading ideals and disappearing landmarks."

Next to Phagan's tomb are two more recent markers. One calls her "Celebrated in Song," a reference to "Little Mary Phagan," the popular ballad written about her by Fiddlin' John Carson and Moonshine Kate, frequent musical accessories to Tom Watson's political rallies. The song is unambiguous about Frank's guilt, and the motive for his act:

She fell upon her knees, to Leo Frank she pled
Because she was virtuous, he hit her across the head

Another marker, presumably erected by the Phagan family, has even more to say. "No Phagan was involved in the lynching," it reads. And, for emphasis: "The 1986 pardon does not exonerate Leo Frank for the murder of 'Little Mary Phagan.'"

Next to the marker, a small stone urn holds a pile of stones, and a red, white, and blue enameled tile of the Confederate battle flag.

Mary Phagan's shocking murder understandably aroused equally intense sorrow and desire for revenge in Georgia and elsewhere; but in this context her death is narrated as a morality tale about the evils of Jews, Black people, and Yankees, and the moral rightness of the Confederate legacy. The most recent marker is simply the latest example of a trend that set in early, whereby Mary Phagan's death was almost immediately repossessed, managed, put in service to a mythology. The language and mise-en-scène of her memorial here lend her murder the specter of a religious sacrilege—she was killed on a high holy day for the Lost Cause: Confederate Memorial Day, 1913.

The city cemetery is part of a larger burial ground that includes one of the nation's oldest Confederate cemeteries. Established in 1863, it is still carefully maintained by local citizens. In addition to the monument erected in 1908 by the United Daughters of the Confederacy to the memory of the 3,000 soldiers "who died for a sacred cause," new monuments are still being erected. Thirty-two tons of granite erected in 2009 list the names of all the known Confederate dead here, in a city-owned park at the edge of the cemetery. Nearby, bronze statues of women representing the Ladies' Memorial Association commemorate their dedication to the "cause." A new monument to "the Confederate Soldier" was erected in 2014. Some visitors have left a row of copper pennies at the soldier's feet, the face of Abraham Lincoln turned outward.

The cemetery remains an active site for the cultivation of Lost Cause myths. Rebel flags punctuate the lawn and fly overhead. It was here that local Confederate sympathizers—including some members of the KKK—came armed in 2017 to protest the "desecration" of Confederate monuments. The cemetery's guest book contains remarks from many visitors, many of which praise the "patriotism" and "principles" of the Confederate war dead. *Deo vindice*, they regularly read. One entry—by Grace from Indiana—does not toe that line. "God bless the souls who once thought it was right to claim ownership over another human soul.

Thank God we as a country are no longer so brutal," she writes. A later, disapproving visitor has crossed out her comment with an X.

The effect of the Confederate Cemetery is numbing. Everywhere you are met with words: explanations, apologias, mini-lectures. This is true of almost every Confederate burial ground, in my experience: they are wordy sites, they take great pains to talk at you, convince you of something, and tell you how right they were.

When someone talks at you that much about themselves, you begin to wonder what it is they have to hide.

Not a mile away from the Confederate Cemetery, the Marietta National Cemetery is a jarring contrast. Visiting them back-to-back brings into relief just how different these two modes of remembering the dead are. Marietta's national cemetery holds the graves of over 10,000 Union soldiers marked by identical white headstones like the ones in every national cemetery. The scale of human grief is vast, overwhelming, staggering. Apart from the names on the headstones, the only words on the entire hilltop site are on a plaque reproducing the text of Lincoln's Gettysburg Address. The rest is silence.

Encircling row upon row of white death stones, like an undulating tide of human loss. For what, we are not told. Bluebirds flit from the arch-topped headstones of the Union dead. A red-headed woodpecker alights on the trunk of a high oak. Their calls pierce the silence. I try to capture one on film but fail. Each time it flits off to another headstone before I can catch it, marking, perhaps, the distance between the dead and who we want them to be.

When John and I first set out in 1997, I don't know enough about most of my ancestors to know who I want them to be. Most of my family on the Candler side are buried in Westview Cemetery on the west side of Atlanta. Family memory has not passed on to me much more than the information on the headstones in Westview, which are sparing and economical. My great-great-grandfather, John Slaughter Candler, was a state supreme court justice in Georgia and the lawyer-in-chief for the Coca-Cola Company. That's about all I knew. After visiting Westview for the first time, I learned that he was born on the same day as me, in the first year of the Civil War, and died two days after Pearl Harbor. But that's it.

I had never heard of Alexander H. Stephens until John tells me about him on US 278 in 1998. The town of Crawfordville east of Atlanta is like many other southern towns we'd seen the previous year: mostly dead, its lifeblood drawn off by Interstate 20 just to the south of town. The town has hitched its fortunes pretty tightly to Stephens, whose image is emblazoned on a mural on Monument Street, offering "A Dixie Welcome to Crawfordville, Ga." It's a general rule of small towns: if you've got someone or something remotely famous associated with your town, whether it be a celebrated bird dog, the boll weevil, or a Confederate general, you flaunt it. Whatever you can do to draw people in, you do it. Just don't invite people to ask too many questions. Hence: Alexander Stephens's home is now a state park.

Our first stop on the 1998 tour proved to be tone-setting. Stephens was the first of many "heroes" of the Confederacy to whom I would devote a totally unjustifiable amount of film to over the next ten days or so. We would come across scores of the tropes of Official Southern Memory as brought to you by the UDC, which present their subjects as uncomplicated champions of right. The monument to Stephens reproduces a passage from his 1855 speech in Augusta: "I am afraid of nothing on earth, or above the earth, or under the earth, except to do wrong—the path of duty I shall ever endeavor to travel, fearing no evil, and dreading no consequences." A typically pious expression of duty, fitting for a monument, perhaps, but not by a long shot the passage for which Stephens is most famous.

Two and a half weeks after the inauguration of Abraham Lincoln on March 4, 1861, Stephens delivered a speech in the Athenaeum in Savannah, in which he made unambiguous the first principles of the new Confederate government formed in Montgomery: "its foundations are laid, its cornerstone rests, upon the great truth that the negro is not equal to the white man; that slavery, subordination to the superior race, is his natural and normal condition. This, our new government, is the first, in the history of the world, based upon this great physical, philosophical, and moral truth."[3] Stephens wasn't just a sympathizer with the Confederacy; he was its vice president. So his words in Savannah were not the off-the-cuff remarks of a private influencer, but amounted to state policy.

Established in 1864, National Statuary Hall in Washington is a repository of monuments to American figures. It's like a memorial Senate: each state in the Union is represented by two statues "of deceased persons who have been citizens thereof, and illustrious for their historic renown or for distinguished civic or military services such as each State may deem to be worthy of this national commemoration." In theory, they are a chance to hold up the best each state has to offer. Georgia's two statues: Crawford Long, the pioneer of medical anesthesia, and Alexander H. Stephens. They were both put there in the 1920s. Stephens's was sculpted in 1927 by Gutzon Borglum, who had first worked on the Stone Mountain Confederate Memorial, and then on Mount Rushmore. Despite some half-hearted attempts to remove his monument in the US Capitol, Stephens is still there.

Elected Georgia's Governor in November 1882, Stephens's term was brief: he died after four months in office, in March 1883. The perennially frail Stephens cut an unusually ghoulish figure, so much so that as he lay in state in the Governor's Mansion in 1883, the *Atlanta Constitution* said that "he looked even better in death than he had in life."[4]

I am telling you that story to tell you this one.

The Judge and I share a birthday. We were born exactly 110 years apart. In 1883, he was twenty-one years old, a Colonel in the Fifth Regiment of the State Militia, and had just finished law school at Emory. The *New York Times* reported on the front page of its March 15, 1883, edition that the day before, Colonel Candler left Atlanta on the 2:00 PM train for Edgewood, "and an hour later was found midway on the railroad, with one leg crushed, a foot mashed, and his head fractured. He had been run over in attempting to jump from the train. Amputation of both legs was performed, and the patient still lingers." The *Times* called it a "fatal leap from a train," and wrote him off for dead.[5] The *Chicago Tribune* was no less decisive: "CANDLER'S BROTHER KILLED," it proclaimed. "Attending physicians say that there is no hope of recovery, and that his death is a matter of only a few hours."[6]

Because local reporting is always more revealing, if not necessarily always more accurate, the *Savannah Morning News* went into much greater detail. "A HORROR ON THE RAILS," it proclaimed. Apparently, the Judge had attended a meeting in Atlanta to organize a new company for the state militia. On the way home he had to take a different train from the one that stopped just near his home, so when the train passed the city limits into Decatur, he jumped off. As one does. "Unfortunately he struck a pile and fell back under the cars, which mashed both his feet and bruised his head. A negro boy discovered him and he was carried to a store near at hand, where Dr. Westmoreland amputated both feet. Later he was carried home, and his death may be anticipated at any moment. Savannah people will remember his boyish, frank face and mourn with thousands here over his terrible fate." Candler "was not in his right mind," according to the reporter for the *Savannah Morning News* who managed to get a word in, and to record his final words. "He could not give an account of himself, simply saying, 'Gentlemen, it is all right. I was doing my duty.'"[7]

Obviously, that is not at all that happened. Within a few weeks the papers were reporting that he was at home recuperating, and nearly fully recovered. He told reporters that his unexpected nondeath and surprisingly swift recovery were due to the fact that he never smoked tobacco or drank alcohol, and that "if he had not in early youth formed the habit of saying 'darn it,' he would have sprouted a new pair of legs."[8]

"The Colonel without Feet," the *New York Times* called him.[9]

But what I could not make sense of was how the future Judge was prominent enough at just twenty-one to be written about on the front pages of the *New York Times*, *Chicago Tribune*, and *Wilmington Delaware*. The Colonel without Feet was not just a promising young lawyer; he was chief-of-staff to Governor Alexander H. Stephens.

My own family's commitment to silence on most of our history has been thorough, and it is staggering to think about the emotional energy generations of my forebears have invested in not talking about any of it. It's staggering because so much of it is public knowledge, and nothing that I have learned in this whole journey has been a family secret. Their prominence in Atlanta society during the early twentieth century has made it possible for me to learn what by my father's generation had become totally suppressed.

It is not hard to understand why any family would remain tight-lipped about darker entanglements in its past. Some southern version of "Let the dead bury their dead" is a common refrain in expressions of White attitudes toward the past, especially in the ever-forward-looking Atlanta. In general, my family's commitment to the "you make a better showing with your mouth shut" principle has been unwavering. But when one is committed to burying one's history it means burying the good parts as well, the examples you'd like to pass on to your children. I can understand why the Judge's involvement in the state's response to a horrific act of White terrorism would not become a staple at the dinner table, because telling that story would require telling the story of Sam Hose, which would require telling the story of Allen Candler, the story of W. E. B. Du Bois, of Milton Candler, and on and on. But that my great-great-grandfather had his legs cut off and lived a very public life for another nearly sixty years with prosthetic feet? How did that never once make the family news?

The Judge's views on race were hardly progressive; his faith was in the rule of law. In 1927, he recalled before a meeting of the Stone Mountain Judicial Circuit Bar Association some of the highlights of his distinguished career as a jurist. In the 1890s, John Candler was both a colonel in the state militia and a superior court judge and inhabited two almost separate personas. With a dash of wry humor, he described how these two offices converged on one occasion. "As Colonel Candler, I was ordered to report to Judge Candler and to make such a disposition of . . . troops under Colonel Candler as ordered by the judge and to protect the prisoner on trial before Judge Candler." Nowadays it might be viewed as a conflict of interest, he noted, but at the time, it "worked fairly well. In one case, he recalled,

> exercising the authority of a colonel, I put a part of the county under martial law, used my soldiers to find out the facts of a lynching, and to ascertain some of the actors in the same. Through this investigation seven white men were found to have been the principal perpetrators of the killing. As colonel presiding over a drum head court martial, I committed them to jail, and as judge I called a special term of superior court of that county, and tried them . . .
>
> I believe that this record made up the first one wherein white men were convicted of murder when they participated in the lynching of a negro.[10]

So whatever the Judge's views on race were when as the young "boy Colonel" on Stephens's staff in 1883, by 1927 he had come to regard trying White men for the lynching of a Black man as an achievement. He wanted his audience at the Bar Association to know that this was his work: seeking justice for a lynched Black man. He declared it a "triumph of justice," and credited the jury with the "vindication of the law." But he also wanted the case to be an example that "might be followed in some other sections in our country at this hour."[11] It may not exactly have been heroic, but it is not nothing.

The Judge was colonel of the state militia in 1899 when he was summoned by his cousin, The Governor, to Newnan to keep the peace around the lynching of Sam Hose. While he didn't discuss it in his address to the Bar Association in 1927, the episode doubtlessly impacted life at the Judge's home on Ponce de Leon Avenue (US 278) in Decatur, just as it did in a stately Victorian home at 224 West Cherokee Avenue in Cartersville.

Cartersville is about as far from Atlanta as Newnan, but in the other direction. Once a remote village on the Western & Atlantic rail line forty-three miles north of the capital city, the town has been either a beneficiary or victim of Atlanta's inexorable sprawl, attracting new residents who want to be close to Atlanta, but not too close.

It's not especially new: Cartersville has long attracted luminaries, and at one time was home to some of Georgia's most influential political figures. In the 1980s, Cartersville belonged to what city boys like me dismissively thought of as "the boonies," but a disparaging appellation is about as much thought as I was willing to give it at a time when I was too ignorant to care.

Between Atlanta and Cartersville is Kennesaw—a mountain town well-known for its 1982 law mandating local residents to own a gun, and the Cherokee burial grounds for which the town and its adjacent mountain are named. If you come to Kennesaw expecting to find the sort of redneck White supremacists that movies and magazines have taught you to expect, Dent Myers's Civil War Surplus and Herb Shop is happy to provide you with an unironic display of Ku Klux Klan paraphernalia and a Rebel flag to take home with you. If confirmation of that expectation is what you're looking for, Dent is ready to oblige.

But turning the bend on South Tennessee Street coming into Cartersville, we are struck by a single roadside marker that hints at a more complicated picture. John—who knows way more about this stuff than I do—notices it instantly, and we pull off the road into a driveway leading up to a modest brick house on top of a hill. The house is older, but not that old. It's clear that the house itself is not what's important here.

John recognizes the name, Amos T. Akerman, which rings no bells for me. It's the first of many *who knew?* kind of moments on this trip, an indication that things are about to take an unexpected turn. It's one reason why we don't travel with much of a plan or a script; by the afternoon of the first day, your plan will be useless. The genie-souls have different ideas for you.

Amos Akerman was born in Portsmouth, New Hampshire, but ended up in Georgia. An opponent of secession, Akerman joined the Confederate Army during the Civil War, but after it was over, he joined the Republican Party, and became one of the state's most prominent advocates for Reconstruction. In 1869 President Ulysses S. Grant appointed him attorney general of the United States, and during his tenure Akerman led the federal campaign against the Ku Klux Klan, which resulted in the Enforcement Acts of 1870 and 1871, ending the Klan's reign, for a time.

When we finish reading the historical marker for Akerman, it is already almost eight o'clock. In the fading light we head over to Oak Hill Cemetery to seek out his gravesite, but are unable to find it before the names have become illegible in the darkness. Early the next morning we return and find a prominent granite tombstone to this famous scalawag in a part of the state not known for that kind of radical politics.

Thirty years after Akerman's death in 1880, a local woman was still seething at the harsh treatment she believed Akerman endured in Washington. "It makes my blood boil to think of it even now," Rebecca Latimer Felton wrote. "This honest man, this upright lawyer, was actually hounded out of General Grant's cabinet by men in Washington City . . . by the pimps and paid agents of [railroad robber barons Collis] Huntington and Jay Gould—and hounded in Georgia by our political desperadoes—organized Democrats."[12]

"I know what I am talking about," Felton insisted. She had been a friend of Akerman in Cartersville, and after her death in 1930 she was buried not far from him in Oak Hill Cemetery.

Felton's tombstone describes her as "Leader in cause of women's suffrage, Pioneer Director of Georgia Training School for Girls, Journalist, Lecturer, and Scholar." And, in all caps: FIRST WOMAN UNITED STATES SENATOR.

Her tenure was short—she served for one day in November 1922—and entirely ceremonial, but the symbolic power of the sight of the nation's first female Senator was enough to draw legions of admiring women and supporters of the nineteenth amendment, passed in the same house three years earlier, into the Senate galleries for a chance to witness the historic occasion. But the throngs of well-wishers proved her undoing: after an over-long lunch, she was waylaid by admirers on her way back to the Senate chamber, only to find it empty, having adjourned for the day. She had lost her one opportunity to speak on the Senate floor.

But the next morning, she got her chance before yielding her seat to the new, duly elected Senator from Georgia, Walter George. Wearing a tasseled and laced black dress stitched together from her own curtains, Felton said: "I commend to your attention the 10,000,000 women voters who are watching this incident. It is a romantic incident, senators, but it is an historical event . . . Let me say that when the women of the country come in and sit with you, though there may be but very few in the next few years, I pledge you that you will get ability, you will get integrity of purpose, you will get exalted patriotism, and you will get unstinted usefulness."[13] Felton's speech "took down the house," but it would be another decade before another woman filled a US Senate seat. Despite Felton's progressive position on women's suffrage and education, her views on race were far more in line with the Georgia mainstream in the late nineteenth century. Those views emerged most prominently around the subject of lynching.

In a speech before the Georgia State Agricultural Society at Tybee Island in 1897, she said that "If it needs lynching to protect woman's dearest possession from human beasts, then I say lynch; a thousand times a week if necessary. The poor girl would choose death in preference to such ignominy, and I say a quick rope to assaulters."[14] She went on: "As long as your politicians take the colored man into their embrace on election day and make him think he is a man and brother, so long will lynching prevail, because the cause of it will grow."

In a letter to the *Constitution* about a week later, Felton protested that she had been misunderstood. She was not, she argued, an advocate of lynch law as she had been depicted in the northern press. She evidently thought the following comment was supposed to correct that impression:

> I am in favor of shooting down mad-dogs when their mouths are foaming after biting their victims, and when a human beast gets ready to destroy my child or my neighbor's child the beast should be taught to expect a quick bullet or a short rope. I would greatly prefer that the law should tie the rope about his neck, but if the law hides behind its "delay" while my child or my neighbor's child perishes in its misery and ignominious condition, then I say there should be home-made law to meet such a case.[15]

Felton's words had power, and a long reach. By the following autumn, "Mrs. Felton's Speech" on Tybee was still reverberating in the ears of African American readers, especially in Wilmington, North Carolina. Alexander Manly, the editor of the *Daily Record*, a local Black newspaper there, wrote a scathing response to Felton in which he accused Felton of hypocrisy. As Ida B. Wells had done in Memphis in 1892, Manly argued that White men had been having "illicit" relations with Black women for centuries, and that some of those accused of rape were actually the products of White rape of Black women. "Mrs. Felton," he wrote, "must begin at the fountainhead if she wishes to purify the stream."[16]

White newspapers ran Manly's editorial ad nauseam in the fall of 1898. In Wilmington, the thirst for Manly's "infamous assault on the white women" of North Carolina was so insatiable that the *Morning Star* reprinted the article at least forty times between the end of August and early November. Democrats began demanding Manly's forcible removal. The "storm of indignation" Manly's piece aroused ultimately led to White mobs' burning of the offices of the *Daily Record*, Manly's flight from Wilmington, and the massacre of at least fourteen, and possibly as many as three hundred, African Americans. The slaughter in Wilmington initiated an explicitly White supremacist regime in the city. Local Democrats violently ousted the Fusionist Party from power in the only successful domestic coup d'état in American history.

Felton's words had come home to roost. Despite criticism of her speech at Tybee, she remained intransigent. Three days before Sam Hose was lynched in Newnan, she wrote to the *Atlanta Constitution*, repeating her earlier appeal to "lynch a thousand a week or stop the outrage." Hose—a.k.a. Sam Holt—was on the run at the time, fleeing for his life. Felton took the opportunity to fan the flames of lynch-lust:

It fatigues the indignation to mention it! Sam Holt needs and deserves no trial. When such a fiend abandons humanity to become a brute, then he shall be dispatched with no more cavil than would prevail with a mad dog's fate, after he had bitten your child. I do not know a true-hearted husband or father who would not help to tie the rope around the beast's neck, with less concern than he would shoot down a poor dog foaming with hydrophobia. In one case there is hellish intent, in the other a hapless disease. The dog is more worthy of sympathy.[17]

Felton's sentiments were quite popular back in Cartersville, where Felton's body is buried a few yards away from a giant, pall-draped obelisk marking the grave of Sam Jones.

He is arguably Cartersville's most famous local celebrity, more well-known in his day than either Felton or Akerman. Jones is often described as the "Billy Graham" of the late-nineteenth century. A circuit-riding preacher of the Methodist Episcopal Church-Southeast, he was a peer of "the Bishop," Warren A. Candler, and the two often headlined Methodist revivals together. He was also a peer and, for not quite a week, a rival of Allen Daniel Candler, the Bishop's first cousin. Jones mounted a short-lived and half-serious campaign for Governor of Georgia in 1898 on a platform of "simple, unadulterated, unpurchaseable, unbulldozable manhood." His improbable bid was possibly calculated "to pressure Candler into supporting temperance education and statewide prohibition." Jones yielded to Allen's popularity, and threw his support behind Candler, with one caveat. "I do not know of but one thing against him," Jones said, "and that is I have heard he cusses."[18]

Jones's most famous convert was Thomas Ryman, a riverboat man and saloonkeeper in Nashville who once attended one of Jones's revivals, where, as Ryman put it, Jones "whipped me with the gospel of Christ." Ryman turned his life around, closed his barrooms and devoted his attention and beneficence to Nashville's down-and-out. He built the Union Gospel Tabernacle, which first hosted a week-long revival led by Jones. It is now the major basilica of country music known as the Ryman Auditorium.

Sam Jones's home, Rose Lawn, is a swank and ornate two-story Victorian mansion on West Cherokee Avenue in Cartersville. It's not the kind of house you would expect for a circuit-riding preacher in the late nineteenth century. It's also not the place I would have expected to see the black dress Rebecca Latimer Felton wore on her one day as a US senator, but there it is, laid supine in a glass-topped case like a corpse an open casket. A museum to Felton is upstairs, which includes a few of her books, her dresses, some photos, and lots of laudatory prose about her pioneering role as a protofeminist but no mention of her career as an unrelenting pro-lynching White supremacist.

The same is true of the materials in Rose Lawn related to Jones, who believed that "Law and order, protection of life and property, can only be maintained by the supremacy of the white man and [his] domination over the inferior race."[19] Despite insisting early on that the rule of law forbade mob violence, the Sam Hose case changed his mind. "Sam Hose deserved to be burnt, but I am in favor of the sheriff executing the criminal, except in cases like Sam Hose, then anybody, anything, anyway to get rid of such a brute."[20]

In Jones's view, the dominion of the devil was a narrowly circumscribed set of "male" behaviors—drinking, gambling, womanizing—and he was an evangelist for the gospel of good, clean, masculine living. In one of his sermons, he exclaimed:

> Good Lord! Give us a strong, sinewy, muscular religion! This little, effeminate sentimental, sickly, singing and begging sort! My Lord God, give us a religion with vim and muscle and backbone and power and bravery![21]

Like Rebecca Latimer Felton, the practice of lynching did not seem to trouble him deeply. Most Black Georgians, he commented, were "peaceable, law-abiding citizens," namely the ones "who know their place and keep it, just as the convicts at Joliet know their place and keep it." He was initially opposed to lynch mobs on the grounds that they operated outside a divinely instituted order of justice and/or vengeance. But he also objected to them because they were unmanly: "whenever I believe a man ought to be licked or killed for anything he has done to me or mine, I am going to go for him by myself . . . If I can't lick him or kill him by myself, he will go unlicked and unkilled."[22] In 1899, Jones complained not that there were too many lynchings in Georgia, but too few. In a dispatch to the *Atlanta Journal* from St. Louis, he asked, "What's the matter down in Georgia? Rape means rope. Have the boys run short on rope?"[23]

The idea that lynching was a just form of vengeance for an unspeakable "crime against Southern womanhood" was apparently a popular sentiment in Cartersville. In 1902, Bill Arp (a.k.a. Charles Henry Smith), a Cartersville-based columnist for the *Constitution*, wrote, "the lynchings will not stop until the outrages do. When a negro dehumanizes himself and becomes a beast he ought to be lynched, whether it is Sunday or Monday. Let the lynching go on. This is the sentiment of our people."[24]

But a more likely indirect target was John Temple Graves, editor of the *Atlanta News* who, at a meeting in Chautauqua, New York convened to discuss "The Mob Spirit in America," claimed that lynching arose fundamentally as a response to "a crime against Southern womanhood." Like Felton, Graves argued that "the cause must be removed before the effect is destroyed."[25] The reasoning was straightforward, if over-simple: when the rape of White women ceases, lynching will stop.

The Bishop was not persuaded. In a strongly worded op-ed for the *Atlanta Constitution* on September 9, 1903, he cited a statistic that showed that out of 128 lynchings in a single year, only sixteen were the result of alleged "ravishing." Unlike Felton, Jones, and Graves, Candler was critical of the party line on lynching that viewed it as a justifiable, if unfortunate reprisal for rape. The data, the Bishop suggested, did not line up, but Candler didn't yet put his finger directly on it. "It is an outburst of anarchy, and not an irruption of righteous indignation against an atrocious crime."[26] And he took implicit aim at Graves in his remarks about "Chautauqua platformers and performers" as "sensation-mongers" who "pour out of their easy-acting mouths" mischief and sophistry.

The Bishop already had a connection to Cartersville: his mother, Old Hardshell, relocated from Villa Rica to Cartersville in 1875 along with her sons Asa and John. Warren himself was named for Warren Akin, a prominent lawyer and statesman from Cartersville. And Rebecca Latimer Felton nursed a long-standing grudge against the Bishop that went back at least a decade. But in 1903, the Bishop was becoming unpopular there, and not just with Felton.

Graves responded to Warren's op-ed with a caustic retort of his own in which he called Candler "the Fat Bishop." But Graves wasn't the only one pissed off at him. In a September 15 letter on *Atlanta News* letterhead, John Temple Graves wrote to Rebecca Latimer Felton thanking her for an "enclosure" that apparently also took aim at Warren.

> I had hit the Bishop so hard and had private information to the effect that he felt himself so hard hit, that I could not, in common chivalry, allow him to receive another blow so crushing as yours...
> The "Fat Bishop" article was generally considered a most effective one and I have been patted on the back by nearly every methodist [*sic*] I have seen.

Graves's reluctance to publish Felton's letter suggests it must have been too inflammatory even for the typically unrestrained editor of the *Atlanta News*. To further irritate the Cartersville contingent, the Fat Bishop became even more direct about the causes behind lynching. He later concluded that "lynching is due to race hatred and not to horror over any particular crime."[27] Eventually the controversy faded away, but for a moment at least, Warren had become a pariah to White supremacists.

Jones's revival week turned out to be a momentous period of sustained intensity in Cartersville, culminating in a bizarre and otherwise ordinary tête-à-tête between two grown men that seemed to bear the weight of competing forces of history coming to blows. On September 6, 1903, Sam Jones hosted his annual week-long revival meetings at the Tabernacle in Cartersville. Later that week, on the heels of his widely circulated antilynching article in the morning edition of the *Constitution* on September 9, Warren Candler preached at the Tabernacle, where Felton was likely in attendance. If the Fat Bishop preached about lynching, it didn't make the news. The last word of the meetings belonged to Jones's masculine gospel of toughness and made headlines around the country. On the final day, Jones took umbrage with the local postmaster, whom Jones accused of selling wine. The two men got into a fistfight in the middle of town: Jones took a punch to the mouth and left a black eye on the face of the postmaster, Walter Akerman, third son of the Klan-busting former US attorney general.

A Field with No Name

The forces that came to blows—literally and figuratively—in Cartersville in 1903 had a backstory. It all went back to a field outside of Newnan in 1899.

I'd brushed by Newnan many times in the past, but never gotten close enough to hear what it had to say—or to hide. Growing up in Atlanta, the Waffle House at the Newnan exit off of I-85 was the exchange point where we would meet my aunt Susie either to ride on with her to West Point or to bring our cousins back with us to Atlanta for a few days.

Newnan isn't just a pitstop town anymore. Whatever Newnan was like during the cousin-swaps at the Waffle House, today it is a lively small town within range of Atlanta. As a result, it's absorbed some of the capital city's commuters along with an uptick in diversity. In central Newnan in July 2019, there are visual avatars of Newnan's self-aware diversity. A series of large photographic portraits by Rhode Island-based photographer Mary Beth Meehan hangs on structures around town. One pictures two Muslim sisters in hijabs. Another, on the side of an aluminum warehouse behind a chain-link fence, features Cliff and Monique, a young African American couple standing in a field that will soon look familiar to me. Taken together, the seventeen photographs represent a Newnan that is richly diverse, and not at all the White stronghold that some of its citizens might imagine it to be.

But not everyone in Newnan wants their city to be remembered the way Meehan has pictured it. The images seem to portend a changing populace that does not entirely square with the old Newnan many locals want to remember. Some fear Newnan will lose its "small-town charm," or become too much like Atlanta, which is a conventionally indirect way of saying "too Black." But the photos have occasioned difficult and sometimes healing conversations among locals about its present, if not necessarily about its past.

Tired and a little haggard from ten days on the road, we wander around the courthouse square looking for something to catch the eye. Nothing takes. I haven't shot a frame of film since Columbus. By the end of these trips, you tend to become more selective about what you shoot. On day one, you click the shutter a lot more than you do on day ten, when you have a better idea about what you are looking for, or what the genie-souls want to show you.

In Newnan, I know exactly what I am looking for. I am in no danger of running out of film, but I have come here for one image. In downtown Newnan, there is—unsurprisingly—no mention of the darker side of this town's history. But a few blocks away from the courthouse is something we did not come looking for but found anyway: an empty lot on Farmer Street shaded with tall poplars and oaks, covered with a carpet of fallen leaves. There is no marker here either, but it is sacred ground. Beneath the soil, intertwined with deep root systems of soaring hardwoods, are the bodies of over 200 enslaved Black men and women. Once endangered by the inevitable forces of development and for a time a playground for unknowing kids in the neighborhood, the site is now undisturbed. If the estimates are correct, it is the largest slave cemetery in the southeastern United States.

As with much of African American history, it is not often permitted by White culture to announce itself. As if not to disturb the comfortable consciences of local White residents or their real estate values, if you want to find it, you're going to have to look for it yourself, or be fortunate enough to stumble upon it. You have to come to these places armed with at least a modicum of curiosity and be prepared to leave them with your presuppositions no longer intact.

Newnan's past—particularly the past at the corner of Roscoe and Jackson—has become the central crossroads for this project, since I first learned that it was the site of Georgia's most notorious spectacle lynching in 1899. On April 11, a local African American laborer named Sam Hose (also referred to as Sam Holt or Samuel Wilkes) asked his employer, Alfred Cranford, if he could go visit his ailing mother in Macon County. Cranford refused, and the two men got into a heated argument. "On the following day, while Hose was chopping wood," as Leon Litwack writes, "Cranford resumed the argument, this time drawing his pistol and threatening to kill Hose. In self-defense, Hose flung the ax, striking Cranford in the head and killing him instantly. A frightened Hose fled to his mother's cabin."[28]

Hose was on the run for eleven days. In the meantime, Governor Allen D. Candler offered a reward for his capture, as did the *Atlanta Constitution* and others. The passage of time between Hose's initial flight and his capture only allowed rumors about his crime to become more and more extravagantly exaggerated in White newspapers. The story had transformed into a tale about "a monster in human form" who attacked his boss without provocation, and raped his wife repeatedly. The newspaper accounts of Hose's alleged crime stoked White fury along with the daily paranoia of an impending race war.

News of Hose's capture on April 23 excited White readers in Newnan and Atlanta thirsty for blood. A special train was commissioned from Atlanta to take spectators forty miles south to Newnan for the anticipated lynching.

On April 23, former Governor William Atkinson, the anti-lynching incumbent defeated by Allen Candler in 1898, ascended the courthouse steps in Newnan and pleaded with a White mob to "let this affair go no further." It was, as he must have known, pointless. A White mob wrested Sam Hose from the authorities, bound him in chains, processed him through the town, crying "Burn him!" and regularly pausing at street corners to hold him aloft for the ladies on nearby porches to view him, wave their handkerchiefs, and applaud.

The mob took him ultimately to Troutman Field. Once there, anticipating the imminent arrival of the state militia, the crowd urgently set to its grim, "fully premeditated" work. "It was no sudden outburst of a furious maddened mob" as Louis P. Le Vin—a Chicago detective work-ing for Ida B. Wells—wrote at the time. "And it was not the irresponsible rabble that urged on the burning, for it was openly advocated by some of the leading men" of the area.[29] Furthermore, Le Vin wrote, Governor Candler "acquiesced in the burning by refusing to prevent it."[30]

By the end of Sunday, August 23, 1899, Sam Hose had been subjected to unimaginable cruelty. White readers who could not attend the spec-tacle themselves were served both horrifying and titillating accounts in the White press. Those further details of Hose's lynching are incredibly gruesome. I do not recommend reading them if your belief in human goodness is not extremely durable. The earliest treatment is in Ida B. Wells's 1899 pamphlet *Lynch Law in Georgia*, a work of courageous journalism that provided much of the groundwork for later full-length analyses.

When, later that day, Allen Candler decried "the most diabolical in the annals of crime," he was referring to the murder of Alfred Cranford, not the torching and dismembering of Sam Hose. He criticized Black leaders, but not White lynchers, of being "blinded by race prejudice." His response was classic Whitespeak at the time (and not uncommon now): express outrage at one Black man's crime and go soft on the sav-agery of thousands of White men.

"The negroes of that community lost the best opportunity they will ever have to elevate themselves in the estimation of their white neigh-bors," Candler said. In his view, it was the responsibility of Black people to participate voluntarily in a legal process that had utterly failed them. Black people in 1899 had no reason to trust that the judicial system would come to their defense, and Candler had little political motive to take their concerns with any genuine seriousness. In language by now de rigueur for White leaders intent on maintaining the White status quo, he said that Black people "must learn to look at both sides."[31]

In my high school physics class, I learned about the principle of momentum and centripetal force: the rule that an object orbiting around a center or gravity will continue in a straight line once its binding attach-ment to that gravitational pull is severed. That is how the Sam Hose story seems to me now. At one time my family's public life orbited tightly around the Sam Hose episode and its aftermath: it was the center of gravity for my distant cousin Allen and my great-great-grandfather John, both of whom were personally involved in the state's official response to the lynching in Newnan. John's brother Warren would become an out-spoken opponent of lynching in the years after Sam Hose. The Governor, the Bishop, and the Judge—each of their lives was caught up in the Hose tragedy, and must have been profoundly altered by it. But in the ensuing decades family—and local and regional—memory moved directly away from those days in April 1899 in a straight and concerted line and—according to the laws of physics and of human memory—seemed destined never to come into its orbit again. But the nature of human experience is far stranger and more unpredictable and inscrutable than physics. The arc of my own particular inheritance of family memory bent back to the Sam Hose episode after a seemingly ordinary lunch meeting with a friend in November 2017, and has been orbiting tightly around it ever since.

The courthouse where Hose was kidnapped is no longer there. A new one was built in 1904. From the square, we retrace the route of Hose's via dolorosa north on Jackson Street to its intersection with Roscoe Road, the site of Old Troutman Field. There is little there to distinguish it: on one corner, a Sunoco gas station. On another, Sprayberry's, one of the oldest barbecue operations in the state, a ghoulish juxtaposition to the site of the site of a human burning. A friend of mine tells me that she is no longer able to eat there, knowing what she does about what happened to Sam Hose across the street.

It is approaching six o'clock in the evening, but the hot July sun has turned the sky into that peculiarly Southern concoction of heat, light and humidity that transforms a blue sky in the morning into an undifferentiated haze of luminous vapor by evening. There is no cloud and no sky. Even before looking into the viewfinder, the scene looks washed out, like the whitewashed history of this particular spot in the universe. I stand alongside Jackson Highway in front of an old phone booth and shoot a couple of poorly composed, overlit frames of the intersection of Jackson and Roscoe. As scenes go, it is uninteresting. In this case, it's not what you see that's the point; it's what you don't. It's also what you bring to the viewfinder.

What I brought to this spot was an intention to record it visually, to mark its new place in my own memory with a kind of celluloid historical marker. Somehow returning to that intersection adjacent to what used to be Troutman Field where Sam Hose was lynched before thousands of spectators cheering "Glory to God" at the sight of a man being burned to death seemed like it would be some kind of reckoning, some act, however inadequate, in paltry restoration of this notorious episode to its rightful place in collective and personal memory. Or maybe as a sort of antisouvenir to counteract the pieces of Hose's body passed around the crowd like perverse relics of a demonic religious sacrifice.

As in film photography, digging into local or family history carries with it a certain amount of risk: you could turn over something you did not expect to find and be either happy with it, or be completely thrown by it.

When I return home to Asheville, I gather rolls of film from the trip to send them off to be processed. Winding the final roll from Newnan back into its canister inside the Nikon, I feel a disconcerting lack of tension, an absence of centripetal force. A palpable sense of dread and regret gurgle in my stomach. When I pop open the back of the camera, the film chamber is empty.

I forgot to load the film.

It is the most boneheaded unforced error a photographer can make, and I make it at the worst possible time. Or over a period of time, since there is a whole segment of that tour for which I have no photographs.

Months later, on returning to Asheville from Columbus, I stop through Newnan again, to make some reparations for my earlier screw-up. With just a digital camera this time—as if to ensure there is no way of repeating my mistake—I finally take that picture of the intersection of Jackson and Roscoe. It's not much to look at, because there is not much to see, which was sort of the point.

Across the street in the parking lot at Sprayberry's Barbecue, waiting for traffic and the clouds to clear, gently leaning up against a beautiful Mercedes 280 ST, I shoot an image or two of the restaurant's catering truck. Suddenly a man's face appears in the viewfinder. Because I am standing in a place heavy with the burden of moral guilt, I am perhaps already attuned to remorse, prepared to be chewed out. I know instinctively that the man forcing his face into my field of vision is the owner of the Mercedes. I apologize profusely in my most Southern and charming way, tell him how much I admire his car. We end up talking for a while, about the barbecue, about what happened in this spot, about how no one around here talks about it. I tell him why am here, to get this shot I didn't get the first time, how I'd failed to load my camera with film.

He looks at me pointedly.

"Maybe there's a reason why you didn't get that picture," he says. "You know? Maybe you weren't supposed to. Maybe there's a reason why you came back."

I cross the street for one final shot, as if hoping something will appear this time.

There is still nothing to see here. Just a white fence, a traffic signal switch box, a thick grove of magnolias sprouting from a field with no name. On this site in 1899 was an act of monstrous white barbarism the city of Newnan does not wish to remember. There are obvious reasons for that. For now, as Chip Arnold writes, the site of Sam Hose's lynching "remains off-limits, an island of jungle in an urban landscape, a cordoned sanctuary where once none was to be had."[32]

But directly across Roscoe Street, there is a sign of what someone thinks we ought to summon to mind: a small granite monument to Duncan's Barbecue, "a well-known and successful Newnan establishment for 44 years." It is a small yet powerful reminder of the way in which public monuments simultaneously ask us to remember one thing and forget another.

As with so many more prominent claimants to collective memory across the South, it seems designed to divert attention, some pleasant memory to displace one we do not wish to be called back to. On this most consequential site, there remains no marker to Sam Hose, no signpost to guide us back into the past with honesty and contrition. I have returned with nothing but a sense that only such a way back into the lived past can enliven our present, and any possible future. Way-marking erased histories, patiently traversing the hitherto anonymous acreage of our shared past, and giving names to it, and coming back again and again, even when we do not find what we think we are looking for: this is how we begin to remember.

Rumbling Man

He had been dead nearly ninety years when I first met Allen Candler on the ground floor of the north wing of the University Library in Cambridge, England, in the late 1990s. I am sure we were both thinking the same thing: "What am I doing here? What are YOU doing here?" I am not sure what I was doing on the north wing—I mostly prowled the stacks on South Wing Four, where the theology section lived. But whatever I was looking for down on the far side of one of the greatest libraries in the world, it wasn't the One-Eyed Ploughboy from Pigeon Roost.

From relatively meager origins I knew nothing of at the time, he seemed to have done pretty well for himself. Allen Candler may not have been landed gentry in his own day, but he does own a fair amount of real estate in the University Library: around thirty or so stout volumes of the Revolutionary, Colonial, and Confederate Records of the State of Georgia. Impressive, if not exactly beach reading.

The truth is, I knew nothing about Allen then apart from the fact that he had managed to get a relatively unspectacular county in the middle of the state named for him, and assumed that like most namesakes of counties, had probably done something equally prosaic to deserve it. Being White and holding office are not extraordinary achievements in late nineteenth-century Georgia, but they are a good way of getting your foot in the named-county door.

It would be another twenty years before I learned that Allen was governor of the state during one of the most notorious lynchings in American history, and whose politics sought to entrench the establishment of White supremacy in Georgia. Since then, Allen has become a case study for me in the ways family and local memory can be dissociated from actual, very public history.

After his two terms as Georgia's governor from 1898 to 1902, Allen retired to a much more sedate life as the state's official archivist and compiler of records. It was kind of like being the historian-in-chief, but in reality the work probably required little more than an aptitude for filing.

The state records project would occupy Allen Candler from late in his tenure in the Governor's Mansion until his death at his home on Edgewood Avenue in October, 1910. The final product is not the sort of thing that you would keep on your bedstand—unless your bedstand is the size of a pool table and you do not use your bed for actual sleeping—it is largely an impersonal and pedestrian record book, but it is the fruit of a highly personal quest, in which Allen Candler looked for himself in the stacks of the Library of Congress.

Before serving as Governor of Georgia, Allen represented Georgia's 9th District in the US House of Representatives. What down time he had—which was a lot, apparently—he spent in the Library of Congress gathering and compiling facts about the family's history in England and Ireland. Those hours led to a short biographical sketch of William

Candler, an eighteenth-century figure who (insofar as he is still thought about) is generally accepted as some sort of important Irish personage in family history, possibly even a legend in a way, and is the patriarch of the Georgia Candlers or something. What little real knowledge of him still circulates in my family is due to a badly faded and little-read typescript of "Colonel William Candler, His Ancestry and Progeny, by His Great-Grandson, Allen D. Candler." Allen never intended the slim volume for publication, but it was published by Foote & Davies of Atlanta in 1896, while he was Georgia's Secretary of State. In 1902, at the end of his tenure as governor, he issued a revised edition, which is the one that I have, bound in a flimsy red high school grade presentation cover.

The text itself, in seventy-five typed pages, is a considerable labor of love. The circulation of the volume, along with interest in it, seems to have basically died out before the digital age; it remains a relic of both an age of hand-to-hand transmission by carbon copy and of a congenital propensity for cost cutting. The copy I have is signed "To Asa," but there are so many Asas in my family it could take a research grant to find out which one is meant. In some places the copier has failed, and there are white blanks that have been filled in with handwriting to simulate type, put back together like a kintsugi tea bowl.

Despite what I know about him now, and despite our differences in political sensibility, we have a few things in common. Like me, Allen Candler came in his forties to believe that the version of family history that he had received was seriously lacking, and began to seek out for himself where and whom he had come from; like me, he found some sort of refuge and wisdom in books and in great libraries; and—for totally different reasons—the lynching of Sam Hose turned out to be a defining moment for both of us.

But Allen's pet project was born in an age when presuppositions about the study of history were totally different from those of my age. In the same library where I first encountered his volumes, I was reading books that undermined the very attitude towards history that Allen Candler breathed in with the air of the late nineteenth century. By "truth" of history, Allen meant "facts": that which could be distilled from "family and official records," "the most authentic historical publications, and, occasionally, unchallenged family traditions." It is the same hard-tack understanding of truth as a series of facts to be surveyed from an objective, all-seeing distance that led Candler to edit, with Clement Evans, the three-volume encyclopedia *Georgia: Comprising Sketches of Counties, Towns, Events, Institutions, and Persons*. The volumes are a gold mine of information, and undoubtedly were a major resource for the WPA Guide to Georgia. But it betrays a perspective especially popular in the late nineteenth century, the age of the encyclopedia: history as compilation and sorting—a glorified form of paperwork—and the kind of distancing from the data of history that is inevitable when you reduce history to data.

Which leaves historical recollection divided into two main types: a reduction of history to "facts" from which the objective observer or author remains innocently removed, and the hagiographical biographies that turn historical figures into morality lessons for future readers. This is, arguably, what happened in the case of Allen Candler, who on the one hand transmitted to posterity an incalculably valuable resource of information, and, on the other hand, contributed to the mythology of the Candler family that I inherited, in abbreviated form. It is no accident that the posture of historical distance popular in the late nineteenth century should lead to a kind of historical schizophrenia: both to a regime of demythologized "facts" and at the same time to thousands of shelf-feet of romanticized family myths distilled for future generations as models of good behavior.

Consider Allen Candler's entry in the *Biographical Directory of the United States Congress*. It reads as an upward series of advancements laden with fact-words: born, attended, was graduated, promoted, promoted, appointed, promoted, engaged in, served, elected, served. They are words that signify action, but the only actions they seem to imply as important are ones associated with institutions of power. It's not so strange: how many of us were taught that history is a series of wars, a sequence of the actions of a set of historical agents, that history is the cumulative effect of the deeds of "great men?" We may have rolled our eyes in school at these history lessons because they were boring; we should have rolled our eyes at them because they were hopelessly misleading and untrue. We didn't know any better, though; I wasn't educated enough then to know that this way of teaching history both conveniently concealed the contributions of "lesser" (nonwhite and nonmale) actors and obscured the fact that those historical agents were human beings with real and often less than noble motivations.

For example: the quasi-mythological story about William Candler's Irish origins came down to me like in a transgenerational game of Telephone: in one hundred years, the already-stilted account given by Allen Candler had become a truncated scrapbook of fabulous factoids. In fact the story of William's Irishness is so glaringly, egregiously untrue that I am grateful to have made it this far without attempting to curry favor with a real Irish person by telling them that I'm descended from William Candler of County Kilkenny.

William was Irish only in the sense that may have been born in Ireland, but how he got there was the more interesting, if less flattering, story. The Colonel William Candler who settled in Wrightsboro, Georgia, fought in the Revolutionary War, served in the Georgia legislature, and died in Richmond County at age forty-eight, my great-great-great-great-great-grandfather, was probably born in Ireland in 1736. That part of the story—with considerably less detail—forms part of the family myth whose actual history pretty thoroughly undermines the illusion of Irishness. William's grandfather was Lieutenant-Colonel William Candler of Northampton, fifty miles east of where I first met his great-great-great-grandson Allen in the library of the University of Cambridge, the same Allen who wrote that Lieutenant-Colonel Candler "served under Cromwell in the conquest of Ireland, and afterward settled in the barony of Callan, in the county of Kilkenny, which had been given to him as a bounty for his military services, about the year 1653."[33]

William Candler was not Irish at all, but so thoroughly and colonially English as to be anathema to actual Irish, the men and women whom Oliver Cromwell's troops savagely routed in 1650.

Allen Candler's nineteenth-century attitudes toward the study of history are now long passé. The same cannot be said for many of the untruths of "history" that he reproduced or passed over in silence. He did not seem as interested in the way this less savory part of family history might have shaped him, how he might have benefited from English pilfering of Irish property and the enforced bondage of Irish people, to say nothing of how—at the very time when he was writing the William Candler book and compiling the state's historical records—he might still be participating in a White colonial regime that enabled and even gave license to the torture and murder of Black men. But Allen Candler was not interested in any of that; he was more into the romantic mythology around William Candler, which, while genuinely compelling, was founded on a smidge of poorly transmitted historical truth.

Only some form of dissociation could make it possible for Allen Candler to describe, on one hand, the alleged crime of Sam Hose as "the most diabolical in the annals of crime," and on the other to call the spectacular torture, lynching, mutilation, and torching of Sam Hose by a massive mob of "respectable" White people simply "a burning." The rhetorical imbalance should shock no one: it is entirely consistent with the majority of White Southern attitudes about African Americans in 1899. But that it should come out of the mouth of someone so manifestly obsessed with the "truth" of history should give one pause.

The German philosopher Friedrich Nietzsche, who died while Allen Candler was in the Governor's Mansion, believed that late nineteenth-century intellectual culture was "oversaturated" with historical knowledge. In his essay "On the Uses and Disadvantages of History for Life," he wrote that "modern man drags around with him a huge quantity of indigestible stones of knowledge, which then, as in the fairy tale, can sometimes be heard rumbling about inside him. And in this rumbling there is betrayed the most characteristic quality of modern man: the remarkable antithesis between an interior which fails to correspond to any exterior and an exterior which fails to correspond to any interior—an antithesis unknown to the peoples of earlier times."[34] We become "walking encyclopaedias." The consequence, Nietzsche thought, is to "take things too lightly," and the "habit of no longer taking real things seriously."[35]

This is not to say that an idea of history is responsible for Allen Candler's racism, but it may help to make sense of how such a contradiction can exist in the mind of one so devoted to historical truth. Nineteenth century fashions in the study of history may have nothing to do with Allen Candler's reluctance to discuss the "horrid details" of the lynching of Sam Hose, or the ease with which he was able to point the finger at "scores of intelligent negroes" who refused to mention "the diabolical crime of Holt [sic]" instead of toward the mob of White people who subjected Hose to unspeakable, ritualized terror. I do not know if the Sam Hose tragedy somehow triggered a later self-reflective impulse in Allen Candler, or if, combined with political fatigue, it prompted a personal movement towards introspection and self-knowledge. He wanted to know the real things about his own history less lightly. But what about Hose? Did he ever come to take those real things seriously?

In any event, the exterior data of history—in this case, the drama surrounding Sam Hose—was all over the local and national press, to be eaten up and to rumble undigested in the bellies of millions of blood-thirsty White newspaper readers.

I do not know if, on his frequent treks across the plaza from the Capitol to the Library of Congress, his prodigiously bearded face sternly set toward discovery, Allen Candler actually looked like a walking encyclopedia or if a casual by-passer could have heard emanating from his sturdy midsection the rumbling, indigestible stones of historical knowledge. I do not know whether or not, in the annals of family and state history, he ever found the self he was looking for.

The truths of family history, as he must have come to realize, amount to far more than the mere compilation of facts: it is possible to know who married whom, who begat whom when, to know where all the bodies are buried and still leave the question of one's relationship to all that knowledge not just unanswered but unasked. As Allen Candler began to show me in the stacks of the Cambridge library, you can know every branch and twig and leaf of your own family tree and still not have the slightest clue who you are.

Mitchell–Dougherty County Line, Georgia. Photo by the author.

ALMOST HOME

MAN ALMIGHTY, my teammate exclaimed during a two-on-two basketball game in the late eighties at Morris Brandon Elementary School in Atlanta. I think he was trying not to take the Lord's name in vain, but our opponents took it differently. They interrupted the game to ask a classic Southern question: if we died that night, where we would spend eternity? *What is uniquely southern about this question?*

If, during that pickup Jesus moment, a wayward jump shot had missed its target, bounded out into the street, and rolled down the hill on Howell Mill Road, it likely would have come to rest along the curb where the road bottoms out in front of a neoclassical home built by the Ku Klux Klan.

The house radiates placid ease and mint julep-scented leisure as if it were custom-built for *Southern Living*. Its legacy has been secured by a listing on the National Register of Historic Places for its architectural merit, which means its actual history should continue to be politely ignored.

Mary Elizabeth Tyler lived there for only three years in the early 1920s, but in that span she helped to rebuild the most notorious organization in American history. Along with her business partner and occasional paramour, Edward Young Clarke, Tyler ran the Propagation Department of the Knights of the Ku Klux Klan. In her first year, she had already begun to rake it in, pocketing $2.50 of every $10 for each initiation fee for new recruits to the Klan, which were plentiful.

Not once in my time in Atlanta did I ever hear anyone talk about this house, point it out, flag its hidden history. I'm not sure how many people even knew then about its Klan association. I'm not sure how many know now. If they did, it was probably mentioned in the same hushed tones that some local White residents also used for the word "Black."

The Klan existed then in an imaginary elsewhere: I did not yet know of its associations with Stone Mountain, where it was revived in 1915, but even if I had it would have helped to locate the Klan comfortably "out there" in the uncultured sticks. And in an elsewhile: the KKK seemed like a string of dead letters, still menacing in their angularity but more a threat in movies than in daily life.

It certainly never occurred to me then that the Ku Klux Klan—during its second wind from 1915 to the mid-1920s—was reborn not in the hinterlands of Atlanta but at its posh and manicured heart: not in Stone Mountain but in Buckhead. My neighborhood.

If, after that game in which I did not really question my eternal destiny, I went home and watched something on television that night, I was not likely to have been historically burdened by it. Mainstream American television asked very little of us in the late 1980s. Ten years earlier, it had shown at least mild historical curiosity, as the shadow of the Korean and Vietnam Wars still fell across after-dinner story lines. M*A*S*H was wildly popular, and its finale is still the single most watched television episode in history. Even *The A-Team* featured a crew of crime-fighting vigilantes who had been members of the same "crack commando unit" in Vietnam.

But by the time I was being asked to consider my eternal future in the middle of a basketball game, even idealized and romanticized history wasn't must-see TV anymore. The primetime lineup was suddenly bereft of automotive dramatis personae like *The A-Team*'s tricked-out black GMC van with a bitchin' red racing stripe climaxing in a totally pointless spoiler, or *Miami Vice*'s characteristically unsubtle Ferrari Testarossa. For some reason, tastes had shifted away from a long and venerable legacy of car-driven TV drivel to cozily homebound domestic fare with occasional flashes of real humanity like *Family Ties* and *Dallas*, and America soothed what was left of its addled conscience about racial inequality in front of a nightly menu of almost entirely White and almost entirely happy families.

Roots was ten years ago. Racism was history, man. We had *The Cosby Show*.

It's possible that there is a relationship between the prominence of cars onscreen and an interest in history. American cars have always been a locus of cultural nostalgia, vehicles for easy-chair recollection that have tended to allow us to fantasize about a past that did not really exist. But that may have been better than indifference: even if automobiles served as proxies for actual history, they were at least a means to the past, however bent by sentimentalism and wish-fulfilment. *The Cosby Show* didn't have a car.

I was ten the year *Knight Rider* premiered. Earlier that winter, laid under with a cold, I watched through the living room window while my brother and neighborhood kids frolicked in the greatest snow event in the city's history. "SnowJam 1982" was a bona fide weather apocalypse in Atlanta terms, and a disastrous time for a kid to be on the disabled list, but for me it was a rare stint spent in a room furnished with formal couches and chairs strategically positioned to hide the yellow stains in the carpet contributed by our young puppy. Apart from Christmas mornings, we rarely ventured into that room. We watched TV in the den.

Like most structures of a certain age in Atlanta, that house is gone now, as is the knotty-pine-paneled den with the black vinyl loungers where I perched myself on an oversized pillow in front of the cathode-ray tube television set. When it debuted in September, *Knight Rider* was the coolest thing my brother and I had ever seen on television. Centered around an impossibly cool Pontiac Trans Am with a British accent, it seemed to be the heir-apparent to the legacy of *The Dukes of Hazzard*, the archetype of the Badass-American-Car-Centered-TV Show.

By the first season of *Knight Rider*, *Dukes* was entering the winter of its years, and unable to keep pace with technologically sophisticated car lust. The precipitating cause was a contractual dispute that led to the replacement of Bo and Luke Duke with the eminently forgettable Coy and Vance. But even when original cast members Tom Wopat and John Schneider returned to set for season five, the die was already cast. For all its 383-cubic-inch V8, 330-horsepower virility and traffic cone orange impudence, the General Lee could not really compete with a black Trans Am with a brain. KITT felt like a business-casual reprise of the Bandit's 1977 Trans Am, but it could talk, and drive itself. Suck it, Lee.

The opening title sequence—KITT barreling camera-ward across salt flats—was the most interesting thing about *Knight Rider*. The pulsing electronic theme song was a notable pivot away from Waylon Jennings's iconic theme for *Dukes* and also a harbinger of everything that was about to go wrong with country music. When the voiceover introduced

Knight Rider as "a shadowy flight into the dangerous world of a man who does not exist," the anti-authoritarian Robin Hood motif was in the same spirit as but considerably heavier than "just a good ol' boy, never meanin' no harm."

The Confederate imagery of the rebel flag and the name of General Lee were accepted in 1982 as part of the White cultural furniture of the South. Like the dog pee–stained carpet in our family living room, it wasn't worth it to think too much about it. Although it might—rightly—shock the cultural influencers of today, good ol' boys straightening the curves in a '69 Dodge emblazoned with a roof-top rebel flag seemed cool at the time. Making our way, the only way we knew how.

And certainly the figure of Michael Knight (played by a consummately White David Hasselhoff) did nothing to evoke suburban anxieties, but that a show named *Knight Rider* did not evoke images of hooded Klansmen roaming the South in search of Black people to intimidate, kill, or purge is indicative of just how immune my generation of privileged White kids had become to the language and mythology of the Confederacy.

There are other more consequential rooms of my own and my city's memory that have been rarely, if ever, visited—similarly furnished with fixtures intended to dress up a city's history in bright colors with slogans laid about the cultural floor to hide the stains. I had grown up with deep familial roots in "the city too busy to hate," trained by my education in private school to look ahead to the future more than at the past, and by my church to dwell in the eschaton more than in the present age, much less in what Thomas Wolfe called "the brown murk of the past."[1]

Which may have something to do with my preoccupation with cars then: always moving forward, sometimes dangerously, they were avatars of American optimism, steel-and-rubber emblems of possibility and engines of progress. And Atlanta was then, and is still, pathologically obsessed with them. Even had I known that such cultural subbasements existed, I doubt I would have had the sense or enough confidence to descend into their musty shades in search of historical knowledge.

If we who were young and White in the 1980s could watch *The Dukes of Hazzard* and not think twice about the rebel flag on the roof of the General Lee—nor of the problems inherent in naming a car the General Lee—we could also easily bypass the racial politics of the flag as they were playing out just to the north in all-White Forsyth County. A series of demonstrations beginning with a march in celebration of Martin Luther

King, Jr.'s birthday in January 1987 led to a much larger march the following week, drawing out thousands of protestors and counter-protestors.
Confederate flags flew, things turned ugly, and it was all televised.

Forsyth had been all White since 1912, when two White women were
allegedly raped in the county. The ensuing fallout followed a familiar
script. The crimes were pinned on local Black men: Ernest Knox, Oscar
Daniels, and Robert Edwards. While the sheriff was mysteriously away, a
White lynch mob stormed the jail where three of the suspects were being
detained, murdered Edwards in his cell, and dragged his body to hang
from a lamppost in the town square that does not exist anymore. In the
following months, white-hooded Night Riders conducted a racial cleansing of the county, forcing out virtually all of Forsyth's Black residents.

What I did not know at the time was how closely connected my own
family's history was to this episode. The Candler Horse Guards—named
for the Governor—were called in to keep the peace. The Judge was mayor
pro tem of Atlanta during the drama up in Forsyth County. His son, my
great-grandfather, Asa Warren Candler—the Major—was the commanding officer of a battalion of Fifth Regiment of the State Militia charged
with protecting Ernest Knox and Oscar Daniels during their trial. It was
the same unit his father had commanded in Palmetto and Newnan during the Sam Hose lynching.   supper

In early 1987, the nightly liturgy of dinner followed by the NBC
Nightly News was acted out in red, white, and blue as defenders of
Forsyth and of "high morals" flew Confederate battle flags—hundreds
of them—to scare African Americans out of town. It became impossible to maintain the illusion that the flag represented "heritage"—it was
manifestly a tool of racial oppression and violence, and you didn't have
to have graduated high school yet to have figured that one out.

The saga in Forsyth could have been an unprecedented teaching
moment, an opportunity for us White kids to learn about how the legacy of White supremacy was continuing to act itself out just a few miles
away from Atlanta. But it didn't. This semi-disclosure represented a
road not taken—while I could tuck away a simple sense that the flags
were designed to menace, it would be another thirty years before I
would come to seriously question the meanings of those flags. Local and
national Black leaders I had hitherto been taught to regard as nonessential had been trying to get our attention for years, but I wasn't listening.
The Forsyth moment passed and left me, at least, believing that White

supremacy was a blood sport for fanatical rednecks and racists out there in the boonies.

Despite an expensive undergraduate education and two graduate degrees, I held this assumption until an embarrassingly late age, when the language of White supremacy began to reenter the cultural conversation. In truth it had never really left; it simply had become the province of authors I was trained—through a combination of formal education and my own self-incurred delusion—to think of as "Black thinkers" and writers, residents of a neighborhood of American intellectual life I had been given little reason to wander into. I recall a moment in the 1980s when, driving with my father en route to a football game in Athens, we stopped in traffic in the town center of Jefferson, Georgia. Lining both sides of the street were hooded Klansmen, passing out flyers for some rally or something. We passed through in silence, did not make eye contact, and did not take a flyer. I rode on, still thinking that White supremacy meant the Klan, and surely that had nothing to do with me.

Perhaps it was an ignore-it-and-it-will-go-away sort of moment, but the Klan didn't really go away, of course. Even if it had, White supremacy would still be with us. In any case, "ignore and it will go away" is terrible advice, and especially when "it" is America's not-so-secret love affair with White supremacy.

The one thing that is guaranteed never to go away no matter how much you ignore it is your own ignorance. Which may explain why I and some of my high school friends could lounge on a summer evening in the late 1980s on the grassy esplanade spreading out from the foot of Stone Mountain like the infinite goodness of God, never once giving much of a thought to where we were. On folding chairs and blankets (the girls could indulge in a luxury forbidden them on our high school campus: ~~laying~~ lying fully horizontally on the grass), with a cooler full of non-adult beverages, we took in an offering of patriotic and family-friendly songs designed to warm the hearts of Georgians for the Peach State. Stone Mountain communicated ease: it was a Disneyesque resort of a kind, a mountain with an undemanding, handrail-assisted climb to the top, and the site of an almost-impossible-to-explain extravaganza on balmy summer nights: the Lasershow.

Lasers were all the rage in the 1980s. Movies and TV shows—*Star Wars, Tron, Battlestar Galactica*—employed them with feverish delight. I roller skated among swirls of them, synchronized with eighties music, at Jellybeans, "the rockin' rollerina on Roswell Road." The Reagan administration dreamed up a plan for shooting down incoming Soviet missiles with them. And in 1984, Chrysler introduced an "executive personal luxury coupe" named after one. So who wouldn't find beguiling the prospect of sitting out of an evening to a whole show of laser beams projected on the side of a mass of solid granite?

I don't remember the main body of the Lasershow at Stone Mountain, but it is impossible to forget the climax: the laser-generated outlines of the three Confederate heroes whose horse-mounted likenesses are carved permanently into the face of the mountain. As loudspeakers blast Elvis Presley's "An American Trilogy"—an emblematic medley in which irreconcilable American myths are put together in the same song and asked to play nice with one another—Robert E. Lee and then Jefferson Davis and Stonewall Jackson seem to take flight: their horses slowly begin to trot in midair and, swords raised, they take off for battle at a determined gallop. In a mild—if sentimentalized and slightly begrudging—gesture to the hell of war, battle scenes follow, at the conclusion of which a not particularly defeated-looking Lee raises his sword once more, only to bring its blade crashing down on his thigh. The broken sword falls to the ground, and the image of the fractured blade transforms into a map of the reunited nation, whereupon Lee resumes his stony pose for all eternity. The grand finale of the entire spectacle is the obligatory blaring of Lee Greenwood's "God Bless the USA," which serves to signify the symbolic redemption of the Confederate "struggle" as ultimately a kind of sacrifice to the American ideals of liberty, justice, and cheesy country music.

It was a clever way of subsuming what I did not know then to call the Lost Cause into a story of noble sacrifice, the altruistic yielding of sectional interests to the greater cause of national union. The Rebels took one on the chin for the team. In retrospect, I don't think it occurred to any of us to talk about just how damn weird all of this was. One fact that certainly never registered at the time was that Stone Mountain was a gargantuan monument to one way of misremembering history, the biggest and most aggressive Confederate monument in the country.

As I leaned back into the warm grass of the esplanade to the sound of Alabama's "Dixieland Delight," my heart strangely warmed, it never once

crossed my mind that my evening of light entertainment was unfolding beneath the very site where the Ku Klux Klan reinvented itself in
1915, that not quite seventy-five years earlier, the first light show at Stone
Mountain consisted of a sixteen-foot burning cross.

I listened to King's "I Have a Dream" speech on cassette tapes countless times in my adolescence and felt myself moved by the idealism of
King's vision—but moved in an abstract way, perhaps, since I never
made the connection then between the lofty Christian nobility of King's
soul-jarring calls for justice and the material realities of where I lived.
Unaware then of the resonances of Stone Mountain as a holy site for
White supremacists and Lost Causers, I didn't think to notice the deliberate power of King's decision to mention it on the steps of the Lincoln
Memorial at the March on Washington in 1963, nor did I consider how
the power of that moment connected to a specific place I was probably
then blithely enjoying seeing lit up with laser beams. But being moved
by King's speeches and sermons is no great achievement; anyone can do
it. King's greatest moments in the pulpit or on the dais had the power to
effect in me a movement of the heart, maybe, but not yet a personal turning of memory. That would come later.

The only noteworthy feature of the carving that struck me then was
how unfinished it so obviously was, the rather lazy pile of cut stone fragments at the base of the mountain where the reflecting pool was supposed to be suggesting some sudden arrest of effort. The horses remain
half-finished, the whole thing a fairly crude and violent imposition of
human artifice and will-to-power onto the largest mass of exposed solid
granite on planet earth. It looked even then like a meticulous scar, the
product of millions of small, surgical hammer strikes enacted by some
interior principle of action I did not know how to name. On the most
charitable reading, the Lasershow could be thought of as an elaborate
effort to make the most out of an irreparable wound of nature; and insofar as anyone fell for the high-tech trompe l'oeil it was at the cost of
being prevented from looking too closely at the human scars the monument is not very interested in.

Only much later, would I start to look again at the monuments to the
Lost Cause that had become like a tasteless fungus in the cultural drinking
water—it was there, and terribly bad for everyone who consumed it, but
most of us White folks just took it for granted or ignored it or weren't even
aware it was there, or what it was doing to us. All of which is deliciously

ironic, given that I voluntarily chose to subject myself to a fabulously tacky display on the biggest Confederate monument in the world.

Stone Mountain has been there for millions of years, but it wasn't until 1915 that it got its close-up, thanks to Hollywood. Following the block-buster premiere of D. W. Griffith's *The Birth of a Nation* that year, Mrs. E. Dorothy Blount Lamar, president of the Georgia division of the United Daughters of the Confederacy (UDC), praised Griffith as "a friend to the truth about those days of reconstruction."

Birth of a Nation was, she said, a "truthful portrayal of the sorrows of those times, it has done a magnificent work for us in setting the jus-tice of our attitued [sic] toward our troubles at that period before an uninformed north."[2] Lamar exhorted all the UDC faithful to "call for it insistently," to get out and see the film, to persuade their local theater operators to screen it. In the same speech, Lamar reported with great excitement the "unbounded enthusiasm of the world-famous sculptor, Gustav Borglum," for his plans for the Confederate memorial at Stone Mountain, which Lamar called a "wonderful phenomenon" to memori-alize "Our Cause." A week later, the *Atlanta Constitution* ran a two-page spread in its Sunday edition, featuring praise for the film from around the country. On the front page of the same issue, a small notice reported: Impressive services of the past week were those conducted on the night of Thanksgiving at the top of Stone Mountain. The exercises were held by fifteen Klansmen who gathered at the behest of their chieftain, W. J. Simmons, and marked the foundation of the invisible empire, Knights of the Ku Klux Klan.[3]

The Klan 2.0 repaid Hollywood's blessing by borrowing the act of burning a cross (used by Griffith for the film) for the first time on Stone Mountain. The film finally made its debut in Atlanta on December 6, two days after the state of Georgia issued an official charter to the Knights of the Ku Klux Klan. At the very same time, the *Constitution* reported a wave of arson attacks by marauding "night riders" in Cherokee County north of the city that led African American residents to flee the county, much as they had done following the racial cleansing of neighboring For-syth County in 1912.

The convergence of these historical episodes is hardly a coincidence; on the contrary, they mark milestones in the authorization of the Lost

Cause version of history, the state seal of approval on a reinvigorated White supremacist regime and a mythological history to support it. By the end of a tumultuous 1915, with Leo Frank lynched, the Stone Mountain memorial underway, and the Klan restored, a blockbuster film celebrating Negro decadence and White virtue was just the thing White Atlanta needed to restore and reinvigorate its faith in the righteousness of its own "cause."

Even if I had become aware at a younger age of Stone Mountain's entanglements with the Klan, it would still have been easy to think of white supremacy at a comfortable distance. Stone Mountain was way the hell out there, in another county, not yet absorbed into the amnesic Atlanta that was swallowing us all.

By the curious civil liturgy of the Lasershow, the world's most obnoxious Confederate monument was made to appear banal—not even really a Confederate monument at all, so much so that we could lounge before three outsize Rebel superstars and not bat an eye. The carving had the air of antiquity, and like many such monuments, disguises its own history. While the initial work on the monument began in 1923, it lay dormant for forty years until it was revived in 1964 at the height of the civil rights movement and at the behest of Marvin Griffin, the segregationist governor of Georgia from 1955 to 1959, who never made any bones about his opposition to *Brown v. Board of Education*'s federally mandated integration of public schools.

I had also assumed that the state flag had always had an embedded Confederate flag. You just assumed that because it was there, it had always been there. Only later did I learn it had been incorporated in 1956, two years after Brown. One of the sponsors of the bill in the Georgia State Senate was named Jefferson Lee Davis.

In my youth, the little park that now marks the center of Buckhead was very different from the epicenter of a new urbanist explosion that it is today. Like many locales in Atlanta, it has a short memory. Bagley Park in the center of Buckhead, the Klan's headquarters, had once been the site of an African American settlement that was eventually bought out by Fulton County to create the diamonds where I played Little League baseball until the sixth grade.

There were still gravestones there, but I never asked about them or wandered among them. And no one I knew could ever explain how Buckhead had gotten its name to begin with. In the 1980s the only actual image of a buck head visible anywhere in the area was atop the marquee for the Buckhead Cinema whose message was unchanging for decades: "ADULT DOUBLE FEATURE."

In front of the nearby Cotton Exchange on Roswell Road, a local gray-haired eccentric known as the Birdman, in light blue short-sleeved Oxford shirt, horn-rimmed glasses, and khakis, regularly rode his bicycle, flapping his arms up and down. The Birdman is long dead, but the Cotton Exchange has survived a frenzy for destruction that has gone on for decades in Atlanta. When it was first built in the 1920s, it was used to manufacture robes and gowns for the Ku Klux Klan, and was the source of a good deal of wealth for Mary Elizabeth Tyler and Imperial Wizard William J. Simmons. I passed it hundreds of times on the way to Henri's Bakery on Irby for turkey on rye before realizing what it was. The original Henri's has been replaced—like almost every other historic structure in Atlanta, it seems—by a chic, new mixed-use development, but the Cotton Exchange is somehow still standing. It is historic, but few really seem to know why.

South on Peachtree Road a mile or so, there is even less of a trace of what once marked the corner of Peachtree and E. Wesley. About the same time Mary Elizabeth Tyler lived in her house, the massive Greek revival mansion that stood on the corner served as the headquarters of the Klan's local and national operations. Simmons used it as a Klan show home and planned for the European-style garden sculptures of famous Night Riders—and one of himself. The headquarters of the trenchantly anti-Catholic Klan was purchased in 1936 by the Roman Catholic diocese of Atlanta for the construction of a new cathedral dedicated to Christ the King. There are no markers to what Atlanta's history was at these sites, but there are also no markers to what it might have become at the corner of Collier Road and Howell Mill.

What is now a city green space named Ellsworth Park straddling either side of Peachtree Creek was to have been the campus of the Klan-sponsored University of America. Many times, I've sat at the window at Fellini's across the street eating a slice of white pizza, looking at what I mistook for just another undeveloped plot of land.

The demise of the Klan in Atlanta in 1923 was not due to federal investigation or massive NIMBY ("not in my backyard") resistance but to internal mismanagement and chronic corruption. Its leaders were vicious White supremacists, but they were also opportunistic charlatans who saw an opportunity to spread their message in a fraudulent and lucrative fashion. While Stone Mountain is a convenient location to which to outsource Atlanta's Confederate and Lost Cause legacy, it's still there in Buckhead if you know where to look.

In recent years, it seems the hellhound on the trail has been catching up with Atlanta: while the city remains the most prosperous, diverse, and powerful city in the South, the hold of the Lost Cause narrative on local identity has diminished. But vestiges still cling to the feet of the myth: four plaques erected in 1920 describing, in classically Lost Cause terms, the "Siege of Atlanta" still stand outside the main entrance of the state capitol building where, for two days a hundred years later, the body of John Lewis lay in state in the rotunda.

The incongruity of the moment that was hard to miss: Lewis, a lifelong foot soldier for voting rights and full citizenship for African Americans, surrounded by the iconography of the opposition, a veritable portrait and statuary gallery of onlooking, now mute secessionists, slaveholders, segregationists, and White supremacists: Alexander H. Stephens, John Brown Gordon, Robert E. Lee, Benjamin H. Hill, Gene Talmadge, Thomas E. Watson, Marvin Griffin, Lester Maddox. Most silent of all, and curiously missing on the day of Lewis's funeral: the portrait of my distant cousin, Governor Allen Daniel Candler. In the spot where it should be is a bare wall, a disencumbered picture hanger.

Allen was the pee-stained living room of my family, a chamber of collective memory visited so infrequently and so habitually kept dark that eventually no one could recall what was in there. Whatever the memory of Allen Candler had been at one time, a hundred years later, the darkness of family ignorance had overcome it.

By the time I really began to learn about him, he had become all but forgotten about in our branch of family lore. He was unknown to me for most of my life until a few years ago, when a single flicker of light in the form of a friend's casual mention of a book about the lynching of Sam Hose began to dispel the darkness, and gradually illuminate the long-unlit corners of Allen's history and legacy to Georgia, and to me. By the time my eyes had adjusted, I had learned that Allen had been

Everyone is a person of color. All skin has color,

governor during the most notorious lynching in the state's history. He had done nothing to prevent it and blamed the episode on Black people. His administration oversaw the implementation of *Plessy v. Ferguson's* "separate but equal" policy on race. Despite the direct pleas of W. E. B. Du Bois made to him in the governor's mansion on Peachtree Street, Candler did nothing to prevent the state's segregation of passenger rail cars. His chief political legacy had been the establishment of the white-only Democratic primary system, a feature of Georgia electoral politics until 1944.

I never had to be troubled by his memory. Perhaps some cruel logic left him out precisely because it was understood that my knowing about his White supremacy would have done nothing to change the system of privilege by which I have come to benefit from his political machinations.

One of the ways I've come to think about White privilege is in terms of the stories that you can get on without: stories about the world, yourself, your family, your city, the past. If you are a person of color, these are stories you need simply to achieve daily existence. For example, the story of Trayvon Martin or Eric Garner or George Floyd or Breonna Taylor—to say nothing of Emmett Till or Medgar Evers or Jimmie Lee Jackson—is a cautionary tale for the purposes of instructing the young and reminding the old that none of your accomplishments nor even your inborn dignity as a human being will count for anything if some representative of the White world decides one afternoon that you are a threat to them. Parents of Black children tell them the stories of Trayvon and Emmett because they know that their child's name could be the next one added to the long list of names of the victims of White brutality, a list they must keep alive for themselves because the state will certainly not do it on their behalf.

Black Atlantans probably are far more likely to know this history than I am. White privilege means there are stories you do not have to be burdened by—neighborhoods of the imagination you think you can casually avoid without damage to your soul. My life as a White person could have turned out differently if I had learned to inhabit a different narrative geography, to be shaped by the practice of alienating mental spaces. But I didn't have to.

Sometimes, though, the black person is in fact the savage. Cf. the first page of "Makes Me Wanna Holler."

My son Charlie is ten that summer. Lately he and his three brothers have been obsessed with the films of the great Japanese animator Hayao

Truth be told, homo sapiens in general is savage, the only true wild animal on Earth.

Mr. You really feel bad about your "privilege"? You should give all your world goods and never, ever, to the poor.

Miyazaki, whose masterful films often deal with the hidden, and even frightful, beauty of nature, and the inveterate human will to dominate and destroy it and one another. I only discovered Miyazaki later in life, so we've gotten into his work together, as a family. We have all grown up with him at the same time.

Charlie and I are headed from Asheville to Atlanta in a Honda minivan. I want to show him some of the places I love, for no other reason than that I hope he will love them, too: Henri's Bakery for turkey on rye; the subdivision that used to be my grandparents' house; the Morris Brandon basketball court. We will take breakfast at the Silver Skillet, ride the streetcar down Auburn Avenue, stop at Ebenezer Baptist, the Royal Peacock. We're also going to see some of the homes built by Candlers during the segregationist era, mainly along the section of US 278 known as Ponce de Leon Avenue, the park-lined boulevard that marked the frontier between Black and White Atlanta. The same street on the White side has one name, and another on the Black side. My great-great-grandfather lived on that boundary at the corner of Ponce and Briarcliff, which becomes Moreland Avenue. His house is long gone, but we will go look for it anyway.

It is worth asking why any of this stuff matters, if at all. Maybe I am interested in family history; maybe I am seeking some place to anchor my own memories, some small plot of earth to which to bind my own wayfaring self. It could be that I am simply trying to manufacture a history I do not really possess, a surrogate past that I might lean on, that might hold steady for just a while longer. The house I grew up in is all gone now, and I have little to return to in the way of a site that still holds a memory of self should I forget. Maybe that's what I am looking for on Ponce. I don't know.

There is something nonsensical in all this, in my desire to give my children a sense of connection to a place where they have never lived, to cultivate in them an attachment to a space inhabited by their forebears they would never have heard about were it not for a random set of coincidences in my own life. It risks being an artificial, enforced attachment and not a real, organic one. But at bottom I just want them to be less naïve than I was, less ignorant than I am. To have a history we can grow up with together. To give them some sign that boundless curiosity will always be met with an ever-greater mystery, that as much as you think you know there is always an infinitely greater knowledge that you do not possess. That as long as you search the grounds of the world for some hint of yourself, you will never fully find it. That you will ever remain a mystery to yourself. That every seeking and finding only prompts more seeking, and that you may often find what you did not seek, and that may be the thing you needed the most.

I have given Charlie a Nikon F3 made about the same time as *Knight Rider*, loaded with Ilford HP5 Plus black-and-white film for the week-end. I tell him to be discriminating with his use of film. It's not like taking pictures with a cell phone, I tell him. You have to be patient, I say, secretly hoping he shoots up a whole roll because he loves the feel of it—the weight of it, the vibrations in the hand from the mechanical click of the shutter—and has to exercise restraint because he doesn't want to stop.

Gainesville proclaims itself "the Poultry Capital of the World." Local hero and global chicken magnate Jesse Jewell (1902–75) revolutionized the industry, and his company employed many people in north Georgia. Just on the edge of the town center, a monument to the city's claim to fame rises thirty feet or so over Poultry Park. It is known as the "Chicken Monument," which makes sense in view of the bronze rooster that tops the obelisk. But it is less a monument to the gallant bird—or the fact that more foods are compared to the taste of chicken than any other food—than a tribute to the ability efficiently to slaughter and process chickens en masse. Gainesville may or may not still be the world's chicken capital, but it is home to possibly the world's most American monument.

It's more than a little ridiculous, but we didn't come here to see a chicken. Down the road a piece is the real goal: the Alta Vista Cemetery. It is getting late in the day: the golden hour of late evening is just beginning. The sky relaxes a bit from its usual late-August gray and returns to a marine sort of blue in which cottony thunderheads show off. One, in the distance, is mildly threatening. Its dark underside seems to ride on a band of golden sky.

One monument in the middle of the burial ground sticks out, but it is not what we came here for either. It is the final resting place of Confederate General James Longstreet. This gravestone mentions only Longstreet's life up until the end of the Civil War in 1865. He lived another thirty-nine years, but you wouldn't know it from this site because he enjoys a conflicted legacy. Beloved by many Confederates and their sympathizers for his military leadership in the Army of Northern Virginia, he is regarded by many of the same as a traitor for allying with the Republican Party during Reconstruction. In 1874, after the election of Republican William Kellogg as governor of Louisiana, members of the Crescent City White League, a white terrorist organization, stormed the US Customs House in New Orleans in an attempted coup of the state government. Longstreet led a multiracial detachment of the Metropolitan Police against the White League in the ensuing "Battle of Liberty Place." He is not on Stone Mountain.

Charlie stands with the Nikon in front of the grave of Governor Allen Daniel Candler, and shoots. The last rays of daylight fall across the name on the tombstone. Unlike me at his age, Charlie knows that name. When the negatives come back a few weeks later, I realize what I already knew. He's a natural. He's got the eye, the patience, the vision. The scene is so dramatically colored that it feels like a sign that we have arrived at our journey's end. But we have a ways to go yet.

On the road back to Atlanta, I-85 is inescapable. Outside Charlie's window, an enormous cumulonimbus, backlit by the lowering sun, against a gradient sky from cerulean to amber. In a truly sane universe, everyone would be stopping in the middle of the eight-lane highway to take in the undeserved beauty of a fire-ringed cloud at dusk. It appears hand-drawn, painted on the back of the sky.

It looks like a Miyazaki, Charlie says.

It's tempting to stop. But what can you do? Make your way, the only way you know how. You can't hold on to the moment. You make some sacrifices, give yourself over to the mad tide of high-speed efficiency. It only goes in one direction. I have to keep my eyes on the road.

Charlie stares out the window at the cloud.

Keep looking, I say to him, hoping that he will see what I cannot.

Acknowledgments

Southbound on US 41 in August 1997, I had a vague idea of someday writing something about this journey but had no idea that many years later these trips would come to determine much of the shape of my creative life. I owe much of that transformation to my dear friend John Hayes, who has been an inspiring traveling companion for twenty-five years. This project is inconceivable without his piercing intelligence, good humor, intuitive navigational sense, deep wisdom, but most of all, his abiding friendship.

Along the way, there have been so many people whom John and I have met, many of whom have become dear friends, some of whom are family. I am especially thankful for my cousin Bruce Lanier and his wife Scottie, who have become regular hosts for John and me on our now-standard stops in Birmingham. I am grateful beyond words for the friendship and encouragement of Sally Mann, an uncompromising and peerless writer and photographer whose example has inspired my own work. I am thankful to the Hillsborough/Sewanee literary family—Allan Gurganus, Tom Rankin, Jill McCorkle, Steve Yarbrough, and the late Randall Kenan—for insight and wisdom they may not even realize they have dispensed.

The origin of this book project goes back to a lunch at the now-defunct Gan Shan Station on Charlotte Street in Asheville in late 2017 with my friend David Moltke-Hansen, who recommended to me Donald G. Mathews's book, *At the Altar of Lynching*, about the burning of Sam Hose. It is not often that academic scholarship precipitates an existential crisis, but I am indebted to Donald Mathews and Chip Arnold, whose scholarly work on the Sam Hose lynching led to a profoundly life-altering revelation.

Over a pasta dinner in Pasadena, Tom Zoellner unwittingly planted the seeds for this project by encouraging me to return to the road and write about it. Through Tom, my work found an early and generous home in *Los Angeles Review of Books*, to which I have returned multiple times. I would never have ended up in Pasadena in the first place were it not for Makoto Fujimura, whose irrepressible capacity for seeing beauty in the broken places of this world has been a constant inspiration to me. For Mako's friendship, and that of the Conrad's Breakfast Club, Curt Thompson and Esther Meek, I give joyful thanks. A final thank you to David Heim, former editor of *The Christian Century*, for the opportunity to cover the opening of the lynching memorial in Montgomery.

My deep gratitude goes to my friend Patrick Weems of the Emmett Till Interpretive Center in Sumner, who lead us through an unusually serendipitous and revealing (even for *A Deeper South*) detour through Sunflower and Tallahatchie Counties. A huge thank you goes to my friend Scott Peacock, who has been a constant source of consolation and good humor to me since an unlikely encounter picking figs in his back yard. I am especially indebted to my late friend Kevin McIlvoy, whose early and persistent encouragement nourished me and got this project off the ground. To the inimitable Peggy Galis, I give my love and life-long gratitude. Finally, I am deeply grateful to Tom and Edwina Johnson, David and Ginger Jones, and Anne Turnbow for support in a multitude of forms.

In a curious way, but which befits the spirit of this book, this book began with a road trip with one Ralph and ended a different road trip with a different Ralph. In 1994, John and I drove from Winston-Salem, North Carolina, to Milledgeville with our then-professor and mentor, my future colleague, and my dear friend Ralph Wood to a conference–festival in honor of Flannery O'Connor. That brief sojourn in O'Connor's hometown would and still does bear fruit for me in incalculable ways. I continue to be shaped by and to aspire to the depth of Ralph's passionate and perceptive reading of the world, in the incident light of O'Connor and other figures to whom Ralph introduced me and led me to love.

In August 2023, shortly before I made the final corrections to the manuscript for this book, I spent a couple of days in the Mississippi delta. The hours I got to spend in the car with W. Ralph Eubanks traversing some very weighty roadways, absorbing his profound wisdom about both his home state and life in this world were a genuine instance of the relentless gratuity of the delta and of Ralph's explosive generosity. As a result of that trip, I returned home having to rewrite much of what I had written about the Emmett Till story, which illustrates for me how no book—and certainly no acknowledgments section—is ever really finished.

The presence of *A Deeper South* in the world is entirely due to Ehren Foley of the University of South Carolina Press, who first pitched the idea to me and who has since shepherded this work from its infancy to its final form. Thank you to Ehren and the whole team at USC Press: Emily Weigel, whose cover design struck gold on the first try; Kerri Tolan, for her patient and painstaking editorial work; Cathy Esposito, for marketing; Michael McGandy, press director, for overseeing this whole project; and former director Richard Brown, for his early support of this book.

Finally, to the innumerable musicians and performing artists whose recorded music has been, often at an unhealthy volume, the backdrop to the composition of this book, and who have often inspired a defiant refusal to give quarter to the demons of self-doubt: I hope this work repays in some measure the life-sustaining power that music has to draw one out from oneself toward something higher, deeper, truer, more beautiful.

I owe a whole separate category of gratitude to my dear friend Rosanne Cash, who for twenty years now has heard something in my own words that has continued to motivate me to keep writing them. Her incredibly generous foreword to this book not only captures my aims better than I could myself but also helped me to better understand myself.

I am so grateful to my brother Matt, my North Star and advocate whose sense of the world constantly expands my own, and my sister-in-law, Virginia, who has likewise been a constant cheerleader and an artistic inspiration. And to my beloved parents, Peter and Shannon, who both have given me more than I could ever articulate in words, I owe love beyond measure.

Finally, this project would be unthinkable without the dedication of my incomparable wife, Meredith, a force of nature and a relentless fighter for other people, a walking (and often cycling) torrent of self-offering who has encouraged these journeys for two and a half decades. For her tenacious faithfulness and her love—and that of our four extraordinary boys, Henry, Charlie, Oliver, and George—I am thankful beyond words. This book is dedicated to the five of them.

Notes

Steak Dinners and Grady Moments

1. William Faulkner, *Absalom, Absalom!* (New York: Vintage 1990), 142
2. Ibid., 289.
3. "Grand Words," *Cincinnati Enquirer,* September 25, 1880, 1.
4. "The Meeting in Tammany Hall," *New York Times,* September 24, 1880, 2.
5. "Grand Words," 1.
6. Henry Grady, *The New South: Writings and Speeches of Henry Grady* (Savannah: The Beehive Press, 1971), 11.
7. Ibid., 20–21.
8. Ibid., 87.
9. Ibid., 102.
10. Ibid., 105.
11. "Henry W. Grady," *New York Times,* December 24, 1889, 4.
12. Sheffield Hale, "An award for all mankind, a dinner for one—the Atlanta Nobel Prize party for MLK, given by the city's image-conscious white leadership," *The Saporta Report,* January 19, 2015, https://saportareport.com/.
13. Juhani Pallasmaa, *The Eyes of the Skin: Architecture and the Senses,* 3rd ed. (London: Wiley, 2012), 14.

Into History through the Service Entrance

1. This essay originally appeared in the *Los Angeles Review of Books,* March 10, 2019. It appears here with permission of the publisher.
2. In 2018, the original Zero Milepost was rescued from the parking garage and installed in a permanent exhibit at the Atlanta History Center. See Claire Haley, "Preserving Atlanta History: The Zero Milepost," Atlanta History Center Website, December 4, 2020, https://www.atlantahistorycenter.com/blog/preserving-atlanta -history-the-zero-milepost/.
3. Toni Morrison, *Playing in the Dark: Whiteness and the Literary Imagination* (New York: Vintage, 1993).
4. *Georgia: The WPA Guide to its Towns and Countryside,* compiled by Workers of the Writers' Program of the Works Progress Administration in the State of Georgia, with a new introduction and new appendix by Phinizy Spalding (Athens, GA: University of Georgia Press, 1940; Columbia, SC: University of South Carolina Press, 1990), 173; *Atlanta: A City of the Modern South,* compiled by Workers of the Writers' Program of the Works Progress Administration in the State of Georgia (New York: Smith & Durrell, 1942), 153.

5. C. Vann Woodward, *Tom Watson: Agrarian Rebel* (New York: Rinehart, 1938), 432.

6. Douglas A. Blackmon, *Slavery By Another Name: The Re-Enslavement of Black Americans from the Civil War to World War II* (New York: Anchor, 2009).

7. W. E. B. Du Bois, *Black Reconstruction in America 1860-1880* (New York: Free Press, 1998), 501.

8. W. E. B. Du Bois, *Dusk of Dawn*, in *W. E. B. Du Bois: Writings*, ed. Nathan Huggins (New York: Library of America, 1986), 602–3.

9. Ibid., 602.

10. Philip Dray, *At the Hands of Persons Unknown: The Lynching of Black America* (New York: Modern Library, 2002), 4.

11. "Colonel Candler's Letter," *Atlanta Constitution*, August 27, 1882, 4.

12. "Governor-Elect A. D. Candler," *Atlanta Constitution*, October 6, 1898, 1. See also Donald G. Mathews, *At the Altar of Lynching: Burning Sam Hose in the American South* (Oxford: Oxford University Press, 2018), 117–19.

13. W. E. B. Du Bois, "The Georgia Negro Again, ca. 1900," manuscript, W. E. B. Du Bois Papers (MS 312), Special Collections and University Archives, University of Massachusetts Amherst Libraries, http://credo.library.umass.edu/view/full/mums312-b212-i001.

14. "What Governor Candler Says," *Atlanta Constitution*, April 24, 1899, 1.

15. "Opening Address of The Hon. Allan [sic] D. Candler, Governor of Georgia," in W. E. B. Du Bois, ed., *The Negro in Business: report of a social study made under the direction of Atlanta University; together with the proceedings of the fourth Conference for the Study of the Negro Problems, held at Atlanta University, May 30-31, 1899* (Atlanta: Atlanta University, 1899), 54.

16. "'Yankee Help Not Needed,'" *Boston Evening Transcript*, April 25, 1901, 14.

Georgia I

1. "Riotous Colored Troops Cause Trouble by Firing at Citizens," *Atlanta Constitution*, March 9, 1899, 2.

2. "What City Is This," *Griffin Daily News and Sun*, March 9, 1899, cited in Edwin T. Arnold, *What Virtue There Is in Fire: Cultural Memory and the Lynching of Sam Hose* (Athens: University of Georgia Press, 2009), 25.

3. "Left Macon Ready for Trouble," *Atlanta Constitution*, March 9, 1899, 2.

4. Ibid.

5. See https://www.youtube.com/watch?v=Hcbgb4gz-DU.

6. Christian Boone, "Hearing Focuses on 1983 Murder," *Atlanta Journal-Constitution*, December 1, 2017, B2.

7. See https://law.justia.com/cases/federal/appellate-courts/F2/154/460/1478559/.

8. "Gene Attacks U.S. Attorneys, Threatens Negro Voters Again," *Atlanta Constitution*, July 13, 1946, 2.

9. Joseph L. Bernd, "White Supremacy and the Disfranchisement of Blacks in Georgia, 1946," *The Georgia Historical Quarterly* 66, no. 4 (Winter 1982), 494–95.

10. V. O. Key, Jr., *Southern Politics* (New York: Vintage, 1949), 106.

11. "'Stay Away from White Folks' Ballot Boxes'—Gene to Negroes," *Atlanta Constitution*, July 12, 1946, 14.

12. "Gene Attacks U.S. Attorneys, Threatens Negro Voters Again," *Atlanta Constitution*, July 13, 1946, 2.

13. "Order Prevails as Negroes Vote," *Atlanta Constitution*, July 18, 1946, A1.

14. Philip Dray, *At the Hands of Persons Unknown*, 379.

15. Erica Sterling, "Maceo Snipes: A Man Whose Death Inspired the Teenager Who Led the Movement," The Georgia Civil Rights Cold Cases Project at Emory University, https://coldcases.emory.edu/maceo-snipes/#f20.

16. Elliott Minor, "Answers Sought in 1946 Ga. Killing," *Washington Post*, February 13, 2007, http://www.washingtonpost.com/wp-dyn/content/article/2007/02/13/AR2007021300121.html; Dan Barry, "Killing and Segregated Plaque Divide Town," *New York Times*, March 18, 2007, https://www.nytimes.com/2007/03/18/us/18land.html.

17. "Kick Up Dust," *Atlanta Constitution*, August 6, 1946, 6.

18. "Take Swift Vengeance," *Atlanta Constitution*, August 22, 1898, 1.

19. "Americus Will Stay in Game," *Atlanta Constitution*, June 19, 1906, 9.

20. "Georgia State League," *Atlanta Constitution*, June 19, 1906, 9.

21. "Georgia State League," *Atlanta Constitution*, June 12, 1906, 7.

22. "Georgia State League," *Atlanta Constitution*, June 24, 1906. Things were not much better elsewhere in the state: "In a very slow game, Waycross defeated Albany today. The game was void of features and the crowd in attendance seemed to be glad when it was over" (ibid.)

23. "South Georgia Teams Will Play in Bowl in August," *Montgomery Advertiser*, August 1, 1923, 6.

24. "Joey the Wanderer Now Snug in Southern Berth," *Battle Creek Enquirer*, July 22, 1923, 15.

25. "Judge Landis Will Not Allow Jackson to Play in Georgia," *St. Louis Star and Times*, July 18, 1923, 4.

26. Guy Cutright, "Shoeless in Americus," *Atlanta Journal-Constitution*, July 25, 1999, G2.

27. "Joe Jackson is Disrupting Baseball," *Tampa Tribune*, July 19, 1923, 8.

28. "Still a Thorn in Organized Baseball," *Jackson Clarion-Ledger*, July 19, 1923, 5.

29. "Americus Has a Headache Over 'Shoeless Joe' and Worry He's Causing All," *Tampa Tribune*, July 19, 1923, 8.

30. "Baseball Notes," *Berkshire Eagle* (Pittsfield, MA), August 27, 1923, 12.

31. Joe Carter, "Raspberries and Cream," *Shreveport Times*, August 28, 1923, 8.

32. Jim Laxson, "Integrated Communal Farm Stirs Controversy," *St. Petersburg Times*, February 18, 1957, 35.

33. Ibid.

34. "Clinton Dynamite Blast Said 'Attempted Murder'," *Greenville News*, February 16, 1957, 2.

35. "Georgia Bureau Looks into Koinonia Farm Activities," *Panama City News-Herald*, February 27, 1957, 9.

36. "Biracial Georgia Farm Said To Have Red Friends," *Baltimore Sun*, April 6, 1957, 4.

37. Dorothy Day, "On Pilgrimage," *Catholic Worker*, May 1, 1957, https://catholicworker.org/722-html/.

38. The Vigilantes of Love, "Andersonville," Track 15, *The Killing Floor*, Sky Records, 1993, compact disc.

39. Walt Whitman, *Specimen Days*, in Complete *Poetry and Collected Prose* (New York: Library of America, 1982), 765.

40. Walt Whitman, *Specimen Days*, 765.

41. Dan 3:1 RSV.

42. Robert Scheer, "The Playboy Interview with Jimmy Carter," *Playboy Magazine*, November 1, 1976, https://www.playboy.com/read/.

43. W. E. B. Du Bois, *The Souls of Black Folk* (New York: Library of America, 1990), 88.

44. Ibid.

45. Taylor Branch, *Parting the Waters: America in the King Years, 1954-63* (New York: Simon & Schuster, 1988), 528.

46. Ibid., 408.

47. "Baker Sheriff Acquitted by Albany Federal Jury," *Macon Telegraph*, November 3, 1945, 2.

48. Cabell Phillips, "U.S. Panel Indicts 9 In Integration Unit For Picketing Juror," *New York Times*, August 10, 1963, 1.

49. Howard Zinn, *SNCC: The New Abolitionists* (Chicago: Haymarket Books, 1964), 211.

50. Branch, *Parting the Waters*, 732.

51. "New Regime," *Charleston Daily News*, March 14, 1870, 1.

52. Lee W. Formwalt, "The Camilla Massacre of 1868: Racial Violence as Political Propaganda," *The Georgia Historical Quarterly* 71, no. 3 (Fall 1987), 414.

53. Isaac Wheeler Avery, *The History of the State of Georgia from 1850 to 1881, Embracing the Three Important Epochs: The Decade before the War of 1861-5; the War; the Period of Reconstruction* (New York: Brown & Derby, 1881), 213.

54. "Opening of the Campaign," *Atlanta Constitution*, September 10, 1874, 3.

55. Ibid.

56. "Recollections of Milton A. Candler's daughter, Claude Candler McKinney, by her daughter Caroline Murphey McKinney Clark," Candler Family papers, Stuart A. Rose Manuscript Library, Emory University, 2.

57. "Life Sketch of Eliza Caroline Murphey Candler, compiled by Caroline Murphey McKinney Clark," Candler Family papers, Stuart A. Rose Manuscript Library, Emory University, 1.

58. Charles Murphey Candler and Mary Hough Scott Candler's eighteen-year-old daughter, Rebekah, unveiled the monument in front of the Dekalb County Courthouse on Confederate Memorial Day, 1908. The monument, which praised the virtues of "a covenant keeping race who held fast to the faith as it was given by the fathers of the Republic," was removed in June 2020.

59. *Report of the Joint Select Committee Appointed to Inquire into the Condition of Affairs in the Late Insurrectionary States, so Far as Regards the Execution of Laws, and the Safety of the Lives and Property of the Citizens of the United States and Testimony Taken* (Washington, DC: Government Printing Office, 1872), 308.

60. Ibid., 321.

61. Ibid., 338.

62. Ibid., 348.

63. Flannery O'Connor, "A Good Man Is Hard To Find," in *Collected Works* (New York: Library of America, 1988), 137.

Florida

1. Harry Crews, *A Childhood: The Biography of a Place* (Athens: University of Georgia Press, 1995), 136.

2. Dante Alighieri, *Dante's Inferno: The Indiana Critical Edition*, tr. Mark Musa (Bloomington: Indiana University Press, 1995), VII, 200–8, 65.

3. Ibid.

4. "Okefenokee Canal," *Atlanta Constitution*, June 27, 1892, 1.

5. E. Merton Coulter, "The Okefenokee Swamp: Its History and Legends, Part II," *The Georgia Historical Quarterly* 48, no. 3 (September 1964), 291.

6. Herschel Vespasian Johnson, *The Probable Destiny of Our Country; the Requisites to Fulfil That Destiny; and the Duty of Georgia in the Premises: An Address before the Phi Delta and Ciceronian Societies of Mercer University; delivered on the 14th of July, A. D. 1847* (Penfield, GA: Printed at the Temperance Banner Office, 1847), 7.

7. "The Correspondence of the Hammond Dinner," *Daily Constitutionalist and Republic* (Augusta, GA), July 28, 1858, 3.

8. *Acts of the General Assembly of the State of Georgia, 1855-56* (Milledgeville GA: Boughton, Nisbet & Barnes, State Printers, 1856), 273.

9. "The Great Okefinokee Swamp," *Atlanta Constitution*, September 7, 1875, 2.

10. "Okefinokee," *Atlanta Constitution*, 15 September 1875, 2.

11. "The Okefenokee Swamp," *Atlanta Constitution*, July 29, 1889, 8.

12. "On to the Sea," *Atlanta Constitution*, April 28, 1892, 8.

13. H. A. Carter, "In Georgia's Fields and Streams," *Atlanta Constitution*, January 28, 1935, 13.

14. Hal Foust, "Trailer Blazes Way to Swamp on Suwannee," *Chicago Tribune*, December 27, 1937, 4.

15. Ibid.

16. Stephen Mufson and Desmond Butler, "Trump Rule Eases Effort to Strip-Mine Near Okefenokee Swamp," *Washington Post*, November 25, 2020, https://www.washingtonpost.com/climate-environment/.

17. Christopher Williams, "A Most Endangered Year: Why do America's Most Endangered Rivers Still Matter in the Wake of a Global Pandemic?" *American Rivers*, April 14, 2020, https://www.americanrivers.org/2020/04/.

18. Del Quentin Wilber, "How a Corporate Spy Swiped Plans for DuPont's Billion-Dollar Color Formula," *Bloomberg*, February 4, 2016, https://www.bloomberg.com/features/2016-stealing-dupont-white/.

19. Hesiod, *Theogony*, tr. Dorothea Wender (New York: Penguin, 1973), 29, 30.

20. C. Kerényi, *The Gods of the Greeks* (London: Thames & Hudson, 1951), 20.

21. Robert Penn Warren, *All the King's Men* (New York: Harvest, 1996), 1, 2.

22. Cecile Hulse Matschat, *Suwannee River: Strange Green Land* (New York: Literary Guild, 1938), 30–31.

23. Ibid., 16.

24. Alexander Sesonske, "Jean Renoir in Georgia: Swamp Water," *Georgia Review* 36, no. 1 (Spring 1982), 30.

25. Ibid.

26. Ibid., 31.

27. Lillian Smith, *Killers of the Dream* (New York: W. W. Norton & Co., 1949; 1994), 224.

28. Ibid., 223.

29. James Weldon Johnson, *The Autobiography of an Ex-Colored Man* (New York: Penguin, 1990), 14.

30. *Florida: A Guide to the Southernmost State*, Compiled and Written by the Federal Writers' Project of the Works Progress Administration for the State of Florida (New York: Oxford University Press, 1939), 361.

31. William Booth, "Together, But Not Equal," *Washington Post*, January 6, 1993, https://www.washingtonpost.com/archive/lifestyle/1993/01/06/.

32. Rebecca Sharpless, "The Servants and Mrs. Rawlings: Martha Mickens and African American Life at Cross Creek," *Florida Historical Quarterly* 89, no. 4 (Spring 2011), 500–29; "Neither Friends nor Peers: Idella Parker, Marjorie Kinnan Rawlings, and the Limits of Gender Solidarity at Cross Creek," *Journal of Southern History* 78, no. 2 (May 2012), 327–60.

33. See Ted Geltner, *Blood, Bone, and Marrow: A Biography of Harry Crews* (Athens: University of Georgia Press, 2016).

34. Harry Crews, *A Childhood*, 25.

35. Stephen Collins Foster, "Old Folks At Home: Ethiopian Melody As Sung by Christy's Minstrels" (New York: Firth, Pond & Co., 1851), 4.

36. W. E. B. Du Bois, *The Souls of Black Folk*, 184.

37. Jan Hinton, "Florida, Where Sawgrass Meets the Sky," Florida Department of State https://dos.myflorida.com/florida-facts/florida-state-symbols/state-anthem/.

38. "Men of the Month," *Crisis* 15, no. 5 (March 1918), 231.

39. Ray Charles, "Swanee River Rock (Talkin' 'Bout That River)," A7, Yes Indeed!, Atlantic Records 8025, 1964, Vinyl LP.

Georgia II

1. Jack Nelson, "Ineligibles Given Surgery; Mental Patients Wait Turns," *Atlanta Constitution*, March 26, 1959, 1, 6.

2. "2 Beat Up Aide, Escape Milledgeville," *Atlanta Constitution*, March 26, 1959, 1, 6.

3. Court of Appeals of Georgia, Stembridge v. State, 82 Ga. App. 214 (1950). 60 S.E.2d 491, 32911, https://law.justia.com/cases/georgia/court-of-appeals/1950/32911.html.

4. "Two Layers Prominent in Legal Difficulties Slain by Georgia Man Carrying 'Grudge,'" *Great Falls Tribune*, May 3, 1953, 2.

5. "Marion Stembridge Murders Rocked 1950s Milledgeville," *Milledgeville Union-Recorder*, September 5, 2008, https://www.unionrecorder.com/news/lifestyles/.

6. "Banker Kills Two Lawyers, Ends Own Life," *Chicago Tribune*, May 3, 1953, 1.

7. Celestine Sibley, "Milledgeville Pageant Traces 150-Year History," *Atlanta Constitution*, May 5, 1953, 14.

8. Michael T. Bernath, "'Independent in Everything—Neutral in Nothing': Joseph Addison Turner, *The Countryman*, and the Cultivation of Confederate Nationalism," *Georgia Historical Quarterly* 96, no. 1 (Spring 2012), 24.

9. Ibid., 37.

10. Joel Chandler Harris, *The Complete Tales of Uncle Remus*, ed. Richard Chase (Boston: Houghton Mifflin, 1955, 1983), xxvii.

11. Alice Walker, "Uncle Remus, No Friend of Mine," *Georgia Review* 66, no. 3 (Fall 2012), 636.

12. Bill Boring, "Chilled Crowd Wisecracks as Rabbit, Fox, Sweep By," *Atlanta Constitution*, November 13, 1946, 1.

13. Celestine Sibley, "Disney Puts 'Tough Audience' in His Pocket," *Atlanta Constitution*, November 13, 1946, 11.

14. Walker, "Uncle Remus," 636.

15. Albert Murray, *South to a Very Old Place*, in *Albert Murray: Collected Essays and Memoirs*, ed. Henry Louis Gates, Jr., and Paul Devlin (New York: Library of America, 2016), 217.

16. Alice Walker, "Uncle Remus," 637.

17. Murray, *South to a Very Old Place*, 217.

18. WPA, *Georgia*, 500.

19. Ibid.

20. Ibid., 211.

South Carolina I

1. Thomas Wentworth Higginson, "The Hamburg (S.C.) Massacre," *New York Times*, July 19, 1876, 4.

2. "The Hamburg Massacre," *New York Times*, July 19, 1876, 1.

3. "The Hamburg Butchery," *New York Times*, August 2, 1876, 5.

4. *Congressional Record: Proceedings and Debates of the Forty-Fifth Congress, First Session*, Volume VI (Washington, DC: Government Printing Office, 1877), 707.

5. Benjamin Ryan Tillman, *Struggles of 1876: How South Carolina Was Delivered from Carpet-Bag and Negro Rule: Speech at the Red-Shirt Re-Union at Anderson [August 25, 1909]: Personal Reminiscences and Incidents* (Anderson, SC: Publisher Unknown, 1909), 15.

6. The frequently cited text is taken from William Henry Trescot's inscription on the 1879 South Carolina Monument to the Confederate Dead on the grounds of the State House in Columbia.

7. South Carolina Writers' Project, *South Carolina: A Guide to the Palmetto State* (New York: Oxford University Press, 1941), 452.

8. See Mark M. Smith, "'All Is Not Quiet in Our Hellish County': Facts, Fiction, Politics, and Race: The Ellenton Riot of 1876," *South Carolina Historical Magazine* 95, no. 2 (April 1994), 142–55.

9. F. E. Thomas to J. H. Aycock, September 21–22, 1876, quoted in Smith, "All Is Not Quiet," 154.

10. "The Southern Massacres," *New York Times*, May 25, 1877, 2.

11. "The Rebels in Power," *New York Times*, October 16, 1876, 1

12. Tillman, *Struggles of 1876*, 63.

13. Drew Gilpin Faust, *James Henry Hammond and the Old South: A Design for Mastery* (Baton Rouge: Louisiana State University Press, 1985), 259.

14. WPA, *South Carolina*, 452.

15. Ibid., 134.

16. James Henry Hammond, "On the Justice of Receiving Petitions for the Abolition of Slavery in the District of Columbia," in *Selections from the Letters and Speeches of the Hon. James H. Hammond, of South Carolina* (New York: John F. Trow & Co., 1866), 37–38.

17. "We use them for our purpose, and call them slaves." James Henry Hammond, "On the Admission of Kansas, Under the Lecompton Constitution. Delivered in the Senate of the United States, March 4, 1858," in *Selections from the Letters and Speeches of the Hon. James H. Hammond, of South Carolina* (New York: John F. Trow & Co., 1866), 318–19.

18. *The Pro-Slavery Argument, as Maintained by the Most Distinguished Writers of the Southern States: Containing the Several Essays on the Subject, of Chancellor Harper,*

Governor Hammond, Dr. Simms, and Professor Dew (Philadelphia: Lippincott, Grambo, & Co., 1853), 108.

19. James Henry Hammond, Letter to the Editor of the *London Spectator*, October 22, 1856, quoted in Elizabeth Merritt, *James Henry Hammond, 1807-1864* (Baltimore: The Johns Hopkins Press, 1923), 112.

20. Ibid., 148.

21. Faust, *James Henry Hammond*, 382.

22. "James Henry Hammond," *Edgefield Advertiser*, November 7, 1878, 3.

23. "Death of Ex-Governor Hammond," *Montgomery Advertiser*, November 20, 1864, 1.

24. *The Buffalo Commercial*, November 22, 1864, 2.

25. Louis D. Rubin, Jr., Foreword to *Secret and Sacred: The Diaries of James Henry Hammond, a Southern Slaveholder*, ed. Carol Bleser (Columbia: University of South Carolina Press, 1997), xii.

26. Hammond, *Secret and Sacred*, 173.

27. Ibid., 177.

28. Ibid., 171.

29. Ibid., 178.

30. Ibid., 176.

31. Ibid., 209.

32. Ibid., 210.

33. Carol Bleser, "Introduction," in *Secret and Sacred: The Diaries of James Henry Hammond, a Southern Slaveholder*, ed. Carol Bleser (Columbia: University of South Carolina Press, 1997), 18.

34. Faust, *James Henry Hammond*, 315.

35. Hammond, *Secret and Sacred*, 254.

36. Ibid., 255.

37. Ibid., 212.

38. WPA, *South Carolina*, 361.

39. Ibid., 362.

40. See https://web.archive.org/web/20141105180816/http://www.screconstruction .org/Reconstruction/Citations_files/GaryCampaign.pdf.

41. Cited in "The Hamburg Row," *Charlotte Democrat*, July 24, 1876, 2.

42. "An Opinion of Hamburg," *Augusta Constitutionalist*, July 16, 1876, 4.

43. WPA, *South Carolina*, 364.

44. *Congressional Record: Proceedings and Debates of the Fifty-Sixth Congress, First Session*, Volume XXXIII, Part 3, February 26, 1900 (Washington, DC: Government Printing Office, 1900), 2243.

South Carolina II

1. South Carolina Writer's Program, *A Guide to Hampton County, South Carolina: A Section of Tall Pines, Fertile Fields, and Good Sports* (Hampton, SC: Hampton County, 1940), 26.

2. WPA, *South Carolina*, 454.

3. Ibid.

4. I am grateful to Ehren Foley for pointing out to me that this same method has been employed in the preservation of two ancient English Elms in Boston, at

a monument dedicated to Robert Gould Shaw and the 54th Massachusetts Regiment which—coincidentally or providentially—arrived in Beaufort in June 1863, and used the port city as its operational base. The Boston Elms are believed to be the oldest living specimens in the Western hemisphere. See https://apps .bostonglobe.com/boston-revealed/series/shaw-elms/.

5. WPA, *South Carolina*, 322.

6. Charles E. Leverett, *The Southern Confederacy Arithmetic, for Common Schools and Academies, with a Practical System of Bookkeeping by Single Entry* (Augusta, GA: J. T. Paterson & Co., 1864).

7. "Old Sheldon Church," *The State*, August 29, 1909, 21.

8. Ibid.

9. Milton Maxcy Leverett to his mother, February 3, 1866, in *The Leverett Letters: Correspondence of a South Carolina Family 1851-1868*, ed. Frances Wallace Taylor, Catherine Taylor Matthews, and J. Tracy Power (Columbia: University of South Carolina Press, 2000), 403.

10. Milton Maxcy Leverett to his mother, February 7, 1866, in *Leverett Letters*, 405.

11. "An Act for the better Security of this Province against the insurrections and other wicked attempts of Negroes and other Slaves," *South Carolina Gazette*, August 18, 1739, 1.

12. WPA, *South Carolina*, 47.

13. "Abstract of the Act, entitled an Act for the better ordering and governing of Negroes and other Slaves in this Province," *South Carolina Gazette*, May 24, 1740, 3. See Walter Edgar, *South Carolina: A History* (Columbia: University of South Carolina Press, 1998), 75-81.

14. "An Abstract of the Act entitled, an Act for the better establishing and regulating of Patrols," *South Carolina Gazette*, May 24, 1740, 3. "The law defined slaves as personal chattels. This was the first precise definition of slavery since the disallowed act of 1690; slavery no longer rested upon custom but upon law." M. Eugene Sirmans, "The Legal Status of the Slave in South Carolina, 1670–1740," *Journal of Southern History* 28, no. 4 (November 1962), 471.

15. Kurt J. Wolf, "Laura M. Towne and the Freed People of South Carolina, 1862-1901," *The South Carolina Historical Magazine* 98, no. 4 (October 1997), 375–405; Akiko Ochiai, "The Port Royal Experiment Revisited: Northern Visions of Reconstruction and the Land Question," *New England Quarterly* 74, no. 1 (March 2001), 94–117.

16. J. Miller M'Kim, *The Freedmen of South Carolina* (Philadelphia: W. P. Hazard, 1862), 11.

17. *Columbia Daily Phoenix*, June 20, 1874, 3.

18. Henry Eichel, "The Reconstruction Era: Pillage or Progress?" *Charlotte Observer*, March 27, 2004, 8A

19. Bill Rauch, "Can the South Make Room for Reconstruction?" *Atlantic*, September 17, 2016, https://www.theatlantic.com/politics/archive/2016/09/.

20. Jennifer Schuessler, "Taking Another Look at the Reconstruction Era," *New York Times*, August 24, 2015, C1.

21. The bill's co-sponsor was former Governor Mark Sanford, whose prior accomplishments included a trip along the Appalachian Trail that was actually a visit to see his mistress in Argentina. You can see where the "you'll never get it" idea

comes from: but not because it makes sense from the inside. Politics in South Carolina is nothing if not weird, and promises a long career of second chances no matter how outlandish you are, so long as you are white.

22. "Bob Smalls Dead in Beaufort," *Sumter Daily Item*, February 26, 1915, 2.
23. Alexis Pauline Gumbs, "Prophecy in the Present Tense: Harriet Tubman, the Combahee Pilgrimage, and Dreams Coming True," *Meridians* 12, no. 2 (2014), 143.
24. Pat Conroy, *Lords of Discipline* (New York: Houghton Mifflin, 1980; Dial Press, 2011), 3.
25. Honoré de Balzac, *Père Goriot*, tr. Burton Raffel, ed. Peter Brooks (New York: W. W. Norton, 1994), 5–6.
26. Douglas R. Egerton, *He Shall Go Out Free: The Lives of Denmark Vesey*, rev. ed. (London: Rowman & Littlefield, 2004), p. 77.
27. Ibid., 99.
28. Ibid., 100.
29. Ibid., 110.
30. Ibid., 121.
31. John Lofton, *Denmark Vesey's Revolt: The Slave Plot That Lit a Fuse to Fort Sumter* (Kent, OH: Kent State University Press, 1964, 1983), 131.
32. *Acts and Joint Resolutions of the General Assembly of the State of South Carolina, Passed in December, 1820* (Columbia: D. Faust, 1821), 22.
33. "By Wm. A. Caldwell," *Charleston Daily Courier*, August 14, 1822, 3.
34. Ethan J. Kyle and Blain Roberts, *Denmark Vesey's Garden: Slavery and Memory in the Cradle of the Confederacy* (New York: New Press 2018), 287–90.
35. "Destruction of the Confederate Monument," *Rock Hill Herald*, June 29, 1882, 2.
36. *Journal of the Senate of the State of South Carolina: Regular Session, Commencing November 25, 1890* (Columbia: Charles P. Pelham, State Printer, 1890), 78.
37. "Gov. Tillman's Inaugural," *The Newberry Herald and News*, December 11, 1890, 3.
38. Christie Zimmerman Fant, *The State House of South Carolina: An Illustrated Historic Guide* (Columbia: R. L. Bryan Company, 1970), 22.
39. "The First Regiment South Carolina Volunteers," *New York Times*, August 17, 1862, 3.
40. Thomas Wentworth Higginson, *Army Life in a Black Regiment*, in *The Writings of Thomas Wentworth Higginson*, vol. 3 (Boston: Houghton, Mifflin, 1900), 78.
41. An opponent of secession and Unionist critic of the Confederate government, Petigru was no abolitionist. A slaveholder himself, he often took cases in defense of the rights of slaves or free Black people. Despite its self-curated reputation for independence and dissent, South Carolina has not remembered Petigru as a model of bucking the status quo. Apart from his most famous one-liner, which is undoubtedly more popular in Georgia and North Carolina than in the Palmetto State, his contributions to South Carolina were significant but not spectacular. Due to his qualified proximity to abolitionists, he was not the sort of character who would ever find a place in granite perpetuity on the lawn of the South Carolina State House.
42. "The South and the Negro," *Charleston Mercury*, July 23, 1868, 2.
43. "A Reverend Ringed-Streaked. Is Arrested for Improper Conduct, Resists the Police and Offers One Hundred Dollars to Be Let Off," *Charleston Mercury*, April 3, 1868, 1.
44. "The Charleston Advocate," *Charleston Mercury*, June 29, 1868, 1.

45. "Orangeburg Delegation," *Charleston Mercury*, February 24, 1868, 8.
46. "The Great Ringed-Streaked and Striped Negro Convention," *Charleston Mercury*, February 27, 1868, 1.
47. "Death of B. D. [*sic*] Randolph, Late Member of the So-Called Legislature," *Charleston Mercury*, October 21, 1868, 1.
48. D. Wyatt Aiken, Letter to the Editor, *Abbeville Press and Banner*, October 9, 1868, 3.
49. State of South Carolina, *Evidence Taken by the Committee of Investigation of the Third Congressional District, Regular Session 1869-70* (Columbia: J. Denny, 1870), 585.
50. Ibid., 496.
51. "Under Which King, Bezonian?" Law and Order, or Outrage and Murder?" *Columbia Daily Phoenix*, February 23, 1869, 2.
52. See Daniel M. Harrison, *Live at Jackson Station: Music, Community, and Tragedy in a Southern Blues Bar* (Columbia: University of South Carolina Press, 2020).

Alabama
1. "Legislators Arrested over Confederate Flag," *Chicago Tribune*, February 3, 1988, 7.
2. James Abrams, "Citizens Seek to Reopen Segregated Pool," *Montgomery Advertiser*, June 17, 1965, 14.
3. Marvin's distant cousin, Mab, would write a famous memoir, *Memoir of a Race Traitor*, about her upbringing among Alabama segregationists. She was sixteen when her cousin shot Sammy Younge. A former professor at Connecticut College, Segrest has devoted her academic work to studies of oppressive regimes, including *Administrations of Lunacy: Racism and the Haunting of American Psychiatry at the Milledgeville Asylum* (New York: New Press, 2020).
4. Ralph Ellison, *Invisible Man* (New York: Vintage, 1995), 36.
5. Albert Murray, *South to a Very Old Place*, 272.
6. Josh Moon, "Groups Plan to Fly Huge Reb Flag," *Montgomery Advertiser*, February 5, 2016, 1A. Alabama State University traces its origins back to the Lincoln Normal School in Marion, Alabama, founded in 1867.
7. From text in a pamphlet distributed at the First White House of the Confederacy, and on its website as late as 2019 (since removed). Some of the text was reproduced in Anthony Izaguirre, "Alabama History Tour Covers Civil War, Cotton—Not Slaves," *Montgomery Advertiser*, May 7, 2017, A10.
8. Hank Williams, "Alone and Forsaken," Side B, MGM K12029, 1955, 7" Vinyl.
9. Hebrews 12: 19–20.
10. Matt 25:35–36 NIV.
11. As the nearby historical marker eloquently describes him. The veneration of St. Jude—one of the twelve apostles and author of an epistle in the New Testament—in this way goes back at least to the fourteenth-century St. Bridget of Sweden, and possibly earlier to St. Bernard of Clairvaux, who was allegedly buried with a relic of the Apostle.
12. "Silence," *Montgomery Advertiser*, March 25, 1965, 4.
13. John J. Winberry, "Lest We Forget: The Confederate Monument and the Southern Townscape," *Southeastern Geographer* 23, no. 2 (November 1983), 107.
14. Alabama Writers' Project, *Alabama: A Guide to the Deep South* (New York: Hastings House, 1941), 287.
15. Ibid., 236, 237.
16. Ibid., 240.

17. Melanie Peeples, "The Racist History Behind the Iconic Selma Bridge," *All Things Considered, National Public Radio*, March 5, 2015, https://www.npr.org/sections /codeswitch/2015/03/05/391041989/.

18. "Selma, Alabama Memorializes Lynching Victims," Equal Justice Initiative website, March 5, 2018, https://eji.org/news/.

19. Ronald Smothers, "Few Neutral on Selma School Chief," *New York Times*, February 14, 1990, A16.

20. "Historic Restaurant Closes in Selma," *Montgomery Advertiser*, April 1, 1985, 15.

21. Carol Dawson, "Lessons Learned from the Civil Rights Movement: JoAnne Bland," *Baylor Magazine*, September/October 2003, https://www.baylor.edu/alumni /magazine/0202/news.php?action=story&story=7595

22. Wes Smith, "Resilient Alabama Town Weaves its Own Magic," *Orlando Sentinel*, December 25, 2002, A1, 15.

23. Michael Kimmelman, "Jazzy Geometry, Cool Quilters," *New York Times*, November 29, 2002, E33, 37, https://www.nytimes.com/2002/11/29/arts/.

24. The New York show followed upon the new attention directed toward Gee's Bend by J. R. Moehringer's Pulitzer Prize–winning article, "Crossing Over," *Los Angeles Times*, August 22, 1999, S1-4.

25. Souls Grown Deep Foundation website: https://www.soulsgrowndeep.org /foundation/about.

26. Moehringer, "Crossing Over," S1.

27. Steve Fiffer and Adar Cohen, *Jimmie Lee & James: Two Lives, Two Deaths, and the Movement that Changed America* (New York: Regan Arts, 2015), 44.

28. Paul Good, ". . . It Was Worth the Boy's Dying," *Washington Post*, March 22, 1965, from *Reporting Civil Rights, Part Two: American Journalism 1963-1973* (New York: Library of America, 2003), 353.

29. Ibid.

30. John Fleming, "The Death of Jimmie Lee Jackson," *Anniston Star*, March 6, 2005, 1E, 3E.

31. Billie Jean Young, Interview with the author, March 15, 2019. Some of the foregoing previously appeared in *Southern Cultures*, September 24, 2020, https://www .southerncultures.org/article/it-was-a-place-of-infamy/.

32. WPA, *Alabama*, 293.

33. David Montgomery, "After the Fall: When a Crash Toppled a Confederate Statue, a Southern Town—Half Black, Half White—Collided with its Past," *Washington Post*, July 20, 2017, https://www.washingtonpost.com/sf/style/2017/07/20/.

34. WPA, *Alabama*, 293.

35. Montgomery, "After the Fall."

36. WPA, *Alabama*, 294.

37. Montgomery, "After the Fall."

38. Sydney Melson, "Segregation Academies' Looking to Overcome Divided Past," *Alabama Public Radio*, July 28, 2020, https://www.apr.org/news/2020-07-28/segregation -academies-looking-to-overcome-divided-past.

39. See Alex Scarborough, "Linden, A Town Divided by Race," *Tuscaloosa News*, September 25, 2011, https://www.tuscaloosanews.com/story/news/2011/09/25/. Marengo Academy closed in 2019; see Edwin Stanton, "Marengo Academy Closing after 50 Years," *Tuscaloosa News*, June 28, 2019, https://www.tuscaloosanews .com/story/news/education/2019/06/28/4785571007/.

40. Goodloe Sutton, "Klan Needs to Ride Again," *Democrat-Reporter*, February 14, 2019, 2.
41. WPA, *Alabama*, 202–3.
42. "Last Slaver from U.S. to Africa. A.D. 1860," Mobile Public Library Digital Collections, accessed October 7, 2023, https://digital.mobilepubliclibrary.org/items /show/1802.
43. Zora Neale Hurston, *Barracoon: The Story of the Last "Black Cargo"* (New York: Amistad, 2018).

Mississippi I
1. William Alexander Percy, *Lanterns on the Levee: Reflections of a Planter's Son* (Baton Rouge: Louisiana State University Press, 1973), 3.
2. Ibid.
3. Isabel Wilkerson, *The Warmth of Other Suns: The Epic Story of America's Great Migration* (New York: Vintage, 2010), 10.
4. Tom Zoellner, *Train: Riding the Rails that Created the Modern World—from the Trans-Siberian to the Southwest Chief* (New York: Penguin, 2014), 132.
5. Birney Imes, *Juke Joint* (Jackson: University Press of Mississippi, 1990).
6. *An Act to Provide for the More Efficient Government of the Rebel States*, March 4, 1867 [Passed over President Johnson's veto on March 2, 1867].
7. Neil R. McMillen, *Dark Journey: Black Mississippians in the Age of Jim Crow* (Urbana: University of Illinois Press, 1990), 41.
8. Janet Sharp Hermann, *Joseph E. Davis: Pioneer Patriarch* (Oxford: University Press of Mississippi, 1991), 55.
9. Janet Sharp Hermann, "Reconstruction in Microcosm: Three Men and a Gin," *Journal of Negro History* 65, no. 4 (Autumn, 1980), 312–35.
10. Joel Nathan Rosen, "Isaiah Thornton Montgomery," *The Mississippi Encyclopedia* https://mississippiencyclopedia.org/entries/isaiah-thornton-montgomery/.
11. Linda Keene, "Mound Bayou," Track H, *Strictly from Dixie*, RCA Victor P119, 1947, Vinyl LP.
12. Ray Lanning, "Night Club Notes," *Cincinnati Enquirer*, October 25, 1942, 54.
13. Lynn Marshall-Linnemeier, "Crowe, Milburn James," *The Mississippi Encyclopedia*, ed. Ted Ownby, Charles Reagan Wilson, Ann J. Abadie, Odie Lindsey, James G. Thomas, Jr. (Oxford: University Press of Mississippi, 2017), 307. See also Constance Curry, *Silver Rights* (Chapel Hill, NC: Algonquin, 1995), 165–66.
14. August Meier, "Booker T. Washington and the Town of Mound Bayou," *Phylon (1940–56)*, 15, no. 4 (4th Quarter, 1954), 396–401.
15. Booker T. Washington, "A Town Owned by Negroes: Mound Bayou, Miss., an Example of Thrift and Self-Government," *World's Work*, vol. XIV (May-October 1907), 9125–34.
16. "A Noble Speech," *World* (New York), September 27, 1890, 1.
17. Ibid.
18. *Journal of the Proceeding of the Constitutional Convention of the State of Mississippi* (Jackson: E. L. Martin, 1890), 69.
19. "A Noble Speech," 2.
20. Ibid.
21. Ibid.
22. Ibid.

23. Frederick Douglass, *The Race Problem: Great Speech of Frederick Douglass, Delivered before the Bethel Literary and Historical Association, in the Metropolitan A.M.E. Church, Washington, D.C., October 21, 1890* (Washington, DC: Library of Congress, 1890), 14, http://hdl.loc.gov/loc.rbc/lcrbmrp.toc13.

24. Ibid., 14–15.

25. James C. Giesen, *Boll Weevil Blues: Cotton, Myth, and Power in the American South* [Illustrated Edition] (Chicago: University of Chicago Press, 2011), 88.

26. Douglas A. Blackmon, *Slavery By Another Name: The Re-Enslavement of Black Americans from the Civil War to World War II* (New York: Anchor, 2009).

27. David M. Oshinsky, *Worse than Slavery: Parchman Farm and the Ordeal of Jim Crow Justice* (New York: Free Press Paperbacks, 1996), 35.

28. Ibid., 49–50.

29. Ibid., 109.

30. Ibid., photographs, 14.

31. *Journal of the House of Representatives of the State of Mississippi* (January, February, and March 1904) (Nashville: Brandon Printing Company, 1904), 562–63.

32. Jerry Mitchell, "Bombshell Quote Missing from Emmett Till Tape. So Did Carolyn Bryant Donham Really Recant?" *Clarion Ledger* (Jackson, MS), August 21, 2018, https://www.clarionledger.com/story/news/2018/08/21/.

33. Federal Writers' Project of the Works Progress Administration, *Mississippi: A Guide to the Magnolia State* (New York: Viking, 1938), 192.

34. "Hearing Tentatively Set for Kimbell," *Jackson Clarion-Ledger*, December 10, 1955, 1.

35. Federal Bureau of Investigation, *Emmett Till*, 2006, 58, https://vault.fbi.gov/Emmett %20Till%20.

36. "Clashing Versions Glendora Shooting," *Greenwood Commonwealth*, December 8, 1955, 1.

37. Aimee Ortiz, "Till Memorial Replaces Sign a Fourth Time. It's Bulletproof," *New York Times*, October 20, 2019, Section A, 13.

38. Saint Augustine, *Confessions*, trans. Henry Chadwick (Oxford: Oxford University Press, 1991), Xxviii, 187.

39. Ralph Ellison, "What America Would Be Like Without Blacks," *Going to the Territory* (New York: Vintage, 1986), 111.

40. W. C. Handy, *Father of the Blues: An Autobiography* (New York: Da Capo Press, 1969), 74.

Memphis

1. The now commonplace claim originated in David L. Cohn's *God Shakes Creation* (New York: Harper & Brothers, 1935), 14.

2. Max Johns and John Chilton, *Louis: The Louis Armstrong Story 1900-1971* (Boston: Da Capo, 1971), 152

3. "Clerk Is Cleared in Sale of Pistol," *Memphis Commercial-Appeal*, October 8, 1931, 4.

4. Thomas Brothers, *Louis Armstrong, Master of Modernism* (New York: W. W. Norton, 2014), 428.

5. Ibid., 2.

6. Joe Sills, "The Unbelievable True Story of How the Memphis Pyramid Became a Bass Pro Shop," *Forbes Magazine*, April 26, 2020, https://www.forbes.com/sites /joesills/2020/08/26/.

7. See Preston Lauterbach, *Beale Street Dynasty: Sex, Song, and the Struggle for the Soul of Memphis* (New York: W. W. Norton, 2015).

8. Preston Lauterbach, "Memphis Burning," *Places Journal* (March 2016): https://placesjournal.org/article/memphis-burning/.

9. Federal Writers' Project of the Works Progress Administration for the State of Tennessee, *Tennessee: A Guide to the State* (New York: Viking, 1939, 1973), 222.

10. Albert Murray, *South to a Very Old Place*, 335.

11. *Journal of the Senate of the United States of America* (Washington, DC: US Government Printing Office, 1977), 1558–59.

12. Progressive Political Action Committee, "Senator Hayakawa Says," *Sacramento Bee*, January 19, 1982, 9.

13. Preston Lauterbach, *Bluff City: The Secret Life of Photographer Ernest Withers* (New York: W. W. Norton, 2019), 42ff.

14. Elinor Kelley, "Statue of Davis Proudly Placed in Proper Park," *Memphis Commercial-Appeal*, October 5, 1964, 1.

15. "President's Message," *Memphis Post*, March 29, 1866, 1.

16. "Civil Rights Bill Passed," *Memphis Daily Appeal*, April 8, 1866, 2.

17. Bobby L. Lovett, "Memphis Race Riot of 1866," *Tennessee Encyclopedia*, 2017, https://tennesseeencyclopedia.net/entries/memphis-race-riot-of-1866/.

18. Dennis C. Rousey, "Yellow Fever and Black Policemen in Memphis: A Post-Reconstruction Anomaly," *The Journal of Southern History* 51, no. 3 (August 1985), 357–74.

19. "The Mob's Work," *Memphis Appeal-Avalanche*, March 10, 1892, 5.

20. Paula J. Giddings, *Ida: A Sword Among Lions. Ida B. Wells and the Campaign against Lynching* (New York: Amistad, 2008), 182.

21. *Free Speech*, May 21, 1892, quoted in Ida B. Wells, "Lynch Law in All Its Phases," in *The Light of Truth: Writings of an Anti-Lynching Crusader*, ed. Mia Bay (New York: Penguin, 2014), 103. See also David M. Tucker, "Miss Ida B. Wells and Memphis Lynching," *Phylon (1960–)* 32, no. 2 (2nd Quarter, 1971), 112–22; Philip Dray, *At the Hands of Persons Unknown*, 65ff; and Giddings, *Ida*, 184ff.

22. "An Outrageous Publication," *New Orleans Times-Democrat*, May 26, 1892, 7.

23. "Vamoosed," *Clarksville Leaf-Chronicle*, May 27, 1892, 3. See also Giddings, *Ida*, 212.

24. Wells, "Lynch Law in All its Phases," 106.

25. Kenneth W. Goings, "Memphis Free Speech," *Tennessee Encyclopedia*, October 8, 2017, https://tennesseeencyclopedia.net/entries/memphis-free-speech/.

26. "A Colored Corday," *Memphis Commercial*, December 15, 1892, 4.

27. Ibid.

28. "Lynched!" *Memphis Appeal-Avalanche*, March 9, 1892, 1.

29. "A Black Mafia," *Memphis Commercial*, October 16, 1892, 2.

30. Brook Thomas, "Adventures of Huckleberry Finn and Reconstruction," *American Literary Realism* 50, no. 1 (Fall 2017): 9.

31. Otto H. Olsen, "Albion W. Tourgee and Negro Militants of the 1890's: A Documentary Selection," *Science & Society* 28, no. 2 (Spring 1964): 188. See also Otto H. Olsen, "Albion W. Tourgee: Carpetbagger," *North Carolina Historical Review* 40, no. 4 (October 1963): 434–54.

32. Lauterbach, *Bluff City*, 253.

33. David J. Garrow, *Bearing the Cross: Martin Luther King, Jr., and the Southern Christian Leadership Conference* (New York: Perennial Classics, 1986), 610.

34. Lauterbach, *Bluff City*, 248.

35. See Lauterbach, *Bluff City*.

36. The Xernona Clayton interview can be found in *King in the Wilderness*, directed by Peter Kunhardt (2018; HBO).

37. See "Episode 8: Memphis Police Officer Guns Down 16-Year-Old #LarryPayne as Sanitation Strike Continues," *The Root*, podcast audio, April 3, 2018, https://www.theroot.com/.

38. Murray, *South to a Very Old Place*, 335.

Mississippi II

1. The story of Paul MacLeod and his Elvis-o-rama was adapted by two native Memphians into a play in 2022 and performed at New York Theater Festival.

2. Herbert Mitgang, "A Talk with Walker Percy," *New York Times Book Review*, February 20, 1977, 1.

3. Flannery O'Connor, "Some Aspects of the Grotesque in Southern Fiction," in *Collected Works*, 818.

4. William Faulkner, *Light in August: The Corrected Text* (New York: Modern Library, 2012), 110.

5. William Faulkner, *Intruder in the Dust* (New York: Vintage, 1994), 48.

6. Ibid., 134.

7. Ibid., 143.

8. Monumental Bronze Co., *White Bronze Monuments, Statuary, Portrait Medallions, Busts, Statues, and Ornamental Art Work: For Cemeteries, Public and Private Grounds and Buildings* (Bridgeport, CT: Monumental Bronze Co., 1882), https://library.si.edu/digital-library/book/whitebronzemonuoomonu.

9. Marc Fisher, "Why Those Confederate Soldier Statues Look a Lot Like Their Union Counterparts," *Washington Post*, August 18, 2017, https://www.washingtonpost.com/politics/.

10. Sarah Beetham, "From Spray Cans to Minivans: Contesting the Legacy of Confederate Soldier Monuments in the Era of 'Black Lives Matter,'" *Public Art Dialogue* 6, no. 1 (2016), 9–33 https://www.tandfonline.com/doi/full/10.1080/21502552.2016.1149386.

11. Mrs. N. D. Deupree, "Confederate Monument at Oxford, Miss.," *Confederate Veteran* 14 (July 1906), 306.

12. *The National Cyclopaedia of American Biography, Being the History of the United States as Illustrated in the Lives of the Founders, Builders, and Defenders of the Republic, and of the Men and Women Who Are Doing the Work and Moulding the Thought of the Present Time*, vol. XVII (New York: J. T. White, 1920), 231, https://archive.org/details/nationalcyclopae17newy.

13. Don H. Doyle, *Faulkner's County: The Historical Roots of Yoknapatawpha* (Chapel Hill: UNC Press, 2001), 330.

14. Kelsey Davis Betz, "'Glorified Shrine of the Confederacy': UM Students, Faculty Fume over Unofficial Plans to Renovate Confederate Cemetery," *Mississippi Today*, June 19, 2020, https://mississippitoday.org/2020/06/19/.

15. The University of Mississippi Department of History, "Statement by US Historians on Recently Released Confederate Monument Plans," June 22, 2020, https://history.olemiss.edu/.

16. Kiese Laymon, "'There Is No Excuse': University of Mississippi Faculty Members Condemn Proposed 'Shrine to White Supremacy,'" *Vanity Fair*, June 23, 2020, https://www.vanityfair.com/style/2020/06/.

17. William Faulkner, *Go Down, Moses* (New York: Vintage, 1990), 165.

18. Long dormant, the building sold for $10,000 in 2015, and was beautifully renovated into the Threefoot Hotel, a Marriott property.

19. WPA, *Mississippi*, 228.

20. Ibid., 230.

21. "The Affair at Meridian," *Hinds County Gazette*, March 15, 1871, 1.

22. "1871," *Atlanta Constitution*, December 31, 1871, 2.

23. Oshinsky, *Worse than Slavery*, 27–28.

24. Michael Newton, *The Ku Klux Klan in Mississippi: A History* (Jefferson: McFarland, 2009), 33.

25. Oshinsky, *Worse than Slavery*, 28.

26. "In A Kenyan Village, a 65-Year-Old Recording Comes Home," *National Public Radio*, June 28, 2015, https://www.npr.org/transcripts/417462792.

27. Amanda Petrusich, "The Magnificent Cross-Cultural Recordings of Kenya's Kipsigi Tribe," *New Yorker*, February 16, 2016, https://www.newyorker.com/culture/cultural-comment/the-magnificent-cross-cultural-recordings-of-kenyas-kipsigis-tribe.

28. Ibid.

29. His nephew, also called Ezekiel Samuel Candler, was head of the Fountain Sales Department at the Coca-Cola Company, and lost his wife Lucy in the tragic Orly crash in 1962. Even this family connection to more recent Atlanta history, however tenuous, was lost on me.

30. "Vardaman Tackles the Race Problem," *Andalusia Times*, April 10, 1907, 2.

31. "A Convention Needed," *Yazoo City Herald*, July 26, 1907, 4.

32. Albert D. Kirwan, *Revolt of the Rednecks: Mississippi Politics, 1876-1925* (Lexington: University Press of Kentucky, 1951), 274.

33. "Candler Misrepresented," *Memphis Commercial Appeal*, August 8, 1916, 14.

34. E. S. Candler to Williams, August 8, 1916, cited in Kirwan, *Revolt of the Rednecks*, 274.

Satellites

1. WPA, *Georgia*, 160.

2. "The Leo Frank Case," *Watson's Magazine* 20, no. 5 (January 1915), 143.

3. "Speech of Hon. A. H. Stephens," *Southern Confederacy*, March 25, 1861, 2.

4. "At the Mansion," *Atlanta Constitution*, March 6, 1883, 1.

5. "Fatal Leap from a Train," *New York Times*, March 15, 1883, 1.

6. "Candler's Brother Killed," *Chicago Tribune*, March 15, 1883, 2.

7. "A Horror on the Rails," *Savannah Morning News*, March 15, 1883, 1.

8. "Evening Echoes," *Wilmington News Journal*, April 11, 1883, 4.

9. "A Colonel Without Feet," *New York Times*, July 1, 1898, 2.

10. John S. Candler, "Judge Gave Orders to Himself," *Atlanta Journal*, November 6, 1927, 14.

11. Ibid.

12. Rebecca Latimer Felton, *My Memoirs of Georgia Politics* (Atlanta: The Index Printing Company, 1911), 94.

13. "Ex-Senator Felton Leaves for Home," *Atlanta Constitution*, November 23, 1922, 2.

14. "Woman Advocates Lynching," *Asheville Weekly Citizen*, August 20, 1987, 2.

15. "Mrs. Felton Not For Lynching," *Atlanta Constitution*, August 20, 1897, 4.

16. "A Horrid Slander," *Wilmington Morning Star*, August 31, 1898, 3.

17. "Mrs. W. H. Felton," *Atlanta Constitution*, April 23, 1899, 18.

18. "Sam Jones' Platform," *Columbus Ledger-Enquirer*, February 22, 1898, 2.

19. Cited in Kathleen Minnix, *Laughter in Amen Corner: The Life of Evangelist Sam Jones* (Athens: University of Georgia Press, 2010), 87.

20. "Jottings by Sam Jones on His Western Tour," *Atlanta Journal*, August 19, 1899, 17.

21. Cited in Mathews, *At the Altar of Lynching*, 225.

22. "'Infernal and Cowardly,' Sam Jones on Lynching," *Atlanta Journal*, July 28, 1897, 5.

23. "Jottings by Sam Jones on His Western Tour," 17.

24. Bill Arp, "Arp Roasts Sledd," *Atlanta Constitution*, August 10, 1902, 2.

25. "Segregation of Races Advocated by Graves," *Atlanta Constitution*, August 12, 1903, 6.

26. Warren A. Candler, "Must Be Put Down by the Mob, Or Be Put Down by It," *Atlanta Constitution*, September 9, 1903, 6.

27. "Lynchings," *Vicksburg Herald*, October 11, 1904, 7.

28. Leon Litwack, *Trouble in Mind: Black Southerners in the Age of Jim Crow* (New York: Vintage, 1998), 280.

29. "Report of Detective Louis P. Le Vin," in Ida B. Wells-Barnett, *Lynch Law in Georgia*, in Ida B. Wells, *The Light of Truth: Writings of an Anti-Lynching Crusader* (New York: Penguin, 2014), 330–31.

30. Ibid., 331.

31. "What Governor Candler Says," *Atlanta Constitution*, April 24, 1899, 1.

32. Arnold, *What Virtue There Is in Fire*, 202.

33. Allen D. Candler, *Colonel William Candler of Georgia: His Ancestry and Progeny* (Atlanta: The Franklin Printing & Publishing Co., 1902), 11.

34. Friedrich Nietzsche, "On the Uses and Disadvantages of History for Life," in *Untimely Meditations*, tr. R. J. Hollingdale (Cambridge: Cambridge University Press, 1997), 78.

35. Ibid., 79.

Almost Home

1. Thomas Wolfe, *Look Homeward, Angel* (New York: Scribner, 2006), 156.

2. "Mrs. Lamar Makes Impressive Report on U.D.C. Year's Work," *Atlanta Constitution*, November 21, 1915, 5.

3. "Klan is Established with Impressiveness," *Atlanta Constitution*, November 28, 1915, 1.

Index

Page numbers in italic refer to images.

Abbott, Robert, 222, 223
Abernathy, Ralph David, 19, 29, 30, 214, 273, 274
Abigail Plantation, 55
abolitionism, 5, 267, 360n41
Acuff, Roy, 173
African American memorials, 155, 348
African American monuments, 118
African Americans: 23, 89, 106, 155, 170, 213, 219; cultural invisibility, 23, 169–70, 318–19; education, 28, 33, 165, 207, 214; foodways, 142, 222, 269–70; political activism, 11, 112; political power, 27, 28, 34, 59, 166, 195, 198, 226, 272, 292; poverty, 52, 149; racist stereotypes, 24, 32–33, 39, 77, 78; subjugation of, 33, 290; voting rights/voting, 28, 41–42, 59, 61, 105, 167, 207, 226, 289, 297–98, 342; and the workforce, 77, 92; see also Black Belt; Black Codes; Black exoticism (alleged); Black soldiers; Blackness; civil rights movement; desegregation; lynching; racial violence; segregation; white supremacy
Africatown (AL), 219
Agee, G. L., 38
agrarian populism, 25
Aiken, D. Wyatt, 159, 160
Akerman, Amos T., 310, 311
Akerman, Walter, 317
Alabama Sharecroppers Union, 185
Alabama State Capitol, 166, 172, 173, 174
Albany, GA, 47, 55–58, 59, 64, 93, 353n22
Aleck's Barbecue Heaven (Atlanta), 18, 19, 34

Alexander, Charles, 260
Allen, Ivan, Jr., 11
American colonialism, 23
American nationalism, 8
Americus, GA, 45–49
Anderson, Devery, 237
Andersonville National Cemetery, 51
Andersonville Prison, 50–52
Andersonville, GA, 49–52
Anglicanism, 126, 135, 136
Antisemitism: 302, 303; see also Frank, Leo
Antley, Jeff, 140
Armstrong, Louis, 90, 260
Arnold, Chip, 323
Arp, Bill, 315
A-Team, 332
Atkinson, William, 32, 319
Atlanta University, 28, 29, 33
Atlanta: xix, 17, 23, 55, 63, 64, 193, 296, 301, 334; and African Americans, 9–10, 18, 28–29, 31–33, 343; civil rights movement, 42, 44, 181, 200, 211, 272–73; Civil War, 26, 342; development of, 20, 30, 101, 149, 234, 341; and historical amnesia, 19, 30, 40, 282, 301, 308, 331, 340; as New South, xix, 4–5, 10, 40, 233–34; during segregation, 10–11, 105
Attaway, Charles, 116
Augusta, GA, 24, 37, 109–13, 117, 121, 306
Austin, J. Paul, 11

Baldwin, James, 285, 286
Balzac, Honoré de, 146
barbecue, 2, 18–19, 34, 56, 203, 321, 322, 323